JOHN W. HOLMES

The Shaping of Peace: Canada and the search for world order 1943-1957

Volume 1

UNIVERSITY OF TORONTO PRESS

Toronto Buffalo London

© University of Toronto Press 1979
Toronto Buffalo London
Printed in Canada

Canadian Cataloguing in Publication Data

Holmes, John Wendell, 1910-

The shaping of peace

Includes index.

ISBN 0-8020-5461-7 (v. 1)

1. Canada – Foreign relations – 1945-
I. Title.

FC602.H64   327.71   C79-094558-4
F1034.2.H64

TO R.G. 'GERRY' RIDDELL
1908-1951
Canadian permanent representative to the United Nations

'His memory and his spirit will help us for the days ahead,
as we work for the things to which he devoted his talents,
his energy and his life.'

L.B. PEARSON

Our contributions to the fashioning of victory have been
far greater than could have been imagined six years ago.
Our part in the shaping of peace may be no less urgent
and no less effective.

MACKENZIE KING
on the Resolution to approve the invitation to
San Francisco, House of Commons, 20 March 1945

Contents

Preface

'The search for world order,' it has been aptly said, 'is nothing but an attempt to conquer turbulence.'[1] No times could have been more turbulent than the latter years of war and the early years of peace when the new order took shape. The contours of that order were to a considerable extent planned but then had to be rapidly adjusted to new and unexpected circumstances. At first the designers, civil servants for the most part, had to contend with those who discouraged contemplation of the peace while there was a war to be won. When in 1943 they went to work on blueprints, the war began to end in stages. Attention had to be diverted to international régimes for conquered and starving peoples, refugees, and disbanding armies. Swift compromises were necessary, furthermore, if firm foundations were to be laid before the wartime alliance suffered the test of peace. The United Nations, established in 1942 as an association of wartime allies with a common aim to defeat the enemy, was seen as a peacetime extension of that alliance; agreement among the Americans, British, and Russians thus became the inescapable priority. We are not dealing here with a philosopher's dream.

The Canadian part must be seen in perspective against this world panorama. It was a part of some consequence, but its quality, such as it was, is to be found not in the proposing of grand designs but in the responses, in constructive amendments and imaginative formulas, in the exploiting of occasions, and in the insistence, usually in company, on certain basic principles. Canadian designs were spun at the outset, but more as a means of concentrating the mind, an aid to consistency, or a point of reference. From this exercise, in continuous review, emerged not a blueprint of world organization but a way of looking at it and a way of fitting Canada into it, a functionalist approach that has endured in Canadian foreign policy. Much of the effort of the Canadian planners went into finding a place in the schemes of things. It was more than just a sordid concentration on Canadian interest, however, because it was highly pertinent to the central theme – the ways and means of agglomerating states of various sizes into a world authority.

The Canadian designers were genuinely interested in creating a workable framework for peace, which they regarded as the first priority in the Canadian national interest. In so far as their calculations were universal in scope they were listened to. They clung, more or less, to the liberal concept, as E.H. Carr described it, that 'every state, by pursuing the greatest good of the whole world, is pursuing the greatest good of its own citizens, and vice versa.'[2] That assumption, of course, saved a lot of effort. It later proved inadequate for the expanded world community, but this limited principle was perhaps all that could be coped with as a start to the United Nations in peace. It was not a communist principle, but, given the balance of power at the time, the Soviet Union also wanted a United Nations of restricted authority. Canadians' hopes and expectations were constantly frustrated by the compromises the great powers exacted of each other and of them, but they tried not to forget that great-power agreement was the *sine qua non* of any order in which Canada could flourish.

This then cannot be an account of ideas as adumbrated in memoranda of officials and speeches of politicians; it must deal to some extent with events. The primary concern, however, is with the ideas; it is not intended as a comprehensive history of Canada's foreign policy. The period in which these events happened and the ideas were fashioned was roughly from 1943 to 1957, but the account spills over at both ends. The first volume is concerned with the winding up of the war and the prospect of a new kind of peace as perceived when the fighting subsided. The second volume deals with what might be called the revised version, the reconsiderations after about 1947 in the light of the realities that were protruding, such as the breakdown of consensus among the great powers and the revealed inadequacy of the economic calculations of 1945. The treatment of themes, however, has been determined more by subject matter than by chronology, and the division is often arbitrary.

International institutions, the United Nations, the Commonwealth, NATO, organizations that were thought about, are the major subjects of concern, but other aspects of policy are included if they illustrate Canadians' views of the systems around them. To grasp the significance of institutions one must consider also the significance of non-institutional relations. No book on Canadian foreign policy can ignore the United States, and the United States as a large international presence plays a leading role in every chapter. Our strictly bilateral relations with the US, however, would occupy little space in a book concerned with formal intergovernmental institutions because we are linked by only a few. It had been Canadian policy, in fact, in its relations with both its closest associates, Britain and the United States, to minimize structures. Why that is so requires attention. Canada matured in a triangle, its economic and security requirements largely satisfied in the Anglo-American entente. It was for Canadians the most concrete reality of their international relations, but it was no more than a concept, deeply though ambiguously felt, and devoid of chartered structure. The shape of the triangle shifted notably during the war and altered thereby Canadian perceptions of the world order that could accommodate their needs.

The study is primarily about official policy and official perspectives, particularly those of the Department of External Affairs. It is intended as one contribution to the expanding literature on Canada's postwar policies. What government leaders and their civil and military servants actually wanted and strove for is an important part of the picture. As one who was a civil servant involved in many of the projects herein described, I have endeavoured to explain official views as I think they were and as they look in retrospect. This volume is not an apologia; to explain is not necessarily to justify, even when the intention may be to counter misinterpretation. One of its purposes is to reveal something of the debate within the bureaucracy. My aim is description and analysis, not judgment, although the book is not without personal reflections on the wisdom of certain attitudes and actions – occasionally inspired by contemplation in tranquillity and by dismay at memoranda bearing my own initials.

Canada's foreign policy towards international institutions is not something to be set forth by its leaders briefly, categorically, and precisely, and it is unwise of historians to package it too neatly. It is imprudent of any country, large or small, to summarize its policy in a speech or a white paper, and it is particularly so of a country that must react to circumstances and policies of countries over which it has little or no control. Certain guiding principles, a way of looking at issues, and a sense, based on experience, of what is likely to work are required. Consistency is not necessarily a virtue. Before the war there was little effort, except in clichés, to define Canadian foreign policy in global terms. It was almost inevitable, however, that with the new self-consciousness after the war an effort would be made to do so. The closest thing was Louis St Laurent's Gray Lecture in January 1947, but it proved more retrospective than prospective. Neither the United States nor the Soviet Union received much attention and in referring to relations with the former he said typically that it was a matter of settling questions day to day 'without dignifying the process by the word "policy." '[3] That shrewd bureaucrat, Hume Wrong, when asked at a press conference on 26 September 1946 whether a statement would be produced on Canada's foreign policy similar to one Australia had just issued, replied, 'we could issue a statement of principles, I suppose, but I doubt if it would be of much value. We follow a fairly consistent pattern at the various conferences we attend, but I don't see what is to be gained by attempting to reduce the matter to a simple code.' To grasp the code of Canada's policies in the shaping of peace one has to look at a spectrum of ideas.

Although I have sought to be as objective as possible and to reappraise in the light of history, I would not pretend to have shed entirely the biases of a Canadian foreign service officer of my generation. I assume that any reader equipped with appropriate scepticism will adjust for that lens. Except for the personal reflections contained in this preface and the conclusion, this is not a first-person account. My part was not consequential enough to justify so narrow a focus. My perspectives, however, may be regarded as raw material for historians and political scientists – traditionalists, revisionists, Marxists, or Whigs – whose job it is to quantify or pass judgment.

The study is not confined to subjects in which I was personally involved, but I have concentrated on them. For that reason there is more about the diplomacy of political and security questions than about economics. My concern is with institutions rather than policy. I had the great benefit of advice and collaboration from Wynne Plumptre, one of the most constructive architects of our postwar economic policies, who not only read drafts and helped me plan the project but relieved me of responsibility by preparing himself a study of foreign economic policies, *Three Decades of Decision: Canada and the World Monetary System, 1944-1975*, which, with characteristic dedication, he completed shortly before his death in June 1977.

My own recollections have, of course, played an important part in the writing of this account. I have to the best of my ability checked the record. The written record is enormous and swallows up those who try to cope with it all. The Department of External Affairs, in accordance with official regulations, has allowed me to consult the files with which I was familiar as a member of the department, a wise provision designed to prevent the alumni from writing historical accounts off the tops of their heads. Needless to say, I found the records in many cases did not confirm the version which had become fixed in my mind. I have graciously left to scholars a considerable range of records unexamined. This study was written while I was holding positions at two universities and an institute, without benefit of sabbatical. It has seemed best to make my account available now rather than to aim for the definitive study in 1984. Footnotes are included in the interests of credibility, but they are intended for the general reader. Admittedly, they do not pamper scholars but they should assist them in tracking documents to the files in which they are now held.

To assist the reader in detecting prejudice – or even special competence – I shall herewith indicate the specific connection I had with the subject matter. My role, especially at the beginning, was junior, but I had the good fortune to work for the men of quite extraordinary ability who play the leading roles: Norman Robertson, Hume Wrong, Arnold Heeney, Escott Reid, A.G.L. McNaughton, Paul Martin, L.B. Pearson, and others, all of them friends as well as mentors, and one prejudice against which the reader should be warned is my difficulty in recognizing that any of them could have been mistaken. Fortunately for this book, at any rate, they were often in disagreement among themselves.

To begin with I was secretary in 1943-4 of the Working Committee on Post-Hostilities Problems and engaged under Hume Wrong's direction in following the plans for the peace settlements and the United Nations being put forward by the great powers, and in drafting position papers on the emerging structures. I served as a general factotum at the prime ministers' meeting in London in May 1944 and on the staff of Canada House, London, during the last period of the war and until late 1947. In London I was involved in liaison with the British Post-Hostilities Planners, in the pre-San Francisco meeting of Commonwealth leaders and later Commonwealth sessions, contact with the Dominions and Foreign Offices on, among other things, the peace settlements, the Council of Foreign Ministers, and the case of Igor Gouzenko. The staff of Canada House was small and my range of subjects during that interesting period broad. I was attached to the delegation to the Preparatory Commission and the first session of the United Nations General Assembly in London. Among other things I made a trip in 1947 to refugee camps in Germany with C.D. Howe which inspired admiration for the humanity of that remarkable man and some views and emotions which show through my account of that subject. Later in 1947 I was sent to Moscow as chargé d'affaires, and a good deal of the material in the chapter on the Cold War in volume II reflects my experience there, which extended to the time of the Berlin Blockade.

I then returned to United Nations affairs, with which I was associated during the rest of my career in External Affairs. After working with General McNaughton, our Permanent Representative to the United Nations, during the Security Council and Assembly sessions in Paris in 1948, I became head of the United Nations Division in Ottawa when I returned in 1949. During 1950-1 I also served twice for lengthy periods as acting head of the Canadian mission to the United Nations in New York, and was on the hot seat when the Korean War started. (Readers should watch for the United Nations rather than the Ottawa bias on Korea.) After two years on the Directing Staff of the National Defence College, 1951-3, during which I acquired a better understanding of defence and strategic questions and saw a lot of the world, from Yellowknife to Bahrein, I returned to Ottawa as an assistant undersecretary, with responsibilities for the next years in United Nations, Far Eastern, and Commonwealth affairs. I attended the Geneva Conference on Korea in 1954 and both then and thereafter was involved in the Geneva Agreements on Indochina and the Canadian role in the International Control Commissions. A good deal of time was spent in New York at Assembly, Economic and Social Council, or other meetings, including notably the sessions of 1955, when the new members issue arose, and 1956, over Suez and Hungary. My supervisory responsibilities required an acquaintance with issues from disarmament or Palestine refugees to the relation of Canada to the Pan American Sanitary Organization, an expertise notable more for its breadth than its depth. Association with the United Nations from its prenatal stage into late adolescence ought to have induced pessimism. Nothing in my career, however, was as exhilarating as United Nations diplomacy in the Hammarskjöld years, and an inextinguishable confidence in the capacity of international institutions to grow and adapt is the most obvious bias in these volumes.

Although most of this study is based on research or recollection at first hand I have made great use of both published and unpublished work by others. There is no need, for example, to describe in depth Canadian defence policy when this has been superbly covered by James Eayrs and Charles Stacey, upon whose work I have heavily depended. The subject matter of most of this study was so ably and reliably recorded by F.H. Soward and Robert Spencer in their volumes for 1944-6 and 1946-9, respectively, in the *Canada and World Affairs* series, by F.H. Soward and Edgar McInnis in *Canada and the United Nations*, and by R.A. MacKay's annotated *Documents on Canadian Foreign Policy 1945-54* that I frequently wondered whether more was necessary. Using their framework, however, I have sought to expand and add details as well as documentary evidence not available when they wrote. I have also taken advantage of much useful work available in unpublished theses, which are duly acknowledged in the footnotes. I have been especially dependent on Douglas Anglin's 'Canadian Policy towards International Institutions, 1939-1950,' a doctoral thesis written in 1956 which ought to have been published long ago. Paul Ambrose, John Kirton, Michael Little, Danford Middlemiss, Kim Nossal, Steven Ruvinsky, and

Michael Tucker not only made their research available but also helped by reading manuscript and offering counsel.

My work was from the beginning enormously facilitated by access to 'A Survey of Canadian External Policy' compiled for the Department of External Affairs in the early fifties from departmental files by Professor F.H. Soward of the University of British Columbia. This comprehensive survey of policy in seven chapters assembled, with Professor Soward's remarkable historical judgment, a great deal of the source material required. In addition to all this, Professor Soward provided critical comment on a great deal of my draft manuscript, increasing thereby the great debt I owe him for information and insight since we worked together in the Department of External Affairs when all this was going on.

The Canadian Institute of International Affairs, of which I was director at the time, requested me a few years ago to write a book on Canadian foreign policy. I was able to get down to work when the Canada Council provided a Killam Senior Research Scholarship. The Department of External Affairs encouraged me to undertake an historical study of postwar foreign policy, and Arthur Blanchette, former director of the Historical Division, provided encouragement and advice and arranged for assistance with my research, greatly facilitated by the good offices of Peter Dobell of the Parliamentary Centre for Foreign Policy and Foreign Trade. With the help of the Historical Division the manuscript in draft stages was submitted to former colleagues whose suggestions and criticisms were of great value. I was fortunate to have a good deal of help from the Rt Hon. Lester Pearson before his death and, through his editors, Alex Inglis and John Munro, he passed to me valuable documentation prepared for his memoirs. My former colleague and mentor, George deT. Glazebrook, generously made available a very useful collection of notes he had prepared on wartime institutions.

The list of those who read parts of the manuscript is long and I am thankful to my readers for saving me from error. I should particularly like to thank Louis Rasminsky, Douglas LePan, and David Mundy for the careful attention they gave to economic sections and to W.H. Barton, Paul Bridle, H.H. Carter, Ralph Collins, Marshall Crowe, Evan Gill, George Ignatieff, D.H.W. Kirkwood, C.E. McGaughey, R.A. MacKay, Escott Reid, and Max Wershof, among others, who read chapters. Robert Bothwell, Charles Stacey, and Norman Hillmer gave the historians' perspectives; and Ruth Russell, the dean of UN historians, very kindly checked the San Francisco material. The Hon. Paul Martin has been, as always, very helpful. None of these friends, however, has read the whole manuscript and no blame should be attributed to any of them for error or offense.

Lois Beattie made an indispensable contribution to the project by searching files in Ottawa with remarkable insight, as did Mary Harrison and Mary Taylor for particular subjects. Dorothy Stepler, Robert Willmot, and Kent Weaver provided research assistance at home base, and Jane Barrett, librarian, and other members of the CIIA staff were, as always, indefatigable trackers down of elusive information.

I was fortunate to have the incomparable guidance of R.I.K. Davidson in shaping these volumes and the editorial wisdom of Rosemary Shipton, also of the University of Toronto Press. Without the collaboration of Gayle Fraser of the CIIA as editor, archivist, transcriber, indexer, and very 'helpful fixer,' the study would not have reached print for many years.

This book has been published with the help of grants from the Social Science Federation of Canada, using funds provided by the Social Sciences and Humanities Research Council of Canada, and from the Publications Fund of the University of Toronto Press.

Abbreviations

AECB	Atomic Energy Control Board
CAOF	Canadian Army Occupation Force
CCF	Co-operative Commonwealth Federation
CCSC	Combined Chiefs of Staff Committee
CDT	Combined Development Trust
CIIA	Canadian Institute of International Affairs
CIPO	Canadian Institute of Public Opinion
CPC	Combined Policy Committee
CRMB	Combined Raw Materials Board
DEA	Department of External Affairs
DP	Displaced person
ECA	Economic Cooperation Administration
ECAFE	Economic Commission for Asia and the Far East
ECE	Economic Commission for Europe
ECLA	Economic Commission for Latin America
ECOSOC	Economic and Social Council
ERP	European Recovery Programme
FAO	Food and Agriculture Organization
FEAC	Far Eastern Advisory Commission
FEC	Far Eastern Commission
FRUS	*Foreign Relations of the United States*
GATT	General Agreement on Tariffs and Trade
IARA	Inter-Allied Reparations Agency
IBRD	International Bank for Reconstruction and Development
ICAO	International Civil Aviation Organization
ICEM	Intergovernmental Committee for European Migration
IJC	International Joint Commission

ILO	International Labour Organization
IMF	International Monetary Fund
IRO	International Refugee Organization
ITO	International Trade Organization
ITU	International Telecommunications Union
JCAE	Joint Committee on Atomic Energy
NATO	North Atlantic Treaty Organization
PASO	Pan American Sanitary Organization
PHP	Post-Hostilities Problems (Canada)
	Post-Hostilities Planning (UK)
PJBD	Permanent Joint Board on Defence
POWs	Prisoners of war
RCAF	Royal Canadian Air Force
SCAP	Supreme commander of the allied powers
SSEA	Secretary of state for external affairs
UNAEC	United Nations Atomic Energy Commission
UNCE	United Nations Commission for Europe
UNESCO	United Nations Educational, Scientific, and Cultural Organization
UNICEF	United Nations International Children's Emergency Fund
UNRRA	United Nations Relief and Rehabilitation Administration
UPU	Universal Postal Union
USSEA	Undersecretary of state for external affairs
WFTU	World Federation of Trade Unions
WHO	World Health Organization
WPB	War Production Board

PART I: PRELUDE

1

Trial and Error, 1914-45

So here I am, in the middle way, having had twenty years
Twenty years largely wasted, the years of l'entre deux guerres.

T.S. ELIOT, *East Coker*

Of the waste of years the historian takes a callous view. It was lives, millions of them, that were wasted by the failure of all efforts between the wars to prevent another slaughter. For the survivors the loss did not have to be in vain. They pondered deeply what had gone wrong and in 1945 tried again. Perhaps they concentrated too simply on doing what had not been done before. Just as generals are accused of planning to win the previous war, diplomats can be accused of planning to avoid it. They did not, however, reject the experiment in international regulation which had been the League of Nations; they reconstructed it with a different name, adjusted rules, and, most important of all, a wider membership.

The United Nations system (more a galaxy than a government) which evolved in the forties has been notable for its endurance and adaptability. Its reputation has suffered from the misrepresentation of those who dramatized its birth at San Francisco too apostolically, who proclaimed it as the final rejection of the failure and betrayal that had preceded it. That version reflects partly the Soviet and American wish to exorcize a League of Nations that had largely been run by others. We suffer a comparable distortion from those who see in the subsequent history of the United Nations a fall from grace, a noble dream of nations united and again betrayed by selfish men. These are romantic views for escapists. It was after all largely the same men who both created the United Nations and later revised it. The purpose of international institutions is to accommodate the legitimate but conflicting interests of nations, which it is the duty of national statesmen and diplomats to defend. The great endeavour is to devise and use the institutions for that purpose, and it is never-ending. It is wiser to regard 1945 as a resumption of the centuries-old experimentation with international structures – if in fact it had ever ceased, because the fighting alliance provided some of the sinews for postwar institutions. The making and remaking of these structures is an organic process; their success or failure is always relative; and final judgments are difficult because the way ahead remains unclear. Progress is not to be calculated as if the fixed goal was 'The Parliament of Man, the Federation of the World.' The unending struggle of mankind to discipline itself moves in mysterious ways. It is essentially a process of adaptation and improvisation. At least, that is the way Canadian policy-makers have tended to see it.

The 'revolution' in Canadian policy towards international institutions can also be over-dramatized. It was a change more of will than of policy, an enforced adaptation to change in international circumstance. There was much that was traditionally Canadian in the response, and, as Raymond Aron has noted, 'There is nothing more "traditional," more molded by the heritage of the past, than the diplomacy of a state, its perception of the world of international relations, and its conception of its role in that world.'[1] Canadians were not unprepared by their own history for the shaping of peace in 1945. Since the seventeenth century they had been calculating how to deal with neighbours and how to survive in a world often at war. Canada's more enthusiastic participation in the details of international life during and after the Second World War marked a notable change of direction, but it was conditioned by what had been learned and felt before. The shock of a second war and the recognition that Canada could not escape commitments was basic to the new mood. Nevertheless, the long experience of empire and commonwealth, of the North Atlantic triangle in which Canada had sought shelter, and the efforts to come to grips with the League were embedded in the subconsciousness of Canadians as they arrived at 'the middle way' of their life as a member of the international community at a time when that community was reshaping itself. Canada was not a young country, even if it was short of ambassadors.

In the years between the wars Canadians had gained a more direct experience than ever before of international institution-building. There was much to be learned in the testing of traditional assumptions against bitter realities, and many of the particular ideas about world order were evolving before 1939. To set the stage it is not necessary to provide a survey of foreign policy in the interwar years, as this has been well done by a number of historians.[2] It is proposed here only to note certain attitudes to the Commonwealth and the League of Nations which help explain postwar perspectives.

EMPIRE INTO COMMONWEALTH

Although in hindsight it can be seen that the Canadian government was reconstituting the Commonwealth for a greater future, that was not the general impression between the wars. Some fond and foolish notions did have to be cleared away, but Canadians sounded pretty negative whenever the architecture of the organization was under consideration. At the end of the First World War there was general satisfaction among government leaders with the Imperial War Cabinet, and it was expected that an imperial conference of sorts would be held as soon as possible to establish a permanent framework. There was a good deal of talk, but nothing concrete came of it. The British were preoccupied with postwar settlements and had little time to spend on getting consensus. Their experience of a commonwealth was as yet limited. It took a long while for them to realize that, even for such loyal subjects as the Australians, an imperial foreign policy was a good deal more complicated than simply the acquisition of agreement from Ottawa, Canberra, or Pretoria to policies which would naturally be devised in Whitehall because Whitehall would know best. The utter impracticality of the idea of a common policy, particularly after the dominions had assumed their separate seats in the League of Nations, ought to have been evident already, but the idea haunted the Commonwealth for another twenty-five years. It did so not just because of British persistence, but because of the continuing demands of the Pacific dominions for a voice in grand strategy and the reluctance of all concerned, including Canadians, to abandon an identity of some kind for the empire.

Mackenzie King was a family man – in his fashion. He argued for a commonwealth principle of consultation, for a continuing effort to seek agreement, but the ultimate right of each government to go its own way. However, he surrounded this sensible argument with circumlocutions to bemuse critics both in Britain and in Canada so that the long-range aim was not clearly evident, if indeed he had one. He did not want to sever the British link, but discussion of the Commonwealth under his régime seemed more concerned with an old relationship Canada was growing out of than a new relationship it was growing into. In opposition the Conservatives sounded more imperial, but in power they did not act very differently. During the First World War Canada had participated in the Imperial War Cabinet because it wanted a say in the way in which Canadians were going to be killed. After the war, as Canada relaxed in its fire-proof house, having a voice in an imperial policy looked too much like getting committed by an imperial government with far-flung obligations. On issues, however, that touched the Canadian national interest or seemed to, or on which the Canadian prime minister felt strongly, advantage was taken of the Commonwealth to establish a position – notably over the renewal of the Anglo-Japanese Treaty which the Canadian government opposed, and the appeasement of Nazi Germany which it favoured. When Bennett's government wanted to fight the high American tariff with a system of commonwealth preferences, he made vigorous use of the empire as a framework.

The Canadian right to press its cases can hardly be questioned, but the results, seen in retrospect, raise doubt about any assumption that Canada's getting its own way would necessarily ensure the triumph of right ideas over wrong. It can be argued that the British rejection of the Japanese alliance set Japan on the way to Pearl Harbor, that King's last-ditch support of appeasement by Chamberlain encouraged the Nazi appetite, and that the imperial preference system only compounded the economic autarky that preceded the bloody war. To do so, however, might be to indulge in a typically Canadian exaggeration of the impact of Canada on the world scene if only it would do the right thing.

The issues were not simple. Sir Robert Borden's experience in power, particularly during the First World War, had made him well aware of the persistent paradox at the heart of the imperial relationship,[3] and subsequent prime ministers wrestled, each in his own way, with the puzzle. A belief that the strength of the empire as a whole was in the national interest of the parts meant that Canada should be willing to commit its military support to the defence of the empire. Such a commitment, however, meant not only a right but an obligation to share in the making of policies that could lead the empire in or out of danger. There could not be a blank cheque. But a principle of shared decision-making was a trap because Britain's role in the world and its authority over a large part of the empire precluded equality. There were inescapable contradictions involved in actually securing agreement among Britain and the dominions, and the process would have been intolerably cumbersome.

This dilemma of decision-making is inherent in any alliance relationship, particularly a relationship with greater powers, as Canada was to find in subsequent associations in NATO and with the United States. The issue, which in one form or another has been an obsession of Canadian foreign policy, is confused by the tendency of politicians and editors to make a contradiction that is in the nature of things look like a struggle between right and wrong, between the weak and the powerful. Blaming the great powers indiscriminately for the postponement of heaven on earth remains a persistent theme in the same vein. Mackenzie King, who did a great deal to straighten out the status issue in the Commonwealth and make possible a sublimated Commonwealth based on principles of consultation, was guilty of obfuscating the issue by shrewd political manipulation. In an anti-colonialist age, the temptation to see Canada's cautious and reluctant acceptance of responsibility for its foreign relations as a 'struggle' for independence was irresistible. What

King did resist, however, was independence in practice from the British diplomatic establishment which would have forced Canada into the kind of expensive and presumptuous foreign service of its own which he deplored. It cannot be said that Canadians emerged from the war as masters of the dilemma, but the long experience of empire and commonwealth had rendered them sensitive when it appeared in new settings and endowed officials with a more sophisticated comprehension of the equations involved. That was some advantage in dealing with the new imperial power, for the Americans had to suffer frustration for many years before realizing that there was a dilemma at all.

The issue of an independent foreign policy was confused in the thirties by the fact that British policy on the basic question of security was not one that the Canadian government wanted to oppose. At the Imperial Conference of 1937 King worked hard for Commonwealth agreement on an issue dear to his heart: so strong was his belief in appeasement and his anxiety to support Chamberlain against Churchill and the other 'warmongers' that he forgot his reluctance to give the British advice on foreign policy. Typically, however, he did this personally and confidentially, and, although he was effusive in public tributes, the full extent of his support of Chamberlain was not revealed until private papers became available after the war.[4]

Once the war started, King's policy on commitments was widely reviled as 'pussyfooting,' but it has been justified – and denounced – as a calculated strategy for bringing Canada as united as possible into a war that seemed inevitable. The judgment of two of the leading historians of this period is as follows:

In many of his opinions on foreign policy, King revealed himself to be unreasonably optimistic, prejudiced and unrealistic. But in his basic perception that foreign policy can be no more effective than one's internal strength will support, he was profoundly right. King's backing and filling, his evasions and hesitations, do not make inspiring reading. But his actions, particularly between 1937 and 1939, indicate his sure grasp of the public mood and his recognition that public opinion cannot be wished into existence simply because one course of action or another is 'right.' When King took a united Canada into the Second World War, he gave Canadians a policy that not only was right to him, but one that seemed right to them.[5]

King's basic philosophy of the Commonwealth was reaffirmed as sound during and after the war, but he was not the man to move it into another and more positive phase after he had set it on the right path. In the meantime, however, the legend was established that Canada was drawn into a war by its attachment to Britain without having had any influence on British policy. The Canadian complaint has been specifically over the British commitment to Poland without consulting Canada, but given King's disposition, well understood in London, to regard consultation as an invitation to commitment, the British action was not without justification. Some deduced that the tie with Britain should be broken or clarified. Others concluded that as Canada would be inevitably drawn into Europe's wars it should get involved before the fighting started. The imperial tie confused the issue. Whereas Canada would probably not have gone to war two years ahead of the Americans for the second time if it had not been linked to Britain, neither would it have done so if Canadian leaders had not believed that the international system which guaranteed Canadian security was threatened. What was needed, as some clear-headed officials recognized, was a new hard look at Canadian strategic concepts and priorities set in a wider framework than the relationship with Britain or France, the Commonwealth, or the North Atlantic triangle. On that basis they began to think about a new international system in which Canada would not only claim its rights but also accept its responsibilities.

THE LEAGUE OF NATIONS

From the beginning of the League of Nations Canadian governments – Conservative and Liberal – made clear their opposition to two interpretations of its function. They opposed the concept of universal collective security, involving automatic commitments, and any pretensions of the League to exercise supranational authority. Their positions were never stated more firmly than by the Conservative statesmen who attended the conference in Paris and the early sessions of the League – although Borden when the treaty was signed defended it as a whole. They well reflected a Canadian consensus. Unlike the belief after the Second World War that only by commitment in advance could aggression again be forestalled, the Canadian mood after 1919 was one of determination not to be dragged again, or at least on a regular basis, into European wars and to take advantage of the peculiar sanctuary provided in North America not only by geography but by the more civilized international habits of North Americans.

There were articulate 'internationalists' and 'imperialists' in both major parties, but their views did not prevail. Late in his term of office R.B. Bennett looked more like a League supporter. He even took advantage of the supranational pretensions of the League system when he used International Labour Organization resolutions to justify federal legislation in what the Judicial Committee of the Privy Council later ruled to be matters of provincial jurisdiction. Partly because of his natural antipathy to the isolationism of the undersecretary of state for external affairs, O.D. Skelton, and a characteristic belief in standing up to be counted, he gave, in the Italo-Ethiopian case, clearer support of League sanctions than was characteristic of other Canadian governments.[6] This apparent disposition to act positively was cut short by the accession to power of Mackenzie King. Bennett's attitude on sanctions, however, was largely emotional and accidental. His government had certainly not been zealous for sanctions in the Manchurian crisis. In any case, his disposition to follow the British lead because he believed in their superior wisdom would more likely have led a Conservative government to support Chamberlain as King did, rather than to a strong stand for collective security.

There were other Canadian reservations about the League. It was not universal in membership. The basis of the Canadian concept of a sound world order was the Anglo-American entente. Canada would undoubtedly have accepted more willingly a league that had as its core the empire and the United States, but when the Americans decided not to join, Canada was left on a limb. It could not and did not wish to give up the seat in the League which gave it international status, but Canadians could not see the practicality of military or even economic sanctions without the Americans involved. Ironically, it was Wilson at Paris who disliked most strongly the Canadian view on Article 10, the article of the Charter which affirmed the commitment to collective security, a view that had been put forward even when it was expected the United States would be a member. Perhaps the Canadians more accurately reflected North American opinion than did the president of the United States. In the Canadian view and that of many Americans the League was Eurocentric. It was a device to get all countries to guarantee a settlement in Europe that had not been determined on grounds of justice and was not likely to last forever. The commitment required was unequal because Canada did not need similar guarantees by European or other powers. When Canada went to war in 1939 it was not because of a commitment to the League or collective security but because of its calculation of the importance of Britain and France to the security of North America.

The opposition to supranationalism took other forms that Canadians are less wont to recall. Canada was very suspicious of proposals that might in any way determine Canadian immigration regulations and bluntly rejected efforts by Japan to enlist the League in fighting racial discrimination in employment. Sensitivity about provincial rights was then, as always, a serious consideration for Canadian delegations, but at a time when there was trouble in the Canadian labour force and a strong current of opposition to aliens, particularly 'orientals,' there were more than simply constitutional reasons for the Canadian position. An Italian proposal that the League consider the more equitable distribution of raw materials was also opposed.[7] The idea of the League as a supranational manager was unacceptable. Some regulation was desirable, as for instance of drugs and epidemics, but only when there was a demonstrated need for it. Canada rejected the suggestion that the League do something to regulate international air traffic. Because there was little air traffic across bodies of water in those days Canadians thought this was a matter for Canada in association with the United States alone to consider. This position, which had some logic to it, is in contrast with the vigorous efforts of Canadian officials at the end of the Second World War to create an international civil aviation organization with what looked like supranational powers. The troublesome propositions raised by the Japanese and Italians have become eventually the dominant issues of the United Nations, but proposals for a New International Economic Order were not foreseen even in 1945.

Canada's strong effort to delete and then to amend Article 10 to make it harmless or inapplicable as far as Canada was concerned created enemies. European and other countries that regarded themselves as much more exposed than Canada considered Article 10 the *sine qua non* of the League and resented the Canadian campaign from a secure hinterland to deny them security. The Conservative government in Ottawa wanted to get rid of it entirely. The Liberals, when they came to power in 1921, did not like the article any better but, realizing there was no hope of expunging it, sought amendment. Among the countries which bitterly disliked the Canadian position were Persia and Estonia, and, perhaps not surprisingly, they were among the few countries that supported an appeal by the Six Nations Indians from Canada to have the League consider their case against the Canadian government – an appeal which was frustrated with the powerful assistance of the British Foreign Office.[8] Canadians also created enemies when, under the strong influence of Senator Raoul Dandurand, they argued for more effective machinery to consider the appeal of minorities. What they had in mind, of course, was the dreadful state of European minorities, but the Polish government hinted that such regulations could apply to Canada as well. It was the beginning of the slow education of Canadians in the basic fact that international politics and particularly the politics of international organizations are a two-way street – a lesson which they will probably grasp fully only after Canada has itself been put in the dock at the United Nations.

In spite of its reservations about the League, Canada did become a member of the League Council in 1927. Whenever it comes to asserting the Canadian right to a seat, Canadian governments then as now tend to suspend their worries over commitment. Mackenzie King, needless to say, was not enthusiastic, but he was pressed by Dandurand and somewhat more surprisingly by Ernest Lapointe, his Quebec lieutenant. The Canadian record at Geneva was, in fact, not as discreditable as legend has it, but the legend was a factor in creating a new climate of opinion. For a small power, Canada played an active role, without however the favourable reputation acquired in the early days of the United Nations. The compulsion of successive Canadian delegates to lecture naughty Europeans on the higher morality of Canada-United States relations, and even to suggest the International Joint Commission as a model for Japan and China,[9] exasperated the Assembly and embarrassed Canadian officials. Canadian objections to collective security as a practical proposition for the League as it existed and the emphasis on the mediatory function look more sensible, however, since the United Nations in practice arrived at similar conclusions.

For Canada to have taken a more active part in proclaiming sanctions against Japan and Italy would have been not only futile but also pretentious. Canada had neither soldiers nor trade of sufficient proportions to offer a meaningful sacrifice and such 'leadership' would have been dismissed by the powers that had to carry the burden as no more than a gesture. When Walter Riddell, the Canadian permanent representative at Geneva in 1935, proposed oil sanctions against Italy during a transition from a Bennett to a King government, he stretched considerably his authority as a civil servant, but he was also the victim of clumsy handling from Ottawa. King favoured economic sanctions to restrain aggressors, but he had, in this situation, come to fear that they would provoke war. Nevertheless his government did pass an order-in-council implementing the sanctions already approved by the League. He publicly repudiated Riddell, who was later replaced in Geneva.

There was warm discussion in Canada, as the incident dramatized the question of Canada's international commitments. In the interwar period dedicated supporters of the League were articulate and eloquent – and somewhat confused – but they remained a minority. The opposition and many other spokesmen strongly criticized the government for backing away from its stand against aggression, but no political leaders wanted to face the possibility that economic sanctions would involve Canada in military action. When war did break out in 1939 and Canada was almost immediately caught up in an effort at collective action against aggression, the 'Riddell incident' came to be regarded widely as Canada's 'great betrayal.' Whether oil sanctions would have done the trick in Ethiopia is doubtful, especially as the French and British foreign ministers were engaged in a 'compromise settlement' behind the scenes. Nevertheless, the case of oil sanctions became a symbol for much of Canada's 'culpability' in the 'failure of the League.'

ON THE EVE OF WAR

Enthusiasm in Canada for the Munich agreement was widespread. Almost anything that would stave off a war was acceptable. The 'internationalists' in the country were victims of conflicting strains of liberal idealism. There were strong believers in the League and collective security like J.W. Dafoe of the *Winnipeg Free Press* who accepted the obligations of collective action. The liberal Left, though professedly favouring brotherhood and internationalism, was obsessed by the will to detach Canada from British 'imperialism' and sounded more nationalist. Some nationalists of the thirties, although normally disposed towards international good deeds, were consistent enough to oppose Canadian commitments either to the League or the empire. Many people, however, especially those who were young and vocal, denounced the failure of 'the powers' to support sanctions against Japan and Italy and the policy of 'non-intervention' in Spain; they called for the overthrow of fascism and vigorously criticized British policies of appeasement. At the same time, however, they opposed military expenditures and argued that Canada, a North American country, should make no commitments to fight against aggressors outside America. In their outlook was a strong strain of anti-militarism and the rejection of war as a conspiracy of Old World aristocrats and munitions manufacturers. The apparent belief that it is for Canadians to denounce sin and for larger and less pacific powers to use force against it has reappeared in many contexts since the war.

The public debate in Canada before 1939 on issues of international organization does not look very good in retrospect, but it was no more confused than that in Britain, France, or the United States. Pacifism, neutralism, appeasement, or universal collective security may seem naïve to a generation that has had a more diverse experience of international efforts to keep the peace, but the League was the first modern effort to grapple on an organized scale with deeply-rooted conflict. The charge of naïveté ignores the conviction of a generation that had lived through Paschendaele that there could be nothing worse than modern war. 'I just can't find the answers to a lot of questions,' Lester Pearson wrote in 1939.[10] It is not easy to identify any group that was right. As the *Vancouver Sun* said in 1942: 'The simple fact is that we were wrong, nearly all of us, before the war.'[11] Professor Frank Underhill, who asked many of the right questions without admitting the contradictions, confessed in the sixties that he had been 'slightly more innocent and considerably more irresponsible than was our Prime Minister.'[12] The men of the thirties did not readily come to terms with contradictions. If anything distinguished the Canadian 'creators' of the postwar world it is a greater disposition to recognize that there is no easy substitute for the endless process of reconciling national and international interests and that an international organization must have the flexibility to embrace paradox.

THE DEPARTMENT OF EXTERNAL AFFAIRS

In the years before the war there was no doubt who determined the foreign policy of Canada. It was the government in general and the prime minister in particular, whether that was Bennett or King. Still, the Department of External Affairs played a significant role. The prime minister set the main lines, but he had not the time to look at the details. External Affairs was small but forceful, staffed with some men of remarkable intellectual quality and a broad comprehension of international issues. It was by no means monolithic in its views on the Canadian role in the international community, but what came out at the top was dominated by the vigorous views of the under-secretary, O.D. Skelton, and in the latter years his 'counsellor,' Loring Christie. These men were convinced of the folly of further involvement in the quarrels of the Europeans. As civil servants it was, of course, their duty to operate within a framework laid down by the government. Their approach was generally in line with the resonant conviction of Canadian governments since 1918, although less so by the end of the thirties. Mackenzie King often sounded like Skelton and Christie, and he agreed with much of their philosophy, but he was playing his game of bringing a united country into a war he saw as almost inevitable. However hard he tried to avoid that war, he had convictions about the ultimate justice of the cause led by Britain. Christie could speak sarcastically of 'an English-Speaking Mission to oversee the universe.'[13] King believed in that mission even though he was reluctant to see it established by force.

Skelton and Christie imposed their own policies on departmental correspondence, slapping down Vincent Massey in London or Hume Wrong in Geneva when they got ideas about positive things Canada might be doing or saying. These exchanges, often penetrating and sophisticated observations on the ways of a wicked world, had a life of their own, but it was too academic to be the stuff of Canadian foreign policy. It could be said that

Skelton and Christie had no policy except to shake their heads – either to say no or to bewail the follies of others, especially the French and the British. The government was strong on denial also, whether it was an invitation to consultation on policy, economic sanctions against Japan or anybody else, an initiative at the League, or the preposterous suggestion from the French that big empty Canada might help with the flood of Spanish refugees. Didn't the French know about unemployment in Canada?[14] In Skelton's and Christie's contrariness may be perceived, nevertheless, some persistent truths. Christie warned Canadian activists not to let their diplomacy outrun their resources. He was cogent on the folly of sanctions without overwhelming force.[15] He argued perceptively that the way to avoid being a 'protectorate' of the United States or the United Kingdom was to pursue a foreign policy based on self-defence plus a diplomacy which sought allies with common interests – a concept developed later into that of 'alliance potential.'[16] If only he had not been so shrill and obsessed, and if he had lived longer, he might have been a useful critic of postwar planning.

There were seeds of rebellion against the prevailing orthodoxy of the East Block, however. They are worth noting because they came from the men who would soon be in charge of the department. From Canada House in London the priorities in 1938 and 1939 seemed a little different from those of Skelton, who could write on 25 August 1939, 'The first casualty in this war has been Canada's claim to independent control of her own destinies.'[17] Pearson in London came to see the inadequacies of the Canadian position. He wrote to Skelton early in 1938 that he now realized the Nazi threat had to be resisted collectively.[18] At home Norman Robertson's powerful intellect and conscience were at work. He had displayed a very different attitude from Skelton's when in 1933 the mission in Geneva asked Bennett if they could take up membership in the Committee of Seventeen, designed to see what might be done to bring pressure on Japan. Skelton was out of town, and Bennett listened to Robertson's argument that a refusal would seem like an evasion of responsibility.[19] Robertson was as always conscious of the limits on what could be done, but he saw these as something to be regretted rather than as valid excuses to avoid commitment. His inventive mind constantly reached for ways of doing something if possible, if only to help the victims. When a conference was held in late 1938 at Evian to try to cope with the refugees from the Nazis, King told the Canadian delegate: 'It is axiomatic that no state should be allowed to throw upon other countries the responsibility of solving its internal difficulties.' There was legitimate fear that an open door for refugees in Western countries would simply encourage not only the Nazis but the Poles and others to drive out all their Jews. Nevertheless, King's perception of the issue is blood-chilling. Robertson, in contrast, proposed that the Nazis be charged with committing 'an international nuisance' and suggested a surtax on all imports from Germany to pay for resettlement schemes.[20] A preposterous suggestion, perhaps, but it was better than just finding good reasons for doing nothing. Hume Wrong was incisive from Geneva, where he had been posted in 1937 as advisory officer and then permanent delegate to the League. His views of the time are worthy of particular examination because of his central influence on Canadian policies in shaping the peace. One can see already in his Geneva calculations the architect of postwar responses. They were the more realistic because they evolved during the years when he was intensely preoccupied with the diplomacy of winning a war and establishing the basis of an appropriate role for Canada.

This concentration on the implications for policy rather than serene judgments Wrong shared with Pearson and Robertson, the other members of the triumvirate most responsible for the shaping of peace, Canadian-style, after 1945. They were a new generation of Canadian 'nationalists,' more assured and less hag-ridden by fear of the British – or later the Americans. They had all learned at Oxford to regard the British as equals. Canada was their country, their base of operation, and their job was to contrive a world best suited to Canadian interests and the ways and means by which a country of Canada's proportions, situation, history, virtues and idiosyncracies, strengths and weaknesses could play its due part in the creation and permanent structures of a peace for that world. That due part, it was recognized, included responsibilities as well as rights. It was a subject for rational calculation rather than just emotional ferment. There was no longer need to agonize over Canada's right to an independent foreign policy. That course had been set, and the arguments about commitments and independence within the Commonwealth or the League were no longer central.

These men were not, in fact, as far from Mackenzie King in theory as his popular reputation suggests. As Blair Neatby has written: 'Autonomy for Mackenzie King ... did not mean independence. He defined autonomy as self-government but saw no inconsistency in a completely self-governing Dominion which none the less had inescapable obligations to Great Britain. Indeed, for King these obligations would become more acceptable and so more secure as self-government became more complete.'[21] Wrong, Pearson, and Robertson would agree with that. The difference was rather in that the older man wanted autonomy to keep Canada out of things and the younger men wanted it so that Canada could do things. They knew they still had to struggle for provisions to guarantee Canada's place in the firmament and against old assumptions and prejudices at home and abroad. Establishing the formulas for this purpose, however, was a matter of intellectual agility and stubborn insistence, not a simple-minded campaign against bullies. These are the men who replaced Skelton and Christie, both of whom died early in the war.

RE-EXAMINING THE LEAGUE

The years 1938-9 were the worst of times, just before the catastrophe, but the best of times for cutting through illusions. There was a somewhat perfunctory self-examination by the League that was on the whole remarkably clear-headed. It was realized by the Geneva community that the League as an agency of collective security could now play little part in the drastic events in Europe, that what hope there was at that stage was in the organization of a European coalition by traditional methods, and that the League as an agency for conciliation could hope to function only after a relaxation of tension. That chance came only after a war had ended the particular set of tensions that existed in 1939. It should be noted, however, that Western members reached the same conclusion within three years of the establishment of the United Nations. Then, however, they had the will and the collaboration of the United States, so they could set up such a coalition and in accordance with provisions they had put into the Charter.

Canada's role as it developed in the postwar creation was adumbrated by Wrong's reflections from Geneva. It was first necessary, he said, to take a hard look at the question of Canada's participation and its responsibilities for protecting its own interests. Here he moved from the fashionable abstractions about rights and wrongs to the policy decisions that actually faced the government. In a memorandum[22] of 7 December 1938 on 'The Canadian Position in the Light of the September [Munich] Crisis,' he wrote: 'We must start from Canadian opinion as it was revealed in September, and not as we might like it to be.' That was always Wrong's approach and it set a pattern. Policy-makers must start from the predicament as it has to be faced rather than rejecting it because it is unpopular or because the circumstances are not of Canada's making. He began with the assumption that the state of Canadian opinion was such that 'no Canadian government is likely to be able to keep Canada out of a great war in which the United Kingdom is engaged.' He cut through the argument of many nationalists by pointing out that although bellicose British adventures that would alienate Canadian opinion were a possibility, 'it is apparent that the United Kingdom will in fact enter no war on the continent of Europe except on a paramount issue.'

Nevertheless, Wrong argued, it was clearly unsatisfactory that the most vital decision in the life of a nation would not be taken in fact as well as in form by the leaders of the Canadian people. He had doubts about the logic of the Canadian solution pursued since 1918 – to limit political commitments and 'to receive information but decline to offer advice.' How could Canada escape from the dilemma that the avoidance of formal commitments had left it still deeply committed to the United Kingdom? Little could be done in a hurry, but a revision of the ends and means of Canadian foreign policy could begin at once to ensure that all vital decisions should be taken in Ottawa. However, it was essential to recognize that a home-made Canadian policy could 'pursue a separate road' or 'stand shoulder to shoulder with the United Kingdom.' Wrong saw clearly that the evolution of independent decision-making had to be separated from the decision for isolation or participation.

As for the League, Wrong looked sceptically at the comfortable assumption that had allowed Canadians to avoid the critical issue – that the League had abolished war or, in any case, as any war would be a League war involving Commonwealth members, the decision to participate would be loyalty to the Covenant rather than the empire. The Commonwealth, he pointed out, had proved hardier than the collective system. Nevertheless, 'Geneva offered, and still offers to a limited degree, a means for the development and expression of a positive Canadian foreign policy.' He was critical of Canada's policy at the League which he described as seeking 'the most modest interpretation of political obligations under the Covenant.' While fully recognizing a good deal of unreality in the idea of League sanctions against the threatened aggression, it seemed wise for Canada to accept sanctions as optional and provide for the possibility of sanctions under the Covenant, giving Canada 'a legal means whereby Canada can enter under her own steam, as it were, a war in which she would in any case be involved as a member of the Commonwealth.' It was an approach which, as he expected, would not work in 1939, but it was central to the predominant view of the United Nations as an instrument of Canadian foreign policy which flourished at the end of the war. In 1950 Wrong, as ambassador in Washington, Pearson as minister, and Robertson as high commissioner in London would be making clear that Canada's participation in the United Nations operation in Korea was from loyalty to the United Nations rather than constraint by the United States, the country which had by then taken over from Britain the role of menace to Canadian independence.

Wrong did not argue for the simplistic conception of universal and mandatory collective security which an articulate minority in Canada advocated because he knew that no nation would accept such open-ended commitments. He saw that in a happier time of eased tension the League could be useful as conciliator, but he knew also that, as the present situation illustrated, there were times when collective force had to be assembled to deter those who defied the international community. In 1938 that force could not be organized by the discredited League, although it would be better if such operations could be under the aegis of a world organization. He knew that what could be done by force had to be related to circumstances. He was wary of dogmas and universal theories, and thought in terms of function.

This functional approach to the League led Wrong to argue also for more attention to economic and social activities. 'More frequent initiative by the Canadian representatives on questions of economic, social and humanitarian importance would contribute towards preserving the practice and technique of international collaboration, now endangered by the extension into nearly every field of the habit of sabre rattling.' The League, he knew, was doomed, but it could be revived 'under some other name in some other city under some other instrument.' As a historian he saw that the essential thing was 'to preserve the habit and technique of international collaboration in a world sadly in need of it' – a cause much older than the League of Nations. For that reason, the 'other functions' of the League should not be discouraged. There was even an argument for over-emphasizing them. The attitudes of Canadian governments became more favourable to the idea of the League having economic and social functions. King saw in his own book, *Industry and Humanity*, 'pretty much the whole programme that now is being suggested for post-war purposes.'[23] Of course, some of this emphasis on the economic function could have been inspired by an anxiety to downplay the military function.

On the eve of the war there was, in connection with the International Labour Organization, evidence of the more constructive pragmatism which differentiates postwar attitudes to international organization from those of the interwar years. When Wrong went to Geneva in 1937 he turned his attention to the problems of what could be done both to serve the Canadian interest and its image and to strengthen the international fabric. Since the Judicial Committee of the Privy Council had in 1937 declared invalid the Canadian government's ratification of three ILO conventions as *ultra vires* of the federal power, Canadian policy had been in a state of paralysis. The constitutional stalemate was both a cause and an excuse. As Wrong pointed out,[24] '... every informed person would agree that the Canadian contribution to the International Labour Organisation has been small and that the most important reason for that has been the limitations of our federal system.' Although as a good civil servant he acknowledged that the question whether a more positive attitude could be taken in prevailing circumstances was a political decision, he pointed out: 'Since the adhesion of the United States to the Organisation, however, our often repeated explanation of our limited activity is not as convincing as it was, since the United States Government has assumed a leading part although hampered by the same sort of constitutional restrictions as Canada.' Largely as a result of his prodding, the parallel interests of the two countries in some provision for the problems of federal states were acknowledged. Consultations took place between Americans and Canadians of a kind which foreshadowed a new relationship after the war in international organization as sharers of certain coincidental interests.

Wrong's memorandum for the minister of labour, dated Geneva, 30 November 1938, and entitled 'Some Proposals Concerning Canada and the International Labour Organisation,' is a masterly analysis of the successes and failures of the ILO, notable for the absence of denunciation and a shrewd assessment of how to build on the successes and write off the failures. It would be best, he thought, to move away from the idea of the International Labour Conference as an 'international legislature' adopting statutes in the form of draft conventions to be ratified by all countries. The ratifications were simply not happening. 'It is better to have a recommendation experimentally applied in a number of States, than to have a convention which only two or three Governments will ratify.' The functions of the ILO, as distinct from the conference, were less spectacular but of real importance and efficiently discharged. The emphasis, he thought, was beginning to shift to the conception of the ILO 'as an international centre of enquiry and research, achieving its results in individual countries more by the influence of its work on individual governments than by securing widespread acceptance of uniform minimum standards set out in conventions.' This was the lapidary approach, the concentration on building from what is possible rather than starting with the grand design.

Skelton waited three months to acknowledge Wrong's memorandum of 8 December 1938.[25] Such positive thinking was not congenial to the masters of the East Block. Skelton had a clear view of the way things were moving, the fragility of Munich, and the inevitability of Canada's going to war at Britain's side. He retreated into an academic disengagement from events to lament the follies of homo sapiens, especially the European species. Christie went even further. His denunciation of the follies of Britain and France, the League, and the whole nonsense of 'collective security' was often devastating. The problem was that, unlike Wrong, there was no recognition of responsibility for a Canadian policy, and his condemnation was from no fixed point of conviction.

Views of the League from the East Block were largely negative. For Christie the objective was 'the elimination, as soon as possible, of the last vestige of our formal commitment, either direct or indirect, to the coercive, alliance features of the League.'[26] J.S. Macdonald, in a departmental examination of the question, recognized some value of the League but doubted if it would be possible any longer 'to justify the payment of $400,000 per annum, which the League at present takes from the Canadian Treasury, to maintain a top-heavy institution at Geneva.'[27] When the Canadian government considered its views on the revision of the League Covenant on the basis of the report to the Assembly in 1938 of the 'Committee of Twenty-Eight' it was not prepared to go even as far as the British, who offered a cool-headed assessment of what was and was not possible now but regarded the system for peaceful settlement of disputes as 'an immensely valuable piece of machinery.'[28] Ottawa feared any effort to revise the Covenant or produce an interpretative resolution lest 'any group of European members would be put in a position to seek to revive the sanctions provisions in a case and at a time that it suits their interests to do so, in spite of having ignored them with respect to wars of aggression in America and Asia.'[29] Finally should be noted the persistent conviction in Ottawa that the Covenant ought to be detached from the unfair Treaty of Versailles, a sound enough view for consideration in 1919 and reconsideration in 1945 but fatuous in the time of the Führer.

What had Skelton and company believed in as a function of the League? They did believe, as Mackenzie King did, in 'economic appeasement.' They shared with many of the liberal internationalists and the 'revisionists' of the interwar years a conviction that the Versailles settlement was punitive, that Germany had legitimate grievances, that France was interested not in collective security but *revanche*, and that Italy and Japan had become aggressive as a result of economic discrimination against them. It was the role of the League not to assemble force to use against force but to tackle the economic, social, and political causes of war and tension. It is hard to quarrel with these beliefs, especially as they have become the doctrine of Canada and most other democratic countries about the functions of the United Nations. Mackenzie King's defence in the Commons in 1936[30] of the League as 'machinery for conference and conciliation' that is always available is in terms that could well have been used about the United Nations by any prime minister after about 1952.

One legitimate question, however, about Canada's espousal of the doctrine of 'economic appeasement' for the League was that its government was slow to recognize any Canadian responsibility, as a rich country, to contribute. In the Canadian view economic appeasement meant freer trade. An External Affairs memorandum of 1936 complained that the League was a failure because: 'In the economic field nothing has been done to prevent tariffs from rising to hitherto undreamed of heights, or to prevent the most favoured nation clause from being vitiated by import quotas and similar restrictions.'[31] By the late thirties, furthermore, there was something very unreal about the insistence of some officers in the department and the more extreme academics that fascism could be cured, or at least could have been cured, by fair treatment for German, Italian, and Japanese exports. The departmental memoranda for the Imperial Conference of 1937 concluded with the injunction to 'fight war hysteria through returning economic prosperity.'[32] The argument was ten years late and it ignored the existence of malignancy in politics. But it was also ten years early.

To give these advocates credit, they had been arguing the case, along with other good cases about Canadian autonomy and Canadian influence, since the early twenties. The temptation of a lesser power that has not got its way, especially a lesser power that can with some credibility regard itself as a fireproof house, to contract out of a mess on the ground that it was not of its making still paralyzes Canadians from time to time. It was not the attitude of the postwar leaders in External Affairs, who recognized that although it was their job to make the world as much as possible like their ideal, they were going to have to go on dealing with a world only partly designed according to Canadian specifications and with crises which they could do little to avoid but perhaps something – even if modest – to help settle. The prime minister, although he liked to cast blame and wring his hands over past follies, did recognize that the world as it existed had to be coped with, that he could not, like Loring Christie, back out. He was still disposed to see Canada as the innocent victim of crises it never made and much less ready to see a Canadian role in sorting out the messes into which the incorrigibles had got themselves. However, he did desperately try to stop the drift to war, which, according to his lights, meant vehemently supporting Chamberlain and appeasement. When that failed, he accepted the obligation to fight.

2

The Wartime Experience

Canadian attitudes to a new international organization were inevitably conditioned by the experience of war. The United Nations grew out of the alliance against aggression. Canada accepted the concept of a continuing alliance as the core of a new security institution and the special obligation of the great powers. However, it was the Canadian view that there had not been in the alliance a proper relationship between the size of the contribution and the voice in decision-making. At any rate, what had been accepted to win a war would not be acceptable in a peacetime institution that must enjoy the willing participation of countries large and small.

THE WAR AND FOREIGN POLICY

The military experience of the Second World War was for Canadians less bloody and frustrating than the First. There was a greater sense of purpose and mission; there was more Canadian control and leadership. At the beginning it was to a considerable extent an imperial effort, but by the end of the war there emerged a world-wide partnership already called the United Nations. Nevertheless, Canadian participation was, as in the 1914-18 war, largely confined to the European front. Canadians again fought for the most part with the British and had little operational contact with the Americans or the Russians.

The reason Canada did not play a larger part in the Pacific war was practical and logistic. By the time Japan entered the war Canada was deploying its forces in Britain and preparing to send further troops to the European front. Although Canada promptly declared war on Japan, splitting the Canadian forces in two at that critical point merely to make a token demonstration would have been bad strategy. The token contribution – made before Pearl

Harbor – of untrained Canadian forces in Hong Kong was bloodily eliminated in the early stages of the war. Unlike the Australians, who felt a need
to protect their homeland, Canadians, in spite of some panic on the west
coast after Pearl Harbor, continued to see Europe as the major threat. The
RCAF played a part in Ceylon, and there was a joint Canadian-American
expedition against the Japanese in the Aleutians designed largely as a gesture. By the end of the war in Europe Canadians were reluctantly preparing
to send forces against Japan. They would be volunteers. Canadians had been
fighting several years longer than the Americans, and had that excuse for
withdrawing. It was accepted, however, that something was owed to the
American allies in the Pacific. Furthermore, it would be unwise for a country
seeking new status in the world and uncertain of its economic future to risk
strong American disapproval provoked by a Canadian refusal to fight in what
the Americans were inclined to consider their war. The war in the Pacific
ended, however, before more than token Canadian forces had been engaged.
This non-involvement in the Pacific war encouraged a Canadian disposition
to leave the Pacific and the Far East to the Americans, a situation which for
some time after the war notably differentiated Canadian attitudes towards
Asia from Canadian attitudes towards Europe.

The Pacific war, nevertheless, led Canadians to a new look at their own
geography and their own vulnerability. It not only made them more aware of
the Pacific as a frontier; it also led them to look upon the North with new
eyes. The focus on Alaska and Iceland and the new threats from the air
raised serious questions about the polar regions as an unbreachable fortifica-
tion. It was natural enough, therefore, to shift after the war from thinking of
the Japanese or German threat in the northeast or northwest to worrying
about an antagonist stretched across the far side of the Arctic Ocean. Maps
with polar projections began to replace the traditional perspectives of Mercator. Collective security took on a new meaning if Canada itself was open to
direct attack.

Drastic revisions in Canadian thinking took place in the alarming summer
of 1940. In spite of brave talk, serious thought had to be given in Ottawa to a
situation in which Britain might be overrun and the Royal Navy largely taken
out of action. In extremis Canadians were prepared even to take a new look
at Pan-American arrangements they had always rejected. Fortunately for
Canada the president of the United States was only too willing to consider
measures of joint defence despite American neutrality and Canadian belligerency. The way had been cleared by the implied commitments to each
other's security exchanged in 1938 between Roosevelt and King.[1] It was in
that critical summer of 1940 that the Ogdensburg Agreement took place,

largely at Roosevelt's initiative, and the Permanent Joint Board on Defence was established.

At the same time, however, Canadians had to face the assertion of American prerogative and priority in determining the defence of the western hemisphere. After Denmark, Holland, and France were overrun, Canadians were concerned about the fate of Greenland, St Pierre, and to a lesser extent the Netherlands and French West Indies. Canadian troops were sent to Jamaica, Bermuda, the Bahamas, and British Guiana. Canada sent a consul to Greenland, but the Americans made clear that the Monroe Doctrine extended to Greenland and it was they rather than the Canadians who would maintain protection over that area. Canadians did not much like this assertion, but there were practical advantages in getting the non-belligerent Americans committed in this way when Canadian troops were urgently needed elsewhere. St Pierre was a different matter. Many Canadians had been fearful of this island where the Vichy authorities commanded a clear view of convoys out of the St Lawrence and were delighted when a Free French expedition liberated St Pierre, but the Americans, who had a deep-rooted dislike of General de Gaulle and suspicion of French 'imperialism,' were infuriated and accused the Canadians of collusion – a charge that was regrettably untrue. The Americans were eventually persuaded not to intervene in St Pierre, but Canadians were uncomfortably reminded of the pretensions of the Monroe Docrine when it extended even to islands more closely associated with Canada or Newfoundland than with the United States.

In these various ways Canada had a broadening experience of diplomatic complications in which it was by its own plight involved. The defence of such Canadian interests could not be left to the British. The Canadian struggle for a voice in the direction of the war and the protection of the Canadian stake was more complex than in the First World War. In the latter part of the war when the great strategic and logistic decisions were faced, the problem of policy-sharing was not just with the British. Canada opened direct diplomatic links with both the Soviet Union and China, but there was never any question of the participation of Canada or of any other of the lesser allies in the great-power discussions at Cairo, Yalta, or Potsdam. Two of the major western strategic conferences were held in Quebec, and the prime minister of Canada was in town for them. Churchill wanted to include King and Canadian officers in the discussions but had to give in to Roosevelt's objections when he threatened to move the conference to Bermuda.[2] The decisions taken, however, even on atomic energy in which Canada was involved, were bilateral Anglo-American decisions. Canadians fought hard, nevertheless, for the control of their own forces and to get some recognition of the Canadian contribution as an independent nation. When it came to questions of supply Canada was a much more important factor, and Canadians won places in several combined boards, largely based in Washington. These wartime exertions to get a hearing conditioned Canadians so that at the end of the war they were accustomed to stubborn insistence on their rights, according to function, in postwar international organizations.

Canada was much better prepared in 1945 than in 1918 to take a constructive part in the peace settlements because it had the professional backing of a well-staffed Department of External Affairs. Whereas in 1939 there was a small but effective department with missions abroad in London, Paris, Washington, Geneva, Tokyo, and Brussels-The Hague, by the end of the war the staff in Ottawa had greatly increased and there were missions in most Commonwealth countries, in Latin America, to the allied governments in London, as well as in Moscow and Chungking. A Post-Hostilities Problems Committee had been set up in Ottawa to consider the shape of peace and Canada's place in the postwar world.[3] Although Canada did not take part directly in high policy planning during the war and in the Dumbarton Oaks meetings preliminary to the establishment of the United Nations, nevertheless it was kept well-informed by the British of their discussions and Canadians were able to put forward views on many subjects in London and Washington and to keep in touch with their other wartime allies.

The new wartime leaders in External had grown restless over the stifling negativism of prewar policy. They sought for things Canada might do rather than things Canada might avoid doing. Hume Wrong left Geneva in 1940 and, after a stint in London, came to Ottawa where he soon turned his attention to the kind of postwar order for which Canada should aim. When Skelton died in 1941, Norman Robertson, aged thirty-nine, took his place as undersecretary. Lester Pearson went from London to Ottawa and then to Washington where his inventive mind was engaged in the United Nations from the moment of its creation in January 1942. With him there was Escott Reid, a skilled and dedicated architect of international structures. Charles Ritchie, who was himself the author of a number of penetrating analyses of the postwar world at the time, described in his diary 'the two most influential senior officials.' Of Wrong he wrote: 'He inspires alarm on first encounter – an alarm which could be justified as he is totally intolerant of muddle, inanity or sheer brute stupidity. He has style in everything from the way he wears his coat to the prose of his memoranda. He is a realist who understands political forces better, unfortunately, than he does politicians themselves.' About Robertson he added: 'Norman understands them very well and has influence with the Prime Minister, but what does not Norman understand? His mind is as capacious as his great sloping frame. He has displacement, as they say of ocean liners, displacement physical and intellectual and he is wonderful company with his ironic asides, his shafts of wisdom and his sighs of resignation.'[4]

Mackenzie King was still very much in charge of External Affairs, but long-term planning had never much interested him and postwar planning was not a subject to which a wartime prime minister could give steady attention. The new team was inspired by a very different perspective on the Canadian role or perhaps on the phase of its history in which Canada stood. They no longer saw Canada as a country developing against odds and in need of protection but as a well-sinewed actor on the world scene, its status assured, its practices still to be worked out. If their sense of Canada's place in the system seems less parochial than that of their predecessors, it should be recognized that a devastating war helps greatly to clarify priorities. As Hume Wrong said, when he addressed the final session of the League Assembly in 1946: 'Those who have lived through the terrors and glories of two great wars are bound to be disillusioned. Disillusionment, in its literal sense the absence of illusions, is a good thing. It should mean that we see more clearly, not that we have lost hope.'[5] Hume Wrong did not look or sound like an 'idealist,' but he was in fact an idealist of the more enduring kind – unillusioned. He worked towards an ideal which would fit an unkempt globe rather than seeking to impose a straitjacket on the world for its own good. He was not daunted, like the less humble idealists, by reverses. After Munich he conceived a better League. During the Blitz in London he wrote:

I have for years thought, and I still think, that war is the worst of avoidable evils. I wonder if that is the right frame of mind. Might it not be better to accept recurrent war as an inevitable feature of life – inevitable not in a strictly logical sense (for war is the most absurd of human activities), but in the practical sense that we can't avoid it because of imperfections of our civilization and had better therefore try to fit it into our scheme of life rather than regard it as the negation of our ordinary aims and purposes? I don't like this idea, but we might make a better peace if we accepted it as true ...

I can bring myself to hope that war will end in an immense fluidity, submerging old loyalties, blurring national and class distinctions. If so, there would be greater hope of salvation, not at once but eventually. We may have to endure chaos in order to struggle through to order. If we can keep a sense of human decency, of toleration, a respectable order might emerge from the chaos in time ...[6]

By the end of an appalling war there was a chance to move ahead. Wrong was ready for that, and he was ready also for the readjustment a few years later when the hopes of security through the United Nations faltered. His particular kind of pragmatic, experimental idealism, based on an acceptance of rather than a denial of original sin, strongly influenced those around him.

The fact that what happened in 1939 seemed to be happening for the second time strengthened the inclination to set up institutions to prevent the same kind of wars. The firm determination to avoid the economic as well as the political situations which had led to war dominated the thinking of the wartime leaders – and their electorates – who created the United Nations. Their fault was not in being militarist or vengeful. They were not. But the double experience had restricted their grasp of the various causes of war and the required conditions for peace. Lest this be regarded as an argument for the constitution of international organizations in tranquillity, it should be noted that without the wartime unity nothing could have been done at all. Later advances in United Nations practice, furthermore – peacekeeping for example – have been forged in times of crisis.

The new perspectives unleashed an unprecedented burst of zeal and invention in Ottawa, an enthusiastic participation in the raising of new structures, the adaptation of old ones, and then, soon after, their remodelling. The mid-forties have been described as 'a relatively Golden Age of international political inventiveness and institution-building.'[7] One of the American architects, Dean Acheson, compared it with 'the Creation' of the world, quoting Alfonso the Wise, King of Castille: 'Had I been present at the creation I would have given some useful hints for the better ordering of the universe.'[8] The Americans loomed largest, of course, throughout this creation, but the Canadians were present, and it is their 'useful hints for the better ordering of the universe' with which this study is largely concerned.

PUBLIC OPINION

The officials, however, could not work in a vacuum. They led and even helped mould public opinion, but they had to adjust their calculations to public tolerance. The uncertain convictions of Canadians are well reflected in an interesting debate in the Commons after the prime minister on 27 January 1943 announced the Casablanca Conference of Churchill and Roosevelt. If it revealed some confusion, that was understandable, for the way was not clear. Conservative spokesmen pressed to know whether Canada had been informed, invited to be a party to the decisions, whether it had concurred, and, in particular, whether the government had advocated to the United

Nations the setting up of a Supreme War Council on which all allied nations would be represented. Howard Green of the Conservatives protested against the growth of a 'small power' complex in Canada, a feeling it must run along behind Britain and the United States. Canada was at a parting of the ways, he said.[9] It could be influential beyond its numbers if it wished, but unless there was a change in attitude Canada would have little to say at the peace conference. That could mean tragedy, as the large nations might decide on a peace which prevented the world Canadians wanted from taking shape. In defence of the government's position over Casablanca, King spoke of the necessary improvisations in creating a War Council. He acknowledged the leadership of Churchill and Roosevelt by saying there was open recognition that all could rally in support of policies on which these two men would have the final word. He admitted anomalies in the evolving organization that should be corrected before a total war effort could be achieved and an instrument for maintaining the peace constructed. Nevertheless, although he hoped a wider organization would develop, it was necessary not to prejudice in the slightest degree the concentration of responsibility for strategic decisions. Although he did not say so, it was one way of avoiding commitments.

It became increasingly difficult to maintain that position in face of the pressure from all sides in the House as well as from his officials, but King's heart was never in the creation of a new world organization. He made the appropriate speeches about the United Nations because he had to, but, as he confessed later to a Liberal party caucus, he 'greatly feared the new organization might in some circumstances be as much of a blind as the League of Nations.'[10] Churchill, the great-power man, stoutly defended the League when King said to him after the Quebec Conference that there would have been no war if the League had not existed.[11] At just about this time, in November 1943, a Gallup Poll indicated that 75 per cent of Canadians favoured an active part in maintaining world peace even if it meant sending Canadian forces to keep the peace in other parts of the world.[12] An External Affairs internal memorandum of March 1943 noted that whereas in the first years of the war 'there had been a widespread tendency to look upon representation in imperial or international councils as entanglements which might involve Canada in commitments in someone else's interest, since the Casablanca Conference there was more concern in Parliament about postwar issues and a realization that unless Canada took part, the interests of other countries would predominate.' Whenever there was talk of an international organization, Canadians were determined to get their rightful place in it. Their conception of their rightful place grew consistently in the latter years of the war, aggravated, as always, by the failure of other countries to recognize it. Not all Canadians felt this way – there were still some who preferred the quiet life. The Hon. P.J.A. Cardin said he was not humiliated because Canada was not invited to Casablanca. 'We had no reason to be there ... we are not one of the main powers conducting the war ... and we must accept the decision of the powers mainly responsible for carrying this war to a successful conclusion ... Let us adjust ourselves to our role, to our position.'[13]

The insistence by the Conservatives and the CCF on a louder Canadian voice was only partly attributable to their ignorance of the difficulties the government was encountering in pressing the case. There was a strong nationalist strain in both parties. The zeal of the CCF was stimulated by their dislike of many allied policies, as for example the support of dubious Frenchmen in North Africa or the wrong kinds of Yugoslavs.[14] They wanted Canada to exert pressure on the Left. They tended to favour a council of all the 'united nations.' They were even more sceptical than King about a Commonwealth front. The Conservatives were less sure what they wanted. They expected more recognition for Canada, but they were always suspicious of King's reluctance to stand up with the empire. They sounded as if they favoured a united empire front within the United Nations, but on the whole they kept empire and United Nations arguments in separate compartments. Rhetorically at least they seemed to like the idea of the Commonwealth as one of the great powers in the postwar organization, but that idea did not survive long enough to become a serious cause. In general, Conservatives were less cautious than King about commitments and demanded a voice in imperial or allied councils regardless of the consequences.

ALLIED ORGANIZATION

The allied war effort was organized through many ad hoc functional committees and commissions operating effectively but without any clearly defined structure. The system was disorderly but it produced a victory. It was not based rigidly on the equality of states. The ultimate authority was always the two or sometimes three great powers and Canadians were reluctant to admit that they had much satisfaction. However, they learned a good deal about how to work the system, how to get their feet in doors, and above all how to go for the arrangement which meant influence rather than mere status.

On general military strategy there was no strong anxiety among the top level in Canada to play a decisive role. The government rested largely on the position that it must be kept informed of all important developments and consulted before any decision directly affecting its interest was taken. It did claim, however, that whenever representative institutions were established, Canada would have equitable treatment. In practice the Canadian interest was best met flexibly, by constant consultation, visits with the principals, and even by participation on the fringes of the Quebec Conferences. When the Combined Chiefs of Staff Committee was set up in January 1942, the British and Americans said no other country could have membership. Roosevelt feared that concessions to Canada would create demands from Brazil, Mexico, and China and he did not want the committee to be 'a debating society.'[15] He had a point. Canadian representatives could attend meetings when the agenda concerned Canada and there were, of course, many bilateral discussions with both British and American chiefs. There was good liaison through the Canadian military headquarters in London and the Joint Staff Mission in Washington. Canadians, although they could not accept such provisions as adequate, tacitly recognized a functional argument in the enormously larger forces of the two major powers and, of course, the need to win the war.

As to be expected, it was on the economic and supply side that Canada was most importunate and more successful. The Combined Raw Materials Board, the Combined Shipping Adjustment Board, and the Combined Munitions Assignment Board were set up early in 1942, but Canada's claim for membership on the first and third was rejected. Later in 1942, however, Canada was admitted to two further boards that had been established, the Combined Production Resources Board and the Combined Food Board. It also got seats on a number of committees the functional justification for which was less obvious – as, for example, the Medical Supplies Committee, Combined Textiles Committee, and a Combined Tires and Tubes Committee. C.D. Howe and those involved with him were less concerned with status and more with the protection of Canadian interests. One problem for Canadians was that both the British and Americans preferred to have Britain represent the Commonwealth on the boards[16] and, to win the war, certain arrangements were tolerated. It was clear, however, that when peacetime institutions were set up, Canada must act on its own. Among the reasons Brooke Claxton cited in 1944 for Canada's supporting international organization was that 'In the absence of international agreement, economic or political differences between Great Britain and the United States may force Canada into closer integration with one country at the expense of our relations with the other.'[17] Ever since the League had been established, Canadians looked to multilateral institutions to rescue them from the dilemmas of excessive bilateralism.

Canada also learned there were other lesser powers to be considered. The American insistence that, regardless of the very different proportions of their war efforts, Canada could not be treated differently from Brazil spurred Canadian officials into a functionalist rationalization. They would not insist on representation on all allied bodies but only on those where they were major contributors. They were even willing to apply the principle negatively. They did not claim membership on the Combined Shipping Adjustment Board, recognizing that Norway and Greece, for example, had better claims. To keep things under control the major powers were cautious about letting Canada set precedents – particularly in the case of the Combined Raw Materials Board.

It was the principle rather than the practice that was the major cause of concern. Canada found that the way it was linked with the CRMB through a Materials Coordinating Committee was effective as a working arrangement. There was towards the end of the war some difference of opinion or emphasis between the practical men like Howe or H.J. Symington, chairman of the Canadian section of the committee, and those who had to keep in mind precedents for the postwar organizations already taking shape. Canadian officials on all levels had established working relationships with their American counterparts and Howe seemed to feel that formal participation in the tripartite board might interfere with his own very effective personal relations with the Americans, not to mention his position vis-à-vis other departments in Ottawa. Symington thought that if Canada were a member of the CRMB it would always be out-voted, that it would be stripped of its raw materials as a powerful bargaining counter. On atomic questions Howe thought it more important to acquire a Canadian position in the Combined Policy Committee or the Combined Development Trust that left him as free as possible to promote and protect the Canadian interest than to insist on a status of equality in policy-making by tripartie bodies.[18]

One lesson learned was that the right to a voice implies commitment. It would also require compromise. Many Canadians, with little experience of the give-and-take of international organization, seemed to assume that the Canadian case, being naturally just, would prevail if it could only be presented. It did not often work out that way, and Canadians did not like being bound by decisions which went contrary to their wishes. By remaining outside the boards, it was easier to maintain autonomy. Canada, therefore, sought more vigorously membership in agencies that allocated supplies it needed than those that allocated products it exported, especially surplus food and raw materials. It was cannily realized, furthermore, that participation on the highest level of allied military strategy was not only unattainable but undesirable. It was bound to be token, except that it would surrender to others the final control of Canadian forces. There was perhaps more to be gained in exploiting a good grievance.[19] A comparable fear of being committed was the dominant consideration in Canada's not accepting Lend-Lease assistance.[20]

Granted the basic value of the wartime experience and the habit of allied collaboration, nevertheless the precedents were in some way misleading. The war machinery was administrative. It allocated. It was directing a large war effort with a strong sense of common purpose. Some of the Canadian planners during the wartime period may well have been thinking of analogies for postwar international 'government.' The prevalent assumption that the enforcement of collective security would be carried on by the peacetime United Nations made more natural the assumption of enforcement in matters of health or aviation or wireless. That was not to be. Wartime boards were based on a recognition of conflicting interests, and temporary compromises were considered acceptable to remove a devastating threat to the greater interests of all. Peacetime agencies must accept, however, the permanence of conflicting interests as the natural order of things and find means of regulating them. The principle of sharing defence production between Canada and the United States, for example, folded when there was no common enemy[21] and reappeared only when a new antagonist was perceived. In a workable United Nations system every member is the prospective partner and antagonist of every other. The system has been most gravely threatened when temporary majorities – the Western powers in the fifties and the Third World in the seventies – were tempted to use it as an instrument against a common 'enemy.' The self-discipline of the economic and social agencies would have to be based on a sense of common interest or common purpose but not a common enemy.

One Canadian weakness was the tendency to judge functional claims in terms of the producer rather than the consumer. Canadians saw the position on various boards as a means by which to insist on their fair supply of scarce materials. They were somewhat too preoccupied, however, with their own role as provider to realize that the stake of those needing provisions was even greater. The Canadian idea of 'responsible government' applied internationally reflected the traditional prejudice in favour of control by the man who paid the taxes. They did not recognize, for example, the rights of their flattened allies in Europe as comparable to theirs in determining the policies of the United Nations Relief and Rehabilitation Administration or the International Refugee Organization.[22] When at San Francisco Canada pressed a functional qualification for the Economic and Social Council, due recognition that the eighteen members should include states of major economic importance, it ran into general opposition on the grounds that small and poor countries had their own perspectives to contribute and that the Council would deal with social and cultural as well as economic matters. The delegation backed away gracefully, with the argument that as the functions of the Council had indeed been broadened there was not the same reason to press the point. Gordon Graydon, who made the statement, was greeted with applause.[23]

If Canada was at times presumptuous in its estimate of its own status in postwar organization, the reason was partly in the special position it had acquired during the war. A.F.W. Plumptre, who was in the Canadian embassy in Washington in the war years, has written of the creation of the International Bank and Monetary Fund:

It was in large measure an American, British, and Canadian affair, but so were a lot of other things in Washington until the end of hostilities, until the French and other European governments became more than exile governments. Washington, indeed, was a surprisingly ABC affair during the war. The Chiefs of Staff were the combined chiefs of staff of the US and the UK, but the Canadians had a large and influential mission attached to them. The Combined Production and Resources Board was an ABC board; the Combined Food Board was an ABC board; the Combined Raw Materials Board was only an AB board, simply because C, Canada, would not go in (C.D. Howe felt we would have more leverage from the outside than by being voted down on the inside). So the international agencies, particularly those that were formed before the end of hostilities, naturally had this sort of cast ... I think that one of our concerns, in looking at the Fund and Bank, is to realize that they still contain certain overtones of that original ABC cast. I certainly feel that, had Bretton Woods come a little later, the European countries would have been more integrally involved in the formation of the Fund and the subsequent activities than, from time to time, they have been.[24]

It should be added that this is not the impression gathered from the memoirs of British and American actors on the scene. References to Canadians are generous but scarce. Memoirists, however, do like to emphasize the big-time company they kept.

UNRRA

It seemed fortunate that the first battle for a voice in United Nations bodies could be fought over the United Nations Relief and Rehabilitation Agency in which Canada had a strong claim because of its expected role as a major provider. It was especially important at that time because the distinction was not being clearly made between relief and reconstruction and all the 'economic proposals' were being lumped together, including those for an international bank and a 'clearing union.' Relief was linked, especially in Washington, to visions of a new world order in which there would be prompt solutions not only for the devastation of war but also for the dislocations that had preceded the war. The European allies were more anxious that their immediate needs be recognized as well. The distinction between short- and long-term action became clearer as the war progressed, and the name United Nations Relief and Rehabilitation Administration was carefully chosen. This organization was not the body to deal with the new world order, but the connection was acknowledged between the way in which a country was or was not restored and its long-term prospects. In June 1943 draft proposals, already approved by the four powers, were made to the United Nations as a whole. The interconnection between relief and reconstruction was recognized, especially as the same men were often involved in each, but they were now to be the concern of separate agencies. There was obviously a distinction between bodies for the actual administration of relief and those which were to recommend to governments plans for a new world order. In the latter category were the conferences being planned on agriculture, money, and civil aviation.

UNRRA was designed to take over after Military Relief. The Canadian contribution to UNRRA was only about twice that to Military Relief, but the nature of Canadian participation became a major political issue. Canada's fortunate position as a producer in the latter years of the war meant that its contribution to relief was essential and large. A refusal to contribute, given the dire circumstances, would hardly have been credible, but other countries had to recognize that the contribution could be affected by the extent of participation in policy-making.

When in September 1941 the Inter-Allied Committee on Postwar Requirements had been set up in London, Canada did not become a member although it was represented at most meetings. After the United States and the Soviet Union became involved in the war, plans were discussed for a UN relief agency. Although the Canadian government approved the idea, it was disturbed by the American draft which provided for an executive committee of the four powers. On the grounds of its expected contribution, Canada vigorously demanded membership on the executive committee or at least the curtailment of the powers of this committee in favour of a more broadly representative council. The Americans, and particularly President Roosevelt, had not as yet learned how importunate the lesser powers were going to be. They were more concerned with conciliating the Russians, and the Russians did not want lesser powers represented. The latter feared that if Canada had a privileged position this might also be accorded to Poland, for example – and an amenable Polish government had not yet been secured. The Americans, as usual, worried over the claims of Brazil. The British were more used to this kind of pressure from Canada and Australia, and they were getting it also from the European governments-in-exile in London. By December 1942 they had accepted the idea in principle of including lesser powers in executive bodies of at least international economic organizations.

In the battle over UNRRA which took place in the spring of 1943 the Canadian interpretation of functionalism was formulated, stated publicly in the Commons by the prime minister on 9 July 1943, communicated to other governments, and, indeed, an effort was made to commit the great powers to the principle.[25] The gist of the theory was stated in the following terms: '... authority in international affairs must not be concentrated exclusively in the largest powers. On the other hand, authority cannot be divided equally among all the thirty or more sovereign states that comprise the united nations, or all effective authority will disappear ... In the view of the government, effective representations ... should neither be restricted to the largest states nor necessarily extended to all states. Representation should be determined on a functional basis which will admit to full membership those countries, large or small, which have the greatest contribution to make to the particular object in question.' It was not simply an argument put forward by diplomatic planners. The prime minister and the War Committee of cabinet were engaged in full cry. In statements and memoranda at all levels it was postulated that the success of Canada's claim in UNRRA was crucial because it would establish the pattern for postwar organization.

Hume Wrong set out the position in a memorandum to the undersecretary of 19 March 1943:

We are, of course, deeply concerned with both the form and the substance of international postwar planning. As to the substance, a good deal of preliminary study has been given here to some of the economic questions ... As to the form, we have hitherto advanced, in our approaches over the Relief Administration and to some extent in connection with the Combined Boards, the principle that representation on international bodies should be determined on a functional basis so as to permit the participation of those countries which have the greatest stake in the particular subject under examination. We have used this principle both to combat the argument that the four largest powers should have a special responsibility in all the fields of planning and organization and to avoid the other extreme which would allow each member of the United Nations to be represented on the basis of nominal equality. I think

that we should stick to this functional principle. If we can secure its general acceptance, it would permit the representation of Canada on most of the bodies in which
we are deeply interested.

Hitherto, Wrong noted, the main concern had been to secure proper influence for Canada in certain of the bodies set up for direction of the war and
also in the so-called Relief Administration which was the only subject on
which postwar planning had reached an advanced stage of international negotiation. They had approached the question singly and improvised as successful methods as they could manage, such as liaison with the Combined Chiefs
of Staff through the Canadian Joint Staff in Washington, membership of the
Production and Resources Board, and of the Pacific Council, and contacts
with the Food Board which had not gone as far as they wished. However, the
United States government had now indicated its readiness to participate in
the series of postwar discussions on a broad economic front – relief, food
consumption and distribution apart from relief, international monetary
arrangements, and other economic questions. They were proposing the con-
vocation on 27 April in the United States of a conference of the United
Nations – the belligerent allies who had been assembled and declared themselves the United Nations in Washington in January 1942 – on food consumption and production. In the monetary field there were British and
American plans which the Canadians feared would become rivals.

The Canadians, like the British, favoured a full-dress conference of the
United Nations. The Americans inclined to a series of ad hoc conferences,
partly because they were nervous of Congressional reactions to postwar commitments and wanted to avoid publicity. The Canadians were hoping the
United Nations as a whole might give the mandate for a programme of international collaboration rather than have it instigated solely by the great
powers. In this way general principles for the participation of lesser powers
would be authorized. From the beginning the argument was seen, particularly on the official level, not simply as a means of frustrating great-power
control but also as a formula which ought to appeal to the great powers
because it avoided the chaos of a system based on equal representation for all
in everything.

The argument over UNRRA began in close association with the argument
over a Canadian place on the Combined Food Board. The British proposed in
August 1942 a compromise on the Food Board by which there would be
Canadian participation in meetings when matters concerning Canada were
under discussion, Canadian membership on all committees dependent on
the board, and a Canadian-United States Committee on Food Policy, but the

War Committee in Ottawa rejected it. At the same time the British were told that the Canadian government took strong exception to the exclusion of Canada from the proposed Policy Committee of the inter-allied organization to deal with European relief. The high commissioner in London was instructed to emphasize to the British that the Canadian desire for effective representation was not caused by considerations of prestige or status. 'We have limited our requests to bodies in the work of which we are inevitably called upon to play a large part. The Government has felt that we should be partners in these bodies and should not merely be afforded means of protecting our direct interests when they come under consideration. A feeling is growing up, not only in Canada, that the direction of the war (except so far as Russia is concerned) is too much of an Anglo-American monopoly. The problem is to find a means whereby sound and speedy decisions can be taken (involving concentration in a few hands), while at the same time sharing responsibility for these decisions among the Governments which are mainly concerned in them.'[26]

The British argued for the enlargement of the Policy Committee from four to seven members to include Canada, a Latin American ally, and a European ally.[27] They were concerned about their European allies, who were being importunate but not likely to agree easily on one country to represent them. Litvinov of the USSR argued against the enlargement of the committee precisely on the grounds for which Canada wanted it – that this would be taken as a precedent. Cordell Hull was affected by the British arguments and Acheson suggested several ways around the problem. One of these was for shared membership between Canada and the United Kingdom, and the other was for establishing a committee of supplying countries. Ottawa did not, of course, like the former suggestion which looked too much like the old idea of a Commonwealth seat. The British also rejected it on the grounds that Canada's was a functional claim of its own. At a later stage the British even offered to step down from the Policy Committee in favour of Canada but, although the Canadians appreciated the gesture, they thought it would have the same unfortunate implications. What was more, they supported the presence of the British on the Policy Committee for functional reasons. Roosevelt's idea of a compromise was that if the British were going to press for membership of seven, the British government could decide whether they wanted their membership to come from the United Kingdom or Canada.[28] Pearson knew how unacceptable this would be to the prime minister, but the Canadian minister in Washington, Leighton McCarthy, was rather impressed with the suggestion – until he tried it out on Mackenzie King who, as Pearson reports, 'gave him a lecture on the structure of the Commonwealth.'[29]

Eden accepted 'the conclusion that the Four Power basis will not normally be appropriate for international organizations dealing with economic problems, while agreeing that it is important that the four great powers "should retain ultimate control over post-war military and political arrangements."' At this stage, however, the Canadians were not disposed to look at any compromises or to restrict their objection to international economic organizations.[30]

The War Committee was adamant. Mackenzie King instructed McCarthy to see Hull and leave with him a memorandum. The committee did not think the External Affairs draft put the case strongly enough, and it was toughened. In this memorandum the government spoke frankly about its own political problems:

There is already a good deal of public questioning over the place accorded to Canada in the various inter-allied bodies which have been set up for the direction of the war. During wartime, problems of this nature are to some extent disguised, because of public concentration on the attainment of victory and because of the secrecy which must surround many aspects of war direction. After the fighting ends, the issues will be seen nakedly. The full activities of the Relief Administration will not begin until the war is over; and it will be very difficult, or even impossible, to persuade the Parliament and people of Canada to accept the financial burdens and other sacrifices, such perhaps as the continuation of rationing and other restrictions on the domestic supply of consumers' goods, which will be necessary for the provision of relief through the Administration on the expected scale, unless they are satisfied that their representatives exercised their due part in its direction.

The practical difficulties in creating representative international agencies were recognized, but 'these difficulties are a challenge to statesmanship; they must be faced and on their solution depends in large measure the possibility of an enduring peace.'[31]

In late February the four powers met in Washington. The Russians budged a little towards an informal intimation to Canada that they would all support its chairmanship of a suppliers committee but they would not abandon the four-power principle. The frank Canadian admission of long-term aims in opening up the policy process had been counter-productive. The British embassy reported to Pearson that it was the intention of the four powers 'to consider the draft in the light of any observations which may have been received from the other United Nations and in the hope that at the subsequent conference of the United Nations to consider the whole matter, the Four Powers may be able to act as a unit in recommending the draft to the other nations.'[32]

The War Committee unanimously rejected the compromise. They would settle for nothing less than direct representation on the Central Committee (formerly the Policy Committee). The Canadian minister was told: 'If we cannot go into the Central Committee by the front we are unwilling to use a side or back entrance.' He was given a quotation from a letter by Clifford Clark, the deputy minister of finance: 'We are still trying to run a democracy and there is some historical evidence to support the thesis that democracies cannot be taxed without representation.'[33] Although the diplomats had been wary about saying bluntly that unless Canada got its way it would withhold its relief or act on its own, the politicians were less sensitive. The War Committee told the Canadian minister 'that it should now be intimated to the United States, United Kingdom, Soviet and Chinese Governments that unless Canada is given in some manner a position in the direction of the Relief Administration commensurate with the expected contribution of Canada to international relief the Canadian government will find it impossible to participate in the work of the Administration.'[34] King told McCarthy to proceed on the assumption that, unless there was some great change in conditions, the Canadian government would refuse to participate in the Relief Administration if its constitution was not altered to meet their views. He was to tell Dean Acheson in the State Department that the government could not accept his argument that this was an isolated problem. If Acheson wanted to come to Ottawa as he had proposed, he would be welcome, not because any arguments he could use would affect the situation but because it would be well for him to receive at first hand the views of the Canadian government. King's insistence that the problem must be faced, not evaded, and that it could not be solved by expedients reveals a lack of awareness of the facts of international life. 'The durability of the post-war settlement depends on its solution. The Soviet Government must be brought to see this and it is greatly in the interest of the other United Nations that this should be done soon. No better opportunity seems likely to arise than this of impressing on the larger powers the importance of sharing control of international organizations with the smaller countries.'[35] That was a point the Russians fully understood.

At this juncture the British became worried. They could not jeopardize the establishment of UNRRA over this issue, however important. Eden was in Ottawa in April where he talked to the War Committee about the desirability of accepting a compromise. He suggested to Canadian officials an exchange of letters between Canada and the United States speaking on behalf of the big four, confirming the Canadian understanding that any arrangements for the Central and Supplies Committees of the Relief Organization would not be a precedent fixing the Canadian relationship to other postwar agencies. Norman Robertson, the undersecretary, was sceptical and argued that the outcome of some months of pretty stubborn and contentious negotiations would be a de facto precedent which would be invoked regardless of any formal reservations of the position which Canada and the other countries might have agreed to. Robertson also told Eden the root of the present difficulties lay in the way the Combined Boards had been shaped as agencies of the United Kingdom and the United States rather than of the United Nations.[36]

Pearson realized the Russians were becoming suspicious that the proposal to expand the committee would lead to domination by the Anglo-Saxons for political purposes. External Affairs was getting worried. It prepared a memorandum for the Cabinet War Committee on 6 April setting out the arguments for and against accepting the compromise of the four powers, but this time the arguments were loaded in favour of acceptance. They said bluntly that there had been a possibility of abandonment of the whole plan because of Russian opposition but the Russians had now made a concession to meet the British-Canadian position. 'The Canadian objection remains, therefore, the only outstanding problem. Its solution should make possible an early United Nations Relief Conference; failure to find a solution may prevent such a conference. We should, therefore, be certain that this failure cannot fairly be attributable to Canada.' The argument showed some shift of ground, emphasizing the importance of the Committee on Supplies which might well become the dominating body with a Canadian as chairman. If that were so, the precedent would represent a valid recognition of the functional principle. They noted also that the Australians had entered the picture by making a plea similar to that of Canada. It was not a plea Canada could easily reject but it was perhaps necessary to grab this special favour for Canada before the Australians had carried the Canadian argument to a too logical conclusion. To assure the War Committee that there had been no backing down, it was argued that the present offer was in accord with the representations made to the State Department on 10 February in which they had insisted on 'the full participation of Canada' in the direction of the administration.[37]

The War Committee agreed to accept the main constitutional provisions of the Relief Administration draft as revised, and the ambassador was told that 'the government's agreement has in large part been determined by the desire that international organization in this field should get under way as soon as possible.' In informing the representatives of the powers the ambassador was instructed to make it clear that Canadian concurrence was on the understanding they would use their best endeavours to secure the election of a Canadian as chairman of the Committee on Supplies and at the same time 'it should be understood that our acceptance of the arrangements in the particular case of the Relief Administration does not indicate any withdrawal from the position we have taken that the four power pattern is not in principle an acceptable form of international organization, that representation on international bodies would, whenever possible, be determined on a functional basis, and that the proposed form of the Central Committee will not be regarded as a precedent in other connections.'[38]

The Canadian government had hoped the United States government would assure them in the name of the four powers that their main points were accepted. What they got seemed better than nothing, but it was of dubious value. It was contained in a letter from Dean Acheson to Pearson dated 12 June, replying to Pearson's letter of 13 April. After expressing the hope that the information contained would meet fully the concern of the Canadian government, he reported that he had read to a meeting of the representatives of the four powers Pearson's letter of 8 April:

All of those present expressed their gratification at the willingness of the Canadian Government to co-operate with the plan set forth in the draft agreement. At the same time they took cognizance of the statement that Canadian acceptance of the proposed plan is based on the following points of understanding: a) that the prospective members of the Central Committee will use their best endeavours to secure the selection of a Canadian as Chairman of the Committee on Supplies; b) that in the view of the Canadian Government the Four-Power pattern is not in principle an acceptable form of international organization; c) that in its view representation on international bodies should whenever possible be determined on a functional basis; and d) that the Canadian Government does not regard the proposed form of the Central Committee as a precedent in other connections.

With regard to the crucial point, d), Acheson stated: 'I believe I can say that there has been nothing in the discussions of the representatives of the Four-Powers to indicate that any of these Powers take [sic] the position that the form of organization proposed in the draft agreement for a Relief and Rehabilitation Administration would in any sense set a precedent for the form of any other international organization.'[39] The bold attempt to have the functional principle endorsed had been taken cognizance of. It might have been considered risky to court thus the possible rejection of the formula. The procedure followed presumably did no harm and might have had some effect on the British and Americans. Subsequent policy of the Russians in particular and perhaps also of the Americans might, however, justify the conclusion that they took cognizance of the principle in order to be wary of it.[40]

The UNRRA case was an early example of a technique to be used often by Canada, and especially Pearson, in dealing with the superpower neighbour. You present the Canadian argument with great vigour, but when you realize that the American will is going to prevail regardless, then you go for a compromise. The compromise does not give you everything you want and you know you will be bound to accept it because you have been involved in formulating it. Still, it is presumably an improvement on the original and the only alternative is feckless opposition. As in this case, you do your best to see that the compromise is not to be regarded as a precedent, but this exercise is intended largely to put you in position for opposition again the next time. You dare not be too exasperating. In defending the agreement in the House of Commons Brooke Claxton made the oft-quoted statement: 'We can apply the functional principle too far. We cannot be on every board there is in the world.'[41]

The four-power draft agreement on the Relief Administration was circulated to all members of the United Nations and, in the light of their criticism, modified to emphasize the authority of the council in which all members were equally represented. The Canadians were encouraged by the indication that their view was shared by other countries, especially those of intermediate rank like the Netherlands and Belgium. There was, however, always a slight ambivalence in the Canadian championship of the cause of the lesser powers, as it was a category into which they were not certain they wanted to be absorbed. The Dutch and others expressed strong resentment against the unrepresentative character of the Central Committee. Their attention was concentrated, however, on reducing its powers, as the question of membership had been clearly settled. Canada could hardly oppose these views of its friends, but it was awkward to take a public stand against an arrangement which Canada had privately secured with the great powers.

In fact, Canada strengthened the functional principle more solidly by making a notable contribution to the success of the institution as a whole instead of simply using its hard-won voice to defend the Canadian interest. The large contribution in money and goods was a justification of Canada's right to representation. Along with the other lesser powers Canada found opportunities for expression on the committees, including the Committee on Europe. Pearson became chairman of the Committee on Supplies and thereafter one of the main architects of UNRRA. The third meeting of the council was held in Montreal, and, although he was still a civil servant, he was chosen to preside over it.

UNRRA, when established, consisted of a Council, to meet every six months, on which each member sat, and the Central Committee made up of the four great powers exclusively. In theory at least the Central Committee, which controlled policy between sessions, had to have its decisions confirmed by the Council. UNRRA, however, had to act fast. There was a Committee on Supplies of twelve countries including, besides the great powers, countries that would properly be chosen on functional grounds: Australia, Belgium, Brazil, India, Holland, and New Zealand, with Canada in the chair. There were regional committees for both the Far East and Europe presided over by representatives of China and Britain, respectively. The director-general, needless to say, was American – first Herbert Lehman and then Fiorello LaGuardia. Each member state which had not been invaded agreed to pay 1 per cent of its national income, at least 10 per cent of which should be convertible. The Canadian government had little difficulty getting approval in April 1944 for its contribution of $77 million. Canada paid up punctually to a total amount of $154 million, third in size to that of the United States and the United Kingdom. It should be noted, however, that UNRRA spent $254 million in Canada for agricultural and industrial supplies.

There was some price paid for the watering down of the authority of the major powers. While the war was on the British and Americans stressed the authority of the wartime machinery of the Combined Boards rather than of the UNRRA Committee on Supplies. Not long after the end of the war, however, they moved towards the dissolution of UNRRA and the continuation of relief on a bilateral basis. As far as the Americans were concerned, it was the difficulty of sharing authority with the Soviet Union rather than the lesser powers which by this time mattered most. Nevertheless, they were not at all used to multilateral control of their funds. In appropriating its second contribution to UNRRA, Congress specified that the Central Committee rather than the Council should be responsible for approving the financial allocations to specific countries. For this and other reasons the Committee on Supplies did not achieve the authority Canadians hoped for at the time of the compromise. As chairman of this committee Pearson attended only some seven of the sixteen meetings of the Central Committee. Nevertheless, he was, by sheer ability, a decisive force in UNRRA. The fact that influence was more closely related to personal ability than formal status was being proved also by other Canadians in these formative years of UN bodies. It permitted a somewhat more flexible stance on the functional principle.

After the San Francisco Conference and the acceptance of France as a great power, it was agreed that France would have to be on the Central Committee. It was tactfully decided to use the occasion to admit Canada as well – in August 1945. The Russians had seconded the United States resolution to admit France and Canada, but they opposed an Australian resolution that would have admitted three further countries, Australia, Brazil, and Yugoslavia. Canada expressed sympathy with the Australian proposal but did not go so far as to resign as chairman of the Committee on Supplies to make way for an Australian.

There was during the creation of international institutions a curious ally-rival relationship between Canada and Australia. Canadians recognized the Australians as valuable allies in the struggle for the rights of middle powers, especially as the Australian style was less inhibited. On the Canadian side there was great respect for the tough Aussies and a close personal association with an extremely able group of Australian diplomats and negotiators. There developed a collaboration in international organizations so habitual it was taken for granted by the 1950s. The Austalians were less subtle and perhaps less far-sighted than the Canadians in their search for independence and a role, but they were also less preoccupied with status as an end in itself. Having a voice in the grand strategy of the war was a luxury that Canadians could forgo, provided they had a decent opportunity to protect the specific interests of Canadian forces and Canadian supplies. For the Australians, however, it was a life-and-death matter to see that adequate forces were allocated to their exposed and lonely front. They needed a say in the direction of the war, and they demanded it without having time to worry about the commitments involved in theory to a common empire policy or a United Nations security scheme controlled by the great powers. At San Francisco and at the Paris Peace Conference the redoubtable Herbert Evatt hollered his way to some considerable influence on the decisions of the time while Canadians were gaining their reputation for moderation and mediation. There was more difference in temperament than in policy, a situation which often made for good team work.

When it came to refugees, Canada's zeal for status was considerably tempered by the government's hesitation to stick its neck out. Although the International Refugee Organization was not set up until after the war, it was, like UNRRA, linked to the war and transitional. The political issues made collaboration between East and West even more difficult. Canada was less enthusiastic about a place of honour because its policy on accepting refugees was hardly straightforward. Nevertheless, Canadian officials did play a useful role and Canada was on the Executive Committee of Nine because it was wanted there and could not decently escape the responsibility.[42]

THE UNITED STATES AND THE UNITED NATIONS

Plans were being laid also during the war for permanent international economic and social institutions to cope with the problems of peacetime.

Although it was hoped to exploit the sense of wartime unity to get them launched, the gulf between communist and non-communist assumptions on economic and social policies was too great. The agencies evolved largely as instrumentalities of the non-communist world – not just the Western world. Without the intimidating requirement of great-power unity, and with Canada's considerable resources, Canadian delegations did quite well in these enterprises.

The role of the United States in the United Nations was a problem. The enormous military and economic power of the United States and its remoteness from the front made a dominant position inescapable. American sponsorship was welcomed by those who feared American isolationism more than American 'imperialism,' but the proprietary stance, accompanied by assumptions of moral superiority, roused some fear and resentment in Europe and also in Canada.

To other countries the United States attitude to the international bodies being set up as the United Nations often looked officious, but Americans tended to see their willingness to act through international bodies, rather than entirely on their own, as a concession to internationalism, a gesture of good intentions. This was particularly true of both the Hot Springs Conference on Food and UNRRA, in which American resources were predominant. Roosevelt had been itching to take over the running of the grand coalition. In the administration of UNRRA and later IRO Americans largely did run the show, with American methods, and little doubt in Washington that that was right and natural. The British and other allies were so preoccupied by and exhausted with survival that there was some compensation in having the powerful Americans move in and assume burdens. Canadians resented the American positions because they thought their per capita contribution was at least as high as that of the United States. On the other hand they had strong reasons for satisfaction in seeing the Americans entwined in world organization – not sufficiently, however, to let the Americans get away with assumptions about their unique mission as God's temporal power on earth. When Roosevelt told King in private how he had thought up the term 'United Nations' in discussion with Churchill, King reported in his dairy: 'The President mentioned it was like adopting the idea of Seeley's Expansion of England. This was the expansion of the United States. The United States had grown into the United Nations, etc.' King commented that 'The pride of authorship is one of the strongest of temptations of most men ...'[43]

The first United Nations conference, that at Hot Springs in 1943, had as chairman a Texas Democrat who tried, as Lester Pearson noted, 'to combine the Congress of Vienna with a Rotary meeting.' 'We opened with a silent prayer and ended by singing, not "Hail to the United Nations," but the

"Star Spangled Banner." "[44] As for UNRRA, Congress scrutinized its activities possessively. Congressmen called its personnel office seeking jobs for constituents and treated it as an American agency.[45] For Hot Springs, UNRRA, and in the original establishment of the United Nations the Americans graciously consulted the other great powers, including China, a great power by American decree, and then even more graciously let the others know what was to be done. By 1945, however, thanks to the resistance of Canadians and Australians as much as any, they had a somewhat better perspective of the star-spangled role than they had held at the dawn's early light. Unshakable, however, was that messianic conviction that the sacred principles of 1776 were the way, the truth, and the light and destined, one day, to be carried to all mankind. Those recalcitrant Northern people whose history had been a superhuman effort to contain that manifest destiny were quick to resent the message. At the same time, if one could swallow the moral arrogance, there was a good deal to be said for democracy American-style. It was certainly preferable to what the Germans and Russians were peddling. The message about freeing the channels of trade, which the Americans regarded as essential to God's plan and had installed as Article VII of all Lend-Lease agreements, was an aspect of the Gospel with which Canadians generally agreed – even if they regarded the Americans as late converts.[46]

At this stage there were some differences between the British and Americans on the approach to shaping a postwar world order to which all the allies were now firmly committed in principle, and which their suffering citizens were determined to have in place of war and depression. The British preferred an orderly timetable and a uniform plan whereas the Americans seemed to want ad hoc meetings and conferences. The effort to get allied agreement on postwar arrangements was plagued by the sensitivity of American officials to Congressional prejudices. Congress was assumed, with justification, to be sceptical of schemes that would lead the United States into interminable obligations to sustain Europeans and the world at large. Between United States officials and those in other countries there were no major disagreements, although the former did not wish to risk everything by frightening Congress. Canadian, British, and other officials recognized this as a genuine risk. In their own long-range interest they were, therefore, susceptible to the American argument, although it weakened their position in the dialogue. The American preference for ad hoc conferences, as Ottawa saw it, was based not on theory but on the anxiety to avoid publicity which could set off adverse Congressional reactions. The administration was trying to lead the United States into internationalism without Congress realizing quite what was happening, and in this aim they had the collaboration of friends in London and Ottawa.

In Ottawa there was a somewhat similar fear of provoking the old isolationism in the cabinet, and officials were shrewdly sensitive to King's prejudices. Mackenzie King was in full charge, however. He might not fully grasp the long-range implications of the proposals being put forward by the officials, but they were careful to seek his approval. It was he, of course, who preferred not to confuse parliament or the public by provoking public debate on foreign policy. The need for broad public acceptance of internationalism was more often mentioned in External Affairs memoranda. The functionalist crusade, however, served domestic purposes. Cabinet was led into firm internationalist commitments because of its determination to assure Canadian status, without always pausing to calculate whether it really wanted to be deeply involved at all. In this formative year of 1943 the ministers were insistent that Canada must get justice, a seat at the table. King and the cabinet regarded External Affairs as too flexible over the UNRRA issue. A change was taking place in the Canadian claim as seen by staunch nationalists – from the right not to be committed by the great powers to the right to sit with the powers. Although American and Canadian parliamentarians shared some of the same hesitations about committing themselves to a quarrelsome and poverty-stricken world, they were at cross purposes. American officials sought to assure Congress that in the postwar institutions the United States could run the show or at least not have to submit to the will of foreigners. That was the kind of institution Canadian politicians and officials were determined to resist. And yet everyone in Ottawa believed that, without the willing participation of Congress this time, there was going to be no brave new world. Canada certainly was not going to pay for it without a United States contribution. Robertson, Wrong, Pearson, and King, from his perspective, did not like or defend this American ambivalence but they recognized it as a fact of life to be lived with.

HOT SPRINGS

In the spring of 1943 Canadians were more inclined to the orderly approach favoured by the British. They had an additional reason. They wanted the new structures to arise from the authority of the United Nations as a whole, not to be products of Anglo-American wartime arrangements or four-power prescriptions. They recognized, however, in the interest of orderly progress, the desirability of the four powers doing a certain amount of steering and initiating, as well as exploring the limits of East-West collaboration. The great powers were going to do this anyway, of course. The Canadian approach on the eve of the Hot Springs gathering was set out in a memorandum of Hume Wrong's of 19 March 1943 which reflected also the views of Robertson and

W.A. Mackintosh of the Department of Finance, and was shown to the prime minister:

I think that the tidiest way of dealing with the present situation would be to hold as soon as possible a full-dress conference of the United Nations with an agenda mainly restricted to the establishment of methods of postwar planning. There should first be a measure of preliminary agreement between the chief participants on what ought to result. The conference might set up a series of bodies of experts to prepare draft plans in particular fields, applying the functional principle to their composition. The occasion might also be used for the formal adoption of some general declarations of purpose, perhaps embodying the economic principles in Article 7 of the Lend-Lease Agreement which were reflected in our own exchange of notes with the United States last November. In this way a mandate could be given by the United Nations for a programme of international collaboration of a flexible character, and we should avoid what I feel would otherwise be the case – a series of disputes like that over the Relief Administration about what countries are to be represented on each body.

The best position to assume, Wrong recommended, was that 'the concept of the United Nations should be embodied in some institutional form, representation on agencies should be extended from the four powers to include those which have the chief contribution to make.' An early agreement was desirable to avoid disputes about the form of international co-operation and this might best be obtained by holding a UN conference charged with setting up expert bodies. 'If this method, however, is not acceptable to the larger powers, it would not be in our interest to press for its adoption.' Wrong was not inclined to waste strength and credit butting against stone walls.[47]

The orderly approach was not to be. Although the British and Americans, and to a privileged extent Canadians, had been engrossed for some time in talks on the expert level about the new bodies to be set up, particularly in the area of relief, food, money, and commerce, the United States State Department was favouring a general international economic conference. Before such planning had gone very far Roosevelt, without even consulting his own secretary of state let alone the British, Russians, and Chinese, announced in February 1943 that a United Nations conference would be held in April to consider long-term food problems. He had sensed that it was time to make clear to the world that the United Nations was moving from words to action. The purpose was more declaratory than definitive – a gala performance rather than a committee meeting. He was not wrong in this, but he was operating on a different wave length from the bureaucracy who wanted to get some clearly defined plans in motion. He and his wife had become interested in a proposal for a 'United Nations Programme for Freedom from Want of Food' drawn up by Frank McDougall, an Australian, with Canadian, British, and American collaborators. He knew that the increased production of food was a theme which would rouse the least controversial support for United Nations action. The British and Russians were not happy, and the American experts had to improvise quickly. The meeting was put off until 18 May to allow for preparation, but no country wanted to oppose it. It was an American production. On his own, Roosevelt invited the non-belligerent American republics, thereby setting a precedent. Against the wish of the Europeans but out of concern for Congressional reaction he insisted that the agenda be the long-range issues and not include the plans for relief now under vigorous discussion among the allies. There was considerable uncertainty in advance, as Pearson commented: 'We knew only that it was to be organized and run by the United States, who would choose the chairman and the secretariat and draw up the agenda.'[48]

This kind of conference did not raise for Canada the acute questions posed by the plans for a Relief Agency. Everyone was welcome at the party. Officials had been doing their preparatory work in Ottawa on food as well as financial issues, and postwar food supply was a subject of enormous commercial concern to Canada. A strong Canadian delegation was sent to Hot Springs and membership was secured on the steering committee. Of greatest consequence for Canada was probably the fact that Lester Pearson, who was at that time a career civil servant with the not particularly exalted rank of minister-counsellor in the Canadian embassy in Washington, was on the delegation and very helpful in the steering. Always aware of the need for inspiration in international politics, he personally proposed to some friends that the conference should issue 'a short, non-technical but inspirational declaration on the determination of the United Nations to deal with the problems of hunger and malnutrition once the war was over; something that would be valuable not only now in the political warfare that was being waged against the Nazis and their allies, but might help also to convince opinion in all countries that, this time, international co-operation and action would not fail after victory was won.'[49] In the end he was asked to draft the statement.

The conference concluded with a ringing declaration that the war against hunger could be won, and in the spirit of the times linked this struggle with the defeat of aggression and maintenance of international security regarded as essential conditions for the tremendous expansion of production envisaged. There was no fear of over-production, and the North Americans got in their strong words about removing barriers to trade. 'In no more succinct way could the popular phrase – "if we can do it in war we can do it in peace" – find expression,'[50] was the comment of the *Winnipeg Free Press* correspondent, Grant Dexter, who well reflected influential Canadian attitudes. No great significance would have been attached to the findings if the delegates had been 'theoretical folk, soft-headed and big-hearted, lacking ... in knowledge of the business of producing, distributing, and selling foodstuffs,' he said, but they happened to represent governments and included experts from every phase of the food industry. Unlike previous international agricultural conferences this was not concerned only with the producers' interest. 'The Hot Springs conference approached the food problem from the standpoint of what is required to feed the people of this world. The approach was wholly the approach of the consumer.' That may not have been quite the assumption of Jimmy Gardiner, the minister of agriculture. Dexter was a large-hearted internationalist, as well as a voice from the wheat country. His was the prevailing mood.

Of great importance to the administrators was the setting up at Hot Springs of an Interim Commission to plan the permanent international food body. Pearson became the chairman of this commission. In spite of his junior status, his extraordinary capacity for reconciling contrary views in apt formulas, his geniality under stress, his tactical skill, and his inoffensive idealism were being recognized. He was exactly the kind of person needed, and he came from the country best designed not only to propose compromises but to be a compromise. Shortly afterwards he was chosen for a critical role in UNRRA and his name cropped up whenever candidates for UN office were being considered. His personal contribution to the acquisition of status by Canada in the United Nations was that he was more concerned with the job in hand than the status of the Canadian representatives, thereby doing far more to raise the latter than those more interested in form than substance. He was not appointed to jobs just because the great powers wearily concluded it was best to appoint one of the Canadians to shut them up.

Pearson had expected that the prime minister would resist his appointment, but such was the zeal in Ottawa for a foot in the door that King agreed. In spite of his heavy diplomatic load as No 2 man in the Washington embassy and, after January 1945, as ambassador himself, Pearson worked diligently and effectively with the commission and its Executive Committee to prepare the required plans. In August 1944 a constitution was proposed which made clear that the agency would be advisory and fact-finding rather than 'administrative,' depending on the co-operation of member governments served by national committees. It was not until 16 October 1945 that the Interim Commission could be dissolved and the new Food and Agriculture Organization set up at a meeting in Quebec City, with Pearson as chairman, an unusual appointment for a mere diplomat. He had also been pressed to be the first director-general of the FAO but he did not want to leave the Canadian service and thought the post should go to Sir John Boyd-Orr, who was a scientist and had done more than anyone else to rouse public and official interest in practical means of coping with hunger.[51]

In spite of this satisfactory Canadian role, parliamentary approval of membership ran into some political difficulty. The problem was not that the Conservatives or CCF opposed Canadian participation in international organization, but they were concerned over the extent to which the implementation of FAO recommendations would be left in the hands of officials. The government met the criticism with some redrafting. It was inevitably the responsibility of officials in all countries to lay the foundations of the new world order in wartime, and they did so with zeal and imagination. They were tempted to circumvent if possible the lumbering political process. Experts had a tendency to favour the role of experts in international bodies, knowledgeable people who would know their business and not play politics. There was pressure within the FAO secretariat to strengthen its authority, but the politicians were reasserting themselves after the special demands of wartime. They had, by and large, accepted the idea of international institutions, but they did not want an international bureaucracy working through national bureaucracies to pre-empt their authority. The FAO debate in Ottawa, just before the organization's Quebec Conference and two months after the end of hostilities, illustrated clearly the difficulties in store if any of the more orderly schemes for 'international government' that had looked good in 1943 had been implemented – even in a body like FAO in which the Russians did not take part.

Canadians could not complain, however, that they had not been given due recognition in FAO. The meeting in Quebec was a calculated gesture, and not only Pearson but the Canadian specialists, in particular Dr G.H. Barton, deputy minister of agriculture, had been duly influential. A seat was obtained on the Executive Committee, to which the government sent a broadly-based delegation, headed by J.G. Gardiner, who was politically if not intellectually powerful, and included experts from the Departments of Agriculture, Fisheries, Mines and Resources, National Health and Welfare, Trade and Commerce, External Affairs, and also, as associates or advisers, representatives of such bodies as the Canadian Federation of Agriculture, the Fisheries Council of Canada, and of the pulp, paper, and lumber industries. The size and quality of the delegation were an earnest of the government's commitment to the cause of an international agricultural agency in particular and to that of specialized agencies in principle. This kind of international exercise was not to be left to diplomats, although they had their function as negotiators, but would involve specialists inside and outside government and, it was hoped, create a community of those who would pursue goals beyond sovereignty and act non-politically. At the same time, of course, the delegation reflected the expectation that, as Canada's staples were involved, there were commercial interests to be advanced or protected.

BRETTON WOODS

There were six legs to the world monetary stool, according to Clifford Clark; 'All six legs are necessary if the stool is to stand up.' These were collective security to end fear, multilateral trade, stability of exchange rates, willingness of creditor countries to accept imports in payment or invest abroad, freedom from wide fluctuations in the price of raw materials, and policies of full employment in each country.[52] That view is constantly repeated in Canadian memoranda and statements, a view shared by many international financial experts. Perhaps the most professional planning being done in Ottawa was on postwar financial arrangements, but the minister of finance constantly reiterated that these arrangements could not succeed by themselves. Canadian officials shared with counterparts in other allied counries the conviction that 'full employment,' which was everyone's stated goal, depended on both the establishment of international mechanisms to assure the stability of currencies and avoid the autarkical habits which had stagnated economies in the thirties and on some kind of lending provisions to tide countries over the difficult periods when they were tempted to put up the barriers.

Because of the widely recognized dependence of Canada on international commerce, Canadian officials had less difficulty with the prejudices of their legislatures than had those in Washington and London. Whereas the United States Congress was wary of efforts by the British and others to drain gold and credit from them, in London there were fears that, in the debtor's position they faced at the end of the war, they would be hamstrung by an institution designed by the chief creditor. Fortunately the leading political figures, preoccupied with grand strategy, agreed in principle that economic multilateralism was the essential counterpart of a multilateral security system, and they blessed the efforts of an extraordinarily wise and able group of financial experts. These experts thrashed out plans for the International Monetary Fund and the International Bank for Reconstruction and Development which may well have been the most revolutionary aspects of the new shape of peace. With much talk several decades later of 'the collapse of the Bretton Woods scheme' and the inadequacies of the bank and fund, it is hard to realize how revolutionary it was. It wasn't the mechanisms themselves; it was the acceptance of international collaboration – now taken for granted to such an extent that its novelty in the forties is no longer apparent. Looking back some twenty-five years later, one of the principal Canadian architects of the bank and fund, Louis Rasminsky, commented:

One of the results of the establishment of the Fund that has not received enough emphasis is the great increase in international consultation and collaboration. This seems so obvious that it may seem jejune even to mention it, but to those of us who saw what international co-operation in these matters was before the war the difference is dramatic ... Before the war, there was great diffidence about discussing any-body's domestic economic policies or the impact of those policies on other countries' positions, and discussion tended to be focused exclusively on 'external' economic policy such as tariff barriers ... If one contrasts that with the frequency and intimacy of the discussions which now take place on the board of the Fund and in other forums one becomes aware of a very major achievement.[53]

One should mention also the bouleversement implied in what may also seem obvious a generation later, the acceptance by creditor countries of joint responsibility with debtor countries to correct a disequilibrium of payments – a reversal of traditional assumptions comparable with the accep-tance a decade or so later of the strategic argument that it is in the interest of a nuclear power that its antagonist should feel secure of its capacity for a second strike.

'The International Monetary Fund and the International Bank were the product of English and American brains, with valuable assistance from the Canadians.' That was the judgment of Sir Roy Harrod, a British economist close to the scene at the time.[54] 'The Canadians,' he said, 'were keen that the British and Americans should think alike on post-war topics; in these talks and throughout the subsequent negotiations the Canadians continued to make valuable contributions. They were represented on successive occasions by able men, including Messrs. Rasminsky, Towers, MacIntosh [sic] and Pearson. Almost alone, outside the ranks of British and Americans, the Canadians seemed capable of understanding the international monetary pro-blem as a whole. Their suggestions were intelligent and constructive, and the British and Americans were always anxious to have them.'[55] With that kind of input the struggle for a voice did not have to be loud and formal.

It was not just the old-fashioned nationalists in Britain and the United States about whom Canada had to be concerned. There were those in both countries who saw the future in bilateral terms. In the United States there were supporters of the 'key currency' approach which envisaged no more than a special relationship between the dollar and sterling, with the countries of the world grouped round one or the other. The British were attracted to this partnership, partly because it would be more efficient and partly, no doubt, because they were desperately clinging to the status which came from association with the new giant. Keynes's original draft proposed 'that the Currency Union should be founded by the United States and the United Kingdom, which would be designated Founder States and given a special position.' However, the Americans took the position that the arrangement must be fully international with no special status for Britain.[56] It need not be assumed that the Americans thereby displayed an enthusiasm for multilateralism as the alternative of bilateralism. Their preference might unkindly be described as unilateralism – or rather multilateralism managed by a single rather than a twin leadership. The key currency idea was described by Rasminsky as 'the monetary counterpart of the Great Power doctrine of international organization generally.'[57]

Although the extent to which the American and British officials worked to a common aim was remarkable, there were stormy sessions. American officials were conscious of the insistence of Congress that the United States be in the driver's seat. They were New Dealers and they had their own itch to run the show in everybody's interest, as well as that endemic suspicion of the British empire as somehow an obstacle to their one world theme – 'theological convictions' about empire preferences, W.A. Mackintosh called them. The British knew how dependent they were, and they were seriously concerned lest the great creditor fail to realize the special needs of debtor countries before the new world was functioning. It was a situation made for the middle man. The Canadian position as a large exporter eager for unrestricted trade to start was closer to that of the United States. But Canada's economic relations with Britain, through trade and investment, were closer than those of the United States and it had, perhaps, a livelier awareness of the time and effort that would be required to get the British economy back on its feet. Personally the Canadian economists had close and good relations with both the British and American officials, which meant that there was a good deal of informal exchange of views in London and Washington before formal talks were initiated with 'the allies.' One service they could perform was to translate for the Cambridge graduates the econo-bureaucratic jargon now infesting Washington like the pox – a lingo which Keynes, the old Bloomsburian, called 'Cherokee.'

To begin with there were two plans, a 'Clearing Union' with an international currency, designed by J.M. Keynes and his British associates, and an international fund, proposed by Harry White of the United States Treasury and his associates, to which members would subscribe gold and their own currencies. Keynes's proposal was shown to Canadians in the spring of 1942. Then, shortly after the British and American officials had started looking at each other's plans, Keynes's ideas were discussed in London with dominions representatives in October 1942. It was in connection with this meeting that Harrod particularly praised the Canadian contribution, and Rasminsky later recalled it as 'the high spot intellectually in the discussions that preceded Bretton Woods.'[58] Canadians had been anxious about the way Britain would move after the war and they were elated by Keynes's sponsorship of the multilateral approach because of his prestige at home and abroad. They were greatly impresed by the design of the Clearing Union but concerned at the way the United States Congress would view it, largely because of the apparently unlimited liability of creditor countries, of which Canada was likely to be one of two. They also saw the White plan, which White gave to Plumptre of the Canadian embassy on a personal basis in November 1942. It originally went much further in providing for supranational controls, allowing the fund not only to fix the initial exchange rates but even to require countries to change their exchange rates. Congress would never have accepted that with its eyes open, and in the end the fund and particularly the bank turned out to be much less supranational than the American planners had at first fancied.

Paradoxically it was the Americans throughout who favoured institutions with managerial powers and the British and Canadians who thought of them as frameworks of agreed rules within which countries would act. As Harrod commented: 'The Americans are in the habit of praising private initiative and inveighing against paternalistic socialism ... Yet, when the Americans turn their eyes away from their own rights under the Constitution towards the international sphere, it is they who have recently tended to be the chief advocates of paternalism.'[59] The Americans, of course, felt they had the power and competence to manage the world for its own good because the American interest coincided with that of mankind. Canadians would probably have conceded that in this the Americans were about half right.

The Canadians produced and published their own plan, which would probably have been labelled a compromise even if it had not been.[60] It was an effort to find ways and means of reconciling Keynes and White and pushing both in certain directions. The British were disappointed that the Canadians did not come out for the Clearing Union. Canada proposed a fund of a larger original amount than White had envisaged and with power to increase its resources by borrowing from its members – a provision that foreshadowed the adoption by the fund of the General Arrangements to Borrow in 1958. It also challenged the extensive veto power the Americans were claiming. It was closer to the British view on the size of the fund while avoiding the virtually unlimited commitment of creditor countries inherent in the Clearing Union proposal. It allowed for immediate withdrawal from the fund if a country wished to do so, thereby covering the fear of those who argued that membership involved a complete surrender of national sovereignty.

Harry White told Clifford Clark it was all to the good that the Canadian proposal had been made public. 'It will unquestionably be widely read in this country and it will contribute to the interest of our people in the various proposals for international monetary cooperation.'[61] Experts from some of the allied countries were also producing their own views, and in April 1944, after a series of meetings culminating in a gathering of delegates from thirty countries at Atlantic City, there was published a 'Joint Statement by Experts on the Establishment of an International Monetary Fund' which formed the basic working document of the Bretton Woods Conference. Although the subject was abstruse and the experts naturally dominated the discussion, there was less secrecy about the debate than there was for most international projects of these times.

There was so much revision and negotiation and honest intellectual groping in this process that it would be hard and also foolish to say just what was Canadian that came out in the end. The view expressed in the *New York Times* that the final agreement most closely resembled the Canadian plan is understandably the opinion cited in Canadian versions. Rasminsky, who contributed as much as anyone, has commented modestly: 'Having in mind the *real* distribution of economic power at the time, my overall impression is that the Americans moved a very great distance, that they did not exploit that power in determining the final version at Bretton Woods. They went a very great distance towards meeting the British view. I would naturally like to think that Canadians played some part in that. I do not honestly know whether we did or not.'[62] W.A. Mackintosh's judgment was: 'There were many points in the International Monetary Agreement at which the Canadians, particularly Mr Rasminsky, made important and clarifying contributions. In successive preliminary discussions we probably had considerable effect in converting the British to a multilateral approach ... On the views of United States officials concerning the British preference we had at least an eroding effect, so that preferential tariffs became subjects for negotiation and not illegal weapons to be given up at the door.'[63]

Rasminsky played an important part in preparing the ground by publishing in the July 1944 issue of the influential quarterly, *Foreign Affairs*,[64] an article in which he demolished with the utmost reasonableness the case against the international approach – and also the bilateral 'key currency' scheme favoured by many Wall Street readers of *Foreign Affairs*. He pointed out to sceptical Americans that a simple return to the gold standard of prewar days was not a feasible alternative, that if they wanted to remove the barriers to trade in accordance with Article VII of Lend-Lease to which they had committed their allies they had to concern themselves with their customers' capacity to pay. The fund was no miracle cure, of course: 'Divergencies between national policies will develop even so; there will be stresses and strains. This will be true under any conceivable arrangement: but I have faith that generally acceptable solutions are more likely to be found through the machinery of consultation, warning and advice provided by an international agency such as the Fund than as a result of the uncoördinated unilateral action of individual countries.' It is a clear early statement of an argument that has had to be repeated constantly: international institutions do not necessarily produce wise policies, but they do provide machinery through which it is possible to achieve wiser policies.

Rasminsky also made several basic arguments for Canadians. First, he stressed the value of the multilateral approach in the ambiguous continental relationship: 'True, the United States is such a colossus in the world economic system that, linked or unlinked, foreign countries cannot help being greatly influenced, for better or for worse, by the trend of affairs there. But it is one thing for a country to accept this predominant American influence when that country is in a position to express some views on the course of events or is free to cope with it with such ingenuity as it can muster, if things do not go well; it is quite another for one country to tie its fortunes inexorably to policies pursued by another, no matter how farsighted and well-chosen those policies might be.' For Canadians, as well as Americans, another point had to be made: the need for a period of transition to the utopian world of unfettered exchange, which was provided for in the 'escape clause' on which Britain and other postwar debtors insisted: 'For Canada, multilateral clearing is the chief merit of any form of international monetary organization, and hope for this is now deferred. Nevertheless, I still think it worthwhile to proceed with the creation of the Fund ... if we are ever to achieve international monetary coöperation we must reach agreement while the atmosphere is relatively favorable. Countries have become used to working together closely during the war. It will require less psychological adjustment to extend these close wartime relationships for peacetime purposes now than would be required five or ten years after the war has ended.'

The United Nations Monetary and Financial Conference at Bretton Woods, New Hampshire, 1 July 1944, was a very different affair from that at Hot

Springs, more concrete and more thoroughly prepared. The Canadian delegation included, in addition to the officials involved in the preliminary discussions, the minister of finance, J.L. Ilsley, and Louis St Laurent, minister of justice and the senior Quebecker in the cabinet. Rasminsky was chairman of the committee to draft the Articles of Agreement and the rapporteur to the Plenary Conference on matters relating to the fund. Mackintosh took the chair in the important committee which dealt with the operations of the fund. The International Monetary Fund agreed upon at Bretton Woods was to consist of a mixed bag of gold and national currencies, with each country's contribution (quota) based on estimates of wealth, trade, and production adapted to meet special circumstances. Canada's contribution ranked seventh. The fund was to be a permanent international institution for collaboration on monetary questions. There was to be a Board of Governors with one representative from each member state and a board of twelve executive directors on which the five largest contributors would have permanent seats. It was specified that there would be two Latin American representatives, a provision Canadians had great difficulty swallowing. There were to be only five other seats. Canada ingeniously argued that this would probably mean a board consisting of eleven debtors and one creditor, and gained acceptance of a provision that the second largest creditor (no doubt assumed to be Canada) should always be on the board. It was probably the neatest victory for the pure functional theory, involving a legitimate principle of general validity calculated to further a Canadian claim.

The Bretton Woods meeting also set up a twin institution, the International Bank for Reconstruction and Development. Although the 'World Bank' has attracted increasing attention, much greater emphasis was placed on the fund at the time. The fund, of course, was concerned with problems of behaviour (exchange rates, exchange restrictions, discrimination) which are inherently more interesting than money. The bank as it emerged had been drastically reduced in scope and resources from the kind of international central bank that American planners had first envisaged. Its importance has grown as the theme of developing the less developed has become paramount, but that is not what preoccupied Canadians and others in the mid-forties. The bank was to have a capital of only $10 billion to provide members with long-term capital for reconstruction and development. Canada's subscription was sixth in amount. Each member paid up 15 per cent of its capital which could, however, be lent by the bank only with its consent. The remaining 85 per cent was a guarantee fund which stood behind the obligations (bonds) which the bank sold in the money markets of the world. This provided a 'safe bridge' which enabled private investors to put their money into risky places, via the bank. The bank was regarded as an agent for speeding reconstruction, the word development in its title being regarded as something for a better day. However, reconstruction was largely accomplished by the United States and Canadian postwar loans and the Marshall Plan. The voice of the developing countries was raised sooner than expected, and the bank turned its attention to a function which, although contemplated by its founders, was not in the forefront of their thinking.

At the inaugural meeting of the Boards of Governors of both the bank and the fund in March 1946 Canada secured election to the boards of executive directors of both institutions. Unlike other specialized agencies, voting in the fund as well as the bank was weighted by the size of each country's quota (or contribution), a form of 'functionalism.' By the original formula Canada had slightly over 3 per cent of the voting power in the fund to 33 per cent for the United States and 16 per cent for the United Kingdom.

In December 1945 Canadian participation in both the bank and the fund was approved on third reading in the Commons by a vote of 169 to 9. Neither the minister of finance nor members of the Liberal or Conservative parties who spoke in favour regarded either of these institutions as the magic solution to their problems. Their preoccupation with trade was evident. Nevertheless, most members seemed to agree with the financial critic of the Progressive Conservatives, J.M. Macdonnell: 'If we can begin by some kind of financial cooperation, it will be a help. It is only a beginning; an understanding in trade is necessary. But we can begin with this act of faith, next summer we may have another act of faith. When trade arrangements are made they will be an act of faith for the moment too.'[65]

The debate was noisier than it would have been as a reflection of broad popular opinion because of the opposition of the Social Credit party. The speeches did at least reveal a hard-core resistance to any abnegation of sovereignty to an international body. They denounced Bretton Woods as a club with which Canada would help the United States 'beat the Motherland to death.' They talked of perpetual bondage to international bankers and Canada losing control of its own economy, themes from the far Right which sound curiously like the interpretations of postwar policies by the 'revisionists' on the Left a generation later. In the Commons debate at the time the CCF were somewhat reserved, but they took a constructive part in the discussions in the Banking and Commerce Committee. However uneasy some of the members were about certain aspects of such a financial agreement, the commitment to internationalist solutions, particularly on the part of their leader, M.J. Coldwell, was such that they would not oppose the grand effort. The only amendment to the bill after discussion in committee was a provision for annual reports on the operations under the act to be made to parliament by the minister of finance, reflecting the same concern of legislators as in the case of the FAO lest their authority be ignored in this vastly fortified level of international government.

The government's view of all these measures as a package was illustrated by Ilsley's announcement on the same day as he introduced the act that the United States had agreed to a loan to Britain and that the British and Americans were taking the initiative in summoning a world conference on trade and employment. 'The proposals on commercial policy,' he said, '... have resulted from discussions among officials that have extended over two or three years, in some of which our officials have participated.'[66] They certainly had. The almost continuous negotiation among Americans, British, and Canadians over war and postwar payments (discussed in chapter 3) had been closely related to the talk about the fund and the bank.[67] The United States loan to Britain would presumably help shorten the transitional period. It would also lead shortly to Canada's making a considerably more generous loan for the same long-range purpose.

The Bretton Woods system was a beginning, but it reflected the restricted vision of the time. John Deutsch who was on the Canadian delegation commented several decades later: '... there was one very important aspect which, as I look back now, we did not understand very well at the time of Bretton Woods. That was the position of the under-developed countries ... At Bretton Woods we were looking for and we thought we were building a universal system ... it has in fact made possible a fantastic growth in trade and production in the industrialized west. But this is in very strong contrast with the rest of the world. The under-developed world really is not part of this system at all. It is still far from clear how this system can be made into the universal system of trade and exchange for the benefit of the whole world. This is one of the great unfinished tasks ahead of us.'[68] It was unlikely, however, that after Bretton Woods there could be an abandonment of the international approach, even if it was on the basis of understandings among regional or functional groups. The zeal for universalism was somewhat fanatical in 1944, but Canadian and other planners had not fully grasped the distinction between the Western world and the universe. They would get the message in part from the very institutions they were creating.

CHICAGO

Of all the issues of postwar international co-operation, none was closer to the Canadian heart than civil aviation. It captured the popular imagination and it involved C.D. Howe in an important aspect of the new international structure. Howe had been minister of transport before the war and was responsible, therefore, for the development of Trans-Canada Air Lines. He retained control of civil aviation during the war as minister of munitions and supply. He was also the guiding genius of the Commonwealth Air Training Plan which gave Canada a special place in the imagination of its citizens and others as well. In the interwar period the fledgling RCAF had been maintained through the austere years because of its role in developing air transport, especially in the north. Technological developments in aviation during the war had a profound effect on Canadian thinking – not only the advances made by themselves and their allies but also by the countries which might threaten them. Aircraft had removed the Arctic barrier in which they had reposed their confidence. It had altered the kind of map they thought by. It brought an unfamiliar feeling of insecurity along with an exhilarating sense of opportunity. 'Aviation has made us a buffer state,' said Grant Dexter in 1944. 'In the air world we are the cock-pit of North America.'[69]

Transport had always been at the core of the Canadian national problem and the Canadian national dream. Aviation offered to a small population the possibility of coping with enormous territory and enormous resources, like the building of canals and then railways in the nineteenth century. In Canada, unlike the United States, the development of aviation, as well as other forms of transportation, was seen as a national enterprise. One reason it had to be national was, of course, to protect the Canadian interest from the free enterprise of a powerful neighbour. The other reason was the relationship of aviation to security, uppermost in the minds of everyone in the forties. It was not just a matter of the defence of Canadian soil. The strategic significance of Canada in world security was dramatized by the Northwest Staging Route reaching up from Edmonton through Alaska to Asia and by the projected Crimson Route in the northeast. When Canadians came to think institutionally about international aviation, they placed heavy emphasis on the implications for security, insisting on a close link with the proposed Security Council. Even if it was a matter of civil aviation there was the vivid recollection of how the Nazis had used (and planned to use further) civil aviation for infiltration abroad and as a screen behind which to develop the Luftwaffe in defiance of the Treaty of Versailles. The British had an even more vivid regard for the airplane as a menace and they, like the Canadians, wanted it controlled. The Americans thought more of the liberation of aviation from control and restriction. That appealed also to the Canadians, anxious to spread abroad their newly found air power.

So it was not an international theoretician of the Department of External Affairs but Howe who said of an international air agreement: 'an enlightened settlement ... can constitute a model for the settlement of other difficult international problems, and create an atmosphere in which the settlement of these other problems will become easier. Failure to devise a working system of co-operation and collaboration ... will prejudice the establishment of an effective world security organization.'[70] He was prepared to set an example that went pretty far for a man supposedly attached to liberal capitalist principles. In Ottawa, as in Washington, London, and in other capitals, there was a strong desire to clear away the national barriers to air transport that had impeded development before the war and would be utterly inappropriate now that transoceanic flights had become an accepted feature of travel. There was little hope of aviation serving the needs of mankind so long as each country could bargain bilaterally for transit of its air space and whole regions could be shut off from competition. Something like 'freedom of the air' to match the 'freedom of the seas' was required, although the difficulties were more complex.[71]

In 1942 studies were authorized in Ottawa and an interdepartmental committee set up so that in April 1943 the prime minister was able to adumbrate a position. 'The Canadian government strongly favours a policy of international collaboration and co-operation in air transport and is prepared to support in international negotiations whatever international air transport policy can be demonstrated as being best calculated to serve not only the immediate national interests of Canada but also our overriding interest in the establishment of an international order which will prevent the outbreak of another world war.'[72] The link perceived with security and the other legs of the new international order was clear. What was also clear in other parts of this statement was the determination to take advantage of Canada's enormously increased significance in international aviation, not only as an air power but as a large space and a crossroads. To this end the government wanted all existing agreements to lapse so they would be 'unfettered by any commitments when it comes to deal with post-war air problems.' Trans-Canada Air Lines would be the government's instrument for international services so that its freedom of action would not be 'limited by the existence of private interests in international air transport services.' This marked a significant difference from prevailing American views. On the government's mind also was the necessity of taking over from the Americans the wartime transport lines they had opened up in Canada.

A particular problem arose vis-à-vis the British. A British perspective was bluntly stated in the Commons on 1 June 1943 by Sir Archibald Sinclair, secretary of state for air: 'After the war we shall either be in a world dominated by the United States or the Soviet Union or the centre of a great Empire bound together by air routes.' When Canada had felt less strong in the field, it had agreed to sponsor a transatlantic air service along with the United Kingdom, Newfoundland, and Ireland. This scheme had not been fully implemented. By 1942 the government had established Trans-Canada Air Lines, capable of a transatlantic service of its own. Its confidence in Canadian capacity was vastly increased, and it preferred to terminate the joint arrangement with the British and Irish. Ottawa was not enthusiastic, needless to say, about proposals for a grand Commonwealth operating company being pressed by Lord Beaverbrook and the imperially-minded members of the British government. When the British proposed Commonwealth talks on international civil aviation the Canadians were nervous. On this subject, above all others, their relations with the United States were *sui generis* and the idea of negotiations with the United States as part of a Commonwealth front was unacceptable.

It was not that Canadians saw their interests and those of the United States as identical or necessarily parallel. In their opposition to American 'free enterprise' they had more in common with the other Commonwealth countries. It was just that the Canada-United States relationship had, for territorial reasons, a dimension of its own. Canadians perceived also that the British might naturally like to negotiate with the Americans as a Commonwealth unit because Canadian real estate would have considerable bargaining power with the Americans. It was the possession of essential bases which Canada regarded as it chief counter in any international negotiations. Curiously enough there were also some Americans who wanted to bargain with the British as a whole Commonwealth as a means of getting concessions from the Canadians.[73] Ottawa was worried over the power of the American air lobby and anxious not to give the Americans ground for complaining that the British countries were ganging up on them. They did not seek to drive a wedge between the British and Americans because they were determined to get a tough and tight international aviation authority and British-American collaboration was fundamental to this object.

There was much skirmishing between London and Ottawa over the holding of a Commonwealth conference on aviation, with the Canadians insisting on American participation. During the Quebec Conference of August 1943 the Canadians found an ally in Churchill, who, in spite of his weakness for imperial solidarity, gave a higher priority to British-American understanding. Eventually, Commonwealth conversations took place in October 1943 in London, with the Americans duly warned of their informal nature. The British did not press an unacceptable imperial scheme, and the Canadians found the talks satisfactory. There was unanimous agreement 'that closed discriminatory systems could only promote disharmony, and endanger the chances of reaching that broad agreement which is necessary.'[74] To make their pure internationalism obvious the Canadian government announced discussions with the United States and the Soviet Union as well as the Chinese. Only those with the Americans took place.

On 17 March 1944 Howe tabled a draft International Air Transport Convention. This proposed an international authority which would encourage and plan international air services. It would be subordinate to the proposed international security organization. It would have power to license international airlines, fix rates, assign quotas, and determine the frequency of service on approved air routes. What proved to be the most important Canadian contribution was the definition of certain freedoms:

1 freedom of transit over the airways of member states;
2 freedom of landing for refueling, repairs, or emergencies;
3 freedom of carrying passengers, mail, and freight to the home state from any other member state, or
4 to any member state from the home state.

Although this plan envisaged unprecedented power for an international body, it rejected the proposal for international ownership and management of international air services, an idea strongly advocated in those heady times by many people, from Henry Wallace in the United States to the Australian and New Zealand Labour governments. Clare Booth Luce called it 'globaloney.' Although many Canadians were attracted by it, the Ottawa planners knew that it would in no circumstances be accepted by the United States and it was wiser to devise something they might be persuaded to go along with. The Canadian plan was circulated for study, as were also British and American plans.

In November 1944 an international conference was held in Chicago on the invitation of the United States. The Soviet Union did not attend, but a large number of neutral and belligerent countries did. A basic document was the Canadian draft convention, revised to take into consideration American and British views and prejudices. The right to fix rates was transferred from the international authority to the operators, and there was provision for a transitional postwar period in which bilateral agreements could be made. The United States plan provided for an international authority with powers limited to technical and consultative functions. The British plan called for an authority similar to the Canadian. When the conference began on 1 November the Australian-New Zealand plan was quickly eliminated. Then it was realized that there was not going to be agreement on any of the three remaining plans. Open meetings were suspended, and from 12 to 20 November the United Kingdom, United States, and Canadian delegations were in almost continuous closed conference, after which they placed before the conference, without committing themselves, draft proposals. The British and Canadian preference for allocating routes and fixing frequencies had lost out. As far as the 'economic functions' were concerned, the proposed body would be purely advisory and consultative. In the end rates and routes were left for bilateral negotiation.

Most of the subsequent controversy was over the 'five freedoms.' The United States had added, as a fifth, the freedom to pick up and discharge traffic at intermediate points. That was critical. The Americans saw the liberation of the airways as a blessing for all peoples, but if planes could not pick up and deposit passengers along the way, there could not be profitable long distance runs and needy countries would be missed. True enough, but, of course, this provision would also enable the well-endowed Americans to capture routes between countries that wanted, as soon as they were able, to get into international flying themselves. As the French representative put it: 'the overwhelming superiority of a competitor, even if he is an absolutely fair partner, might provoke protective reflexes in smaller nations, the aerial sovereignty of which is unquestioned.'[75] Agreement on the five freedoms could not be reached, and it was decided to open for signature a Two Freedoms agreement and a Five Freedoms agreement. Many more states signed the former than the latter, which was abandoned a few years later. Canada signed only the Two Freedoms agreement which did cover the essential freedom of transit. The sovereignty of a country was never questioned, of course. What was provided was a reciprocal, multilateral guaranty of rights. Canada refused to concede the rights involved in the third, fourth, and fifth freedoms, except as part of a worldwide multilateral system which would promote the kind of orderly development of air transport they had sought from the beginning. In fact they kept fighting for multilateralism for some time afterwards. The Chicago Conference produced also a Convention on International Civil Aviation that modernized the law of the air, a standard form of bilateral agreement for the exchange of air routes that brought some measure of consistency, an impressive series of technical annexes that provided the basis for technical and operational uniformity, and an International Civil Aviation Organization to supervise and develop further what had been agreed at Chicago.

The Chicago Conference was in a sense not a United Nations conference. The Americans planned and ran it. The staff were American, and the prescribed language was English. The chairman, Adolf Berle, was far from impartial. The French and Chinese vice-chairmen were not able to throw much weight. The results, however, were not what the Americans wanted, although little got through that they did not want. Canada had a powerful delegation headed by C.D. Howe, with H.J. Symington, president of Trans-Canada Air Lines, J.A. Wilson, director of Air Services, and an unbeatable collection of technical advisers from Transport, National Defence, and other departments. The Canadian draft was used not just because of its intermediate position but because of the thoroughness and detail with which it had been prepared – a product largely of the master hand of Escott Reid. Adolf Berle said in his closing remarks: 'let me also pay tribute with particular affection to the Delegation of Canada, which tirelessly worked to reconcile the different points of view. Indeed, to the Canadian thought and the Canadian draft we owe the language we are using.' The British, he said, approached the problem primarily from the point of view of order in the air. 'We on our side approached it from the point of view of freedom of the air.'[76] There was something of both approaches in the Canadian attitude, so that the role of middleman came naturally. It is a generalization which might have been made about the positions of the three powers towards the postwar economic structure in general.

The Chicago final act provided for an interim body for three years. The Canadian draft had envisaged an International Air Transport Board to consist of representatives of the eight states of chief importance in international air transport plus the nationals of four states elected by an assembly. In arguing for this position the Canadians found themselves closer to the great powers than to the smaller powers, displaying thereby their bias in the application of the functionalist principle. The political strength of the smaller powers, especially the Latin Americans, was such that a compromise was necessary. The eventual agreement was on an annual assembly and a council of twenty-one elected for a period of three years, to be in continuous session. The council, composed by a more flexible interpretation of the functional principle than Canadians usually advocated, was to include states of three categories: those of chief importance in air transport, those which made the greatest contribution to the provision of facilities, and those which represented the main geographical areas of the world. Canada was elected in the second category, which was functionalist enough.

The experience of this election early in the process of establishing international institutions had a considerable effect on Canadian thinking about the functional principle and also about its so-called 'neighbours' in the western hemisphere. Since the Latin Americans and the Arabs combined could command nearly half the votes of the Chicago Conference, they were able almost to dictate the slate of candidates elected to the interim council. What particularly disturbed Canadians was that they simply ignored the criteria for membership that had been carefully adopted. Mexico was elected as a world air operator and Canada, although it was the fourth military air power among the United Nations, was not. Seven Latin American and two Arab states were among the twenty elected to the council, and these included El Salvador. There were only five Europeans and four Asians. India was omitted altogether, but Cuba finally withdrew in its favour. Egypt was the only African member. The majority of these states had approved the functional principle incorporated in the Air Convention without intending to abide by it. Nothing could be done. An election could not be contested on the ground that the state elected lacked the requisite qualifications. What happened in Chicago stiffened the Canadian resolve to make provisions for membership according to function on the Security Council. It might better have provided a warning that the functional principle could not be successfully prescribed.

The first session of the Council of the Provisional International Civil Aviation Organization was held in Montreal in June 1945 with an American as president and a Frenchman as secretary general. In May 1946 the first meeting of the interim assembly was held, also in Montreal, and at that session it was decided to make Montreal the permanent site of ICAO, which came into existence in April 1947 after thirty-five states had ratified the convention. Not surprisingly, Canada became a member of the Permanent Council of twenty-one. It continued vigorously but unsuccessfully to press the case for a multilateral system, arguing that a network of similar bilaterals was not multilateralism. In the meantime, however, it proceeded to negotiate what were in fact reasonably consistent bilaterals with the United Kingdom, Ireland, Newfoundland, the United States, and Australia. When Newfoundland entered confederation in 1949, Canada was saddled with commitments previously made, and for the first time exchanged fifth freedom rights with the United States and the United Kingdom.

The civil aviation negotiations posed squarely for Canada the challenge of American New Deal internationalism, that ambivalent mixture of idealism and imperialism personified in Adolf A. Berle, the assistant secretary of state in charge of, among other issues, international civil aviation. It is a phenomenon of the mid-forties perhaps better understood a generation later when one can see in it the source of the flourishing family of United Nations agencies that could not have been launched without American leadership and resources, and also the source of the appalling miscalculation in Vietnam. To regard Berle as the typical American planner of that era would be an error. He was held in check by other American traditions, less arrogant and more conservative, but is illustrative as caricature. As a political appointee, a New Dealer among the State Department pros, with links to Roosevelt and

Hull, however, he was a part of the act. His brand of moral imperialism was to be found in doses of varying proportion throughout Washington and coast-to-coast. There was much of it in the president himself, although his humanitarianism was less xenophobic. Berle was an anti-imperialist imperialist, *genus Americanus*, not to be confused with the nationalists whose single dedication to the assertion of United States military and economic interest was easier to cope with. In the First War, as he saw it, the United States 'came so into the English camp that ... we got not one thing that we really desired in the ensuing peace.' This time it should be the other way round. 'We have the ultimate strength. We also have the ultimate consistency of principle; we are the inevitable economic center of the regime which will emerge – unless, of course, we all go under.'[77]

In his diary for 22 February 1944 Berle jotted: 'The last few days, working on two separate jobs, although they sound the same: the development of a postwar civil aviation policy; and the collection of a string of bases designed to take care of United States security after the end of the war.'[78] He took for granted that the United States must have assured access to air bases in all strategic parts of the globe, for reasons of strategy and commerce and the stability of the great globe itself. He had been passionately aroused over Canadian, British, or French 'plots' to take protective custody of Greenland or St Pierre during the war, yet he could note in his diary: 'The bases in the Japanese mandated islands ... we will not negotiate for; I hope we shall simply go out and take them. We shall have some negotiations to do with a few British islands ... Just as soon as we get reasonably started in Brazil and Mexico, I propose to go to work in Canada.'[79]

Berle saw a sinister dispostion of the Europeans to carve out their empires in the air, begat of cartelization and socialism in the face of the American doctrine of the liberation of trade. It had been this American attitude that provoked these countries to insist at Bretton Woods on a transitional period of financial and commercial protection until they could get on their feet. Berle accepted the need for a transition period in aviation, but he did not want to dismantle the world-girdling network of military transport the Americans had set up, especially as he believed that the British were planning to exploit their wartime system. That the removal of barriers to the flight of planes all over the world must work to the particular interest of the United States he could not admit. In any case, the United States would operate in the interests of all. Freedom was, after all, a holy cause. As the chief of the Aviation Division in the State Department expressed it: 'It need not stop at the water's edge, or hesitate at mountain barriers. To do so is to deny its God-given right of universal entry.'[80]

The Americans would not concede, however, that if the British made available bases in their maritime empire, the United States should open up its great land empire – Chicago for Singapore. An American interest in opening up Canada was a major cause of anxiety in Ottawa. That is why Canada resisted the Fifth Freedom agreement which, unless it was part of a broader scheme, could have permitted Pan American to pick up passengers at Montreal or Edmonton en route abroad. The realization that the Americans could easily dominate air transport in Canada if they got a foothold was clear to Howe.

Because he was the zealot most likely to draw the United States, in spite of the howls of isolationists and private interests, into an international aviation structure which Canadians staunchly believed to be the best guarantor of their interests, Berle had to be supported. But he and his kind had to be treated warily. He represented, after all, not only internationalism but a messianic continentalism. His anti-British prejudices prevented him from understanding the ambiguous phenomenon that Canada was. His comprehension is illustrated by his gleefully noting, at the outbreak of war, that Mackenzie King had taken a more neutral position than had Lord Tweedsmuir in his speech from the throne.[81] Canada did not fit his simple view of the righteous republic and the wicked empire – except, of course, as a people straining for freedom in the American way. Although the Canadian plan at Chicago, with its extensive international control, was contrary to the basic American concept, Berle was less harsh on Canadians than on real foreigners. Berle believed in the western hemisphere as his community. He was no crude annexationist. He did want to see the hemisphere politically completed, but he saw it more as a community of nations. After a talk in Ottawa on 18 March 1941 with Hugh Keenleyside of External Affairs about what was to become the Hyde Park agreement for mutual exchanges in defence production, Berle noted: 'Keenleyside realizes that this is now one continent and one economy; that we shall have to be integrated as to finance, trade routes, and pretty much everything else; and in this I so thoroughly agree with him that it is refreshing ... This at least is a new order which can exist without hatred and can be created without bloodshed, and ought to lead to production without slavery.'[82]

Canadians were more inclined to envisage a postwar Utopia dominated by the Commonwealth and the United States, but their assumption about the moral superiority of 'the English-speaking world' had something in common with Berle's assumptions about America. Some Canadians could be accused of wanting multilateralism under neither unilateral (US) nor bilateral (US-UK) but rather trilateral leadership. That is perhaps what the Chicago Conference was. Discussion was directed to the three plans. There was also the Australian-New Zealand plan. No meeting could be smoothly trilateral if the Aussies were there, but they made themselves ineffectual by divorcing themselves from the main stream. As the official report of the proceedings makes clear, the American-British-Canadian conference within a conference was the centre of the action. The Russians had refused to attend at the last minute, and their absence removed the compulsion to preserve the great-power front. The French were attending their first conference as a Paris-based government and were not ready to assume a leading role in a highly technical negotiation.

In spite of this sterling performance by Canada – a stature and status probably never again reached in a broad international conference – did the Americans triumph regardless? They successfully resisted the Canadian and British hope for an international body with stricter regulatory authority and got instead a body that would be advisory or consultative. However, the Americans may have had the better argument. Howe insisted that what Canada wanted was no more than what the Americans had at home in their Civil Aeronautics Board. The Americans pointed out the very great difference between a board of individuals appointed by the elected president of a state, with a set of guiding principles, and an international board composed of the representatives of states who would inevitably be advocates.[83] In their enthusiasm for international institutions 'with teeth' and in their trust in the role of 'international men' Canadians were hoping there could be international 'government' by wise and expert men detached from a political constituency. But the responsibilities of any international authority would inevitably be political. It was a lesson Canadian imperial experience had taught them, but they were tempted to think the United Nations would be different. In 1944 the Canadian conception of a United Nations structure was more authoritarian than what proved possible. The original Canadian plan for civil aviation envisaged, for example, that the Security Council could call upon the Air Authority to 'take the measures concerning technical services, operating facilities and bases which the international security organization has directed should be taken' or even 'to operate air services on routes or in regions designated from time to time by the international security organisation.'[84]

Experience proved, however, that states would work together without enforcement provisions when they had good selfish reasons for doing so – a fact the Universal Postal Union had been proving for three-quarters of a century. What was produced at Chicago was a basic agreement on the essential freedoms and an organization to oversee and further develop the rules and regulations to which nations now conform, not because they are called 'compulsory' but because it is in their own national interest to do so. It seemed like a watering down of the vision, but its importance, like that of Bretton Woods, was the commitment to the international consultative approach. There would still be bilateral deals and cut-throat competition, but the world was not going to be cut up into closed zones. Freedom of the air had, as was so often said, in one jump reached the status which had taken several centuries to achieve for the seas. The Chicago Conference is of great historical importance because it set a pattern for what has become the essential function of the United Nations – providing a framework for multilateral diplomacy so that sovereign members can bargain with each other in accordance with universal principles. It foreshadowed the accomplishments within the General Agreement on Tariffs and Trade and the United Nations Conferences on the Law of the Sea, the boldest effort yet to solidify an international community.

The success of the delegation ought not to be judged in terms of the number of points scored for Canadian aviation. Canada could have single-mindedly held its broad territory for bargaining but said instead that 'it would be willing to forego a bargaining position in order to contribute to increased freedom of the air that would promote international harmony.'[85] At Chicago the Canadian government notably achieved an important aspect of its functionalist philosophy. 'The Government has felt,' Hume Wrong wrote to Vincent Massey in 1942, 'that we should be partners in these bodies and should not merely be afforded means of protecting our direct interests when they come under consideration.'[86] It was their critical role in bringing about a general agreement that best served the Canadian interest. It is a role that requires a certain detachment from narrowly national advantage. In fact, there was no serious sacrifice of advantage. Canada would have to negotiate directly with the United States for reciprocal rights, but the Americans could claim no conceded 'freedom' to fly beyond border points in Canada. When he first presented his plan to the Commons, Howe said: 'If any such framework for international cooperation in the field of air transport should be developed ... it would seem that cross-border services, such as those between Canada and the United States, should be considered in a special category, and dealt with specially by the two countries concerned, since services originating in the one country and terminating in the other are primarily trans-frontier extensions of domestic air services.'[87] In spite of a diffuse feeling that global international organization was a counterweight against the continental pressures, Canada preserved in practice an assumption that continental international relations were a thing apart.

FUNCTIONALISM

In the creation of these international institutions in wartime, the Canadian philosophy (if one can use such a grandiose term) of a United Nations was being shaped before the position papers were drafted for the Charter conference in San Francisco. The theory which emerged in King's statements on functionalism of 9 July 1943 during the discussions over UNRRA, and then again on 4 August 1944, had been largely a conception of Hume Wrong, formulated in constant colloquy with his colleagues. Whether King meant what his officials had in mind may be doubted, because theirs was an argument not just for Canadian rights but by implication for wider responsibilities, but when asked if he agreed with the argument set out in detail in a memorandum of guidance for an UNRRA Council meeting, he wrote, 'entirely so.'[88] In the context of relief he was probably seeing this as the principle of no taxation without representation. He had been predisposed in favour of the general 'functionalist' approach to international organization because of its apparent emphasis on economic and social rather than on military activities.

There were two meanings of the term 'functional international organization,' as Wrong pointed out to the prime minister. The special Ottawa meaning had been that effective international authority in a given matter ought to be concentrated in bodies in which the countries mainly concerned were represented. He added, however, that, 'there is another meaning given to the term, used especially by Professor Mitrany in a study recently issued by Chatham House.[89] He argues that the world should be bound together by a large number of different international institutions organized to deal separately with the many functions requiring international co-operation. The two meanings overlap and are not essentially inconsistent but the variation in the use of the term should be borne in mind.' There was no doubt a general acceptance of Mitrany's assumptions in Canadian policy, and what King and his officials meant by 'functionalism' was by no means incompatible. Nevertheless, 'an analytical distinction must be made,' as A.J. Miller has aptly put it, 'between the theory of functional representation and what, for lack of a better term, shall be called functionalist internationalism.' He adds, 'The essence of functionalist internationalism, as distinct from functional representation, is a belief in international economic and social co-operation as a means of reducing the likelihood of conflict in the building of human accord, ultimately to the point of world government.'[90]

The concrete steps towards 'functionalist internationalism' taken at Bretton Woods and Chicago made the principle of 'functional representation' more important to Canadians. The statements of 1943 had not been approved in advance by cabinet, as the significance they were to have as basic documents of Canadian foreign policy was not foreseen. Although they did not cause a loud public stir, the speeches were noted with interest by the diplomats of other lesser powers, and support came quickly from the representatives of Belgium, Brazil, the Netherlands, and New Zealand, as well as from the redoubtable Evatt, who visited Ottawa a few days later. Canadian editors recognized the significance of the functional principle, which got favourable mention even from usual critics in the *Gazette* and the *Globe and Mail*. Thus encouraged, government spokesmen gave the principle full treatment and King developed a new regard for the advice he was getting from External Affairs. As Douglas Anglin has said: 'Most important of all, functionalism was readily adaptable to the exigencies and uncertainties of the war and post-war years. Indeed, the functional approach was so natural that it was never formally adopted; it simply emerged.'[91] To some extent it was a matter of making necessity into a virtue – an attitude characteristic of much of Canada's emerging foreign policy.

PART II: ENDING THE WAR

3

Relief, Rehabilitation, and Reconstruction

The new world order was not conceived in tranquillity, and to this fact is attributable some weakness but also much strength. Because it was forged in conflict, the inevitability of conflict would not be ignored in brotherhood phrases. The structure would undoubtedly have been better-looking if there had been harmony at the time, but there wasn't – then or later – and harmony could not have been imposed by a more platonic Charter. Canadians worried particularly about a too close link between the new United Nations and the peace settlement and about the imperfections that would be perpetuated if the institutions were determined during the turbulence inevitable at the end of a destructive war. They preferred to think in terms of a transitional period and an interim United Nations. Nevertheless, the winding up of the war permanently affected the shape of things to come. There was some immediate advantage to Canada in that its status and functions in the new world were to an important extent determined by its considerable role in relief and reconstruction – although the question must be asked whether it did not also distort the Canadian situation. For purposes of calculation, the times were not at all normal.

THE CANADIAN PERSPECTIVE

One of the basic problems of Canadian foreign policy in the postwar years has been the adjustment of Canadians to being rich. The immediate postwar period when Canadians could hardly deny that they were relatively, if in their minds only temporarily, better off than others was a useful training experience for more acute trials in the last third of the century. In his preface to *Canada's Immigration Policy* in 1957 David Corbett quoted Rousseau from *The Social Contract*: 'How can a man or a people seize an immense territory and keep it from the rest of the world except by a punishable usurpation, since all others are being robbed by such an act, of the places of habitation and the means of subsistence which nature gave them in common?'[1] It was not until the acute realization in the seventies of the world's under supply of resources and over supply of people that Canadians began to be aware of the full implications of their enviable situation. By that time, although they had not abandoned the habit of lamenting their lot, it was hard to deny, even to themselves, that absolutely or relatively they were rich. In the immediate postwar period, while acknowledging their relative good fortune, they clung to the image of themselves as a thrifty, hard-working, pioneer people who would do their Christian duty to their fellows but could not afford the generosity of the élite powers. The difference between the Canadian and American income was such that this attitude was from one perspective justified. Unlike the United States, furthermore, Canada was heavily in debt to the rest of the world and running a deficit, most of the time, in its current account balance of payments. Vis-à-vis the British, however, the new situation was harder to grasp. In spite of Britain's straitened circumstances, Canadian politicians, King and especially St Laurent, could not shake off the old expectations of the opulent imperial power.

Judged by their own perspectives, Canadians were generous in their policies of mutual aid during the war, and in relief and rehabilitation assistance at the end of the war. Comparisons are not only odious but hard to compile. Just what do you include as aid? In 1948 Walter Lippmann said that with one-twelfth the American population and one-eighteenth the American national income, Canada's contribution to recovery was one-fifth of the American. Canadians were not disposed to dispute these figures and Lippmann's comment, justifying the use of Marshall Plan funds for purchases in Canada, was often quoted: 'The truth is that man for man, family for family, taxpayer for taxpayer the Canadians have borne a heavier part of the burden of European reconstruction than we have.'[2] Books, speeches, and editorials of the time are self-congratulatory about Canadian philanthropy and willingness to sacrifice. The attitude, however, betrays the persistence of the voluntarist approach. It was a good record for a country which could have escaped war entirely if it had wanted and whose contribution even at its best was bound to be supplementary rather than decisive.

In the early months of the war Mackenzie King had told the British delegation proposing a Commonwealth air training plan that although Canada had 'lost no time in ranging herself on the side of Great Britain and France ... it was not Canada's war in the same sense as it was Great Britain's, and it would do more harm than good if they were pressed to do more than they felt they were able to do.'[3] That attitude was considerably altered by the course of the war in which half the world was ranged on the allied side and the North American stake became more obvious. Nevertheless, there persisted the tacit assumption that Canada, not having been responsible for the war nor its intended victim, should not be expected to interpret literally the principle of equal sacrifice, or at least that its contributions should be regarded as somewhat beyond the call of duty. Caution was required in the case of relief and reconstruction. It could be argued logically that Canada and Britain should suffer equally in a common cause, and this assumption lurked in the British attitudes during the long haggling over postwar loans. The fortunes of war had weakened the British and strengthened the Canadian economies, but there were long-range historical trends involved as well. Where should the line be honourably drawn between rehabilitating Britain or Western Europe and being saddled with the continuing burden of sustaining economies over which Canada had no control? The Americans were faced with the same dilemma, but they could aspire to more influence over the recipients.

The problem of how to behave towards the less fortunate in other countries troubled Canadians in their official and private capacities through various phases. During the war there was the inescapable necessity to keep the British and other allies solvent so that the common struggle for victory could be carried on. Then followed the period of emergency supplies, to keep not only allies but enemies alive and get them working again. Relief, however, was one thing; reconstruction was another. Vast sums of money were then needed to get the European economies moving so that relief could be suspended. Canadian motives were frankly acknowledged as a compatible mixture of charitable instinct and the calculation of advantage for a trading nation dependent on healthy markets. By the early fifties, when the European countries were stumbling to their feet, attention switched to the other continents where drastic changes were taking place and new threats to stability perceived. Although few people failed to acknowledge the difference between the reconstruction of a mature European economy and the construction of rudimentary economies in Asia and Africa, nevertheless, much of the simple optimism of the successful reconstruction programme in Europe, culminating in the Marshall Plan, stimulated the ventures in foreign aid and development in the fifties.

Because of its earlier involvement in the war and in particular in the survival of Britain, Canada provided help when it was most needed and least noticed – that is, during and immediately after the war. While the American administration coped with more refractory public attitudes and the division of powers, the Canadian government was able to provide financial support to stave off a British collapse in 1946 and 1947 while Congress pondered. By the time the Marshall Plan was approved in 1948, Canada had, in so doing, virtually bankrupted itself. There was in 1947 a very serious exchange crisis. Canada was an indirect beneficiary of the Marshall Plan because the Europeans were thereby enabled to pay for the supplies Canada had previously been providing them on highly uncertain credit. The Marshall Plan is remembered by Europeans with gratitude, and properly so, while the Canadian assistance is recalled, if at all, only by elderly ex-officials.

WARTIME AID

Well before the approval of Lend-Lease by the United States Congress Canada was financing British purchases in Canada and enabling Britain thereby to assist other Commonwealth and foreign countries. In the beginning transactions were on a normal commercial basis, but as war supplies were more desperately needed the British were unable to pay. The flow of arms from Canada could not be stopped in mid-war, and the Canadian government was forced to improvise various ways and means to provide the cash. In March 1942 a billion dollars were put at the disposal of Britain for the purchase of vital war materials. This was an outright gift, but it was usually described officially in other terms to appease a critical attitude in Quebec. There was also an interest-free loan of 700 million dollars. However, it was regarded as natural to require some repatriation of Canadian securities held by residents of Britain and to ensure that the proceeds of the sale of any non-repatriated securities be used to finance British purchases in Canada. It seemed to some cabinet ministers a good chance to do what their successors have wanted to do with American investments – bring them home. Control by London was the bogey. This insistence on a hard-pressed ally divesting itself of its assets may have reflected a persistently colonial attitude to the imperial economy and a failure to foresee the Canadian interest as perceived years after the war, when Ottawa was concerned both with the inability of the British to earn Canadian dollars and the unhealthy preponderance of American investment in Canada. At the time, however, it looked more like one of the desperate expedients to which recourse must be had. Unlike the United States, Canada did not repatriate direct investment, and the British remained in a creditor position vis-à-vis Canada after the war. Long-term investment in Canada owned in the United Kingdom was $2476 millions in 1939 and $1670 millions in 1945.

Directing military aid to Britain made sense in the early years of the war, but by 1943 it was recognized as more appropriate to have a 'United Nations

Mutual Aid Act' which empowered the government to spend money on war supplies for any of the United Nations considered 'essential to the defence and security of Canada and the cause of world freedom.' Mutual aid agreements were negotiated not only with the United Kingdom but also with the Soviet Union, China, Australia, New Zealand, and the French Committee of National Liberation. Because of an anxiety not to get involved again in the terrible problems of the repayment of war debts and recognizing that in a common effort Canada should be giving and not lending, mutual aid agreements did not provide for repayment or redelivery of war supplies although there were certain reasonably flexible provisions about handling materials in the pipeline at the time of the termination of hostilities. Altogether Canada provided economic aid to its allies of over five billion dollars which, in view of the fact that it exceeded the national income of 1939, was a considerable feat. It was fortunate, for political reasons, that it was broadly based on a vast expansion of the economy across the nation.

In return for mutual aid the beneficiaries were obliged in each case to sign the pledge. They promised to follow after the war economic policies that would lead to the 'adoption of measures designed to promote employment, the production and consumption of consumers' goods, and the expansion of commerce through appropriate international agreements on commercial policy.'[4] Canadian politicians and officials, like the Americans, were determined to create a postwar system in which the barriers to trade, which they both believed had been major causes of depression and war, would be removed. Canadians, not being under the same strident political pressure as the Americans felt from their Senate, did not engage in the sordid pressures that distinguished the negotiations over Article VII of the Lend-Lease agreements which pledged the recipient to expansionist economic policies and the elimination of 'discriminatory treatment in international commerce.' Still, Canadian politicians wanted their government to get terms not significantly different from what Washington was demanding.

Canadians, like Americans, would regard this as 'aid without strings' although that phrase had yet to be coined. A commitment to virtuous behaviour in the motherhood terms of the day was not regarded as a string, although the signatories thought it was. Certainly the Canadians, no less than the Americans, were convinced that their aims for a free-trading world were as much in the interests of the other parties as they were of Canada and the United States. They were prepared to open up their own markets. They had, by gifts and interest-free loans, showed their concern that the erstwhile trading partners would not be unduly handicapped. The British and others knew, however, and postwar experience was to prove them right, that during an extended period of recovery they would have to protect their economies and the free-trade gospel of the North Americans was better suited to the American and Canadian economies which at the end of the war would be bulging with increased capacity in industrial and natural resources. The Canadian taxpayer did have to be promised some reward, however, and in particular some reason for the easy terms. The overseas market was so stubbornly regarded as the essential condition of Canadian prosperity that fewer questions would be asked if aid were related to it. Although the House of Commons gave overwhelming endorsement to the various mutual aid appropriations, there was significant opposition from a small group of members from Quebec.[5]

MILITARY RELIEF

Mutual aid ceased at the end of hostilities, and it was explained that relief funds were being provided through other sources. One of these was what was known as Military Relief. As Canadian forces were liberating areas in Europe and had their quota of Civil Affairs officers, they were inevitably involved in programmes to help the civilian population survive until civil régimes could be established. Not only food but medical supplies and other commodities were required, if only to enable the fighting forces to maintain security in their rear. In Italy this was a lengthy process, but Military Relief was less protracted in other countries. Allocations were in the hands of a Combined Civil Affairs Committee (Military Relief) financed by the United States, the United Kingdom, and Canada. Each government had undertaken to pay for the supplies it provided, but this meant an undue share for Canada. A new formula was worked out that allowed for Canada's paying roughly in proportion to its part in the invasion of Europe. The total Canadian contribution to Military Relief was in the neighbourhood of $95 million. Inevitably, in view of the dominant role played by the British and Americans in military policies, Canada had little share in the major decisions of this programme. As this was a winding up of the war rather than the shaping of the postwar era, precedents were relevant to the past rather than the future.

The United Nations Relief and Rehabilitation Administration was designed to co-ordinate relief efforts as territories were liberated. As described in chapter 2, its establishment was of critical importance in the evolution of Canadian positions on UN structures. UNRRA was not only a cause on which officials worked out their new theories, it was one that roused the support of the Canadian public. The government had little trouble getting the approval of parliament; questions from the opposition tended rather to strengthen than to weaken the position the government was taking. The fact that Canada was relatively fortunate was questioned by only a few. At the second reading of the bill calling for Canadian participation in UNRRA there was some suggestion that it was too limited in scope, that it should go beyond relief and rehabilitation to involve recovery lest it merely lead to indefinite relief. That was a note struck frequently, and it was accompanied by a full recognition that the economic interests of Canadians were involved in the recovery of Europe. The fear expressed in the United States by Senator Vandenberg that UNRRA would pledge 'our total resources to whatever illimitable schemes for relief and rehabilitation all around the world our New Deal crystal-gazers might desire to pursue' was reflected in Canada, but less bluntly. Gordon Graydon, for the Conservatives, wanted 'some limiting clause with respect to the length to which these nations banded together are going to go in matters further than relief and rehabilitation provisions.'[6] Like others, he feared a domestic food shortage. The cessation of Mutual Aid immediately after the end of hostilities before moving on to the recovery phase was evidence of this cautious approach.

Public opinion may have only vaguely comprehended the new functionalism, but the fine-spun theories of the specialists did reflect a national mood. It was a mixture of a reinforced nationalism along with a new conviction that internationalism was the only way to assure peace. This first of the new United Nations family to get under way provided a challenging opportunity for Canadian diplomats because they were less dispensable than usual. By the internationalization of the relief programme the public vaguely sensed a practical means of diffusing the awful responsibility of feeding the destitute indefinitely. Canadians were neither strong nor self-confident enough to face alone such complex issues as supplying the inscrutable Russians, deciding whether or not to let the Germans starve, not to mention the horrendous political implications of assistance to the fragile and distracted coalitions struggling for power in the European capitals. Political trouble over aid to dubious régimes in Eastern Europe could be averted. It was ironical that although it was anxiety to feed the starving peoples of Europe that had inspired the governments of the UN to set up a relief agency, in the end UNRRA did not operate in the liberated West European countries because of the principle that it would aid only those countries unable to pay. The Dutch, Belgians, and others were regarded and regarded themselves as capable of financing their own relief supplies. At the Atlantic City meeting of the Council in 1946 Pearson urged that food should not be a weapon of international politics, and when post-UNRRA relief was discussed in the UN Assembly in 1946 Canada took the lead in getting the supplying countries to provide relief without regard to 'race, creed, or political belief.'[7] A Canadian brigadier, C.M. 'Bud' Drury, was head of the UNRRA mission in Poland. The great advantage of an international organization for this problem and for the many problems looming in the future was that they removed the necessity of unilateral or bilateral decisions. Isolation from the world's problems, it was fully realized, was no longer a possibility. Internationalized responsibility was the other way out.

For all these reasons and because UNRRA had clearly put Canada on the map – and one Canadian, Lester Pearson, in particular – Canadians were reluctant to see it dissolved. The reasons the United States Congress wanted to deal with relief bilaterally were the reasons why Canadians did not want to do so. When the UNRRA Council met in Geneva in August 1946 Canada took the lead in the adoption of a measure asking the General Assembly to consider the problem of post-UNRRA relief. The British, somewhat reluctantly, supported the Americans. So did the Dutch. In the 1946 autumn session of the General Assembly the Canadian delegation, led by Paul Martin, strongly favoured an approach to the problem 'which will rest on concerted action by the United Nations.'[8] Although Canadians wanted action through the UN, they were not entirely happy to pass beyond the UNRRA phase. It had become a vast affair. 'Admiring its success as we do, we cannot help but shudder at its present complexity.'[9] Many recipient governments were now on their feet and able to make trade agreements. However, 'one of the purposes for which the international organization of UNRRA was established is still present: namely that there must be some international machinery for the screening of requirements and the balancing of competing claims.'[10] It was made clear also that Canada, the third largest contributor to UNRRA, both in sharing costs and supplying goods, now wanted a broader base of contributing countries.

There was a candid note of grievance in the Canadian position. Contributing and receiving countries were admonished for not living up to their commitments and burying political differences. The Canadian spokesman mentioned that Canada's ability to contribute had depended on special conditions, notably a wheat surplus. Now reserves had been reduced below normal. 'In this connection, I might mention that we are still rationing butter and meat in addition to sugar.'[11] The Canadian position was close to that of Denmark, Brazil, and other lesser powers and of Fiorello LaGuardia, the American director-general of UNRRA, who denounced his own country's position. A majority, which included the East European countries, fearing they would be cut off relief, opposed the British and Americans, but the latter would not give in. So the Canadians realized again that they would have to bow to the inevitable and make the best of it. In the General Assembly a Canadian compromise resolution was passed unanimously. It called for a 'special technical committee of experts ... [to] be established by the Assembly to study the minimum import requirements for the basic essentials of life of countries which might be in need of relief, to survey the means available to each to finance such imports, and to report on the amount of financial assistance required by each of these countries.'[12] The Canadians expressed 'understanding' of the United States position. Their private view, however, was better expressed by a well-placed Canadian journalist, Max Freedman, who commented that 'it is a pity, however, that she [the US] lost her way and abandoned the shining vision before the task was done.'[13]

POST-UNRRA RELIEF

UNRRA's activities were duly wound up in 1947 and, in spite of the good intentions of Canadians and the others, not much in the way of international co-ordination through the UN was provided for post-UNRRA relief. The Assembly designated ten governments, including Canada, to appoint an expert each to the committee. This body, convened by the secretary-general, said that European countries would need additional assistance of $583 million for 1947. The principle instrument for continuing relief was to be the United Nations International Children's Emergency Fund which had a budget of $450 million for 1947. By this time, however, Canada was beginning to feel the pressure of the drain on its dollar reserves and its generosity was considerably less than it had been. In these days Canada was still adjusting to the revolutionary programme of social welfare and family allowances introduced by the King government during the war – and beginning to realize its cost. There were postwar taxation troubles as well. Caution was observed, therefore, about commitments to programmes, however worthy, which implied a continuing international obligation to social welfare in the world at large.

Whereas Canada pressed for obligatory support by all members of temporary relief agencies like UNRRA or the International Refugee Organization, when it came to the United Nations International Children's Emergency Fund, which might carry on indefinitely, they wanted to make contributions voluntary. In fact, Canada was not enthusiastic about UNICEF as a permanent institution and in 1950 actually voted against the resolution to continue it for another three years because it was impossible to give relief to hundreds of millions of children and it was better to act in emergencies. Nevertheless, UNICEF had the strong support of a number of Canadian officials and also of

Canadian private agencies.[14] In the critical 1947-8 period the government contributed only 1.1 per cent of UNICEF's budget. The country's reputation was partially saved by the millions of dollars ($18 million between January 1947 and April 1948, for example) raised for relief by private organizations in Canada. Government support, needless to say, was heavily directed to the purchase of Canadian produce.

Parliament in 1947 appropriated $20 millions for post-UNRRA relief. Five million dollars of this went to UNICEF and the rest to Austria, Greece, and Italy. None of this relief went to the East European 'satellites,' as they were now being called. Soviet hegemony was becoming clearer, and the charge was being made that relief funds would be used for Communist party purposes. Communist representatives in the UN attacked the aid policy of the Western countries on the grounds that it was granted for political reasons rather than on the basis of need. Although the Canadian government had not renounced its view that aid should be non-political, it could probably not have got parliamentary support for sending relief to the régimes now being installed in East European countries. It was Europe, of course, to which Canadian attention was still directed, not only because of the historic fixation and the conviction about the economic and security priority of that continent, but also because the challenge of relief to the suffering millions of Asia was better not thought about. If Europe might prove insatiable, Asia was certainly the bottomless pit. In a very few years, however, it would be membership in the United Nations, as well as the Commonwealth, that would force Canadians to think about the unthinkable. That was a consequence of the passion for participation in international institutions not clearly recognized at the time – although it may have been foreseen all too clearly by Mackenzie King.

It should be added that as Canada's financial position improved in later years and it was obvious that the UN, with its present balance of power, was not going to rush headlong into global welfare, the government accepted the existence of such bodies as UNICEF and supported them, if not to the limit of its resources, at least well enough to compare reasonably with others. When it came to specific – and presumably emergency – relief programmes such as the United Nations Korean Reconstruction Agency and the United Nations Relief and Works Agency for Palestine Refugees, the Canadian contributions were among the worthiest.[15]

FINANCIAL AID TO EUROPE[16]

Canadian motives for contributing to relief, rehabilitation, and reconstruction were mixed and fully acknowledged to be so. Even without the conviction that a restored Europe would be good business, it is hard to believe that Canada could have stood idly by. The programmes of Military Aid and UNRRA were obligatory, less related to calculations about the needs of the Canadian economy. By the time they were exhausted, however, the economies of Western Europe, including especially Britain, were still desperate, far from being those of profitable trading partners. There had been an investment that needed much more money before it could pay off. It could not be written off, partly because a restored British and European market remained central in Canadian calculations, but also because, however exasperating the effort to establish terms with the bankrupt, no Canadian government could be ruthless enough to turn its back – especially when the Americans were not doing so. The situation did not differ greatly from that which obtained during the war when the movement of goods and services led the way and then some respectable financial cover had to be found.[17] After the fighting had ceased, however, practices accepted in wartime would come into question.

That Mutual Aid would not go on after the fighting stopped should probably have been taken for granted. Its abrupt ending in September 1945 was harsh – and would have seemed harsher if the Europeans had not already suffered several weeks earlier the shock of Washington's cessation of Lend-Lease. Canada obviously could not afford to be the one source of free assistance when the Americans had shut off the flow. In making his announcement the minister of finance, J.L. Ilsley, pointed out that Mutual Aid was a wartime measure to end when victory came. 'The government has always endeavoured to make this clear to parliament and the Canadian public, as well as to the allied nations receiving Mutual Aid.'[18] However, this would not end or delay the flow of essential civilian supplies to the allies. The government would continue to buy such supplies for allied governments if they requested them and undertook to reimburse Canada for the costs so incurred. Ilsley recognized that most countries would require credits, and negotiations were proceeding with a view to the provision of credits under the Export Credits Insurance Act. Britain, he acknowledged, was a very special problem.

Even in 1945 the illusion persisted that the British could get back on their feet soon, and there followed a series of desperate measures to prop up the British economy and permit the British to continue buying food and other products that were still pouring out of the enormously expanded Canadian economy. It became a long sad story and a classic illustration of how indebtedness affects old friendships. The British were strapped, with little room for manoeuvre, but when they had to bargain stiffly over the terms by which they would accept Canadian assistance, the Canadians were understandably irked. There was persistent and wide-spread sympathy for the British in their tribulations, a feeling that geography and British courage had forced them to pay an undue price for victory. Cold winters and shortages of food and fuel in 1946 and 1947 stirred compassion among comfortable Canadians. At bottom was a simple realization that they could not let a people to which they were so deeply, if ambiguously, attached sink into a slump. King was of two minds. In his diary he records his irritation with the British over the loan. His views swung from those of St Laurent, who was for tougher terms, to those of Ilsley and the financial experts who thought it best that a loan not be saddled with interest at all. That he was, nevertheless, Britain's best friend, King never doubted. 'It did not seem to me it was fair to future generations to mortgage the future in that way though I was prepared to agree that had Britain become a debtor nation in the war, and we had become a creditor nation, that we must recognize an obligation to help to restore Britain's future. This did not mean our going the length of risking the defeat of the Government itself ... I said it was my first duty to see that the Government was sustained. It would be little help to Britain or anybody else if we were out of office.'[19] He was probably right. A Conservative government with its imperialist reputation could less easily have marshalled support across the country for a loan of this proportion to Britain.

In his speech of 11 April 1946 announcing a loan to the United Kingdom of $1,250,000,000, Ilsley stressed the crucial importance for Canada of the rehabilitation of Britain. The triangular trade on which Canada had flourished was at stake. The irresistible pressure of consumers flush with money and short of goods had enormously increased imports from the United States. The needs of Britain and Europe were such that exports were pouring in that direction, but they could be paid for only by credits. He expected Britain would be going through about five years of transition. There was a broader principle at stake, however, than simply balancing the Canadian budget. 'Because of this large and central place which Britain occupies in world trade, British policies in regard to trade are of critical importance to exporting countries and particularly to Canada. In addition, British policies will influence and largely determine the policies of many other countries, including particularly the countries now in the sterling area and probably the countries of Western Europe.' The British were seen as facing two alternatives, one liberal and one restrictive, and it was of the utmost importance to Canada that Britain give the lead in the direction of liberal trade.[20]

A determining factor in arranging the loan to Britain was the fact that the British were at the same time negotiating with the Americans. Canada could not afford to be as generous – or so Canadians thought – as the rich United States, but where Britain was concerned they would be expected to be. They would not want to compare unfavourably with a country outside the family. The United States Congress expected them to be more generous and the assistance offered by Canada was regarded as important by those in the Washington administration trying to get legislative approval for aid to Britain on the best possible terms. Canadian legislators, on the other hand, especially those less well disposed to the 'Mother Country,' had an eye on the terms the Yankees were getting. What Canada offered was in proportion very much larger, $1.25 billion as compared with $3.75 billion for the United States. The interest was the same, 2 per cent, although the cost of borrowing was higher in Canada. In addition, after much argument, the British debt of $425 million on the Commonwealth Air Training Plan during the war was cancelled. The $700 million loan of 1942 was extended to 1951, still interest-free. Ironically, the ground was cut from under the feet of the Canadian officials when the British in their loan negotiations with the Americans agreed to the insertion of a clause by which they undertook not to accept any loan from a Commonwealth country on terms more onerous than those incorporated in the loan agreement with the United States. This, of course, made it impossible for Canada to give them better terms.[21] Although the Canadian agreement, like the American, called for non-discrimination and the convertibility of sterling, the terms were less harsh and specific. The Americans made no secret of their desire to end the imperial preference arrangements as the major barrier to the brave new world of freer trade. Even Canadians who would have been happy to exchange imperial preference for something wider and better preferred that it not be abandoned without being used as a bargaining counter with the Americans, whose professed devotion to removing barriers had yet to be tested in the practice of Congress.

The Anglo-Canadian wheat agreement of 1946 should be seen in this context. It was not strictly speaking an aid-to-Britain scheme, but there was a tendency to see it in that light as it followed soon after the loan. The British desperately needed wheat and they had to get it economically. Canadians wanted them to get it as cheaply as possible and remain the stable customers. A bilateral deal of this kind ran counter to the Canadian argument for multilateral arrangements, but it could be excused as a temporary necessity. Political pressures from Western Canada made a wheat deal with Britain obligatory for any government. Britain was the historic destination for Canadian grain. Sending foodstuffs to Britain had been a habit during the war. In the depression before the war the prairies had suffered bitterly from low farm prices. The British could not afford to pay much for wheat now when it was a scarce commodity, and Canadians were prepared to concede a low price provided they could get some commitments from the British to go on buying at a fair price later when supplies were expected to be more plentiful – and prices were expected to decline. Some far-sighted officials, such as the high commissioner in London, Norman Robertson, realized that such an arrangement would be storing up trouble, that the British recovery would be slow, and in such circumstances it might be very difficult to insist that they go on buying wheat at a price that could be well above the market price.

The inevitable happened. According to the agreement Britain would take more wheat than it would normally require, at least 160 million bushels in each of the first two years and 140 million in each of the next two years. The price stipulated, $1.55 in the first two years, was considerably lower than world prices. It was to go down to not less than $1.25 and then $1.00, respectively, in the third and fourth years, but the prices negotiated for the last two years were to 'have regard to any difference between prices paid under this Agreement ... and world prices' for deliveries in the first two years. Wheat prices did not fall and the price agreed upon for the last two years was $2.00. However, the new international Wheat Agreement in 1948 set a ceiling of $1.80, and then when the Marshall Plan got into operation in 1949, North American wheat was available to the British free. The British thought that, as they had paid a price well above the specified minimum for the last two years, they had paid off their obligation. Canadian wheat farmers thought they had got a raw deal and pressed the government to get an additional payment from the British. After much sour haggling, the Canadian government paid the additional sum, $65 million, itself. Robertson had been right in his fears. Like all of the British-Canadian financial negotiations in this period, the perspectives on what was right or wrong, fair or unfair, could not be brought into focus. Too few people in London or Ottawa could see it as Pearson noted in a memorandum for cabinet of 9 December 1947 at a time of near deadlock with the British: 'We agreed that both sides were facing facts which were difficult to reconcile, and that the facts of the situation and not any lack of goodwill on either side was responsible for our present difficulties.' That kind of perception was the essence of his diplomacy.

Britain was crucial, but the other European countries – and potential markets – were not forgotten. It was as 'a measure to facilitate and develop trade between Canada and other countries' that the Export Credits Insurance Act had been introduced on 28 July 1944. Although it was a boon to the recipients, it ought not to be classified as aid. It provided for insurance of ordinary short-term commercial credits that could be used only for Canadian goods and services.

On 3 December 1945 Ilsley secured approval both for the provision of $750 million for credits to France, the Netherlands Indies, and Norway and also to enable the government to conclude negotiations with Belgium, China, and the USSR. In this speech he again stressed the importance of 'reviving and developing our export trade during the reconstruction period.' He saw also a security angle, for 'If Europe and Asia are economically healthy, wars are less likely to break out.' He recognized there was a risk, but Canada was prepared to accept the risk rather than pass it on to the receiver. Recipients were asked to purchase part of the requirements in Canada for cash, normally one-fifth or one-sixth, but the requirement was waived in the case of Czechoslovakia which could not pay cash.[22] After the huge British loan in April 1946, the drain on reserves made officials more cautious about Canada's leading role in reconstruction. In 1946 the government discouraged applications for further assistance from France, Czechoslovakia, Greece, Denmark, Finland, Hungary, and Turkey. The Poles did not make known their interest in this kind of assistance until the appropriations had been almost exhausted, but the troubled relations with Poland over the admission by Canada of Polish soldiers as refugees and the Polish state treasures still held in Canada[23] were of some relevance. This programme had a very successful record as far as repayments were concerned. Although the Export Credit procedure was designed for a postwar situation, it continued and developed into the Export Development Corporation.

As the war ended, the continental position was for Canada quite satisfactory, thanks to the favourable balance resulting from the Hyde Park Agreement. By the middle of 1946 Canadian reserves had reached a substantial figure beyond that of prewar years, and the government felt confident enough to return the Canadian dollar to parity – a measure primarily intended to insulate Canada from importing inflation from the United States. In 1947, however, the reckoning came. The British were drawing more rapidly than expected on the loan – a result in part of the delay of Congress in ratifying the American loan – and the reserves of gold and dollars deteriorated seriously. The government was still reluctant to change its policies, and post-UNRRA aid was extended during that year. However, by February the governor of the Bank of Canada was warning that 'Canada cannot continue indefinitely to sell on credit in overseas markets while she is incurring a substantial cash deficit in her balance of payments with the United States.'[24] In their postwar need for materials Canadians were importing heavily from the United States, but unlike the prewar years they were not able to compensate by payment from exports to the United Kingdom. The Americans were concerned with the recovery of Western Europe and not disposed to take Canada's difficulties seriously. In June 1947 General Marshall made his famous speech, but the promised massive American assistance for European reconstruction was a long time coming. In the absence of American help, the British continued to draw so rapidly on the Canadian loan that Canada was facing a crisis. The British were pressing Canadians for more generous terms and warning that they would have to discriminate more severely against Canadian imports.

Canadian officials saw the collapse of their dream of a transition from temporary difficulties to the era of world-wide trade expansion, and they went off to Washington to put pressure on the Americans to do something. They in turn had to threaten the Americans with discrimination against American imports and the effect that would have on their version of the dream. Officials in Washington were understanding enough, but they were clearly concerned over Congress. British demands for Canadian help got more shrill, and Canadians, beset by their own difficulties, got less sympathetic. The American officials were unable to find a solution, although they did help Canada get a line of credit of $300 million from the Export-Import Bank in November 1947. In spite of the anxiety in Ottawa to seek broader international solutions, they were caught in the old triangle. The world market was slow in opening up. It was clear that Canada would have to restrict dollar imports, and this was especially unfortunate as it had to be done just as the General Agreement on Tariffs and Trade was signed in Geneva on 30 October. The Americans were equally concerned over the impact on GATT, and the Canadian announcement of the restrictions was stage-managed in collusion. It stated the government's intention to administer the controls in a manner consistent with GATT and remove them 'at the earliest possible moment that circumstances permit.' The State Department issued a press release that concluded: 'In terms of her continued contribution to world reconstruction Canada's action should be considered as a short term measure which does not mean abandonment of the long term objectives shared by the United States.'[25]

The period between the end of the war and the middle of 1948 was a curious lull between the hot war and the cold war. During this time everybody seemed to be desperately trying to get back to the prewar world, even though they proclaimed their will to something better. It was a cantankerous and frustrating period, and the spirit of wartime community was draining rapidly. From this corrosion the Atlantic economies, including the Canadian, may have been saved by the blundering Russians.[26] The Prague coup in

March 1948 moved the United States Congress to pass the Foreign Assistance Act in April. The argument in Ottawa, as well as in Washington, on the loans to Britain had been largely economic. Now political and security calculations became important. Just after the coup in Prague the Canadian high commissioner in London pointed out that the altered political situation, as well as the resulting probability of more rapid action by Congress, were arguments for a somewhat more generous Canadian attitude on credit to the British. In this way, he thought it would be possible for Canada 'to share in this additional but comparatively modest way in the risks involved in attempting to safeguard Western Europe from further encroachments and infiltrations.'[27] In Washington Wrong, who had been appointed ambassador in September 1946, was finding the Americans critical of Canada's unwillingness to help the British further. The political circumstances were only going to make Canada look worse. On 25 March the Canadian government agreed that the United Kingdom might draw on the Canadian credit at an increased rate, with the additional concession that the offer was to hold good whether or not the European Recovery Programme in Washington came into effect before that date. Louis St Laurent was now assuming control as secretary of state for external affairs and, although he had been less disposed to concession to the British, he was more susceptible than Mackenzie King to the political-security argument. In September 1948 he suggested in a joint meeting of the cabinet External Trade Committee and the Interdepartmental Committee that the United Kingdom and Western Europe should now be regarded not so much as a market but as a buffer between the Iron Curtain countries and the western hemisphere which should be helped to self-sufficiency.[28] It was a time, of course, when St Laurent and his advisers were contemplating the moves that shortly produced the North Atlantic Treaty.

Statistics for the Canadian contribution to relief and recovery were produced in February 1948 by the new minister of finance, D.C. Abbott. In addition to the money provided Britain, Canada had under the Mutual Aid Act provided goods and services to its allies to a value of approximately $2,200,000,000. This he regarded as part of the war effort. It was in addition to further wartime aid amounting to $1.3 billion, postwar relief direct and through United Nations agencies of over $275,000, and postwar credits of about $1,857,000,000. This was on the eve of the Marshall Plan and Canadians were justified in pointing out that on a per capita basis they had made a very much larger contribution to European recovery than had the Americans.

There was, however, another aspect of postwar relief that required decisions much more difficult and much closer to political sensitivities than the mere provision of money. What was to be done with the millions of people displaced during the war, many of whom were unwilling to return to their homes?

REFUGEES[29]

Although there was much talk from Ottawa in the later years about the need to surrender sovereignty to the new world organization, there were certain reservations about sensitive areas on which the Canadian government was as unyielding as it had been when confronted with the League.[30] 'If there is one idea held more tenaciously than another on our side of the Atlantic, it is that we must retain control of our own internal affairs,' declared Newton Rowell to the First Assembly of the League. The abstractions of the post-World War II leaders were different. In his address to the first session of the United Nations General Assembly St Laurent did not stress national sovereignty but said rather that 'Sovereignty must not mean liberty to defeat the purposes of international peace and security.' He went on to say that 'If this be the way to world government, then the Canadian delegation wholeheartedly supports world government.'[31] This could be misleading. From the private memoranda of the time it is clear that international control of the immigration policies of member states was so far from the minds of Canadian politicians that they were not even preoccupied with it as a threat. When they talked about the subordination of national sovereignty they were thinking of collective security in conventional terms or, as St Laurent made clear in this speech, the need of desperate measures to control atomic energy. When it came to international security Canada was a consumer, but in matters economic Canada was a producer. They were strongly emphasizing the role and the authority of the United Nations Economic and Social Council, but its function was to be co-ordination. It was, of course, a liberal's, not a socialist's, view of 'world government.'

Within the civil service the facts of life, including the conservatism of cabinet on population policies, were recognized as setting limits to policy proposals, even though External Affairs officials in particular were aware of the handicap placed on their vision of the country by Canada's insensitivity to the plight of refugees, its archaic immigration regulations, and the racism clearly evident in practice. External Affairs battered vigorously against what they regarded as the defensive mentality entrenched in the Immigration Branch, sought to warn the cabinet of the desperate realities they saw in Europe, and to encourage an imaginative approach to a population policy for Canada.[32] To avoid the exposure of hypocrisy, External Affairs thought that the less said in international bodies the better. At San Francisco the Australians and New Zealanders threatened to go out on a limb over a proposed limitation on the domestic jurisdiction article of the Charter (2:7) which they thought might threaten ratification by their legislatures, fearful of implications for immigration laws. Robertson and Wrong saw that the Australians and New Zealanders could not change the great-power draft and would serve only to draw loud attention to a possible consequence that would be as unhappy for the Canadian parliament as for theirs. The fuss would do no good. They got the prime minister's approval for a policy of lying low and supporting 'any text which could be agreed between the United Kingdom and other Commonwealth countries and the United States.'[33] This was not a topic on which to be put on the spot. It was rarely difficult, of course, to get King's approval for a policy of lying low.

The idea of a world body actually assigning the world's population on the basis of available space and resources has always been more a bogey than a threat.[34] As an abstraction it can be supported or opposed on moral grounds, but in practice the closer one approaches it the less real it becomes. As a cause it had and still has, nevertheless, a significance which rallies the righteous and makes the guilty tremble. In their defiance of immigration pressures, parliamentarians betrayed only occasional sensitivity on the subject. The imaginary threat of being forced to accept hordes of people of someone else's choice undoubtedly inhibited the more humanitarian feelings that might have been expected for the victims of that tyranny younger Canadians were fighting to destroy.

Some one million refugees were in the care of UNRRA at the end of the hostilities in Europe. They included refugees of long standing and the millions of persons displaced by the war, crowded into camps in Germany and uncertain about returning to Eastern Europe. Canadian officials were active in the creation of international structures to cope with refugees, specifically an International Refugee Organization that would be functionally effective and provide for an equitable sharing of the financial burdens. The response of the government was muted. Sharing the finances was one thing; sharing the refugees was another. It touched upon an unresolved dilemma of the Canadian economy of this period. The government was dominated by men who had only recently survived the depression of the thirties and it could not, in these uncertain times, shake loose from the inhibition about immigration written indelibly into party policies during the period of desperate unemployment. Whereas the expectation of postwar unemployment after the dismantling of the war machine encouraged generosity in the reconstruction of the European market, it discouraged a policy of welcoming newcomers. The old caution was countered by the expansionist nationalism of young politicians and a large part of the senior bureaucracy, who took a Keynesian view of population.[35] Their conviction that a more populous country would be a wealthier country was widely expressed as Canada entered the postwar period, but it did not sway government policy until a few years later when it looked as though, contrary to widespread speculation, the transition from war to peace economy would not entail severe unemployment. By that time, however, the period of desperate emergency in the refugee camps had passed.

REFUGEES: WARTIME MEASURES

The nervous attitude towards refugees in 1945 resembled incredibly that displayed before the war. While the number of desperate people fleeing from Germany, Italy, or Spain had mounted in Europe during the thirties, Canada's immigration regulations admitted only British and American citizens and agriculturalists who could be self-sufficient. Hitler's treatment of the Jews was deplored, but a boatload of Jews escaping from Germany was denied admission to Canada, as well as to the United States and Cuba, in the summer of 1939.[36] A scheme to bring Sudeten refugees to Canada for which the British would have paid was so hesitantly embraced that the Nazis overran Czechoslovakia before their victims could escape.[37] At the end of the depression officials did not want to add more names to the welfare rolls, and there was a widespread feeling that relief funds should be spent on Canadians. There was also a nativistic fear of increasing the percentage of any racial group except the British and the French. A memorandum to cabinet from the Immigration Branch, 29 November 1938, said: 'We do not want to take too many Jews, but in the present circumstances, we do not want to say so. We do not want to legitimize the Aryan mythology by introducing any formal distinction for immigration purposes between Jews and non-Jews. The practical distinction, however, has to be made and should be drawn with discretion and sympathy by the competent department, without the need to lay down a formal minute of policy.'

When Roosevelt called a conference at Evian in 1938 to establish some international action on refugees from the Nazis, Canada was invited. The Canadian delegates were instructed to see that no country would be expected to take more immigrants than were permitted by existing legislation and reminded that few refugees were of the agricultural class, that they had usually been deprived of their citizenship and their capital, both of which were required for immigrants to Canada so they would not be a charge on welfare and could be sent home if necessary.[38] In the decade 1933-42, when hundreds of thousands of people were desperately trying to escape from Nazi-dominated territories, some 9000 people were admitted to Canada by special orders-in-council – mostly refugees. The total number of immigrants in that period was 39,000.

Even during the war the attitude to refugees remained exceedingly cautious – although problems of transportation reduced the pressure. Canada took over some interned enemy aliens from Britain, but a distinction was made between wartime sanctuary and permanent settlement. Canada was not represented at a conference in Bermuda in 1943 to deal with refugees, but asked to be kept informed. It was a British-American affair to which, King said, Canada had not been invited. King did say Canada would receive a number of additional refugees *until peace is restored* and 'individual applications for permission to remain in this country after the war will be given full and sympathetic consideration.'[39] Willingness to play a full but unspecified part was a favourite formula of King's when dealing with issues on which he believed that the less said the better – a category that included most questions of external affairs. Members of parliament raised questions but the prime minister and J.A. Glen, who as minister of mines and resources was timidly in charge of immigration, took evasive action – one formula of King's being to deplore the raising of such a question when there was a war to be won. He said Canada would be glad to play its full part as soon as the proposals were presented to the United Nations – another pious excuse frequently invoked to justify procrastination on ticklish issues. He promised participation in the revised and strengthened 'Intergovernmental Committee' although this gallant body, seeking to operate from London during the war, had received little help from Canada.

King was reflecting hesitation among the general public to throw open the doors. Quebec members of parliament said bluntly that they did not want hoards of refugees, either because they would distort the balance within the country or because they were people who would not be easily assimilable in Quebec. That usually meant Jews, a sentiment also expressed by some Social Crediters and more politely by some others. Canadians were horrified by the treatment of Jews in Germany but they did not necessarily want to increase 'disproportionately' the Jewish population of Canada. Polls taken in 1946 show a resistance to the admission in particular of Japanese and Jews.[40] There was the traditional xenophobia of a conservative society that had, in the first quarter of the century, absorbed an enormous number of strangers and achieved precarious equipoise, fearful now that the ruined civilizations of Europe would spew forth their desperate millions to threaten Canada's bucolic and abstemious way of life. Fear of displaced persons was not merely anti-semitic. There was legitimate concern that some had been collaborators with the Germans. There was fear in labour unions that Canadian employers might exploit their desperation by importing displaced persons as cheap labour, a fear encouraged by a storm over the importation of Polish girls by a Quebec industrialist to work in his textile mills under contracts reminiscent of the age of indentured labour.

THE INTERNATIONAL REFUGEE ORGANIZATION

A few hundred refugees were reaching Canada at the end of the war. The government was co-operating in its fashion with the Intergovernmental Committee on Refugees. Through its contributions to and its work in UNRRA Canada was, of course, offering some assistance in the immediate problems of the refugees. It is notable, however, that in all the extensive debate over Canada's role in UNRRA there was little acknowledgement of responsibility to provide refuge for the homeless victims of the war. In all the justifications, public and confidential, of Canada's right to a major voice in UNRRA, it is Canada's role as a producer of foreign exchange assistance and supplies which is stressed. There was less awareness of a con-comitant obligation to share with the European countries the burden of the refugees. Canada did agree that the Intergovernmental Committee was in-adequate to deal with the enormous refugee problem and that the question should be referred to the United Nations. In February 1946 the General Assembly established a committee on refugees. The Economic and Social Council took up the question and began preparing an international refugee organization.

On matters of general UN policy Canadians were, as usual, zealous and mediatory. The important committee dealing with budgetary and financial aspects of the refugee question had as its chairman Senator J.G. Turgeon of Canada and met in London in 1946. The Canadian attitude was still to hope that politics could be kept out of the refugee question, but it became a forum for one of the most vehement clashes between East and West. The Russians insisted that the organization should assist only in the repatriation of refu-gees, with the Western countries arguing that repatriation must be volun-tary. Canadian delegates in the committee and later in the General Assembly made desperate but futile efforts to put forward compromise solutions, but no matter how understanding they tried to be of legitimate Russian feelings after such a war – or aware of the practical advantages for Canada of the repa-triation of the troublesome 'displaced persons' – they could not agree to the forced repatriation of Ukrainians, among others. Canadians were denounced for their pains by Vyshinsky, and the Polish representatives expressed sharp criticism of Canada's taking Polish soldiers from General Anders' army.

When the General Assembly voted on the creation of the International Refugee Organization the motion was passed by only 30 votes to 5 with 18 abstentions. Canada supported the resolution, but with typical caution proposed that it not come into force until it had received the support of fifteen states contributing 75 per cent of the organization's budget. While Canada favoured voluntary contributions to UNICEF, it was insistent on the obligatory principle when it looked as if the large financial burden of the refugees might fall unduly on those able and willing to pay. The new organization, it was said, would not be able to carry passengers. The proposal was accepted, but contributions to the expensive projects for long-range settlement were to be voluntary. Canada favoured the IRO going as far as possible to meet Soviet objections. The IRO, it was agreed, would not force repatriation but would provide that refugees be fully informed concerning existing conditions in their countries and produce valid objections 'such as a rational fear of persecution, compelling family reasons, or reasons of health.' The IRO would not help 'war criminals, quislings, and other persons guilty of collaboration with the enemy, or, of participation in organizations hostile to members of the United Nations.' It would also not help 'persons of German ethnic origin.' This was not good enough for the communist states, however, and they would not participate.

In July 1947 the IRO took over responsibility from UNRRA and the Intergovernmental Committee. There were only eighteen members. Canada was a member of the Executive Committee of nine. Its contribution was set at 3.2 per cent of the administrative budget and 3.5 per cent of the operating budget, which might be compared with Britain's contribution of 11.48 per cent and 14.75 per cent, respectively. In July 1947 the government established a quota of 5000 DPs to be admitted to Canada provided they were capable of filling positions in Canadian industries experiencing labour shortages. This was raised to 20,000 by the end of 1947 and by 1949 to 40,000. By the end of 1947 7345 DPs had been admitted to Canada. Although the number Canada could or was prepared to take was relatively limited, some effort was made to help maintain the others. In June 1948 a grant of $5,415,000 was made to the IRO to maintain DPs in camps and for other costs.

Altogether, during the life of the IRO until 1951, Canada accepted 123,479 refugees. Sixty per cent of these were workers and their dependents and 40 per cent were nominated cases. This total number compares reasonably favourably with that for the United States, 329,851, but Australia took 182,851. When one considers, however, that this was the cream of the DPs skimmed in UNRRA camps where in 1946 they numbered 1.4 million, it is not impressive as a contribution to 'relief.' In any case the motives by 1951 were by no means strictly humanitarian – although they were enlightened. By that time Canada was looking for good immigrants to build up its population. One might assume that many of the immigrants who came to Canada from Germany and other countries at a later stage were originally inhabitants of the DP camps. Altogether it was an investment which the sceptics of 1945 hardly deserved – an injection into the blood stream of an extraordinarily qualified group of people whose contribution to the economic, intellectual, and cultural life of the country has never been equalled. It is not easy to determine who exactly is or is not a refugee, but the rough official Canadian figure of the number of refugees admitted during the whole postwar period from all areas is over 300,000. The United States gives a figure of over one million and Australia claims to have admitted some 354,000 refugees.[41]

Contemporary accounts dealing with Canada's role in accepting suffering refugees speak with the restrained satisfaction about the Canadian performance that was becoming typical. It was generous if one accepted the approach that what Canada did to help the Europeans was beyond the call of duty. In the light of the oratory accompanying the victory over Nazi bestiality and the revelations from Belsen, Canadian policy seems incredibly calculating. There were formidable practical problems in the way of rescuing victims of the war who could not be repatriated. The lack of shipping was serious and the insistence on giving a priority to the return of Canadian forces and their families acquired in Europe was inevitable. To these legitimate excuses government spokesmen always paid the greatest attention. The realization that Canada was better placed than any other country in the world to take a risk on these wretched people was only dimly perceived. However, the more Canadian spokesmen opposed, with emotional public support, the forced repatriation of anti-communists, the more difficult it became to do nothing about those left. Public opinion – at least among the articulate – may have run ahead of the government in changing its attitude to refugees. At the extended hearings of 1946 in the Senate Standing Committee on Immigration and Labour representatives not only of religious organizations but of labour and of management displayed some recognition of Christian obligation and of national advantage in an open-door policy. By August 1947 51 per cent said in a CIPO poll that Canada needed immigrants, with supporters of the CCF considerably less enthusiastic than Liberals or Conservatives.

The president of the United States made his 'statement on admission to the U.S. of DPs and refugees' in December 1945, but no Canadian offer of refuge was made until 7 November 1946. Not only the well-populated United States but also the over-populated and distressed United Kingdom were recognizing the urgency of the problem. The Australians, similarly situated to Canada but less bountiful in their prospects, inaugurated a very active policy of bringing refugees from Europe. The Australians, of course, had had a shock and the realization of the need for more people in their isolated continent was a powerful spur. In spite of an increasing awareness of their greater vulnerability to attacks by air, the Canadians had still that comfortable feeling of security in the Anglo-American bosom. They were only dimly beginning to recognize the vulnerability in an over-populated world of an under-populated country. David Croll was one of the few MPs to make refugees a cause. In a strong and well-documented speech in March 1947 he pleaded for accepting DPs not as an immigration policy but as a limited short-term humanitarian act arising out of obligation. 'Since the end of the war we have shipped our old clothes and surplus food, but that is not enough.'[42] Curiously enough, the most timid of leaders in this respect, Mackenzie King, acknowledged when he presented his immigration policy in 1947 that it was dangerous for a small population to attempt to hold 'so great a heritage as ours' – a gesture which is probably attributable to the civil servants who drafted the speech. But it would take another quarter of a century before the full significance of that remark was to become apparent.

The few refugees who came during the critical period were admitted partly for humanitarian reasons and partly because some gestures were unavoidable, but an economic justification had to be found. Much was made in Canadian statements of the admission of about 3000 veterans of General Anders' Second Polish Army, the only substantial group of immigrants from Europe to arrive in 1946, but these were selected by representatives of the Department of Labour from among 4500 who did not want to return to Poland but did want to come to Canada. They were all sent off to work on farms where they were needed. As it was assumed, however, that Canada was doing the British a favour by taking these sturdy allies off their hands, the United Kingdom provided the shipping and paid the cost of transportation. Any DPs who would be permitted to come, it was assumed, would be selected like good beef cattle with a preference for strong young men who could do manual labour and would not be encumbered by aging relatives. The latter presumably could sit in camps in Germany until the strong young son made his fortune and sent for them.

By 1947, however, attitudes towards immigration had changed and shipping was becoming available. External Affairs, particularly members in the field, had been insisting for some time that shipping could be found and that its scarcity was being exaggerated by immigration officials for purposes of stalling. The voices of Canadians whose blood-brothers were in the camps were beginning to be heard. The inhumanity of separating families was increasingly recognized when some of the single men arrived. Regulations concerning families became more lenient. However, the most desperate problem as the IRO came to an end was the fate of the so-called 'hard core,' those no country would take because they were ill or elderly and required welfare, or those professional people, such as doctors, who were not accepted by the professional establishments in receiving countries. While Canada selected the best, the Europeans in their distressed state had to look after the vast majority of the refugees until they had reached saturation point. In a few years, however, the DPs were becoming reconciled to abandoning Europe and any hope of returning home and Canadians were having revised thoughts about their value to a young nation.

AFTER IRO

The attention of the IRO was devoted very largely to European refugees. It did have a hand in repatriating a few Chinese, but the vast dislocations of population in Asia were too overwhelming to be faced. If Canadians felt daunted by the thousands of Europeans who needed new homes, they did not dare turn their eyes towards Asia. In official circles at least there was an unspoken realization that the IRO as a United Nations body was discriminatory in its attentions to a world-wide problem. The practical argument was that when something at least could be done about the wretched in Europe, the whole operation ought not to be swamped by taking on a burden with which no administration of the time could cope and which was a problem of the ages rather than just of postwar emergency. It was quite clear to those determining policy in Ottawa that the Canadian public, which had some reservations about admitting European DPs in large numbers, was not yet prepared to alter drastically its firmly entrenched policy of discouraging 'orientals.' It was best, therefore, not to think or say much on the subject.

However, as the non-European countries became more vocal and influential in the United Nations, the IRO could not continue as it had done. It had been intended as an emergency body, and rather than expand its mandate it was wound up with two successor institutions taking over some of its work. The office of the United Nations High Commissioner for Refugees was set up by the General Assembly in 1950 and although in the early stages its work was directed largely towards the remaining refugees of the European war, in later years it became more and more involved with refugees in Africa, Asia, and the continents where the wars were then taking place. As for those countries interested mainly in European immigration, including Canada, the solution was to set up, as they did in 1951 outside the United Nations framework, the Intergovernmental Committee for European Migration. ICEM was not devoted strictly to refugees but sought to provide international assistance to any people who wanted to emigrate from Europe. By this time Canada was taking a more favourable view of European immigration and as ICEM suited its purposes it was for the first decade an active supporter of the committee. In 1962 Canada withdrew from ICEM on the grounds that its function had become of marginal use to the country.

CONCLUSIONS

The experience of relief was educational and sobering. It had elements of nobility, but it often looked a little sordid in contrast to the high resolve of postwar rhetoric, especially as most of the quarreling and jostling was among friends and allies. The financial crisis resulting from the loan to Britain and the consequent need for American help graphically illustrated the limitations on the Canadian role. Although the issues were not basically between East and West, Canadians, in UNRRA and the IRO, were faced directly with the frustrations of negotiations with the Soviet Union and understood better than previously attitudes of the British and Americans that had looked somewhat rigid.

Certain ambiguities about international institutions were already being revealed. On the question of responsibility for IRO, for example, the Canadians pressed their more idealistic principles. It should be directly under the control of the Economic and Social Council, they argued, thereby making every United Nations member responsible for it and subject to annual assessment. In theory it was a good idea, a desirable precedent for the United Nations in general, but it revealed an early illusion about the extent to which strong member states would ever agree to participate in causes to which they objected. The view that prevailed, however, saw the IRO as an ad hoc specialized agency which could be operated independently by those who supported it and removed from broad United Nations policies. This prevailing view, which was applied by the United States, was, in fact, much closer to the 'functionalist' approach that Canadians later came to advocate, often against the more absolutist Americans.

The double edge of international institutions, as instruments to be used and commitments to be accepted, was becoming more apparent. For a country as vulnerable as Canada to demands for help, worried, with some justification, about endless philanthropy and unassimilable immigration, the value was evident of a United Nations framework to spread the burden and alleviate the anguish of unilateral policy decisions. At the same time, involvement in UNRRA and the IRO, which status and self-respect required, increased the moral pressure for appropriate contributions. Without for a moment recognizing the right of any international organization to determine Canada's immigration policy, a new and powerful element had entered into the Canadian decision-making process. When Mackenzie King finally announced a more liberal policy for immigrants in general in February 1947 he cautiously recognized the new factor: 'Canada is not obliged, as a result of membership in the united nations or under the constitution of the international refugee organization, to accept any specific number of refugees or displaced persons. We have, nevertheless, a moral obligation to assist in meeting the problem, and this obligation we are prepared to recognize.'[43] In time these club memberships would play their part in leading the country to alter drastically its rules about immigrants. Members of the United Nations and the Commonwealth are free to legislate as they wish, but it is much harder for them to practise racial discrimination. King was probably correct when he said: 'There will, I am sure, be general agreement with the view that the people of Canada do not wish, as a result of mass immigration, to make a fundamental alteration in the character of our population.'[44] It would be some years before the Diefenbaker government would begin to dismantle the racial priorities in immigration. To join an international organization is, in some ways, to light a time bomb.

4

Peacemaking

Along with the facts of life learned over relief and reconstruction came the bitter lessons of the peacemaking. The functionalist principle was refined in the fire. It survived, but with the functional expectations considerably altered.

THE RIGHT TO A VOICE

After the Second World War Canada's international status had been more firmly clarified than at the end of the Great War. It was a country of larger consequence in world politics as well as in the war effort, and it had a professional establishment much better prepared on the details at issue in the peace settlement. And yet Canada had a less satisfactory role in the peacemaking than in 1918-19. It may be that the part played in 1919 has been exaggerated because it was the establishment of Canadian status hitherto unacknowledged, whereas what happened in 1945-6 seemed like a checkmate to a country on the rise. What had happened in 1919 was, in the opinion of Loring Christie, who later became the supreme sceptic, highly satisfactory. The dominions, he said, were much better placed than other small powers. They '... were prominently represented on the various Commissions of the Peace Conference, and at times the Prime Minister attended the Council of Ten, while in addition the Prime Minister of Canada on a number of occasions took part in the work of the Council of Four and the Council of Five. More than that, every Commission Report, every aspect, every section of the Conditions of Peace was first considered in meetings of the British Empire Delegation (whose personnel was the same as that of the Imperial War Cabinet) before the assent of the British Empire was given. The Dominions' participation in the making of peace has been substantial indeed.'[1] King was less anxious than Borden to involve himself in grand strategy. His intent was to defend specific Canadian military or economic interests. He was more hesitant than his own professional advisers to take stands on the settlements in Europe or Asia, although he defended Canada's right to do so.

The essential difference in 1945, however, was not that Canadian leaders failed to press their case. It did not matter greatly that Canada had changed in status and power. Circumstances in the world at large were different. There was no great single peace conference as in 1918 and no conference at all on a settlement with the major enemy, Germany. In 1918 the great powers had been divided, but in 1945 they were threatened with even more serious division. It was the desperate necessity to avoid a split of devastating consequence that prevented them from opening their negotiations to lesser powers.

Why did Canadians, both official and private, insist so strongly on the Canadian right to a voice in the peace settlement and why did they express dismay at the treatment received? Smaller European countries or Australia, for example, had convictions about specific national interests that would be overlooked if the national voice was not listened to. Canadians had views about the kind of world they wanted, in which the Germans would not be able to do this again, and there was some disposition to retribution. There was, however, no particularly Canadian territorial or economic interest at stake. Canadians were more concerned with general questions of collective security. One does not sense an urgent need to put across a unique national message as a principal motive for wanting a proper voice.

The theme on which Canadian spokesmen kept harping was that of justice. The war, as far as most Canadians were concerned, had proved one thing conclusively. Whether they were involved in European affairs or not – or even Far Eastern when they thought about them – they were going to be involved in foreign wars. Their participation in the war, they constantly reminded their allies (one hesitates to call them their listeners), was without stint. 'No question of partial participation arose,' said the Canadian statement to the Council of Foreign Ministers. It was undeniable in simple justice, therefore, that they had dearly bought the right to a position of equality in the settlement. King told the Paris Conference on 2 August 1946: 'We also wanted Canada's contribution to be of an order which would entitle us to share effectively in the making of peace ...'[2] It was offensive in that hour to be treated as second-class pleaders. It was not a simple emphasis on status; it was a cry for fair treatment. If one was to judge by speeches and editorials, the Canadian public backed the government in its claims and protests. The Progressive Conservative leader, John Bracken, spoke of an insult and indignity if Canada was excluded,[3] and the Montreal *Star* warned the great powers that a peace which did not carry the judgment of the Canadian people was bound to affect Canada's foreign policy in the future.[4] Because there was no specific Canadian content in the Canadian demand, however, public resentment was not long sustained. The fate of Germany or of Japan did not touch them directly. They were more interested in demobilization of the Canadian armed forces and the restoration of the Canadian trading position.

Officials in the Department of External Affairs and the defence ministries, however, were concerned. They had had some modest involvement in early planning. The interdepartmental Post-Hostilities Problems Committee, set up in 1943, had been receiving information regularly from the British about the discussions at Yalta, Potsdam, Quebec, and other exotic places concerning postwar planning for the defeated states.[5] Views on substance and on the mechanics had been consistently put forward to the British and shared often with the Americans and the allied governments-in-exile. For the most part, this was merely a question of commenting on drafts. Hume Wrong, who had a sensible view of what was possible, wrote to Wilgress on 13 May 1944: 'it would be wasted effort for us to contribute any comprehensive plans of our own, for Canada, as a secondary power, would not have a great enough influence to make our views prevail. We should, however, be in a position at least to decide what is not acceptable to us, and to advocate changes in accord with our interests, through appropriate channels, in the plans of the Great Powers.' It would be impossible to calculate the amount of Canadian 'input,' but the close relations with British, American, and other colleagues provided some part in the continuing explorations of policy options. Of this incalculable influence there may have been as much Canadian as that of any other lesser powers. The form mattered, however, when what was at issue was a claim for justice. Canada did not only have to be influential, it had to seem to be influential.

However galling to some Canadian nationalists to obtain information from the British Foreign Office, it was of considerable advantage to do so. Canadian officials received through these regular sources not only copies of British papers on the subject of the settlement but also a regular flow of telegrams and despatches from British embassies in sensitive places which gave officials in Ottawa a sophisticated understanding of the forces as they existed. The rudimentary nature of the Canadian external service at that time made this kind of detail from another source essential. And to be really useful, it had to come from a great power. The danger, as some might see it, of being brainwashed, was minimal. Canadian officers were well able to assess what came out of a Foreign Office with which they were very familiar. Few national foreign services have a point of view. The British voices to which Canada was able to tune in were varied. At any rate there was a good opportunity to compare what they were saying with what the Americans, the Free French, and others were also whispering or shouting in their official ears. Whether they liked it or not, and they didn't much, the major issues of the peace settlement were being decided by the four or five great powers, and the Commonwealth communications system enabled Canadians to know much more than they would have known otherwise. It was useful because it was a system on which Canadians could count. The Americans were prepared informally to tell them a good deal when they wanted to. Officially, however, the State Department had to be careful about treating Canada more favourably than the Latin Americans.

Of the five great powers, the only country that cared much about the position of the secondary powers was Britain. The Russians considered the peace settlement a closed affair for the great powers. The Free French had been desperately anxious to have an equal seat at the table and were generally supported in this claim by their wartime friends, the Canadians. However, once the French had been accepted as a great power, it was clear that their previous interest had been in the position of France, not of lesser powers. The concern of the British Foreign Office for lesser powers was not entirely inspired by a magnanimous and democratic view of international politics. The most clamorous lesser powers were the Canadians, New Zealanders, and Australians and they could make loud noises in London's political circles. The British also would have liked Canadian support in their occupation role in Germany.

In the early stages post-hostilities planning tended to encompass everything. The Canadian concern over its position in the peacemaking must be seen in the context of its concern with the new world order. As Mackenzie King told the House of Commons, they must not acquiesce in the wartime practices by which the great powers arrived at 'private settlements.' 'Every possible precaution should, therefore, be taken to see that in this particular the war-time pattern is not perpetuated in the framing of the peace settlement and in the United Nations organization.'[6] Canada wanted peace settlements in the name of the United Nations. The British proposal on which the post-hostilities planners in Ottawa first went to work called for a United Nations Commission for Europe and the Canadians wished to be part of that not just because they wanted a voice in the peace settlements but also because they saw it as an important arm of the emerging United Nations structure.

OCCUPATION FORCES IN EUROPE

The connection between the provision of occupation forces and a voice in the European peace settlement was apparent to planners in the Department of External Affairs in 1943 when an enquiry was received from the British government as to whether Canada would want to contribute forces to police Germany. The departmental planners were interested in playing a justly allocated part in the European settlement, but Hume Wrong could see that not only would military participation be required for membership in the UN Commission for Europe but the maintenance of that position could require the indefinite retention of forces in Germany or elsewhere.[7] Although in the Department of External Affairs they were disposed to pay that price, it would be unwise to get trapped in commitments for which their political masters were not really prepared.[8] With this cautious position the military planners were impatient. They already worried about the dismantling of the armed forces, as had happened after the First World War, and an extensive and honourable commitment to postwar obligations in Europe might be some guarantee against instant demobilization.[9] External Affairs was aware that a blunt refusal to take part at this stage would seriously threaten the Canadian campaign to be involved in post-hostilities planning and might also encourage a return to the isolationist mood that had kept Canada out of international activity between the wars. The government did agree to send something less than a negative reply, noting that Canada would be contributing substantially to the pacification of Europe but pointing out that its expected large-scale participation in relief and other civil activities should be taken into consideration as well. 'The nature and extent of the Canadian contribution to the "policing of Europe" would depend on the circumstances of the time and on the definition of that phrase.'[10]

The political considerations for caution were not easily dismissed. Many Canadian units had been away from home longer than those of any other country and they and their families wanted a speedy return. There was also worry about the contribution Canada might have to make to the war in the Far East when Germany had been dealt with. The government remained cautious until it was realized that there was no possibility in any case of the Canadian forces returning instantly because of the acute pressure on shipping. They would have to remain in Europe for quite a long time and this factor might be exploited to get some credit for occupation. In December 1944 the Cabinet War Committee approved a programme for occupation forces in Germany, including eleven squadrons of the RCAF and an army group of about 25,000. These would be allocated to the British zone of occupation and committed for what was known as Stage II, a term covering only the period of adjustment and disarmament immediately following the operational occupation of Germany.[11] The British, who were counting on this assistance in occupation because they had some of the same political problems, were told at the beginning of 1945 of this intention but warned not to count on occupation forces indefinitely as the matter would be reviewed again in 1946.

During 1945 the political arguments for withdrawal became stronger. Canadian forces were not required in the Far East because Japan surrendered. Transportation became a subject of constant debate and there was concern over the restlessness of the troops in Europe. One reason occupation duties had been accepted was that it was considered better to have the troops doing something while they waited for ships. The astuteness of a few Canadians in such activities as trading cigarettes for art masterpieces worried the authorities lest they endanger relations with friendly countries, especially Holland. In December 1945 the British government was informed that the Canadian Army Occupation Force would be withdrawn during 1946. The British were upset. Prime Minister Attlee made several strong pleas to Mackenzie King, at least for a postponement into 1947. In the course of his argument Attlee unwisely suggested that Canadian forces in Germany would help free British troops which had world-wide obligations. Although Louis St Laurent was no Anglophobe, he was a Quebecker and this plea for assistance in the maintenance of the British imperial role made him uncharacteristically angry.[12] In any case, there was no possibility of Mackenzie King relenting. He was in a snit over heavy taxation and the way in which Canadians were bankrupting themselves for the relief and reconstruction of Europe.

King would probably have had political difficulties if he had, at British request, changed the date for repatriation. In a CIPO poll of 8 May 1946, 46 per cent approved withdrawal to 37 per cent opposed, but outside Quebec only 40 per cent approved and 43 per cent opposed. The government had explained to the British that one of the difficulties was that of administration. There was no doubt that maintaining an administrative tail for these forces was considerable, and there was also concern about having their forces on duty in a zone where they in no way shared policy responsibilities with the British. The opposition was sceptical of the administrative argument. They also saw a connection between the exclusion from a voice in the peace and the precipitate withdrawal of Canadian forces. In a debate on the subject of Canada's part or lack of it in the German peace settlement in March 1947 St Laurent made his memorable comment that the Canadian forces had been 'kicked out.' This was reported as 'kicked out,' but he was too gentlemanly to like that language on reflection and he had it altered in Hansard to 'left out.'[13] His apparent argument was that Canada had refused to maintain occupation forces in Germany because they had not been allocated a fair share in policy-making or in the control machinery. It was not an argument that could be made cogently and it bothered the officials who recognized its weakness. The government did produce a statement and even published the despatches to London of 9 January and 8 December 1945, which proved merely that the British had received fair warning not to count on Canadian occupation forces. St Laurent's outburst should not be taken literally. He was still irritated over Attlee's suggestion and he had been goaded. A more convincing point was made in the same debate by the minister of national defence, Brooke Claxton, that there was no proof 'that the presence of any force Canada might have in Europe would change our position by so much as an ounce of more power or weight.'[14]

Although the great-power planners who were busy concocting schemes for the control of Germany and the maintenance of peace in Europe would from time to time include the possibility of Canadian and other Commonwealth forces in their calculations for postwar policing, at no time did they ever seriously consider allowing any country except the wartime big three and France in the control machinery.[15] Canada might have put up a better case if it had, before the war ended, tied a specific promise of so many troops to the allocation of a seat on some body, but it is hard to believe that the Russians would have agreed and it is almost certain that the provision for the voice of the lesser powers would have been without great substance. Undoubtedly irritation with the way in which the major powers were ignoring Canada's right to a voice on Germany played some part in the decision of December 1945 but the real cause of anger on this score did not come until 1946. The decision of December 1945 would probably have been taken in any case, but the position of the Canadian government in defending it might have been more difficult if a shiny seat polished in accordance with the best functionalist principles had been awaiting it in some well-balanced control council for Germany or for Europe as a whole.

Mackenzie King was still prime minister and he knew that involvement in European politics was unwise for Canadians, however much they thought they had a right to it. There is a canny Canadian political instinct to recognize that although the arrogant claim of the great powers for special responsibilities is quite unacceptable, there is, nevertheless, something to be said for it. From the perspective of a later generation it is hard to see why Canadians would have profited at all from involvement in the long, troubled question of occupation – or contributed much. The yearning for an activist European policy was a legacy of the postwar logic that because the security of Europe unquestionably affected the security of Canada, Canadians must seek a national involvement in matters pertaining to the security of Europe. There may be no escaping the consequences to Canada of a disturbance of European security, but it is hard also to escape the conclusion that the security of Europe will be determined by the Europeans and the Americans and there is little Canadians can do or need do about it – other than provide forces when needed.

PARIS PEACE CONFERENCE[16]

There was a peace conference of sorts in Paris in 1946, but this was to deal only with the treaties with Italy and the minor enemies. The peace conference with Germany has never been held and that for Japan came some years later. At most peace conferences of recent centuries the great powers have dominated the proceedings, but the role of the lesser powers was rarely so formally limited as it was at this meeting in Paris in the summer of 1946. The main lines of the settlements had already been worked out by the great powers, and the recommendations of the conference, which included all those who had been at war with one or all of the enemy states under consideration, were merely recommendations to the Council of Foreign Ministers of the great powers which the latter did not have to accept. Canada took the conference seriously. The brief for the delegation had been in preparation for over a year. It was an impressive delegation but there was no great expectation of a dramatic role. The commentary for the Canadian delegation noted that: 'The procedure for the preliminary drafting of the Peace Treaties, as it was worked out at Moscow, and the convoking of the Conference accords closely with what might be expected at any large Peace Conference. In fact, the concentration of authority and responsibility for preparation of preliminary drafts in the representatives of the Great Powers had a precedent in the practice adopted at Paris in 1919.' There had then been a Council of Foreign Ministers as well as a Council of Prime Ministers and a Conference of Ambassadors (of the great powers) set up to supervise the carrying out of the terms of the Treaty of Versailles.[17]

Under the terms of the Moscow communiqué, the five treaties (Italy, Romania, Bulgaria,[18] Hungary, Finland) would in the first instance be drafted by the signatories of the relevant surrender terms. Canada was not a signatory of any of the armistice agreements, which the Canadian government regarded as military instruments imposed on states by the commanders of the allied forces. At the time the government had reserved its position in relation to the negotiation and signature of the final peace treaties. The instruments of surrender provided for a form of association for the United Nations at war with the respective enemy states other than the signatories. The way in which the great powers assumed these rights, never delegated to them by the allied powers acting as United Nations, had been another source of irritation in Ottawa.

When Mackenzie King announced to the House of Commons on 12 July 1946 the names of the delegation he made it clear that the Canadian delegation would take an interest only in the general nature of the peace treaties and not in the specific issues such as boundaries, population transfers, war damage and indemnities which were of direct concern to the European states. Canada's role, he suggested, would 'lie in helping the countries more directly concerned to work out agreed solutions which are fair and will be likely to endure.'[19] Needless to say, he informed the plenary session in Paris that Canada's role in the conference would be 'a modest but constructive one.' He was resuming somewhat the traditional Canadian role of observer of the European scene, willing to be helpful and, of course, morally above the battle as Canada had no special interests or claims for territories or reparations.

In spite of all this modesty a small but talented delegation was sent to Paris. The prime minister himself was there at the beginning and, when he departed, he left the minister of national health and welfare, Brooke Claxton, in charge. The alternates were Robertson, Wilgress, General Maurice Pope, and the advisers included some of the best brains in the department. Most of the European delegations were much larger. There were never more than ten Canadians available at a time, rather few for all the commissions and subcommissions during a ten-weeks' conference. No members of the opposition were present as they had been in 1945 at San Francisco. Mackenzie King raised the question at a cabinet meeting and St Laurent advocated having the opposition represented. King opposed this, however, 'on the score that Canada's interests in the Conference itself would not justify that.' On this point he 'found all the other Members of the Cabinet with me.'[20] The quality of the delegation and its relative objectivity was in fact recognized in some small ways. Claxton was made chairman of the important Legal and Drafting Commission. A particular recognition of Canada's disinterested position was the appointment of General Pope to chair a special meeting to discuss the frontier between Hungary and Czechoslovakia.

The most important Canadian contribution to the conference was probably a procedural one made by the prime minister himself in the initial plenary session. A fact which daunted the conference was that it could do no more than make recommendations which would then be considered by the Council of Foreign Ministers. King made the suggestion, which he himself credited to Claxton, that the Council of Foreign Ministers should endeavour to save time in completing the treaties by meeting at intervals in Paris to review and discuss proposals developed during the conference. This suggestion, which was ultimately adopted, did help to lift the conference above the level of the slanging match it had been at the start. According to Harold Nicolson: 'It was Mr. Mackenzie King, who, before he returned to Canada, advised Mr. Bevin that things could not possibly continue as they were. Mr. Bevin acted promptly on that advice. He persuaded his three colleagues that only failure would result unless they met together in secret, reaffirmed their solidarity, examined how the machinery could be speeded up, and made it clear to the small Powers, who were ganging up behind them, that the agreement reached between the four Foreign Ministers must be maintained at the Conference of 21.'[21] According to a Dutch press report King's proposal received the biggest ovation at the conference because he had appealed to the conscience of the world with the authority of an experienced statesman.[22] It was a trying conference, nevertheless, for a statesman who saw himself as Solomon. When the Belgian and Yugoslav delegates were nominated for chairman of the Committee on Procedures, King voted for a Czech motion that the two hold office alternately, commenting in his diary that he was 'glad to have a chance at the outset to cast a first vote which showed no antagonism toward anyone.' This noble motion was lost 12-8. King then voted for the Belgians, saying in his diary that everything seemed to be done in the wrong way with no guiding spirit or direction.[23]

This excellent delegation certainly did not throw its weight about. Claxton reported in a broadcast to Canada on 16 October that members of the Canadian delegation made only eleven speeches, three in plenary session and eight on major issues discussed in commissions, and none exceeded fifteen minutes in length. Some of the credit won by the Canadians may have been inspired by contrast with the extraordinary performance of the Australian External Affairs minister, Herbert Evatt, who made himself ridiculous by introducing an enormous number of Australian amendments, practically all of which were defeated. King's inclination to take a moderate line was reinforced, and the Canadians kept out of the procedural debates which started the peace conference off on a bad note. Canada was discovering methods which later distinguished its middle-power diplomacy, such as keeping clear at an early stage of partisan commitments so that its credit was more acceptable at the bargaining stage. Claxton reported that Czechoslovakia, Poland, and Yugoslavia had invited the whole delegation to ceremonial lunches. 'This may be a coincidence or result from the fact that we are less committed to positions than most delegations here ...'[24]

As the Canadians were there, however, even though the subjects under discussion were European they could hardly keep out of them altogether.[25] They gave some support to Austria in stating its case on the frontier dispute with Italy (South Tyrol-Alto Adige) and they secured unanimous approval of a motion for a joint session of the Hungarian and Romanian representatives. They tried to persuade the Yugoslavs to take more 'reasonable' positions in their frontier disputes with Italy and the Czechs in dealing with Hungary over the Bratislava bridgehead and the transfer of Magyars. Canada supported modification in the political clauses of the treaties of the Balkan countries and Finland, the most important of which was an amendment for the guarantee of minority rights designed to protect the Jews. A concern for the protection of all religious and racial minorities was displayed. On the subject of the Free Territory of Trieste the Canadian delegation showed an interest that was to reappear on subsequent occasions, in connection with Jerusalem or Berlin, for example, in the experiment of independent municipal entities under the authority of the United Nations – a precedent created by the League for Danzig. When this failed, however, Canada decided to support the three western powers in their proposal to return Trieste to Italy.

The Canadian delegation was hardly satisfied with the results, especially as they had hoped this might be an occasion to narrow the breach with the Soviet Union. Claxton summed up the treaties as 'generally just and workable if there is the spirit to make them work ... in any event they are the best that could be obtained.' He saw the Paris Conference 'as a proving ground to show numerous mistakes to be avoided in making the much more important peace treaty with Germany.'[26] It had been a chastening experience for the delegation and when they returned to Ottawa they recorded some of their impressions. They had been struck forcefully with Soviet determination to maintain the monolithic solidarity of its bloc and were pessimistic about the prospects of an early East-West rapprochement. They were also very much concerned about the continuing weakness of France and the other European allies and concluded that European economic recovery was going to be harder and take longer than expected. This raised the question: if Europe needed help what would or should Canada's attitude be? In the economic sphere, there would be no financial help available after May 1946 with the exhaustion of the last export credits. They were pondering the answers in the political and strategic sphere as well. What would be the implications for

Canadian policy of greater American involvement in Europe and also the British quest to establish understandings across the Channel?[27]

ITALIAN COLONIES

As disposition of the Italian colonies could not be settled in Paris, it was referred to the United Nations. In the General Assembly Canadians found themselves several years later taking part in a forum where the distinction between great powers and medium powers was less evident. It was still difficult, nevertheless, to have a strong Canadian position on matters concerning Northeast Africa. In such a setting the Canadian anxiety to achieve a settlement, not regardless of cost but somewhat impatient of the cost for others, encouraged a disposition of Eritrea more expedient than just. The Canadian interest has always been in the reduction of tension, the settlement of disputes, a good intention which encourages at times a belief in the virtue, as an end in itself, of getting troublesome matters off the United Nations agenda. In such situations people like Eritreans are expected not to be tiresome about their fate. There may be nothing particularly Canadian about this attitude in international politics, but it is a temptation to a country whose vested interest in international tranquillity supersedes other national interests. The question of Eritrea is worth noting,[28] because it raised moral issues too little perceived at the time. It typified an issue which has perturbed the United Nations ever since.

At Paris a guilty feeling of obligation to Ethiopia was evident. As the head of the Canadian delegation noted: 'Ethiopia was one of the first nations to suffer the full force of aggression in consequence of the failure of collective action, which had been established precisely to prevent such an occurrence and, consequently, Ethiopia should be one of the first to receive redress.' The commentary for the delegation, moreover, had described Eritrea as an 'artificial creation of Italian imperialism,' parts of which had been detached from Ethiopia and the Sudan. Nevertheless, after the deputies of the Council of Foreign Ministers decided to send a four-man commission to investigate conditions in the former Italian colonies, the Canadian attitude changed a little. The secretary of state for external affairs sent a cautious telegram to London saying that the Canadian government was 'inclined to support the union with Ethiopia of that portion of the highlands of Eritrea in which the majority of the people wish to be included in the Ethiopian Empire. The remainder of the territory would be placed under trusteeship ... Where Italian settlers are welcomed by the native inhabitants, facilities should be provided for the settlement of former residents of Africa now living in Italy.'[29]

The UN General Assembly sent a commission of its own to Eritrea to find out more about the state of local opinion and asked the so-called Interim Committee of the Assembly to study the commission's recommendations. These, received in 1950, took the form of three different proposals. The one which the Interim Committee thought might be the basis for an agreed settlement provided that Eritrea should be set up as an autonomous unit federated with Ethiopia under the sovereignty of the Ethiopian crown, enjoying a constitution, a government of its own, a separate legislature and judiciary, and equal representation with Ethiopia in an imperial federal council.

Canada joined in sponsoring the resultant resolution, which the Assembly adopted. It represented a very Canadian approach to the issue of historic rights. There were still nagging doubts in Canadian minds, however, as to whether or not Eritrean separatists could be brought to co-operate or Ethiopia induced to treat Eritrea as an equal partner in the federation. Another worry assailed the Canadian representative in the Interim Committee. The four powers had promised to put the Assembly resolution, whatever it was, into effect. This meant that in its recommendation on the disposal of former Italian colonies the General Assembly was coming about as close to international legislation as it had ever come and there were doubts about its authority under the Charter to do so. A proposal before the Assembly prescribed a bill of rights for residents of Eritrea which recommended constitutional features not only for Eritrea but for Ethiopia as a whole. The analogy seen in the department was a situation in which the opponents of confederation in Newfoundland might appeal to the United Nations and the General Assembly, in order to achieve an amicable settlement, would prescribe a union of Newfoundland with Canada which obliged the Canadian government to recognize certain fundamental rights in the province of Newfoundland and set up a particular kind of federal council.[30] There was little doubt that Canada would have protested that this was intervention in domestic affairs, contrary to Article 2(7) of the Charter.

The Canadian representative in the Interim Committee raised with the British and American representatives the question of the extent to which the General Assembly would be obliged to enforce its system in perpetuity on Ethiopia. The British and Americans were, however, so intent on getting an immediate agreement that they could not spare time for speculating about the long-range implications of what they were doing. It seemed to the Canadian representative that the Assembly was either moving well in advance of the intentions of the founders or else being hypocritical. In the corridors other representatives agreed that the Assembly could not interfere with a member's desire to alter its own legislation, but this meant of course that the federal solution in no way guaranteed the rights of Eritrean minorities. It was not the sort of subject, however, on which a remote North American middle power would stick its neck out – and certainly not in 1950 with the Korean war raging. That it might have been justified in so doing, however, has been proved by the disregard by Ethiopia of Eritrean autonomy and the armed resistance of the Eritreans a quarter of a century later.

GERMANY AND AUSTRIA

Canadians in general were not much interested in the settlements with the minor enemies. For them the war had been almost entirely against Germany – even when they fought in Italy. It was in this context they felt most keenly their right to a major position. The British idea of a United Nations Commission for Europe suited Canada as it provided for bodies dealing with armistices, occupation, and relief responsible to the UNCE. The commission would have a Steering Committee of the great powers but it would be open to any European ally or dominion prepared to contribute to the policing of Europe.[31] Such an admirable arrangement did not survive the exigencies of the final military phase. Canada did not press for membership in the Advisory Council for Italy or the European Advisory Commission in London established by the great powers at the Moscow Conference. It sought an appropriate role in a UN body. By late 1944 Canada was expressing uneasiness over the appearance of a tripartite High Commission for Germany.[32] And so it went. Disappointment was perhaps keener among the officials. When the War Committee considered a memorandum about the Canadian part in UNCE it was cautious. The view was expressed that it was important to avoid commitments which would involve extensive use of Canadian forces after the end of hostilities and heavier burdens than the Canadian people would be inclined to accept after the long strain of war.[33]

On 13 October 1944 Pearson had predicted accurately from Washington that 'whatever may have been the UK Government's own views on the subject, they have had to yield to the views of the U.S. and, above all, of the USSR, that the armistice terms and the German settlement are to be matters for discussion and decision by the Three Powers alone. An occasional bone of participation will be thrown to the European allies and the Dominions, but it will be done without enthusiasm and there will be little mention of it.' In spite of this discouraging forecast the interdepartmental Post-Hostilities Problems Committee gave the subject of Germany major attention. The consideration was detailed and exhaustive, touching on all aspects of the future of Germany. It was a good academic exercise, although it was largely wasted.

Some of the Canadian ideas, for an international Ruhr Authority for example, did attract interest from the major powers. In retrospect, it is hard to understand the concentration on a subject which, however important for the peace of the world, was not one on which Canada had any reasonable expectation of being decisive. The explanation was partially sheer intellectual exuberance, the inability to keep one's hands off a subject of admitted importance. And then there was the need to do what had to be done to prove a right.

What Canada wanted, particularly after the experience of the Paris Peace Conference, was in the first place an opportunity to discuss the German settlement before it had congealed in four-power agreement. And in the second place, to have a real give-and-take discussion. What they got was even less satisfactory than the Paris arrangement. At Potsdam the four powers had indicated a willingness to discuss the German settlement with the lesser powers. Their greater rigidity on the subject, when they got round to this phase early in 1947, was the consequence of the even greater difficulties they were having in reaching agreement among themselves. It was not that they were callously unaware of the claims of Canada and the other countries. If they could reach any kind of agreement with the Russians, they were not going to forfeit it by exposure to the Australians.

Canada did argue, with some justification, a special case as the fourth power arrayed against Germany, but there was no way in which an exception could be made for Canada alone. In one respect Canada did get a deserved rebuke. Its claim that it had a greater right even than the occupied countries on the grounds of its greater war effort was grossly lacking in imagination. Such a claim reflected that bias in favour of the producer as opposed to the consumer that was notable throughout the Canadian interpretation of functionalism. As the secretary of state for the dominions pointed out to Ottawa, the occupied countries may have been unable to produce a war effort comparable to that of an unoccupied Canada, but certainly their stake in a German settlement was greater.[34] However, the Soviet position, which made some minor provision for committee discussions with representatives of 'interested states,' defined those with direct interests as countries whose territory had been occupied during the war. The Canadian reaction was to regard this as preposterous.

In late 1946 the Council of Foreign Ministers (US, USSR, UK, France) began to consider a German peace treaty and appointed deputies to hear the views of the other allies. The Canadian government was duly invited to submit its views in writing to the deputies and given one week's notice to do so. The written submissions could be supplemented by oral presentations. A

Canadian note was sent requesting a larger part along with the other allies in considering matters of procedure and substance. Such was the interest of the opposition and of editors across the country that St Laurent gave a full account to the House of the negotiations, together with the text of the communications, emphasizing that Canada had tried to be 'moderate and constructive' and make 'practicable suggestions for alternative measures.'[35] The deputies were unable to agree on a reply, but the Canadian high commissioner in London was invited to present the views of the Canadian government to the deputies on 25 January. This placed the government in a difficult position. They did not want to acquiesce in this unsatisfactory procedure, but if this invitation were rejected the possibility of pressing further claims when the foreign ministers met would be jeopardized. First the government tried to get assurance that the submission of preliminary views at this point would not prejudice the chance of discussing the settlement higher up at a later stage. The deputies, however, said they had no authority to give this assurance. So a written submission was made which was called preliminary and the Canadian insistence on having a further opportunity was spelled out.[36] In the submission the Canadian claims on questions of procedure were firmly put along with views on substance.

As reflected in editorial opinion the mood of the country was resentful. The tendency was to blame the government for not having more loudly proclaimed and insisted. In fact, the charge that the government had been slow to make its views known in appropriate quarters is hard to sustain. The British and Americans were made well aware of the Canadian view by the Canadian representatives in London and Washington and by the loud statements in Ottawa. The Canadian ambassador in Moscow had been making the case with Molotov. The government did stick to what St Laurent called a 'moderate and constructive' tone throughout. It was a posture more congenial to the minister, but it was also calculated to persuade the foreign ministers that Canada had no intention of being a nuisance like Evatt.

As might have been expected the deputies were unable to agree on procedure and they simply sent a report to the Council in which the views of the various allies were included. The foreign ministers then met in Moscow in March and again there was deadlock. Bevin and Marshall did try to find a way to satisfy the lesser powers, but Molotov got some support from Bidault in his view that the allies might merely submit their views on a subcommittee level before the peace conference. What happened then was that the occupying powers began to make arrangements for their own zones, which quite clearly meant that the future of Germany was going to be determined by their ad hoc practices.

The Department of External Affairs saw the chance to play a role in a peace conference slipping out of its hands and continued to remind the great powers of 'the necessity of making adequate provision in the near future, before the general lines of the peace settlement with Germany have become fixed, for the active participation in the process of peace making of those countries, like Canada, which contributed effectively to the prosecution of the war.'[37] The perpetuation of this argument about a right based on wartime effort was becoming not so much tiresome as irrelevant. Attitudes to peace and to the postwar position of Germany shifted drastically during 1947 because of the realization that the great powers were not going to agree. Robertson, from London, advised against reviving the old issue of appropriate participation and pointed out that the 1939-45 lines of neutrality and belligerency had been completely cut across by the movements for 'Western Union' and the Marshall Plan. He thought the Western occupying powers would need all the elbow room they could get to cope with the Russians. Premature pressure for a peace settlement would confirm the division of Germany and end the faint possibility of an agreement with the Russians.[38]

Because Canadian perceptions of Soviet policies were similar to those of the Western Europeans and Americans, they were susceptible to the argument that the Western great powers should not be inhibited in the quick and desperate measures they might have to take to cope with what was generally seen as a calculated Soviet effort to engineer, in one way or another, a communist Western Europe. Some Canadian officials were, furthermore, attracted to the concept of Western European Union, not only as a means of restoring the European economy but also as a framework within which Germany might safely be revived. On 5 May 1948, in the House of Commons, St Laurent summed up the revised Canadian position with a sensible distinction: '... we have not wished to appear to be attempting to put forward technical claims which might require the occupying powers, in order to give offence to no one, to invite all those who had declared war against Germany; this in our opinion would have had a delaying effect on the measures the occupying powers are trying to take to bring about some semi-permanent solution of the problem. But we are still insisting that when it comes to the making of the final peace with Germany the powers who took a substantial part in the winning of the war shall be given a role proportionate to their importance in the conflict.'[39]

Ottawa did not cease, however, to bombard the powers with memoranda. An indication of Canadian zeal had been the setting up of a Military Mission in Berlin in January 1946 under the direction of one of the shrewdest military men, General Pope, who continued to make his presence felt in Berlin and Ottawa. The last-gasp Canadian effort was directed to Berlin. When it was learned in early 1948 that the three Western military governors in Berlin would continue secret studies of the future of Germany, the heads of Commonwealth military missions in Berlin were told by the British they could present their views then. Nothing daunted, the Department of External Affairs set up a series of interdepartmental panels and came up with extensive prescriptions for the political and economic life of Germany. The papers were respectable contributions but considerably beyond the call of duty. As it happened the secret Working Party in Berlin completed its report so quickly that the Canadian position could be slipped in only as an addendum. An extensive paper on the establishment of an International Ruhr Authority did attract some attention in London, Paris, and Washington. The Americans incorporated some Canadian sentences in their draft proposal but did not like Canada's canny suggestion that provision be made for the accession of other powers to the Authority, lest this tempt the Russians to claim membership in a body concerned solely with the Western zones. At any rate the new Authority was established late in 1948 and in Ottawa it was thought it agreed in all major points with their own commentary.[40]

Futile as all this work may have been, the papers do provide an indication of Canadian views, at least on the official level, on Germany and Europe during that strange interlude before NATO took over.[41] The approach to the future of Germany was, as might have been expected, one which avoided extremes. The concept of a deindustrialized Germany advocated by Henry Morgenthau, Jr, the former United States secretary of the treasury, was rejected. The best hope was seen in 'a moderate and democratic government in a united and relatively prosperous Germany.'[42] By the time formal views were presented in 1947 this emphasis had been strengthened by the gradual – although reluctant – transition to the concept of Western Germany as a bulwark. Towards the Germans themselves the attitude remained hard, but in the political and economic confusion of Europe at this time the belief was strong that Germany ought not to be in so depressed a condition that it would serve as a centre of infection. Canadian planners were afraid of the spread of communism, of course, but their liberal view was that communism was more likely to be the product of misery than of Soviet machinations. General Pope, from the devastated city of Berlin, feared 'a German state so politically and economically oppressed that she will be a constant threat to the peace and economic stability of the world.'[43]

The Canadian submission to the Council of Foreign Ministers argued that the primary consideration in a treaty should be the welfare of Europe and the world and not merely 'the position of Germany or her relation to any one of her neighbours.' The prescription was for a nice democratic government and a mildly but not too prosperous economy, federalized so that it would not be too strong (an interesting Ottawa perspective on federalism circa 1946), with a constitution that could not be amended for a number of years without consent of the United Nations. It outlined suitable forms of democratic government for people with a perverse disposition to naughty behaviour, and was even so nationally doctrinaire as to point out the superiority of a system of 'responsible government.' There were all the correct views of the time about breaking up cartels and the emergence of what became a dogmatic belief in Western European Union. In 1947 the Canadian government favoured the complete demilitarization of Germany, with only police forces left.

In the light of the political realities of the time, much of this prescription for German good behaviour sounds pedantic. More to the point was the contribution of Norman Robertson whose inventive mind produced the idea of an international statute as an alternative to a peace treaty which was unachievable. This would serve a number of purposes. In the absence of a German government, it would provide a constitutional basis for the new state. Having in mind the recent German attitude to the Weimar Republic as the work of traitors, Robertson thought there was some advantage in having a constitution provided for the new political leaders. The new German government might itself later adhere to the statute. It was a means also of making peace by instalments, starting with the bare minimum on which there was a consensus and then moving on as agreement could be reached.[44] From the Canadian point of view this procedure had the advantage also of permitting the lesser states to be associated by membership in various functional committees. It was consistent also with the Canadian idea of building the European peace settlement into the international framework of the United Nations. Those who drew up the treaty should regard themselves as trustees for the world community. It was only within the United Nations system of collective security that there could be any real protection against German or any other aggression. The proposal is interesting as an illustration of the lapidary approach to institution building which increasingly characterized Canadian thinking as it moved away from the blueprint stage.

The idea of a statute was overtaken by events. It probably never had a chance because the gap between the great powers was already so wide that there would not have been even the minimum consensus necessary to get started. The concept of the all-embracing United Nations looks, from a later perspective, illusory. Nevertheless, it was a serious effort to grapple with real politics. It was original and imaginative and served to justify the Canadian insistence on a voice. Within a year, however, the same officials were contemplating a different kind of immediate procedure, a North Atlantic security pact, although even this they were anxious to fit into the concept of a universal security system under the United Nations.

A settlement with Austria was also a responsibility of the Council of Foreign Ministers and their deputies. As the great powers had regarded the Anschluss as null and void, Canada, like the other allies, did not regard itself as having been at war with Austria. The issues there seemed somewhat more remote, but the government regarded it essential to submit views in order to maintain the rights of the lesser allies. There was no question of a peace treaty or a peace conference and the Council instructed its deputies to prepare the terms without any provision for consultation. The Canadian submission, made to the deputies in February 1947, was called a statement 'on the proposed treaty for the re-establishment of an independent and democratic Austria.' The earlier part of the submission was devoted to restating the Canadian case on procedure. This was followed by some very general principles calling for a free, democratic, and independent Austria, withdrawal of all occupation forces, and prohibition of union with Germany. One interesting and typically Canadian section was the following: 'Canada does not, however, consider that the signatories to a treaty should be asked to secure the future integrity of Austria, but rather that any threat to Austrian independence should be dealt with by the united nations. If the four occupying powers, however, wish to go beyond this and themselves make such a guarantee it is a matter which would not concern the Canadian government.'[45] Canada proceeded to establish normal diplomatic relations with Vienna, although a 'state treaty' between the four powers and Austria was not agreed to until 1955. Canada acceded to the treaty in 1959.

JAPAN

The government's attitude towards the peace settlement with Japan differed in many ways from its attitude towards the settlement with Germany. There was a similar desire to avoid sending forces for occupation, rendered easier by a dissimilar reluctance to play an active role in control, supervisory, or even just advisory bodies. Although Canada had trade and other interests in the Far East, it had never had to determine a coherent policy in that area and had judged events in Asia more in terms of their effect on relations between the United Kingdom and the United States or on the League of Nations. The war in the Pacific Canadians had left to the Americans for good tactical reasons. It was recognized that a failure of Canadian troops to go to Japan after the victory in Europe would cause a serious rift with the Americans, but King was determined that this be a volunteer effort. J.W. Pickersgill's comment in volume I of the *Mackenzie King Record* was that 'the war against Japan had never really caught the imagination of Canadians, and any plans for participation in the fighting in the Pacific had no political pressure behind them.'[46] Little attention was given to the Far East by the post-hostilities planners in Ottawa. Although the Dominions Office referred copies of British-American exchanges concerning postwar policies towards Japan, the prime minister never approved the sending of Canadian comment. External Affairs assumed that this meant he did not want to intervene in that sphere.

The British showed insensitivity to Canadian prejudice in August 1945 which can be attributed, perhaps, to the confusion of changing governments at Westminster. A request came to the prime minister of Canada for assistance in many tasks resulting from the Japanese surrender which included the statement, 'indeed, we regard your assistance as indispensable.'[47] Before this there had been proposals for a Commonwealth occupation force to reoccupy key areas and take part in the occupation of Japan. A misguided effort to be sensitive had even led to the suggestion that since Canada had shared in the defence of Hong Kong a Canadian ship might like to take part in the surrender of that colony, the ship of course to sail with the commander-in-chief of the British Pacific Fleet. All have the earmarks of proposals designed by the British military. Attlee would never have authorized them after he had experienced Mackenzie King.

Canada replied on 15 August[48] that HMCS *Prince Rupert* would join the fleet to repatriate POWs from Hong Kong and carry relief supplies. The Canadian military attaché at Chungking would accompany United States General Wedemeyer's land force from China to Hong Kong. No brigade would be supplied for occupation or other special duties in the Pacific theatre. 'We now have considerable occupation forces in Europe and we are not ready to undertake any further commitments of this nature involving our Army or Airforce units.' King went further: 'I regret to have to say that I consider that any mention to the United States Chiefs of Staff of the possible participation of Canadian troops in such a force should have been deferred until you had been informed of our views ...' Under instructions the Canadian ambassador in Washington passed on this exchange to the State Department on 18 August, but he added that it was uncertain how long the occupation forces in Germany would be kept there since the firm commitment was to provide only an occupation group of some 25,000 during the fiscal year. The Americans were not to get the notion that although Canada used its occupation duties in Europe as the reason for not sending them to Japan, any troops released from Europe would be available in the Far East.

Nevertheless, Canada would be jeopardizing its claims to a voice in the postwar world if it were to reject a seat at a council table. The war was, after all, one war and Canada had been holding its assigned front. Canada was a Pacific country, as the British Columbians kept insisting, and there had been some contribution to fighting the Japanese. Late in August Canada was informed that it was included, along with Australia, New Zealand, the Netherlands, and the Philippines, with the great powers in membership of a Far Eastern Advisory Commission. There was no suggestion of a United Nations Commission as had at first been contemplated for Europe. The FEAC had been a proposal of the great powers in the Moscow Declaration, but this membership list was proposed by Washington. The FEAC was to be responsible for formulating policies for Japan to fulfil its surrender terms and the steps necessary in the machinery to assure compliance by Japan. Hume Wrong recognized that although a United States initiative to include smaller countries was welcome and the offer would be difficult to refuse, nevertheless it was desirable to be cautious because the United States suggestion 'may have been in part prompted by a desire to enlist the direct responsibility of as many countries as would have anything to contribute, while retaining for themselves the actual execution of policy in Japan through the supremacy of the American Commander there.'[49]

The department suspected also that the United States wanted the FEAC to forestall Soviet pressure for a four-power control council in Japan and thereby avoid another Berlin situation or a stalemate by veto. That was an American wish Ottawa had no interest in frustrating. They recognized the realities of American power and the inevitability, therefore, of American responsibility. The Canadian representative on the FEAC was told that what was most desirable was retention of a single United States military command and an allied body to lay down general lines of policy.

The principle of according to the United States a position of primary military responsibility avoids the practical difficulties inherent in setting up separate zones of occupation or in other forms of four-power administration. Moreover, there is an advantage in having the United States, as a power with both the means at her disposal and a reasonable degree of willingness to cooperate with smaller nations, made responsible for the execution of Allied policy. At the same time the exclusion of other countries, particularly the Soviet Union, from any real share in the control of Japan is difficult to justify. Indeed, it might well encourage the formation of spheres of influence which it is in the general interest to avoid as far as possible.[50]

The FEAC did not go far because the Soviet Union refused to participate so long as it had a purely advisory role. The United States was exceedingly reluctant to have an allied council established with veto powers that would shackle the work of the Supreme Commander for the Allied Powers. Nevertheless, they were anxious to get the Soviet Union involved. At the Moscow Conference of foreign ministers in December it was agreed to replace the FEAC with a Far Eastern Commission, which was to be no longer an advisory body but was charged primarily with the task of formulating policy for the fulfilment of the surrender terms for Japan. However, there was an Allied Council for Japan in Tokyo to advise SCAP on policy formulation by the FEC and there the veto applied.

In connection with the Allied Council Canada ran again into the problem of participation as part of the 'British Commonwealth.' This time it was not the British who made the proposal but the United States secretary of state, the Americans no doubt thinking this would all be neater. The argument the Canadians used against this proposal in talking to the British was that the Soviet government might use it as a precedent for resisting separate Canadian representation in situations of considerably greater importance to Canada. Therefore, Canada considered it important that the United States be discouraged from making such proposals in future.[51] There was a British Commonwealth seat in the Allied Council but Canada did not participate in the arrangements.

If Canada wanted to escape involvement it would have been wiser to reject membership. Membership involved taking positions. Canada was represented, even in the FEC, by ambassadors like Pearson and Wrong as well as deputies who were specialists in Far Eastern affairs and if they had to take part at all they could not resist taking part intelligently. Seldom, however, did work of the FEC receive consideration at a high level in Ottawa. The Canadian contribution in Japan was considerably greater than intended because the Canadian on the spot happened to be a remarkable person, E.H. Norman. Herbert Norman had grown up in Japan and been educated at the renowned Canadian Academy at Kobe. He had studied also at Toronto and Cambridge, published works in both English and Japanese, and although he was still in his thirties he was recognized in Japan and abroad as a unique scholar.[52] He had been involved during the war in special work dealing with Japan in the Department of External Affairs and shortly after the end of hostilities in the Far East he was sent to Manila to head the Canadian group arranging for civilian repatriation from the Orient. From there he went to Japan where the United States army was anxious that he remain so that his extensive and special knowledge of Japanese political conditions could be made available to General MacArthur's staff. He was allowed to remain and played a leading part in counter-intelligence work.[53]

When the FEC moved to Japan at the end of 1945 the prime minister agreed that Norman should represent Canada even though he would be junior to the representatives of other countries. As an adviser on SCAP's staff his freedom of action had been restricted, but as the Canadian representative he gained the confidence of MacArthur himself and of other leaders in the United States headquarters to a remarkable degree. Canada had had a legation in Japan for some years before the war, in one of the largest and best equipped buildings in Tokyo which had miraculously survived. The government was anxious to set up a civilian mission and put Norman in charge of it, but the Americans were unwilling to receive any civilians who were not attached to SCAP's staff. There was a typically exasperating hassle when MacArthur grudgingly agreed that the Canadian representative might go to Tokyo with the proviso that he could not be accommodated in the Canadian legation as the building was required for other purposes. After strong complaints to the State Department, the situation was worked out. The mission was wanted to look after relief of Canadian nationals in Japan and other consular and commercial duties as well as political liaison with SCAP. The mission in Tokyo, unlike that in Berlin, was civilian.

The FEC had two principal functions: 'To formulate the policies, principles, and standards in conformity with which the fulfilment by Japan of its obligations under the terms of surrender may be accomplished' and 'To review, on the request of any member, any directive issued to the Supreme Commander for the Allied Powers or any action taken by the Supreme Commander involving policy decisions within the jurisdiction of the Commission.'[54] The supreme commander was of course MacArthur, the sole executive authority for the allied powers, who was able permanently to circumvent Soviet objections by having recourse to interim directives. In the commission there was theoretically at least a chance for the lesser allies to state their pieces and exert their will. However, in spite of its wide authority with respect to the post-surrender policy, the commission's freedom was considerably handicapped by the fact that the main outlines had already been drawn up by the Americans before the FEC got into action. The commission could review or modify these policies, but the practical opportunities were distinctly limited by the chaotic situation of Japan and by the fact that all authority was in the hands of the Americans.

Canada played its part in drawing up the basic post-surrender policy, which was somewhat miraculously agreed upon. It was in general a declaration for all the accepted virtues and there was no particular Canadian angle to be noted. Differences however did begin to develop over the reform of the Japanese constitution and related issues. Australians and New Zealanders played a more active role, which Canadians were happy to concede to them. However, there was a tendency for an informal Commonwealth front to emerge in the pursuit of what might be described as more liberal positions. Australia, New Zealand, and Canada, with more reluctant support from the United Kingdom, expressed some opposition to the early date set for the elections in the belief that it did not allow time for the more democratic forces to organize themselves. Canada joined in a stubborn opposition move behind a New Zealand resolution on this subject, but SCAP convinced a majority of the commission that such questioning of his position would undermine his authority dangerously. That was the only time Canada went along with a resolution that could be regarded as critical of SCAP. This kind of argument by the Americans was at first resented in the commission, but the Canadians and their Commonwealth colleagues were more inclined to submit to it as they became more concerned over Soviet policies elsewhere. Hereafter the opposition continued to question American policies but to do so privately, to seek amendments without public differences in the commission that might undermine SCAP. The commission was far from being a docile body and the Canadians were active and conscientious, constantly seeking to strengthen all the democratic elements as they saw them in constitution-making. In the end, however, they submitted to American domination not because it was imposed or because they always agreed but because, when it came to the final assessment, they did believe in the ultimate priority of maintaining SCAP's position in perilous times. They recognized also, of course, that the Americans were providing all the force and the economic assistance, the Canadian contribution to both was virtually nil, and the government would not want to change that happy situation.

In their attitudes towards the reconstruction of Japan and towards reparations, the Canadians tended to agree with the United States. Canada had little interest itself in reparations and could be more impartial than those who had suffered directly from Japanese aggression. Consistent also with their position on Germany was the belief that the best guarantee against communism in both cases was a reasonably prosperous country. In Japan there was less inclination than in Germany to see a new market for Canadian goods because the traditions of Canadian trade with Japan were more ambiguous.

A typical contretemps took place in the autumn of 1948 concerning the policy of the Japanese government prohibiting strikes. At issue was a FEC directive of 1946 in which the right of Japanese workers to join unions of their own choice, bargain collectively, and strike was affirmed. The lively Australian member of the commission took a strong stand in opposition to what had been done and he certainly had the sympathy of the Canadians and the somewhat reluctant support of the British. Open criticism of such policy in the commission, however, would have been regarded as an attack on

SCAP, who had allowed the Japanese to act thus. The Soviet delegation was anxious to discredit SCAP on every possible occasion and would welcome such an opportunity of support. The American argument was that SCAP had been confronted with the threat of a strike that would have endangered the safety of the occupation – an argument that may have been a clever debating point or may have had substance. None of the friendly governments was in the end prepared to challenge the United States on the matter in the commission. Because the same considerations continued to apply to almost all issues before the commission the body declined in importance.

In July 1947 the United States proposed a conference of the eleven states who were members of the FEC to draft a peace treaty for Japan, decisions to be adopted by a two-thirds majority. All agreed except China and the Soviet Union, who wanted to preserve the veto in a treaty drafted by the Council of Foreign Ministers. In August and September 1947 representatives of Commonwealth governments met in Canberra in the first meeting outside the United Kingdom, the first to include representatives of India, Pakistan, and Burma, and the first major effort to have a genuine consultation on foreign policy without the assumed necessity to establish a common policy. Although the communiqué was careful to note a similarity of views with those of the United States, there was a difference of emphasis which was to characterize a Commonwealth approach on Asian matters during the fifties. The members were agreed on pressing for a peace settlement as soon as possible. Canada urged the desirability of a peace treaty and of getting Japan set in the ways of self-government at the earliest possible moment, but the Russians continued to insist on the priority of the Council of Foreign Ministers.

On 16 November 1949 Pearson said the absence of a treaty with Japan was one of the causes of uncertainty in the Far East. 'Much as the United States occupation of Japan has done for that country, I myself am inclined to think that military occupations as a rule quickly reach a point of diminishing returns ...'[55] Between 1947 and 1950, although Canada continued to believe that a peace treaty was not only desirable but necessary, it deferred to the delaying tactics of the United States, attributable to the conflicting views of the State Department and the United States army.[56] The Canadian view was clearly expressed by the secretary of state for external affairs in the House of Commons a few days later: '... it is clear that the Japanese have fulfilled pretty well the requirements that have been imposed upon them by the occupation, and it seems to me that from here on we must give them some incentive to maintain and strengthen the democratic way of life, and to wish to maintain close and friendly relations with the western world.'[57] He went on to speak of the dangers of punitive peace treaties in general terms which indicated that Canadians were still influenced by the view that the revival of militarism in Germany could be traced to the harsh terms of the Treaty of Versailles.

The Korean War confirmed the view that something must be done about Japan. Japan had assumed enormous importance as a security base for the United Nations operation, and the Korean War had assisted greatly in the revival of Japan as an economic power which was becoming of considerable interest to Canada, among others. The action taken against North Korea also encouraged the non-communist powers to act on their own when faced with indefinite resistance from Moscow and Peking. Early in 1951 President Truman sent John Foster Dulles to Tokyo and other countries to prepare for the negotiation of a treaty with Japan. In March Canada was invited to express views on an American draft. An invitation was issued in July to all countries that had been at war with Japan. The peace conference was held in San Francisco in September, and the treaty was signed on 8 September 1951. Fifty-four nations had been invited. For various reasons India, Burma, and Yugoslavia did not accept. Neither Chinese government was invited. Of the fifty-one countries that were present, forty-eight signed. The Soviet Union, Poland, and Czechoslovakia participated but refused to sign. The procedure was not much more conducive to lesser-power participation than was the Paris Peace Conference of 1946, but the arrangements were less offensive. It was a non-punitive peace treaty along the lines Canada preferred, and there was no strong sense of frustration in Ottawa.

In various speeches in the House of Commons and elsewhere the prime minister and the secretary of state strongly defended the treaty. In stressing the desirability of Japan's being allowed to take its place in world commerce they recognized lingering Canadian doubts about Japanese trade practices. In a speech to the House on 22 October 1951 Pearson outlined Canada's attitude to the treaty and incidentally took some credit for Canada in seeing to it that although they had not managed to have a fisheries agreement included in the treaty, Japan was obliged to begin discussions with Canada and the United States for a fisheries arrangement.[58] St Laurent told the Women's Canadian Club in Victoria on 5 September 1952[59] that Canada must learn to buy from Japan in order to raise the living standards of the peoples in Asia. He said the Japanese would be prepared to agree by treaty not to take salmon, halibut, and herring in the North Pacific Ocean and added that as long as goods were not dumped Canada should be prepared to buy its share of goods made by those with lower living standards. On 11 February 1953 Pearson told the House that Japan was already Canada's fourth best customer, that Japan brought from Canada only one-eighth of what Canada sold to

Japan, and the balance was paid in United States dollars, an exceedingly valuable commodity at that time.[60] Canada was well on the way to a new and special relationship with its North Pacific neighbour. The mission in Tokyo became the Canadian embassy in November 1952 and in June of that year a Japanese ambassador reopened as an embassy the legation in Ottawa that had been closed the day of Pearl Harbor.

REPARATIONS AND WAR CRIMES

At the Paris Peace Conference Canada, along with other Western allies, waived all reparation claims against minor belligerents. During the discussions in the Economic Commission on Italy the Canadian representative pointed out that Canada was not only asking nothing for itself but had already contributed substantially to the recovery of Italy through its support of UNRRA and its grant of over $28 million in military relief. The Canadian government had also been the first to allow its people of Italian origin to send relief supplies to their relatives. In November 1945 the governments of France, Britain, and the United States invited representatives of fifteen governments that had fought against Germany to study plans for allocation of reparations from Germany. General Pope represented Canada. The meeting established the Inter-Allied Reparations Agency to ensure equitable distribution. The Canadian ambassador in Brussels represented Canada, and Canadians continued for some time to take part in the work of subcommittees which interested them.

The Canadian representatives sought to protect Canadian interests, but it was not a matter of great importance to Canada and the participation was not vigorous. It reflected also the increasing Canadian interest in security through a modest revival of the German economy. The IARA allocated Canada 1.3 per cent of category B assets (capital goods and merchant vessels) and 3.5 per cent of category A assets (all other forms of reparations). Canada later agreed to a reduction of the number of ships it received and then renounced rights to industrial capital equipment. The government did not feel it had much claim on surplus industrial equipment and Canadian industry was not much interested. It was a policy consistent with the general view on the subject expressed in the Canadian submission to the Council of Foreign Ministers: 'On the question of German reparations, it is the view of the Canadian government that existing agreements will have to be reviewed in the light of the level of economy and standard of living which is to be permitted to Germany in order to prevent Germany continuing to constitute a centre of European economic depression. Reparation deliveries agreed upon should then be implemented as expeditiously as possible in order that the Germans may know what industrial capacity is to be left to them. The Germans should then be made to realize that within the framework of allied control it will be possible for them to reestablish favourable living conditions only through their own efforts.'[61]

In Japan Canada was more interested in the restitution of property belonging to Canadian firms. Brooke Claxton stated in 1947 that Canada held Japanese external assets of about $5 million and claims filed against these assets were of about the same amount. He pointed out that Canadians had the biggest life insurance business of any foreign country in Japan before the war.[62] These were a subject of concern to Canadians in the treaty, although they never disputed the claims of those who had suffered more directly. In his statement in the House on the treaty, Pearson said: 'The allied powers recognize in the treaty that Japan should in principle pay reparations for the devastation and suffering she caused during the war. They recognized in addition, however, that Japan lacks the physical capacity to recompense her former victims if at the same time she is to achieve a viable economy and contribute to the economic health of the Pacific area.' He noted also that Japan had agreed to make available its assets to indemnify prisoners of war who had suffered undue hardship, a matter of concern to the Hong Kong survivors in Canada.[63] Some modest and specific compensation of this kind seemed worth pursuing, but the Canadian attitude to reparations in general was to count on them very little for financial help and to regard them as an aspect of political policy towards the former enemies. It was a duly functional approach. To those who suffered most should go the most reparation.

In the prosecution of war criminals Canada was not very active. There was a good deal of interest in seeing that those who had maltreated Canadian soldiers and prisoners were brought to justice, and Canada joined the United Nations War Crimes Commission set up in October 1943. However, it did not adhere to the Charter set up by the International Conference on Military Trials in 1945 consisting of the four major powers. Altogether nineteen states in addition to the drafters signed, but Canada was prepared to leave this matter to the countries that had had the Germans on their soil. The high commissioner in London participated in the work of the United Nations War Crimes Commission, but Canada took no part in the Nuremberg trials. On 13 September 1945 the prime minister stated that Canadian military courts would deal with offences against Canadian armed forces, the courts would be established in accordance with military law and the principles of justice, with safeguards to assure fair trial.[64] Seven cases came before Canadian military courts in Aurich, Germany. There were no military courts in Japan as Canada had no forces stationed there. Japanese who were accused of atrocities against Canadians were tried by British and American military courts, but in each case a Canadian judge sat; Canadians assisted in gathering the evidence and in the prosecution. Whereas there was no Canadian at Nuremberg, a Canadian judge, Mr Justice E.S. McDougall, was a member of the International Military Tribunal in Tokyo. This apparently greater interest in Japanese than German crimes was less a matter of deliberate policy than a reflection of the Canadian sensitivity about its unequal part in the German settlement.[65]

THE LESSONS

Before the fighting was over, planning for peace was inevitably abstract, based on assumptions about the cause and cure of war. The conception of the Canadian role was also based on postulations about participation and justice. If these plans seem naïve, the naïveté was not peculiar to Canada. The great-power planners were equally abstract – the Americans incredibly Utopian – although their expectations were constantly adjusted by the exigencies of negotiations among themselves. If Canadian officials adjusted also, it was not from a failure of idealism but from a need to cope with the onrush of events in a world which, after what it had been through, was chaotic. Canadian attitudes of 1944 and 1945 reveal an identification on the one hand with a group of allies facing common enemies and on the other with a layer of lesser powers demanding rights from a consortium of great powers. As the East-West split came swiftly, there had to be a reconsideration of priorities. The early Canadian memoranda make clear that Canada was not counting with assurance on postwar unity among the great powers. However, they thought it important to make all efforts to maintain unity in spite of the odds against it. The insistence on lesser-power rights continued, but the priority was conceded to the perceived need to maintain the strength and unity of the Western powers. It was not a shift made under pressure, and it was based on eclectic assessments – an obvious enough comment, required, however, by the persistent legend that Canada and its European allies were hypnotized into a Cold War mentality by the Americans.[66] Elemental problems of security and economics took precedence. The postwar world took shape in the emergency measures required after a holocaust.

The 1945 Canadian memoranda spoke of the way in which the Germans might be allowed eventually to grow up within a democratic strait-jacket imposed by the occupiers. In 1947 Canada was recognizing the German government set up in the Western zones. The main reason for this change is obvious, the reluctant recognition that there could be no more than rudimentary co-operation with the Russians. Fear of another war exaggerated the similarities between the new challenge and that which had just been so bloodily repulsed. Feeling the need of allies with a considerable population and even some capacity to fight, the Canadian view of both the Germans and the Japanese changed rapidly.

A second reason for the change was that the assumptions of the constitution mongers of 1945 dissolved under the pressures of cold and hunger and fear. Given the attitudes of 1945, the Germans might have been left to starve in their ruins. However, when their vanquishers assumed responsibility for government they became involved in keeping the Germans alive and making it possible for them to earn their own living. Canadians were not occupiers but they shared this concern. The future of Germany lay in the hands of the administrators. Whatever vantage-point Canada may have had in 1945 to claim a voice in the disposition of Germany had disappeared by 1947 – only to reappear in a different form in 1949 as a member of NATO. Another former enemy, Italy, was also an ally shortly after the end of the war. There was no alliance to embrace Japan, but Canada and Japan evolved a special relationship, based on mutual economic and political interests, a tacit alliance. There was little doubt felt of the desirability for Canada and the world at large of unrestricted international trade and the strengthening for that purpose of the liberal-capitalist system, wherever it could flourish. Retribution seemed pointless if the Canadian interest was best served by self-reliant, free enterprise German, Italian, and Japanese economies.

Over peacemaking Canada had its early lessons in the new diplomacy of participation. Claxton regarded the Paris Conference as 'a proving ground to show numerous mistakes to be avoided.'[67] That could be said of the whole experience of settling with the late enemies. Viewed in the light of Ottawa's expectations and demands it was not a success. The expectations, however, were wishful. Canada's place during the war had been abnormally large, and the process of influencing postwar policy was infinitely more complex than it had been when Canada's world was triangular. There was the old problem of relating influence to rights and to participation. Now new ways and means had to be worked out: how to combine with others, when to be stubborn and when to be complaisant, how to use a committee, at what point to speak out. Canadians profited from the experience and earned a reasonable reputation for serious and practical contributions and, above all, a sense of responsibility for the long-range issues rather than just the national angle. The ad hoc mechanisms of peacemaking, however, were less satisfactory for Canada than the fixed but flexible framework being provided in the United Nations.

In peacemaking one had to plead for a chance to speak, argue for a general conference, forestall great-power fiats, waste time and energy on mechanics rather than substance. United Nations bodies were more comfortable for lesser powers. A seat and a chance to speak were provided; the challenge was to use the opportunities effectively. It is no wonder that Canada pressed whenever possible for a UN role in the peacemaking.

A practical lesson of the experience was not only that a country's diplomacy should not outrun its resources but also that it should not outrun its personnel. The multiplication of obligations to participate in all kinds of bodies connected with the settlement of the war and the establishment of new international structures came on top of the need to provide staff for a considerable number of missions which had been agreed to in principle during the war and served until then by a single mission in London. There had been no recruiting of permanent officers during the war, and it took time for the postwar crop of veterans to be recruited and trained. Between 31 December 1944 and 31 December 1946 diplomatic staff increased from 72 to 138, but in 1946 128 officers attended various international conferences abroad. Concern was being expressed in the department and elsewhere in the government structure about the proliferation of agencies and meetings and the heavy strain on government departments. This helped to induce a mood of scepticism about some of the new agencies and institutions and also about putting too much effort into bodies like the FEC where there was a minimum chance of having influence.

A neat moral would be how Canada learned from the peacemaking that to get a voice in policy-making a country had to pay its way. But the argument that Canada had already paid its way by its wartime effort was never rejected – not even by the Russians. There were other reasons for great-power dominance, and being deserving was irrelevant. Did Canada forfeit its influence by refusing to take part in occupation duties? Some good will from the great powers was perhaps lost, but would Canada have enjoyed a better audience if it had responded affirmatively? How would one tell anyway? There was no special Canadian content for the settlements by which to judge success. Influence is hard to measure. In diplomacy it is rarely to be judged by formal provisions. A country has as much influence as it can expect if it involves itself not only physically but intellectually, constructively, and assiduously in the variegated channels of policy formation. It is less a question of being in there fighting as being in there thinking. Some very able External Affairs men were so involved, contributing in a thousand conversations to weaving the web of ideas and policies, making their presence felt at the creation.

PART III: THE TRIANGLE REORDERED

MANIFEST DESTINY REVISED

Canada grew up in a triangle – isosceles, of course. Some of its neurotic quirks may be attributable to having been the product of a ménage à trois – what with two mother countries and an over-weening uncle. In 1945 the need to understand Canadian history as a continuing triangular relationship had just been persuasively stated by J.B. Brebner in his *North Atlantic Triangle: the Interplay of Canada, the United States and Great Britain*. In the eyes of some Canadians, Canada had been crushed between two rival powers. Others would argue that Canada survived and prospered by skilful exploitation of this rivalry. In either perspective Canada's international predicament was seen as three-sided. Whether Canada should lean towards Britain or the United States or pursue its own path was a contentious, if somewhat unreal, issue during the war and postwar decade. What was not a subject of much contention was that Anglo-American goodwill and co-operation were the best guarantee of Canada and of peace in general. It was a conviction that had ripened over a century. The British had been more convinced of its wisdom at first than the Canadians, because Canadians, as in the Washington Treaty of 1871 or the Alaska Boundary award, thought they were being asked to make sacrifices to appease the Americans and perpetuate the entente. By the Second World War, however, the virtue of the triangle was accepted wisdom in Canada and a primary theme of Mackenzie King. He saw the Ogdensburg Agreement not as a simple continental arrangement but as 'part of a new world order based on friendship and good will.' In an interesting twist of an American formula he stated in the House of Commons on 12 November 1940: 'In the furtherance of this new world order Canada in liaison between the British Commonwealth and the United States is fulfilling a manifest destiny.'

The altered positions of Britain and the United States on the world scene were an historical development which profoundly affected Canadian policy and the Canadian predicament. The shift in power to the United States was not something Canada willed. It was a fact to which Canada had to adjust. A shift was not entirely to Canada's liking, and much of Canadian policy in economics and security was intended to shore up the old happy balance. Canada had for a century been in a sense an Anglo-American 'protectorate.' After the war one could argue that both Britain and Canada had become American protectorates – or that in the age of nuclear deterrence Canada was in reality a Soviet-American protectorate. Terms like protectorate, dependency, or satellite are best avoided. Such over-simplifications of complex relationships have done more to obscure and prejudice than to clarify. The standard pronouncement about Canada's having switched from being a British to an American dependency misrepresents the past and the present and Canada's association with each of the powers. The purpose of Part Three is to clarify the triangular relationship by complicating it.

A paradox is that although this study is primarily concerned with the institutional framework which Canada sought zealously to construct for international relations, the Canadian attitude towards its relations with the two major partners was anti-institutional. Canada resisted efforts to establish formal structures for the Commonwealth. Aside from the Joint Board on Defence which was intended to be 'Permanent,' wartime Canada-United States bodies were dismantled and no concerted effort was made at the end of the war to institutionalize the relationship. There was, furthermore, little interest in bringing the continental relationship within the jurisdiction of the United Nations. A policy of non-institutionalization was not a policy of neglect or antipathy. Nor was it unstructured. Canada had a good idea of the kind of Commonwealth it was shaping. The avoidance of institutions, in the case of North America, was perhaps more instinctive than calculated, but it was not without design. The transformation of the triangle was itself an alteration of structure, even though the triangle was a concept without institutions. There were during the war certain so-called ABC (American, British, Canadian) bodies, but they were ad hoc, functional, and temporary. The subject of this section is the relationship rather than the relations, with attention directed to aspects which illustrate the complexities.

5

The Commonwealth, 1944-7

Whether one thinks the Commonwealth was weakened or strengthened by the Second World War depends upon the perspective from which its history is viewed. Certainly it could never be the same again. It matters, however, whether we think we have witnessed the decline and fall of the British empire or the sublimation of an organism, glorious or inglorious but anachronous, into a new kind of Commonwealth, fitted to play a valuable part in an age of transition.

The war weakened the trunk and strengthened the branches. Militarily and industrially, Canada, Australia, and even India took great leaps forward. To begin with the organism had its finest hour when the dominions rallied of their free will to a common cause. The British Commonwealth Air Training Plan, successfully run in Canada, was a major source of inspiration. The prestige of this kind of Commonwealth was high during the period when its members stood almost alone against the acknowledged enemy of all Western civilization. (The English had a habit of spoiling the effect by speaking of how Britain – or even England – stood alone. Mackenzie King reprimanded Churchill several times for doing this, but he kept on.[1]) When that stand became in 1942 the common cause of the 'United Nations' the Commonwealth as a political ideal was justified, but its incapacity as a strategic – or economic – institution to stand on its own was evident. In particular, the essentiality of United States power to the survival of its parts was made clear – although this was not so much a new as a previously concealed factor. The shift of balance within the Commonwealth and in relation to other powers meant that its days as a power on its own in the world were clearly numbered – if it ever had been in that position. The fact that it had acted so splendidly as an entity in a crisis unfortunately obscured for some, especially in Britain, the reality.

Although there was emerging another and a valuable function for the Commonwealth as a power for good within broader international structures, the wartime experience stimulated the hope that the empire could be revived as a Commonwealth of Nations united before the world. This was not to be the old empire run from London. It was in many ways a splendid vision of equality, but the premises were false and it could have run the Commonwealth into a dead end. The alternate future, for which Canada was to a considerable extent responsible, was not seen clearly enough even by Canadians. They found it difficult to shake free of antiquated attitudes to the empire and to Britain, whether these were filial or rebellious, and to recognize sooner the opportunities provided by the shift of power from the centre. Canadian nationalists were still obsessed with status vis-à-vis the British and tended to emphasize Canada's North Americanness as a corrective, a proclivity which later nationalists mistakenly interpret as calculated 'continentalism.' For the most part they did see the Commonwealth dimension as a part of the Canadian identity, provided it could be kept in proper balance – and it looked more useful to them as the American dimension loomed larger as a challenge.

Issues of Commonwealth relations were in many ways similar in the Second World War to those in the first, especially in the early years. The major Commonwealth countries had, however, now established themselves as internationally recognized entities. Canada had the status and resources to act more independently and a keener awareness of a distinct national interest. There was, nevertheless, continuing anxiety on all sides to maintain a common bond, the mysteriousness of which was a favourite theme. In spite of the changes since 1918 and the fact that Canada, by ostentatiously declaring war on its own, had demonstrated that it was not automatically committed to take part in British wars, the same basic problem emerged: How to manage a common enterprise – with participation of the dominions not only in the fighting but in the policy-making? It was increasingly evident in the World War II setting that the members had a common interest but also quite different regional priorities. There was the fact also that they were not equal. Britain was the most populous, militarily the strongest; it had a prestigious role and more experience in international diplomacy. The war may have undermined its position as a world power, but the international community did not fully absorb this fact until about a decade after the war was over.

There were, as always, paradoxes which could not be explained away by abstract talk about arrogance at the centre and the democratic rights of lesser powers. That the dilemma of policy-sharing in an association is inescapable and not peculiar to an empire was made clear to Canadians in the course of the war when what had been largely a Commonwealth enterprise became an allied coalition. By the time the war ended arguments which for Canadians had been imperial in context had been transformed into issues that were to persist in their relations with foreign allied powers and, particularly, the United States. However blind and unimaginative Westminster had seemed to be at times on the question of the Canadian voice, the Commonwealth had been a good training ground for all concerned. The British had had much experience of clamorous associates.[2] The Americans tended to assume that although Canada and other lesser powers would have such problems with a real imperial power like Britain, they would be bound to understand that the United States was the vicar of all democracies.

The Australian prime minister, Robert Menzies, approached Mackenzie King directly in July 1941, expressing his concern about the lack of dominion participation in the direction of the war and suggesting something be done – 'not some practical impossibility like an Imperial War Cabinet but effective Dominions' representation in a British War Cabinet.'[3] He also wanted a meeting of dominion prime ministers. King's way, as always, of rejecting such proposals was to praise existing means of consultation as well as to point out the 'grave political and constitutional objections' to including in a cabinet responsible to Westminster ministers responsible to other governments.[4] Smuts told Churchill he supported King's 'outspoken condemnation of agitation for an Imperial Cabinet.'[5] The matter was settled by Churchill's agreeing in January 1942 to the Australians accrediting a minister of their government to attend meetings of the War Cabinet. He told Canada they could have the same arrangement if they wanted. In fact, as King pointed out to the House of Commons,[6] any dominion prime minister could attend the War Cabinet when he was in London. He did say that although existing means of consultation were working well, Canada might if necessary have its views presented by an accredited representative.

In the Second World War Canada maintained strong enough establishments in London, both political and military, so that, with much better means of communication, the Canadian ideal of a permanent Commonwealth 'cabinet,' with the capitals in constant touch with each other, could be better justified than in the Great War. If the Canadian voice, however, seemed to have been more resonant in the First World War this may have been because in the second Canadians were less perturbed about the military direction of the war than they had been in the first. In 1916 Borden had complained: 'It can hardly be expected that we shall put 400,000 or 500,000 men in the field and willingly accept the position of having no more voice and receiving no more consideration than if we were toy automata.'[7] King did not talk like that. There were persistent and unavoidable problems about the way in which Canadian forces could be fitted in with the British and allied forces. According to a good judge, General Maurice Pope, 'so far as the army, and the army only, is concerned the British in providing a place for a Canadian army have been as magnanimous as they have been farseeing and wise.'[8] The experience of the other services was perhaps less happy, but in spite of friction the war was won.

The entry into the war of the United States and the Soviet Union raised new questions. Canada had to resist suggestions coming from various quarters that there be a Commonwealth entity in international institutions, both those for running the war and those being designed for the postwar world. These were the product not just of a British interest in magnifying its power but also of an American preference for a tidy arrangement that would avoid a lot of problems, along with their innocence of the nature of the Commonwealth. For practical reasons the American military insisted on working bilaterally with the British. No other country could have membership on the Combined Chiefs of Staff Committee set up in 1942. Canada did not in fact accept the right of the British to act for them in the CCSC and arranged for their own representative to be heard when necessary. The objections in principle were pressed less vigorously because the results, as far as Canada was concerned, were reasonably satisfactory. The same can be said of the ad hoc means of handling issues of supply.[9]

Canadian officials were sensitive about suggestions that the Commonwealth act as a unit and were slow to recognize the advantages of the practice of consultation, the virtues of which they emphasized, however, when it was convenient to do so. When the British pressed for Commonwealth discussions on economic and other postwar matters, Ottawa saw difficulties. In October 1942, for example, a group of Commonwealth experts met in London for a preliminary discussion of postwar international economic relations in general and specifically on some proposals that John Maynard Keynes had for an international clearing union.[10] On international economic questions, where Canadian relations with the United States were close and important, there was resistance to any suggestion of a common Commonwealth position. The Canadians were reluctant not only because they disliked the idea of a common voice but also because they were afraid of upsetting the Americans, who were suspicious of a Commonwealth front on trade preferences and might draw the wrong conclusions when it came to matters of representation of Commonwealth countries in the postwar structures.

This was particularly the case over international civil aviation where Canada's interests were much involved on its own continent. It was not that it had a common interest with the United States but rather that in negotiations with the United States it did not want to be hampered by attachment to a somewhat unreal Commonwealth position.[11] When the Canadians finally did have Commonwealth talks on civil aviation in London, many of their fears proved unfounded and in fact it was a very useful discussion. The 'imperial sky' idea, which was being pressed by the British Right wing, especially by Lord Beaverbrook, did not win out, and the conference unanimously took a stand against discriminatory systems. Some excessively nationalist Canadians took a perverse pleasure in the foolish imperial schemes perpetrated by peers and potentates and assumed a conspiratorial connection with the British government in very much the same way as a later breed of nationalists have enjoyed selectively citing Southern senators, mid-western editors, or over-zealous generals as evidence of the malign designs of the United States government. The experience over civil aviation was useful in getting the Canadians over their neurosis. From then on they were inclined to agree to preliminary discussions as, for example, before the Bretton Woods, San Francisco, and Paris Peace conferences. When it had become clear that these were for the clearing of minds and the exchange of opinions, their value as trial runs was proved. A new era of serious Commonwealth consultation was being launched.

The conceptual problem with the Americans is illustrated by Harry Hopkins' account of how he, Roosevelt, and Welles opposed in March 1943 a British proposal for separate representation of Canada and Australia on the Central Committee of UNRRA. 'I said I believed by this technique we would be constantly outvoted, and that I thought we should put our foot down in the very beginning in this Food Conference and insist on the main committee of four members only and let the British decide whether they want their membership to come from England or Canada.'[12] The American draft air convention of October 1944 provided that the Executive Council would be composed of two members appointed by the government of the United States, two by the government of the Union of Soviet Socialist Republics, two by the British Commonwealth, and one each by Brazil, China, and France.[13] In both cases Canada successfully resisted until some Americans began to realize that they had got the wrong idea about the empire.

HOW MANY VOICES?

The issue of a common voice was raised on the highest level in the latter years of the war and persisted for a time afterwards until it was buried forever in the transformation of the Commonwealth by the accession of India and Pakistan. There were various pressures for unity, some of them British, some of them Australian, and some from Canadian Conservatives.[14] Britons perceived already during the war that they were unlikely to emerge from it an unquestioned great power. To keep their place among the great they would have to represent something more than an island with diminishing resources. This theme varied from the purely rhetorical to some concrete suggestions for institutionalizing the Commonwealth so that it could be the designated great power on the United Nations Security Council. The Canadian government rejected any such inference from the beginning. They were quite happy to accept the position of the United Kingdom as a great power on the Security Council and wanted only to be recognized as an independent middle power with its own functions. The idea of a common foreign policy and some kind of institution to formulate it was more enthusiastically sponsored by those remote from the realities of diplomacy. The secretary of state for dominion affairs[15] and the Foreign and Dominions Offices in London could see the difficulties involved in seeking assent to the hundreds of decisions that make up a foreign policy. They could see the risks, furthermore, for Britain in having its policy in the new United Nations Council determined multilaterally. Unfortunately, however, political leaders found mystical adjurations to unity irresistible, and their pronouncement stimulated and prolonged a scholastic debate over a proposal which was a dud.[16]

The British Foreign Office people could, of course, see the advantages of some mystification of Britain's role and would have been willing to go along with schemes which provided for a special role on the part of the dominions. That they could even think in such tems is attributable to their inability to take the dominions very seriously. They were shielded from the importunate Commonwealth by a Dominions Office which they did not take seriously either. It was unfortunate for both Britain and the dominions that at this time few people in the Foreign Office had ever been posted in the Commonwealth. Foreign countries were their preoccupation. Some of them were unable to understand why the 'Doms' bothered to have their own diplomatic services when they were so liberally supplied with the 'gen' from Whitehall. Others, because of their experience of some of the first-class Commonwealth diplomats in the course of the creation, developed a regard for their contributions to both information and policy formation and, on the whole, a good relationship was established both in London and in the field. The Canadian Department of External Affairs had inherited much of the style and analytical approach of the Foreign Office and, in spite of differing perspectives and sometimes divergent interests, especially on economic issues, the

British and Canadian professionals had much in common in their views of the postwar structure. One important conviction they shared was the priority to be accorded to the relationship with the United States.[17]

The discussion of unity in all its mystic forms came to a head at the May 1944 meeting of Commonwealth prime ministers in London. Prime Minister Curtin of Australia, desperate to protect Australian strategic interests, had let it be known that he would propose the establishment of a Commonwealth council with a secretariat. He was not specific in his proposal. What he emphasized was a standing consultative body rather than an executive, but such consultation 'must be consistent with the sovereign control of its policy by each Government.' His interest seemed to be more in seeing that the Australian case got a hearing and the British did not make important decisions on their own. He did not stress the 'common foreign policy' theme for its own sake, but many of those who were interested in this end supported him for that purpose.[18] Shrewd minds in Whitehall realized that although such a council might promote the idea of Commonwealth unity, which was in their interests, it had little chance against Canadian and South African opposition. Support in Britain was strongest in the press and parliament.

Mackenzie King made clear that this was not the kind of proposal that appealed to him. An ill-advised speech in Toronto by the British ambassador to Washington, Lord Halifax, seemed to link this highly pragmatic Australian proposal with a move to establish a united empire as a great power, thereby challenging the dearest held of King's views.[19] The speech stirred up a commotion. On 31 January 1944 King said in the House that he was unable to agree with what was implied in the argument of Lord Halifax. We look forward, he said, 'to close collaboration in the interests of peace not only inside the British commonwealth, but also with all friendly nations, small as well as great.' External Affairs officers were less inclined than the prime minister to espy a conspiracy, but they were not in the mood to think of restricting themselves to diplomatic effort within a Commonwealth unit. Lester Pearson, commenting from Washington in a personal letter to Norman Robertson on the Halifax speech, said that as it was clear Canada had been involved in the results of British policy, 'surely we should seek to influence British policy in some way when it appears to be going in the wrong direction.' That did not mean adopting 'certain ideas being thrown out at this time.' 'If we act as a unit, I do not see how we can also act separately and maintain the national and international position we have gained ... The Prime Minister was, in my opinion, absolutely right when he deprecated this talk of a Commonwealth unit in foreign affairs; talks based on views held, I'm afraid, in pretty high quarters, in the White House, in No. 10. Acting in unison as separate States is one thing; acting as a unit is quite another.'[20]

Mackenzie King could not resist the opportunity to posture as the defender of Canada against another imperial plot. His emotional approach was exacerbated by the fact that he was regarded by the supporters of 'unity' as the villain, even the sole obstacle in the way of a great opportunity. This view was perpetuated by those like Geoffrey Crowther, editor of the *Economist*, who accepted the fact that, given Canadian opposition, the plan must be dropped. Crowther insisted on regretting the lost opportunity and like others nourished a grudge in spite of the efforts of Canada House to put him straight.[21] A legend persisted for years that Canada had spoiled the chance of a glorious future for the Commonwealth.[22]

Discussion of the Curtin proposal at the prime ministers' meeting was, in the light of all the hullabaloo, anti-climactic. It was a useful conference, proving the value of consultation. Most of it was devoted to hearing a review of the war situation from Churchill and the chiefs of staff and discussing foreign policies. According to a Canadian report of the sessions, 'the Prime Minister of Canada expressed warm approval of the foreign policy pursued by the United Kingdom since the beginning of the War and satisfaction with the way in which they had been kept informed.'[23] In the discussion of strategy Curtin explained very effectively the severe supply problems Australia faced. 'Many questions were asked, but there was general agreement on the main lines of Allied strategy.' The most valuable discussion concerned the new world organization. Again there was agreement on the approach of a Foreign Office memorandum. King called it 'excellent,' but was careful here as at all times to establish his principle by saying that he did not wish to commit the Canadian government to specific proposals without consulting his colleagues in Ottawa. So much agreement on foreign policy relieved the pressure for new machinery and seemed to validate the Canadian argument that all was well. 'Our present discussions,' King said, 'have confirmed our confidence that the policies of our governments will be in substantial agreement on the major issues of war and peace.'[24] The Foreign Office memorandum spoke of the desirability of one member of the Commonwealth in addition to the United Kingdom having a seat on the UN Council, clearly implying that they did not see the Commonwealth sitting as a unit.

King, on several occasions, made clear his belief that the United Kingdom should sit in its own right. Churchill agreed, although he fudged the issue by saying there 'would be obvious advantages if she [the UK] were in a position to speak on the world Council for all the Dominions, of course, after the closest consultation with them.'[25] Curtin and Fraser of New Zealand were worried about the UK speaking for itself alone, but Curtin did not press his proposal for a secretariat. He and Fraser, as well as Cranborne, made various proposals for improving means of consultation, especially on defence matters. The prime ministers expressed general agreement with a suggestion for monthly meetings of the British prime minister with the high commissioners – a practice of which King had been very sceptical before the war – and agreed to consult their governments on the other proposals put forward. Curtin had revised his proposals and the British ministers had determined their attitude in the light of the negative attitude expected from King.

As was often the case King was less forceful on such issues in London than in Ottawa and had to be prodded by Norman Robertson to state his position in the meetings. On 11 May he made a statement, prepared by his advisers, stressing the positive and constructive aspects of the Canadian position on the future of the Commonwealth. It was a succinct outline of the approach to the Commonwealth in a new postwar setting which was being developed in Ottawa. The aim was to find a valid role for an institution which many Canadians prized and which offered advantages as well as traps for the new Canadian diplomacy. This would have to be formed by emphasizing not its exclusivity but its universality, an international institution of proven strength which could play its part in holding together the perilously inchoate world body which the United Nations were preparing to launch.

The draft prepared for King was delivered in the context of a discussion of the new world organization. He stressed the importance of the United Kingdom's having a firm and decisive voice, which it could not have 'if every issue must be decided on the majority vote of countries, some of which are not directly in touch with the affairs of all parts of the world at once.' Britain's strength had always been in its 'alliance potential':

This alliance potential she is able to command when her policy is such that her interests are those of her allies. Her most faithful allies in the past two wars have been the other nations of the Commonwealth, and no nation who wishes to attack Great Britain can dare to ignore the lessons of 1914 and 1939. Nor need we fear that Great Britain will fail to give due consideration to the interests of other nations of the Commonwealth, for she will want our continuing support. But this is true not only of Great Britain. It is true for all of us. None of us can defend ourselves by ourselves, and we shall all seek so to coordinate our policies that we can count on support in times of crisis. Are we stronger and more impressive in the eyes of the world this way, or bound together in such a way that our differences may be magnified and our disputes advertised?

The inflexibility of the common-voice principle was presented as a threat to Commonwealth solidarity. Canada cared about the health of the Commonwealth:

The prestige of the British Commonwealth was never higher than it is to-day, and that is particularly true in the United States, despite friction and jealousies that sometimes obscure their fundamental friendliness. The prestige is based upon a belief that in the British Commonwealth there has been evolved a unique alliance of a peculiarly tough and enduring kind whose members act together, unlike so many allies bound by explicit treaties, not because they are compelled to act together, but because they have the will to act together. What is more our friends have discovered that the primary objects for which the members of the Commonwealth act together are objects which can be shared by other countries of good will. They have realized that the Commonwealth is not a Power bloc exploiting its own selfish interests but a group of like-minded nations whose close association has in the past and may in the future form the most reliable element within the framework of the world order.[26]

There persisted considerable discussion about a common voice, but it was taken more seriously in the press and in parliaments than it was by officials, who were increasingly aware of the gap between idea and reality. It would, if it were to work, require an enormous amount of extra effort and the postponement of decisons that could not be postponed. The British especially were much too busy winding up the war to pay more than lip service. The Foreign Office and the Dominions Office, rechristened in 1947 the Commonwealth Relations Office, continued to keep the dominions as well posted as possible on their doings among the great powers and invited comment. They got a good deal of comment, listened to some, but inevitably made up their own minds in the end.

The man who did more than King to kill the idea of a unified foreign policy was probably the rambunctious minister of extenal affairs for Australia, Herbert Evatt. He professed agreement with the Canadian position, but his actions suggested that if he could largely determine Commonwealth policy in the Pacific, he would concede a priority to the British in Europe, an argument which did not prevent him from raising a row about Australia's right to a voice over Trieste. The idea of regionalizing Commonwealth policy kept cropping up. Churchill had fancied it and King had had to argue with him its impracticality.[27] The idea that Canada would have a priority in determining policies of Britain and Australia in North America might have promised new power and influence but neither King nor his advisers were susceptible to that alluring trap. The experiment of having the Australian representative speak for the Commonwealth (except Canada) in the Allied Council for Japan dismayed the Foreign Office. When the Australian representative, a distinguished professor, sent back his first message saying he assumed his role was to mediate between the Russians and the Americans, the British pointed out that their collaboration with the United States in other parts of the world was of such outstanding importance that they were not prepared to be committed in advance to such a policy of mediation. The professor was told to request instructions in all cases.[28]

In the meantime extensive consultation, exchanges of views, and sometimes combined representations meant that the Canadian concept of the Commonwealth was being put into practice. The dominions, having acquired more extensive and on the whole ably staffed foreign services of their own, were able to make a contribution to the pool of understanding which British officials came to appreciate.[29] The British Labour party, when it came to power at the end of the war, did not flatly rule out the idea of a common voice, but it was less imperially minded than its predecessors. Labour style facilitated a give-and-take relationship. King found Attlee an easier man to deal with than Churchill. The departure of the Conservatives removed some of the suspicion of imperial plots which had made it difficult for Canadians previously to discuss the subject of Commonwealth collaboration in a rational way, although British Conservatives, by constantly pressing the Labour government to prove its Commonwealth loyalty, forced ministers to use language that affected Canadian sensibilities. King remained cautious, of course, and suspicious. When the question of Commonwealth defence was raised at a prime ministers' conference in the autumn of 1946 he acted suitably shocked. He might well have recognized that the Australians and New Zealanders had good reason to want to talk about Singapore and all that even if he did not. Instead, he acted as he often did, like a teetotaller at a party into which alcohol has been introduced.[30]

CONSULTATION

There was much talk of conferences in 1945-6. The opposition Conservatives and much of the press in Britain badgered the Labour government to have an imperial conference in full panoply to show the world that the empire was a great power, but it was hard to arrange such a grand affair. King naturally did not like this sort of thing, and he was busy. His professional advisers were asking whether the value of the Commonwealth association was not better assured by the almost continuous series of functional conferences which accomplished the work with less fuss and better timing.

Although Clement Attlee, the new prime minister, and Lord Addison, the secretary of state for dominion affairs, could not entirely shut their ears to the internal pressures in Britain, their thinking on the whole was sympathetic to the Canadian conception. When the Council of Foreign Ministers of the great powers met in the autumn of 1945 to consider the peace settlements[31] the new Labour government sent out a discreetly-worded invitation to Commonwealth capitals for those who might want to send ministers or others to be on hand for discussions with the British who would be taking part in the council. King did not wish to come, but he sent a gracious response. Canadian participation was through the High Commissioner's office, although Vincent Massey was on home leave in Canada. There was some suspicion in Ottawa that this was an effort by the new government to put Britain in the position of speaking for the empire. In fact, it was an effort by Attlee and Bevin to organize some kind of input from the importunate dominions to the peace settlement with Germany in spite of the arbitrary attitude of the other great powers. As one Dominions Office staff member told Canada House: 'This is not the Halifax plan for a single voice. The members of the new government are anxious to meet representatives of other Commonwealth Governments and inform themselves of the general trend of their views on international policy.'[32]

External Affairs was increasingly realizing that, whether they liked it or not, the big decisions were being made among the great powers and the best channel of information as to what was going on at those levels, and also of providing some outlet for Canadian views, was the British bureaucracy, which shared its confidences with the Canadians and Australians in a much more familial way than was conceivable at that time from Washington. If the bogey of a single voice could be laid, then the advantages of the Commonwealth association could be exploited. As Canada House saw the Attlee proposal: 'It could be argued that they are seeking a guarantee of Canadian and Australian support for their policy in the Balkans and elsewhere, and Canada would naturally be reticent about signing any blank cheques of this kind. I feel reasonably convinced that the Labour Ministers really do want something else. Just as they are always anxious to know the views of the French and the Americans before they act, they wish to make sure that they do not make irrevocable decisions without being assured that their policies are generally acceptable to the other Commonwealth countries.'[33] That would seem obvious enough, but the obvious was not always evident to those in Ottawa whose minds had been overstimulated on the subject of Commonwealth relations.

The state of transition was reflected in 'the meeting of Prime Ministers and other Ministers of the British Commonwealth' which took place in London between 23 April and 23 May 1946. There were nineteen meetings divided into three series. Different sets of prime ministers attended each, depending on the exigencies of their timetables and also on the subjects they were prepared to discuss. The Canadian prime minister, needless to say, would not open his ears to talk of Commonwealth defence, but the Australians and New Zealanders wanted to talk about it and were given the chance trilaterally. It was all very functionalist in a way designed to appeal to Canadians. What was more, the agenda concentrated on world issues, everything from Egypt and the Italian colonies to Palestine and the disposal of the Polish armed forces. This was consultation, not navel-gazing.

Only a short time at the final meeting was actually devoted to the subject of consultation and co-operation. 'The reason,' according to Canada House's report of the meetings, 'was the remarkable degree of agreement among the representatives of the Commonwealth.' The communiqué made clear that members considered the flexible methods being practised preferable to any centralized machinery, which might even hamper effective co-operation. The report added: 'It should be emphasized that this expression of opinion did not represent simply the triumph of the Canadian point of view against opposition. The United Kingdom and other Commonwealth representatives made their satisfaction with the present system emphatically evident. Field Marshal Smuts expressed the hope that something might be done in order to inform the public as to the efficiency of present methods in order to forestall the agitation which is constantly taking place for new machinery. Mr. Attlee and Lord Addison expressed their entire lack of sympathy with those who were constantly wishing to reorganize the Commonwealth.' It was further noted that, in spite of the small but vocal group campaigning for centralization, the Conservative party as such was not going to campaign for new machinery. 'Mr. Eden accepted Mr. Attlee's definition of the principles of consultation. Whatever some of his backbenchers might say, he and Lord Cranborne ... can be counted on to prevent this matter from becoming a Party issue.'

Among the practitioners if not among the editors the idea was disappearing that Commonwealth meetings were intended solely to determine the nature of the Commonwealth. In the discussion of so many different topics the idea of a united front or a single voice vanished not so much because of constitutional arguments against it as because it was irrelevant. It would have died sooner if it had not been for the editors of the *Sunday Times* and a few other papers obsessed with their imperial design. They were all the more difficult to combat because they did not represent merely an old-fashioned view of a British-dominated empire. Many of them were the contemporary spokesmen of the Balfourian Commonwealth in which unanimity would be spontaneous rather than imposed. They saw themselves as advocates of the rights of the dominions to a voice and the end of domination from London. Canada House had to remind Ottawa that these eminent journals which had been looked upon for so long as representing semi-official opinion were no longer on the inside. The only voice of Labour, the *Daily Herald*, was not interested in this campaign.[34]

IMPERIAL DEFENCE[35]

The idea of imperial defence was more persistent than the idea of a common voice. The Australians and New Zealanders wanted defence co-operation and planning for reasons of basic national interest as they saw it. Canadian governments had long rejected the idea of an imperial defence system except in the sense that by tending to the security of their own vast region they were contributing to the defence of the empire as a whole. They repeated that argument now, but they also stressed the importance of the American factor, not only for Canadian defence but also because of the significance of the United States in any concept of the far-flung empire as defendable. Ottawa was still clinging to the triangle and not anxious to opt solely for a continental defence system. Canadian officials were busy at this time resisting arguments from the military in Washington[36] even though defence of North America made more strategic sense than defence of the thin red empire. They made clear to the British that the establishment of the Permanent Joint Board on Defence with the United States was basic, that they wanted to make it compatible with the Commonwealth association, but, without saying so too bluntly, it was the former which would have to have the priority if necessary. (Later Ottawa was to make even clearer that it was the NATO defence association that had first priority and that Canada could make no greater contribution to imperial defence than to put its efforts into the maintenance of the North Atlantic life line.) Above all, Canadians insisted that security for the scattered British lands would depend on the success of the plan for collective security within the United Nations.

Nevertheless, Labour governments in London, Canberra, and Wellington were stuck with far-flung responsibilities that could not be immediately sloughed off. Attlee's government had the foresight to see the ultimate answer to the impracticality of 'imperial defence' when India and Pakistan were created as independent nations, but in the meantime the garrisons had to be maintained. Whatever the prejudices in Ottawa against the empire, Canadians, and Americans likewise, were concerned not just over the dangers of communism but of anarchy and for the time being at least a precipitate breakdown of the imperial structures in Asia was not to be regarded with equanimity. In the circumstances, however, the idea of a self-contained imperial defence structure was absurd. The British chiefs-of-staff paper prepared for the 1946 conference did try to see the empire as a unit, even recommending the dispersal of industries and manpower from the United Kingdom to the dominions for this purpose. The latter was not an idea which appealed to the Labour government, but Attlee put the Commonwealth representatives on the spot by producing statistics illustrating Britain's near bankruptcy and the appalling burden of maintaining the minimum number of forces required to maintain obligations in Europe and other continents. Attlee foresaw total annual military expenditures of over a billion dollars, compulsory military service for two years, and a drain on the finance and manpower of the country which would seriously affect its ability to rehabilitate its economy and overseas trade. That was an argument which affected Canadians. The Labour government was too sensitive to suggest that other countries of the Commonwealth should contribute to a common pool, but expressed the hope that the other countries might accept defined regional obligations which would reduce to some extent those of the United Kingdom.[37]

Such a formula would be acceptable to Canada only if its regional responsibilities were defined on its own terms and not as part of an imperial strategy. They were not inclined to stretch this even to include the West Indies, fearful that it would involve them in intervention in the internal affairs of the islands for which they had not, and did not want to have, any responsibility. In every memorandum and statement of the time the Canadian government and its advisers insisted that they regarded the security of the United Kingdom as vital to the security of Canada. However, a combination of old prejudices and a regard for strategic realities made them exceedingly leery of any commitments to defend other parts of the dependent empire. That is why they were particularly cautious about involvement in any 'Commonwealth' responsibilities in the Far East or the Middle East. The British chiefs were not unnaturally thinking of the problems faced early in the war when the Commonwealth had had to stand alone and unprepared. Canadians were aware of that dreadful lesson as well, but they assumed that once the United States had cast off isolation there would not be a situation like that of 1940 in the future. The obsessive suspicion in Ottawa (in government rather than military circles and by the prime minister more than his colleagues) of anything that looked remotely like an imperial chiefs-of-staff prevented Canada for the time being from looking closely at even the kind of arrangements for liaison officers in London which the Labour government was putting out, not as the nexus of an imperial body but as a sop to the heady empire-builders in the British forces and in the opposition. There were proposals affecting other parts of the Commonwealth discussed in the sessions which King did not attend. Canada House pointed out that although they might not be acceptable to the Canadian government as they stood, they were different from those made in the past. 'In the first place they recognised the fact that no centralised Imperial body for the direction of Commonwealth defence is practicable, and that any arrangements must make it possible for members of the Commonwealth to conclude their own arrangements with foreign countries – in particular with the United States. It is specifically recognized that in any future war the Commonwealth would have to rely on the active assistance of the United States, and that any Commonwealth defence system must therefore include machinery for co-operation with the United States.'[38]

Although a sentimental attachment to the imperial fraternity lingered in the defence forces not only of Britain but of Canada as well, and even India or later Nigeria, the British military in a few years, when NATO was being created and the Korean War fought, moved closer to the Canadian idea of priorities. It may be symbolic that one way in which the common military traditions of Commonwealth forces paid off was in the collaboration which was possible among them as a Commonwealth Division in the UN force in Korea and in peacekeeping operations in Indochina, the Congo, and elsewhere. It was, in a sense, the fulfilment of the Canadian idea by which Commonwealth defence would be sublimated in the North Atlantic or UN security systems. In defending the Canadian contribution to imperial security it was pointed out that the North Atlantic shipping lanes were a great deal more crucial than the Suez Canal. Canada's record of good advice on Commonwealth defence had not been noteworthy, but the British might have avoided some of the miscalculations of the next decade if they had given some of the Canadian views of this period more patient consideration.

COMMERCIAL POLICY

Discussion of commercial policy took a surprisingly small amount of time at these Commonwealth meetings. The Beaverbrook press and other Tory organs, whose calculated distortion of the purposes of the 1946 conference was a subject of some vigorous complaint by Canadian officials, sought to give the impression that the Commonwealth ministers were coming together to strengthen their devotion to the principles of imperial preference. This was another subject Canada did not wish to discuss in this context. The United Kingdom government shared the Canadian view that questions of imperial preference were at that point proper subjects of discussion only among experts – a view that was not entirely shared by the other prime ministers and in particular by Nash of New Zealand. The Canadian experts were doctrinally dedicated to freeing the channels of world trade. They did not much like imperial preferences, partly because they were imperial and partly because they were obstacles to purer forms of trade. They knew, furthermore, that the Americans were obsessed over imperial preferences and any combined Commonwealth effort to strengthen or defend them might drive the Americans in their own preferential direction. Nevertheless, in the parlous state of Canadian overseas tade there was no disposition to surrender those advantages which the preference system did provide and a canny recognition that this was at least a bargaining point to be maintained. According to the reports of the prime ministers' meetings sent from the acting high commissioner in London, 3 June 1946: 'it was made clear in the discussions that all Commonwealth Governments are agreed that Imperial Preferences might have to be reduced or removed in the interests of wider international trade, but that they would be surrendered only in exchange for appropriate tariff concessions on the part of the United States and other countries.' As the same report noted, 'discussion of commercial policy occupied only part of the time at the concluding meeting.'

Despite King's insistence on equality, other members of the Commonwealth might well have argued that their agendas were determined to a large extent by the will and whims of the Canadian prime minister. It was perhaps significant, however, that whereas the British Conservatives had submitted to King's will out of deference to the strength of his voice within the Commonwealth and his power of veto, Attlee and Addison did so to a large extent because they agreed with him. There had been worry that Canada would find itself something of an outsider in view of the ideological fraternity of the Labour régimes in London, Canberra, and Wellington. In foreign policy generally the British Labourites and the Canadian Liberals seemed to have had more in common. Canada House thought King's reasonable style would be appreciated. 'He [Evatt] is probably going to find that he cannot bully the new Government as he could bully the old, in spite of the ideological harmony. He knew he could abuse the old Etonians because their code required them to take it, but Bertie might just make one pass too many at Ernie [Bevin]. The Labour men are more apt to look at this thing on a man to man rather than a mother and daughter basis, and daughter will have to make adjustments as well as mother.'[39]

If King's presentation of the argument for a consultative Commonwealth had not been accompanied by what looked like petty sensitivities Canada might well have been acclaimed sooner, as it deserved to be, as a principal begetter of the new Commonwealth. There would certainly have been no Indian and Pakistani applications for membership on the basis of a common voice. A vestigial Commonwealth of the white members would have lost momentum and become an ineffectual old boys association. The multiracial Commonwealth phase (which will be considered in a subsequent volume) may have been a formula only for a generation, but it was an idea that averted bloody struggles during a precarious period of transition both for the empire and Commonwealth and for Britain. Acclaim for Canada did come later from new members of the Commonwealth and somewhat belatedly by its supporters in what was unofficially known as the Old Commonwealth.[40] The transformed Commonwealth did somewhat unexpectedly provide a counterweight, if not in defence and economics, at least in diplomacy, a sublimation of the 'British connection' into something more relevant to a new world and a new Canada.

6

North America

An understanding of Canada's changed and changing relationship with the United States at the end of the war does not begin in Ottawa. The essential change was not in Canadian foreign policy but in the role of the United States in the world at large. The relations of Britain, Europe, or China with the United States were dramatically altered as well. The international situation limited choice. There was a certain inevitability, as well as broad consensus, about Canadian policy towards the giant neighbour. Relations were on many levels, between governments, between officials, and between people, infinitely more complex than they had ever been before, but there was not here the deliberate effort to institutionalize them that provides the main theme of this study. There is no need here to provide a detailed account of defence and economic policies on which specialists have already published the results of considerable research.[1] It is proposed only to relate these subjects to the theme – Canadian designs for the web of a world at peace – and to look for filaments.

Because this study is concerned with the shaping of international institutions, it must pay some attention to reasons for non-institutionalization. Canada's postwar planners were constructivists by nature. At the drop of a gavel they would conceive a new international organism. Functionalist rather than Utopian they may have been, but these organisms were usually seen as deliberative and administrative bodies with at least some rules of procedure. How does one explain, therefore, why the planners had no concrete structures in mind for the international association which loomed as the most important of all – that with the great continental partner?

The two major bilateral institutions, one old and one new, would, it was taken for granted, remain. The International Joint Commission had been affected very little by the war. It was a consultative body empowered only to make recommendations to two sovereign and equal governments, although it had potential quasi-judicial powers. It was superbly functional but had none of the authority to prescribe, if not impose, collective decisions after which the planners seemed to hanker for the multilateral bodies they were proposing. The Joint Board on Defence, established by a press release at Ogdensburg in 1940, had been called Permanent and it would be retained. It had been useful in planning for common purposes and protecting the interests of the minor partner. Furthermore, as it was based roughly on the same principle as the IJC, it did not challenge Canadian sovereignty. Nevertheless, litle attention, if any, was given at this time to enlarging the scope of these bodies or setting up others in accordance with a pattern which, experience seemed to prove, had been well calculated for co-operative endeavours between unequal powers locked by geography into functional complicity of one kind or another. That Canadians and Americans were bound to get more mixed up together in their various activities was taken for granted. Why then was more thought not given to the creation of structures to cope with the inevitable? A memorandum of the Post-Hostilities Problems Committee referred to the PJBD as 'a practical working model of a regional defence system where weight of counsel is dependent on function rather than on net power.'[2] One would have expected dedicated and inventive functionalists to play with such models.

Explanations are many. Basically there was the endemic nervousness about 'constitutional' links of any kind with a power which, however neighbourly, still trailed an aura of manifest destiny. It was showing awesome muscle, and the future was too unpredictable for confident planning. Furthermore, the Canadian enthusiasm for multilateral creation was to some extent a wish to make continental institutions unnecessary. By entwining North America in multilateral institutions Canada would find greater flexibility, breathing-space, and counterweight. This was rational enough, but there was withal an element of nostalgia for the North Atlantic triangle which had in so many ways seemed ideal for Canada. Canada's almost ideological antipathy in 1945 to regionalism in international institutions reflected worries about the North American region into which it might be cast.[3] In matters of security, for example, Canada was one of those that insisted on the ultimate authority of the UN Security Council so that regional organizations such as the Pan American Union could not be managed by a regional superpower.

However, when it came to specific practices Canada showed no interest in having the world body 'interfere' with Canadian-American relations. If the United States were ever to behave outrageously, an appeal to the Assembly or ECOSOC, the International Court, or the Inter-Governmental Maritime Consultative Organization could presumably be made. An appeal to the Security Council would be a very tricky affair to be considered ad hoc. In the meantime it was best to assume it would never be required. The United States had a veto, but so had Britain and France. There was no question of merging the IJC or the PJBD into universal structures. A century or more of successful co-existence had apparently given Canadians the assurance that they could handle the United States best on their own and perhaps also a belief that there was a superior North American way of doing things that ought not to be upset by the quarrelsome habits of others. The only outsider that had ever been involved in these continental disputes was Britain, and the Canadian legend had it that the other party had always, for reasons of 'power politics,' favoured the major North American power. There was a good deal to be said for encasing United States commerce or civil aviation or even its military operations in broad international regulations, but if it came to an appeal to a United Nations body in a Canada-United States dispute, the smaller power might get the sympathy but Santa Claus would get the vote.

Circumstances required that Canadians get a new perspective on the meaning of North America in their lives. This more powerful and assertive continent had to be fitted into a new assessment of the world at large. It would be too much to expect that the view would be free of contradictions. The situation was volatile, and various patterns had to be envisaged to provide for the turns Washington – or Moscow or London – might make. When Canadian policy must be essentially reactive, it is folly to pretend otherwise. Neat schemes for the dovetailing of regional and global structures were useful to perceive directions, but Canada's position was unique. Ad hoc decisions were forced by events. There was risk in the functionalist approach, but greater risk in the rigidity of adhering to broad schemes. The historian must be careful not to iron out the ambiguities.

It is difficult for later generations, knowing how the United States bestrode the world like a Colossus, to grasp the uncertainties about the States which preoccupied Canadians and others as the war ended. To some extent they were wary in view of their neighbour's swollen power. Perspectives, however, were conditioned by the United States of the thirties, not the sixties, by the experience of war and depression neither of which, it was thought, would have been so ghastly if the United States had not isolated itself. The priority must go, therefore, to enmeshing the superpower that was 'on our side' in international commitments from which it would not want to run away. That the United States would self-righteously try to run the show would not surprise those who had survived two centuries of the

American mission and a war effort which the United States had presumptuously taken over when it had become belatedly involved. There had been considerable practical advantages in having the Americans run the war, however galling it had been, and there were similar practical advantages in letting the only power with sufficient resources assume 'leadership' in the postwar world. For all their hubris and their heresy, they did stand for moral and political values basically the same as those of Canada or Britain, Belgium or Australia, and even of the non-Western powers such as India.

The Americans were, however, brash and impetuous. The Canadian view of a pax Americana was succinctly expressed in 1946 by Mackenzie King to the secretary of state for the dominions who had enquired about Canadian attitudes to the United States maintaining its chains of bases in the Atlantic and the Pacific: 'In short, we regard it as in the interest of Canada and in the general interest of the Commonwealth and the United Nations Organization that the United States should have extensive rights and responsibilities outside her own territories. However, we also are dubious about the timing of some of the requests which they have put forward especially as they may encourage the Soviet government to make undesirable demands.'[4]

In spite of anxieties about the future, it was a time of national self-confidence for Canadians. The war effort had encouraged it. However frustrating the effort had been to gain a voice in allied councils, Canadian officials had done not at all badly in getting the Americans to listen to them. Having somewhat more realistic expectations of influence and independence than a later generation, they were less easily depressed. Those worried about Canada's image were still more concerned about being regarded as a British colony than an American satellite. That there could in the mid-forties have been sincere anxiety about freedom of action vis-à-vis Britain may now seem as absurd as it was in fact. There was, however, enough loose talk about a single-throated empire to provide evidence for those who enjoyed conjuring up imperial spooks. Even among these old-style nationalists, however, there was a growing recognition that the triangle would be hard to restore and that the economic and security relations with the United States of one kind or another that would have to be cultivated would provide a more substantive challenge than the Commonwealth to Canada's maturity.

This chapter is concerned with Canadians' vision of their continent as they emerged from the war. The counter-theme of preparation and adaptation for new challenges begins almost immediately, but that new order will be left for later treatment. In order to comprehend what the war had done to the relationship, a look will be taken first at the wartime association in defence and defence production. Economic relations have been discussed up to a point in chapter 3 in the context of postwar reconstruction. To illustrate the contradictions with which Canada was now faced, this account will be extended to its climax in the Marshall Plan. Finally, a look will be taken at the significance in diplomacy of Canada's having become an ally of the United States, aligned as it had never been before – with both common and cross purposes – in search of a congenial world order.

CONTINENTAL DEFENCE[5]

The concept of 'continental defence' against an actual assault was developed by President Roosevelt when, in the late thirties, he became seriously concerned about a military challenge from Japan.[6] Canada had been tacitly regarded as part of the area to which the Monroe Doctrine applied, but the significance of its frozen wastes in the defence of the United States was not a matter of serious concern. American defence planners had been largely preoccupied with Latin America. Roosevelt's pledge in 1938 that if Canada were attacked the United States would not stand idly by was a calculated step in his vision of continental defence, and Mackenzie King's reply that Canada would not be a base for an attack on the United States fitted neatly into his plan for northern coverage. However calculated it was on the American side, it was a clarification of principle so sensible and so mutually advantageous that it has remained the basic commitment on both sides ever since. Roosevelt was popular in Canada and the menace of the Nazis was looming. Canadians by and large saw Roosevelt's tactics as a guarantee of their security, not an 'imperialist' threat. Caution in any military association with the United States was deeply ingrained, but the 1938 declaration called for none, although some preparatory discussion seemed a logical means to the end. King was shy about talks before September 1939, and then the Americans had to be wary of military discussions with a belligerent.

It was not until both countries, in the summer of 1940, had to face the stark possibility of their being isolated and threatened by a Nazi-dominated Europe that they were ready to face the challenge of military collaboration. The president and the prime minister came together at Ogdensburg that summer to accept what seemed the inescapable principle of co-operation in defence and to set up the Permanent Joint Board on Defence. This was followed in the next year by an agreement at Hyde Park on defence production.

Even before Pearl Harbor the PJBD went to work grimly on a scenario in which North America faced the world alone. The summer of 1940 was a traumatic experience for Canadians. They worried over the implications of this last-ditch strategy while the Battle of Britain was going on. Nevertheless, there was virtually unanimous support for a defence arrangement with the Americans in such circumstances and an acceptance of continental defence as the ultimate necessity. When Roosevelt suggested American air and naval bases in Nova Scotia, King said facilities would be made available on a kind of 'limited free port' basis.[7] The Ogdensburg initiative had been almost entirely Roosevelt's. There is no evidence of pressure from the military whose concern was directed towards Latin America. The American military, in fact, did not want to divert their limited resources to the northern regions. Canadians stoutly resisted proposals by which Canadian forces would be placed under United States command, except in the hypothetical situation of fighting in North America.[8]

Although the word integration was loosely used, wartime defence association was mainly an exercise in co-operation, co-ordination, and trouble-shooting. During the middle years of the war, when the threat not only from the Japanese in the Aleutians but also from the Germans in the northeast preoccupied defence planners in both countries, the PJBD was kept busy planning projects like the Northwest Staging Route, the defence of Newfoundland, and organizing co-operation on many levels. It kept away from issues such as the protection of Greenland and the Free French seizure of St Pierre and Miquelon because these were sensitive political issues between the two countries. The PJBD was organized in two national sections, each with its own chairman and independent administrative machinery.[9] The board was based on roughly the same principles as the IJC (except, of course, that the PJBD assumes a common cause and the IJC assumes perpetual contention) and its role was to make recommendations. It had no executive functions, although in the pressures of wartime the two sections with their close telephonic communications did act informally and unofficially as quasi-executive bodies seeing that programmes were carried out. Towards the end of the war, with the two countries as allies, the board was less active, although it retained its status. The broad plans had been laid, and day-to-day collaboration was the responsibility of the chiefs of staff and the many liaison agencies.

The PJBD and the whole Ogdensburg arrangement were geographically limited and did not constitute what might properly be called an alliance. There was obviously no commitment to be military allies, as Canada was belligerent and the United States intended to remain neutral. The provisions had to do with the defence of the northern part of North America but not even all of the United States. In practice it involved the United States in the defence of Canada, but it did not involve Canada in the whole of United

States strategy. While this might appear as an asymmetry dictated by the larger power, Canadians had no more desire to get mixed up in United States commitments in the Caribbean, for instance, than the Americans had to share their policies. There was no question of the United States having any say in Canada's military operations in Europe except later through the Supreme Allied Command. As the war against the enemies was carried on further and further from the coasts of North America there was an inevitable lowering of the priority for continental projects, and before VE Day liquidation of major operations in Canada was already taking place.

DEFENCE PRODUCTION[10]

Whether the wartime experience of 'integrated' defence production was a unique and limited experience, the beginnings of absorption into the American economic empire, or an interesting straw in the wind, it is the subject of animated debate – and for that reason requires some examination. A.F.W. Plumptre, who watched it from Washington, concluded: 'It has been suggested that there was some far-reaching integration of the whole North American economy for wartime purposes. This was not the case; but there was a real and effective coordination of wartime economic planning and wartime controls in the two countries.'[11]

In 1940-1 Canadians were trying to involve the Americans in support of Canada's war and Roosevelt wanted to be helpful. United States neutrality legislation forbade dealings with a belligerent, but the administration, recognizing the particular effect on Canada because of its close financial ties, bent the rules to accommodate Ottawa. There was some risk entailed, as Michael Little has pointed out: 'It was to the Canadian national advantage to curry favor with the American economic colossus in time of war. Thus, in many respects, the very satisfactory high level American image of Canada was to result, in no small part, from premeditation on the part of the Canadian officials concerned with the United States. However, this practice also entailed a certain danger, in that American satisfaction with an accommodating Canadian Government might well reinforce the American propensity to take for granted their access to and use of Canadian territory and its environs should a strategic threat to North America become palpable.'[12]

The Canadian British payments position vis-à-vis the United States got increasingly desperate, and the Americans were preparing Lend-Lease for the British. Secretary of the Treasury Morgenthau thought it would be neater for Canada to accept this formula.[13] The Canadian government, however, did not want to be obligated by an arrangement like Lend-Lease which would require commitments on postwar commercial policy and the liquidation of Canadian assets[14] in the United States. Canadian officials, therefore, presented to Adolf Berle, United States assistant secretary of state, a proposal looking at the 'possibility of arranging for co-operation between the war-expanded industries of Canada and the United States or for their co-ordination or integration.'[15] Berle saw this as the dawn of 'a new order.'[16] Others in both countries had their eyes more firmly fixed on loading the convoys to Britain in the spring of 1941. In April King went to Hyde Park where the president and he made a declaration agreeing 'as a general principle that in mobilizing resources of this continent each country should provide the other with the defence articles which it is best able to produce, and, above all, produce quickly, and that production programs should be co-ordinated to this end.'[17] It was not so much a calculated step towards economic integration as an arrangement to benefit the Canadian economy without the entanglements of Lend-Lease.

The Hyde Park declaration looked like a functional agreement, but King placed a significance on it that was far from routine. What he saw was more international in implication than Berle's dream of an integrated continent. He told the House of Commons that the declaration was 'a further convincing demonstration that Canada and the United States are indeed laying the enduring foundations of a new world order, an order based on international understanding, on mutual aid, on friendship and good will.'[18] Roosevelt, concerned above all with sustaining the allied cause, understood the significance of helping the Canadian war effort. Cordell Hull was dedicated to postwar liberalization of trade, to the conviction that any removal of barriers to trade was a way of preventing postwar autarky. King saw the agreement in the context of a new world, not just a new continental order, and thereby supported Hull.

Whatever the lurking implications for Canada of this kind of continental enterprise, there was no doubt of the immediate advantage. The Canadian balance-of-payments deficit with the United States, which in 1941 was $162 million, became within one year after Hyde Park a surplus of $136 million. In 1943 the so-called Morgenthau-Ilsley agreement sought to control excessive surpluses on either side. In spite of this and subsequent agreements according to which Canada assumed larger responsibilities for sharing costs under its own Mutual Aid programme, Canada ended the war with a considerable balance in its favour.

Neither Hyde Park nor Ogdensburg was a formal treaty. The Ogdensburg Agreement had set up a continuing institution, the Permanent Joint Board on Defence, but there was no provision for a committee to implement Hyde

Park. What was accomplished was done in a highly pragmatic way. Barriers such as the 'Buy American' Act, tariffs, and export controls were removed not by treaties and legislation but by the extraordinary ingenuity of administrators. Congress and parliament were more docile in wartime. The lack of an institutional structure might suggest that the defence-production sharing experience was shallow, but functional integration can be more constructive or insidious (according to value judgment) than formal intergovernmental institutions which usually guarantee sovereignty and set limits on integration.[19] In this case the implementing committees on a high level petered out or failed to meet whereas subcommittees flourished. The Joint Economic Committees established were in fact two committees, one American and one Canadian, which sometimes met jointly. The Joint Economic Committees gave birth to a Joint Defence (later War) Production Committee in September 1941 which was to report to the president and the prime minister. This body did little more than draw up a Joint Declaration of Principles a few days after Pearl Harbor.[20]

The action was in the subcommittees on tanks and automotive vehicles, artillery, ammunition, and small arms. There developed an old-boy network of effective operators conspiring together to win the war by short-cutting diplomatic procedures and existing legislation. Officials and businessmen who work this way are impatient of sovereignty when there is a common enemy. In Ottawa in particular there was a determination to avoid the usual diplomatic procedures. The testimony of the Canadians involved concerning the very satisfactory treatment of Canadian interests because of the good will shown and the common approach to problems is convincing. Two of them, S.D. Pierce and A.F.W. Plumptre, concluded: 'In short, the United States trusted us, liked us, understood us, had no reason to fear us, and shared with us the common objective of defeating the enemy.'[21] That specific judgment sparked a sceptical professor of a later day to remark: 'This is close to being a classic formulation of the "good neighbourhood" theory of continental relations, but some of it may be true for all that.'[22]

The special circumstances do, of course, have to be borne in mind. R. Warren James, who also had the Washington experience and gives the same testimony about the values of personal contact, cautions:

The virtue of informal understandings can be exaggerated. Casual agreements are not very satisfactory when a crisis develops and the national interest becomes involved. As it was, the path of economic co-operation between the two countries was smoothed because, in general, consumption was increasing in both countries. If it had been necessary to reduce consumption in both countries to austerity levels over a wide range of essential commodities, it is certain that domestic political pressures would have strained even the formal agreements between the two countries. This would almost certainly have meant that almost all intercourse between the two governments would have had to be conducted at the highest levels, ie, there would have been much heavier reliance on diplomatic negotiations.[23]

The arrangement with the United States was seen in the context of the triangular relationship with the United Kingdom. Canada had gained a place on several of the United States-United Kingdom boards.[24] However, in the field of defence production, as distinct from the actual fighting of the war where Canadians were largely 'integrated' with the British, what was evolving was not so much a triangle as a continental 'team,' which the United States naturally dominated, in a bilateral relationship with the British. This was somewhat the reverse of the pattern in atomic questions where Canada was part of a British team.[25] What C.D. Howe was interested in was not the proper form but the best way to see that Canadian interests were advanced in the allied directorate. He was prepared for a Canadian to sit as a British representative in the Combined Development Trust (Atomic) or on an American body for war production if that was the best way to get results. In the official history of the United States War Production Board it is recalled that Canada declined to present its requirements to the United States Board of Economic Warfare because it objected to being considered a foreign country. 'It was willing to become a member of the Requirements Committee, but this was generally objected to by the committee on the ground that, although the Hyde Park Agreement ... made Canada a part of the American economy [sic], it was, in fact, a foreign country and foreign representation on the Requirements Committee was undesirable.'[26] The problem was resolved by utilizing what was called the 'Canadian and Foreign Divisions of the WPB.'

An important implication of the principle of a common effort was common sacrifice. Canadians and Americans would have to submit to roughly comparable controls. The economies were so different, however, and they started off the Hyde Park era at such different stages of involvement in the war that this could be done only on a basis of parallel or comparable national regulation. It was, of course, an important aspect of the period of decontrol at the end of the war. Inevitably an agreement for war production spread into production for civilian purposes. To begin with, United States officials had tended to think the scheme meant that Canada would simply modify its defence production programme in accordance with United States plans and be regulated by United States priorities, exports, and allocation controls. It proved to be much more informal than that. There was simply a generally accepted feeling that the Hyde Park spirit should be maintained, but there was no intergovernmental policy directive. There was no legislation. The Canadians often acquiesced in United States proposals because that was the best way of getting the benefits of collaboration, but, as Danford Middlemiss observes, '... the long-run implications of excessive economic defence co-operation were not lost on Canadian officials and the lofty ideal of integration was accordingly never fully realized, or, for that matter, fully attainable.'[27]

The programme of joint production was undoubtedly justified as a wartime measure. The Canadian operators may or may not have been heedlessly weaving a pattern of permanent continental integration, but the long-range consequences were not the first thing on their minds. They were trying to win a war and see that Canada got the best deals. The programme helped lay the foundations of a vastly more competitive Canadian industrial base, designed more than it otherwise might have been to fit a continental pattern. The declaration was intended to be more than just a negative agreement to remove barriers to trade. The intention was the maximization of the continental product to strengthen the allied cause. To achieve this end there would have to be positive government direction of the two economies. The wartime situation was extraordinary in that both countries had controlled economies and the need and capacity to co-ordinate regulations was much greater than it would be in normal circumstances. It was not possible, however, to develop 'a single war production programme for North America' because the two countries' programmes were planned independently. They were not initiated at the same time and Canada's was designed to meet the needs of the United Kingdom.

Canadian dependence on United States industry was a consequence of the war, not of Hyde Park. Hyde Park was a means of organizing that dependence in the Canadian interest. The promotion of reciprocal trade was a far less demeaning relationship than the acceptance of Lend-Lease or loans. It was, nevertheless, a new chapter in the continental relationship, an experience beyond the earlier experiment in reciprocity. The conclusion of John Kirton is that the appropriate metaphor is 'not one of a silent surrender of sovereignty but a selective suspension of self-reliance for a temporarily limited period.' He adds: 'This is not to deny the original Canadian ambitions to extend the Hyde Park "system" into the post-war period. Yet as the external conditions which had produced the original two-stage agreement began to erode with the decline of the axis powers, and as the benefits of the cooperative endeavour began to accrue disproportionately to the junior partner, the corresponding inter-governmental and societal alterations in the relationship were produced without undue difficulty.' Canada had, as a result of wartime economic co-operation, accumulated the resources to buy its way out of the arrangements which had interfered with its sovereignty: '... the 1941-1944 period appears as a classic example of "integrative immuniza-tion," in which limited amounts of sovereignty are surrendered to attain the capabilities by which it is ultimately to be preserved and enhanced.'[28] Depen-dence, after all, was not one-sided. Canada got good deals at Ogdensburg and Hyde Park because it had what the United States needed. Having mobilized sooner and with less haste, Canada's economy was less over-heated. These advantages, along with King's conviction and his clever diplomacy, got for Canada arrangements which left the country at the end of the war with a surplus. Without that surplus, the forces of continental absorption would surely have been less easily resistible.

STRATEGIC APPRECIATIONS

Before the war ended the strategic position of Canada in the postwar world was considered jointly in the PJBD and the Military Co-operation Committee and somewhat more candidly by the PHP Committee. This latter was an all-Canadian examination and its report entitled 'Post-War Defence Relation-ship with the United States' was approved by the War Committee of the cabinet on 28 February 1945.[29] It was a cool assessment which regarded the maintenance of friendly relations with the United States as being in the Canadian interest, favoured close co-ordination of the defences of Canada with those of the United States, and the continuation of the PJBD as an in-strument of co-ordination – even if it had little to do and was not much more than a symbol. At the same time, the report foresaw that although Canada-United States relations were unlikely to prejudice friendship there was a pos-sibility of the United States being moved to exert undue pressure on Canada because of differences of attitude towards events in other parts of the world.

The Canadian experience during the war confirmed the view of the PHP committee that Canada should take an active part in maintaining defences in Canada as well as in Newfoundland and Labrador to forestall an inclination of the United States to proceed on its own. The war had brought about a new set of defence relationships. Opinion in both countries, they thought, had gone far towards recognizing that the two oceans did not provide full protec-tion from attack and further that the ultimate security of the continent depended on the maintenance of peace in Europe and Asia. Both countries accepted the fact that they must have adequate protection against airborne attack, especially from the north, northeast, and northwest. Canada would continue to be vital to the defence of the United States and, as aviation developed, the northern routes would increasingly become world commercial highways and at the same time potential routes for hostile powers with designs against the United States. Conceivably, also, they could be used by the United States for offensive purposes. The United States, the committee held, might be expected to take an active interest in Canadian defence policy and on occasion express it 'with an absence of the tact and restraint customarily employed by the United Kingdom.' In view of Canada's position astride 'the overland route' between the United States and the USSR, any serious deterioration in their relations would be an embarrassment to Canada. Canada's best hope was in the establishment of a world security organization, but in any event Canada and the United States would have to co-ordinate their defences and such a policy could 'take its place as part of a plan of universal security.' For that purpose the PJBD was a suitable instrument. Canada should not base its defence policy exclusively on collaboration with the United States, but should accept a fair share of responsibility in an international security organization. Finally, it was agreed that the new vulnerability of North America made it compulsory for Canada to accept increased defence responsibilities and maintain larger armed forces than before the war.

As basic strategic principles these proved far-sighted and continued to guide defence policy for some years, even though the plea to maintain larger armed forces was ignored by politicians in Ottawa – as well as in Washington – anxious to demobilize. A point to be noted is that the argument for participation in defence of the continent was established before the Cold War on the grounds that Canada and the continent had become more vulnerable to an extracontinental threat. The planners certainly had in mind the danger of United States-USSR confrontation, but their calculations were based on considerations of more permanent validity than anti-communism. Through the Canada-United States Military Co-operation Committee an effort was made before the war ended to agree on a new set of principles to replace the so-called ABC-22 which had been designed for wartime. Although the cabinet War Committee agreed in February 1944 on certain principles, the pace was relaxed when the war ended and the Americans were told not to press.[30] It was early 1947 before a joint statement on defence co-operation was reached, but that belongs to a later chapter when the prospect had drastically altered.

Canadians were getting after 1940 a new geo-political vision of themselves which altered their perception of North America. Maps were becoming popular which showed the world from a polar projection rather than the familiar prospect according to Mercator. The conviction remained deeply rooted, of course, that Canadians, by travelling straight east, would first encounter the British and the West Europeans and then, if they kept on going, the Russians. The idea that Europe was the place where wars hatched and were fought persisted – and was to be later reinforced by the Europe-based strategy of NATO. Nevertheless, in 1945 Canadians were trying hard to absorb the idea that they had an 'Arctic frontier.' The building of the Alaska highway, joint concern over the Japanese threat from the northwest, the prominence of Edmonton in wartime as the take-off point by air for the Soviet Union, the shock felt in 1940 over the possibility of Greenland and Iceland falling to the Nazis – all had a considerable effect on Canadian ideas of their own sovereignty. Canadians felt exposed and vulnerable as they had not since they gave up worrying about an American invasion. The deductions, however, were not clear-cut. There was an argument for perpetuating the closest links with the United States in Fortress America, but there was also an argument to do everything possible to prevent the Americans and the Russians from staging an aerial war over Canada.

The Arctic frontier posed squarely for Canadians the double edge of defence policy. They had to defend themselves against any hostile outsider and they also had to defend themselves on another plane against their defenders. There were two aspects to the latter concern. They had to put up at least a show of defence themselves lest the Americans seek to do it for them. They also had to keep a wary eye on the sovereignty of their own vast territory. The small band of Canadian arcticians who had pleaded the cause of the north without much success over the years profited considerably by the wartime activities in that area and they now had the powerful argument of security. There was a considerable flurry of interest in the north marked by a number of articles in journals and scholarly quarterlies. The Canadian public became aware that their sovereignty over the Arctic archipelago was by no means universally recognized and that it would have to be assured by a more active occupation or at least surveillance. It was, as an External Affairs memorandum said, 'unchallenged but not unchallengeable.'[31] A lot of Americans had been in the Canadian north during the war and there was an increasing number of reasons for them to return or stay there. Canadian sovereignty was becoming a matter of some political consequence. There was not the acute popular sensitivity that erupted several decades later when the resources of the Arctic, especially oil, became significant. It was muted by the fear of being left alone and defenceless.

The policy of a carefully calculated defence partnership with the Americans in the North, as eventually adopted, was an effort to resolve the contradictions. When after the war the Americans expressed interest in maintaining and developing weather stations in the Arctic for both military and civilian purposes, there was uncertainty in Ottawa. It was recognized that the project would be in the Canadian interest, and there was much to be said for co-operating with the United States, which could contribute money and technical resources. All Canadian departments, including National Defence, were adamant, however, on the need to affirm Canadian sovereignty. National Defence worried about Soviet actions if Canada showed doubts of its own sovereignty vis-à-vis the United States, and External Affairs worried that if the United States was turned down they might seek their ends by actually challenging Canadian sovereignty. Eventually the officials recommended a cautious but affirmative reply to the American request. Cabinet refused to be rushed, arguing that all aspects of North American defence should be considered together.

There was hope in this predicament that the United Nations could be the answer. National Defence wondered why there could not be a regional defence agreement with the United States as provided in the Charter. Similarly, when the Canadian section of the PJBD produced plans for a revision of ABC-22, both Pearson and Heeney objected that it had not been regarded as part of the UN plans for international security.[32] The multilateral framework had priority and whatever bilateral arrangements might be necessary must be fitted into it. To begin with there was some hope that the existence of a UN system of security would obviate the need for bilateral defence with all its problems. In any case it provided for a time an excuse for procrastination.

The question of territorial waters, which also became a major issue a generation later, arose at the end of the war. Whereas in the seventies it was to be Canada that took the initiative in asserting control of waters far out to sea in the name of conservation, it was the United States that did so in the forties. During the war, in accordance with Roosevelt's wishes, talks had been initiated with the Canadians on measures to conserve the fisheries beyond the territorial limits. These were still proceeding when the United States developed at the end of the war a parallel interest in asserting its rights over the continental shelf, which was beginning to have importance as a source of oil. The State Department argued against unilateral action until those other countries most directly concerned had been consulted, and this advice was accepted. Canada and Mexico were recognized as primarily interested, and it was clear that Canada was given a priority over all others. As the

Canadian chargé d'affaires, Merchant Mahoney, explained, Canada was in the middle of an election and a governmental opinion would be hard to get. When no response was forthcoming, the possibility of postponing action until after the Canadian elections was actually considered. It was a classic case of good behaviour by the Americans, making sure that Canadian views were considered before taking action that would obviously affect Canadian interests, but Canada muffed it. The Canadian government did not in fact object to United States policy because it saw advantage for Canada in the principle but the Department of External Affairs thought that, in light of the commitment to drafting new international law through the United Nations, it would have been better to approach the subject multilaterally.[33] One advantage Canada gained was that when the Americans protested in 1970 against the Arctic Waters Pollution Prevention Act which asserted Canadian control over a one-hundred-mile zone, the declaration by President Truman of authority over the continental shelf in 1945 was cited as a precedent for unilateral action.

LIQUIDATION

As the war ended on both fronts Canadians surveyed their experience of continental defence. There was little inclination to abandon the concept or its instrument, the PJBD, but the defence production arrangements, which had been less formal and designed for an emergency, were wound up quickly. The experience of co-operation with the Americans, particularly on the official level, had been reasonably satisfactory, although the American military, preoccupied with their responsibility for winning the war, had often seemed insensitive about sovereignty. In order to remind the visitors of the authority of Ottawa, the government had in 1943 appointed a special commissioner for defence projects in the northwest, resident in Edmonton, and officially at least the Americans had welcomed the step for the better liaison it provided. For both old and new reasons Canadians were determined to liquidate entirely American military establishments on Canadian soil and make unnecessary the presence of any American troops. The scaling down of American garrisons in Canada and Newfoundland began in 1943. In that same year the withdrawal began of the engineer troop construction force on the Alaska highway which at one time had exceeded a strength of ten thousand. Nevertheless, a good many American civilians remained in Canada and there were expressions of Canadian uneasiness over what was glibly referred to as the 'ocupation forces' based in Edmonton. As early as 1 February 1943 the prime minister stated: 'It is not contemplated that the contribution which the United States is thus making to the common defence will give that country any continuing rights in Canada after the conclusion of the war. Indeed, with regard to most of the projects that have been undertaken in this country by the United States, agreements have already been made which make the post-war position completely clear.'[34] The government was careful to avoid any note of antagonism in declaring its policy, and the Americans displayed no strong disposition to resist.

The liquidation was virtually a *fait accompli* before the Pentagon began, at the end of the war, to look at continental defence from a new perspective. They had had other things to worry about in 1944. The American politicians were mollified by the extraordinary experience of an ally offering to pay. According to the American military historian of the period: 'On the U.S. side, no responsible official had envisaged a position of special privilege for the United States in Canada as a result of the wartime operations there, and therefore the offer of unanticipated payment for U.S. expenditures was readily gratefully [sic] accepted.'[35] By late 1944 the Canadian Department of Transport was taking over facililties from the Americans and a year later only a few United States personnel remained. A ceremony at White Horse on 3 April 1946, in the presence of the chairmen of the PJBD, wound up the transfer. Airfields in eastern Canada were released from August 1945 on. The United States was reasonably satisfied with its reimbursement and Canadians for their part had acquired airfields and other facilities at only a fraction of their original cost. On 1 April 1946 the Canadian army took over the care and maintenance of the Canadian section of the Alaska highway. The RCAF assumed charge of all facilities on the Northwest Staging Route as American personnel departed. Although Canada assumed full control, continued collaboration with the United States was, of course, not ruled out.

One important function of the Hyde Park arrangement had been clearly stated from the beginning – to assist the parties through the transition to peace. By 1944 Canadian officials were concerned over the consequences of war production. Canadian industry would still need United States components during conversion and the very acts of decontrol would have to be co-ordinated. Decontrol was, however, not a joint operation but parallel action by each government based on consultation and co-ordinated timing. In May 1945 there was an exchange of notes 'Providing for the Continuation of the Principles of the Hyde Park Declaration into the Post-War Transitional Period with Special Reference to the Problems of Reconversion of Industry.'[36] The United States at this stage was most interested in continuing Canadian co-operation in the war against Japan and in Canada's not restoring the old barriers to trade. Canadian motives were more strictly economic and immediate. However, the exchange of notes certainly indicated that both parties were still thinking of continuing defence production co-operation in peacetime – whatever that would mean.

When the war actually ended, however, there was a reaction against defence production in both countries. The conviction of a common cause was suspended, at least for a few years, and efficiency no longer had the absolute priority over other considerations. The infrastructure could not be dismantled immediately. There were still scarcities, and the controls in each country had to be balanced so that continuing sacrifices were commensurate. Canadians were dependent on the supply of many American materials, and, in particular, on shipping, and they had their own needs for a staged dismantling. A large American war effort in the Pacific, furthermore, would keep the Canadian arms industry rolling during a change-over. But that war ended sooner than expected, and after VJ Day there was a rush from a wartime to a peacetime order. The Materials Coordinating Committee was dissolved in December 1945 and the Joint War Production Committee in January 1946. The wartime officials who had worked so well together went home as soon as they could.

The beautiful thoughts which Mackenzie King and others had had about the removal of continental barriers as an example to the world and the development of common resources for the common good seem to have dissipated as conflicting interests and fears emerged. Among the Canadian politicians anti-militarism was more important than anti-Americanism as a motive for dismantling, but the actual experience at first hand of the American driving force had sobered somewhat the earlier enthusiasm for integration as an abstraction. The government was not going to be rushed into long-range defence commitments of any kind. For the moment Canada had its surplus from wartime defence production exchanges. Without a common enemy, the raison d'être of 'integration' vanished. If there was to be an integrated continental economy in peacetime, it would have to be on the basis of a new philosophy for which neither side was prepared in 1945. The belief in collaboration with the United States in defence, including defence production, was not rejected, and the need to be prepared was upheld. Other things, however, seemed more important.

Mackenzie King had fits of suspicion about American intentions and insisted that there be no military agreements with the Americans with which the British could not be associated as well. He did, of course, exploit the triangle to avoid commitments. Having taken a very negative position on all proposals on Commonwealth defence, he nevertheless pleaded the need for co-operation and consultation with the British to stall proposals from the

PJBD for continental defence.[37] Much of the effort to maintain defence preparedness went into the effort to achieve military standardization on a trilateral basis. When the Americans proposed to the PJBD in June 1945 a number of joint projects, including 'the standardization of equipment and forces,' General McNaughton refused to consider anything that would not provide for British participation. What King wanted was 'standardization of equipment in training and military research between U.S. and the U.K. and Canada.'[38] McNaughton pressed the issue hard. He and his colleagues recognized the inescapable necessity of being able to work with American defence industries, but they did not want to cut themselves off from the traditional link with British industry. The lessons of 1940-1 were not forgotten, when the circumstances of a real war had made it impossible to depend on British supplies and therefore essential to secure sustenance from a source vastly better endowed and closer at hand. After several years of tough negotiating, at which McNaughton was a master, there was achieved on 18 November 1948 an accord on an American-British screw thread. By that time, of course, standardization was being regarded in a wider NATO context and Canada was seeking to encase its defence relationship in the broader alliance to ease the pressures.

TRANSITION

In 1945 Canada and the United States were in a summit period of their alliance relationship, a status attributable not so much to Ogdensburg as to their commitments as 'united nations' fighting a war. However, the relative simplicities of that alliance relationship were on the point of giving way to the historic dilemmas of two unequal powers with many interests in common and many in collision. During the period of transition from hot to cold war the special arrangements of wartime were largely abandoned or fell into desuetude. Both countries, but Canada in particular, reached towards what was regarded as normal. For Canada this meant demobilization and a drastic reduction in the priority given to defence considerations. Although the Ogdensburg and Hyde Park agreements were reaffirmed, political leaders in Ottawa saw them more as a means by which Canadian rights and interests could be preserved in the 'reconversion' than as a base on which important new peacetime structures of economic and defence co-operation should be built.

Canada wanted to reduce the uncomfortable dependence on North America which had been essential during the war and restore as quickly as possible the old balance by which trade with Britain and Europe would correct the imbalance of trade with the United States. There was plenty to export to Britain during the war and after, but Canada had to lend the money for repayment. It was not just the old triangle they wanted to recover. That was still basic, but the counterweight to continental pressures would be sought also in wider markets opened up by a new international trading system. Trade discussions were held with the Americans in Ottawa in the summer of 1945 at which the Canadians argued for a 'multilateral horizontal tariff cut' or at least 'a series of bilateral trade agreements among the leading nations.'[39] The wartime experience may well have encouraged Canadians to greater confidence that they had an industry which was competitive if there were minimal United States restrictions and Canada would use its special neighbourly status to lessen those restrictions. Some people at least were thinking of bilateral arrangements for freer exchange, even if it was only an alternative to fall back on.

One factor which drew the United States and Canada together was a similarity in their predicaments. Both had to help the victims of war get on their feet, and that meant co-ordination not only in UNRRA but also in bilateral aid programmes. A United States-Canada Joint War Aid Committee had been set up to co-ordinate Canadian Mutual Aid and United States Lend-Lease so that countries could not play off one against the other. This wartime measure had been stimulated on the American side by the Chinese making direct appeals to Ottawa without Washington knowing what they were up to.[40] That sort of thing could happen again. The common predicament also produced similar attitudes towards the reduction of trade barriers and in the exploitation of the greatest new resource, atomic energy. The mutual perpectives, however, did not abolish friction, for Canada had many specific interests to protect and could not, therefore, simply join forces under the American banner. It was largely a matter of coincidental rather than common interests. In spite of Canada's relatively healthy financial position, worry about the dislocation of its markets prevented Canadians from acting like an assured economic power. The surplus in trade with the United States disappeared rapidly, and there was no surplus with the United Kingdom to counterbalance it.

As for the Americans during that period, there was some specific concern in the Pentagon. Those who thought about the north wanted to maintain and expand the continental defence system worked out during the war and they wanted Canadian co-operation. The economic advisers in Washington thought about Canada most often as a country which could share some of the obligation for relief. The 'creators' in the State Department took Canada more seriously, some of them because Canadians had proved good fellow workmen and others with an eye to attaching Canada to the American sphere. The Canada-watchers thought that Canadian fears for their British markets would drive them to economic collaboration with the United States. In Washington W.L. Batt, vice-chairman of the War Production Board, said: 'I am authorized to take the position for the State Department that to treat Canada like any other foreign Government would be contrary to our policy. It is their view that the Canadian economy should be treated as nearly as possible like our own in peacetime, as well as in war, based always on mutual reciprocity.'[41] In Congress Canada could always count on a few friends and a few axe-grinders. The prevailing mood was friendly but opposed to special favours for a country which had not been damaged by the war.

Attitudes on the highest level returned to the banality characteristic of the White House before Roosevelt had turned his shrewder and more knowledgeable eye on the north. President Truman's approach is illustrated in his remarks to members of the National Conference of Business Paper Editors, a conference which included some of those good folks and neighbours from that country they just don't think of as foreign. The relationship was benign, President Truman said.

It is one that has prevailed for more than a hundred years, ever since old Daniel Webster and Lord Ashburton had a meeting ... to discuss the situation of the boundary between the United States and Canada from Lake Superior west. And old Lord Ashburton and old Dan came to the conclusion that that part of the country wasn't worth anything anyway – and this was after they had a few good cocktails – and they took a ruler and ran it down from the middle of Lake Superior and said you take this and we will take this. And it turned out to be a very satisfactory settlement ever since.

It is not necessary for either one of our neighbors to be in the least bit nervous about what we may want to do to them. They are most likely to think what can we do *for* them. And that is the way we want them to feel.[42]

When the president used words written for him by the wiser boys in the State Department he was more interesting. In a letter to the president of the Senate concerning the St Lawrence Seaway he said: 'our security depends also upon a vigorous and prosperous Canada, an ally in both world wars.'[43] It was fortunate for Canada during this period that it had a few staunch friends in the State Department who felt considerable good will, reinforced by serious calculation. These were the internationalists in the State Department who wanted Canada as an ally in creating international institutions and in particular supporting liberal trade, who also wanted a willing Canada as a partner in continental defence, and who argued bluntly in Washington that the United States had enough collapsed economies in Europe to rehabilitate without having another one to the north. They appreciated the way in which Canada was helping to keep the British economy from collapse. They could hardly help being attracted by the idea of a continental economy, which one of them said had been 'an objective of United States foreign policy since the founding of the Republic.'[44]

To call such people covert annexationists would be to make their aims too specific. They were understandably happy to see Canada moving into their sphere, but their interest in restoring Britain kept them from grosser forms of seduction. They were internationalists to the world at large in that blissful dawn, and their attitude towards Canada was of a piece with their conviction on the need to lower barriers everywhere, to combat 'narrow nationalism,' and limit sovereignty. They were battling the protectionism of their own government and needed Canada as a good example. It is not surprising some friends in Washington assumed that what Canadians wanted was a continental economy which they could penetrate. Their own disposition to Canada being so benevolent, it was hard for them – or their president – to understand why Canadians might be 'the least bit nervous' about any arrangement that was reciprocal and presumed therefore to be fair.

Canadians also opposed protectionism and talked the same lofty language about taming nationalism and sovereignty. It was their hope, if less and less their expectation after 1945, that freeing the channels of trade would work miracles. Those who speculated – usually off the record – about free trade or other special relations with the United States did not see them as exclusive and continental. As Norman Robertson put it in December 1943: 'a comprehensive and thoroughgoing trade agreement with the United States ... could be the first major instalment of the multilateral programme which nearly everyone recognizes as the desirable goal.'[45] In economics, as well as in security and diplomacy, multilateralism was seen as a counterweight to bilateralism. The bilateral relationship with the United States was inescapable on many levels. If something had to be done about it, however, whether in economics or defence, it could be regarded either as part of the larger edifice or as a regional step towards a global goal.

These hopes and fears and tentative designs were put to a severe test during the difficult days of 1947 and early 1948, when Canada's financial position was sorely strained. Canadian officials pressed the Americans to consider their plight along with that of the Europeans because Canada's crisis could be attributed largely to its greater speed in rushing to the help of the Europeans. American officials did not disregard this argument, as they were anxious to encourage further Canadian assistance to European recovery. Congress was being reluctant about the Marshall Plan and it was essential it be convinced that Canadians were playing their part.[46] Before the passage of the so-called European Recovery Programme, Canadian officials were desperately trying to get some assurances of help from American counterparts in order to justify carrying on just a little longer their help to the British. Cripps and Robertson favoured a joint approach to Washington about allowing purchases from Canada under the plan, but Wrong and Pearson advised against it. From the officials Wrong could get only pessimistic responses about an offshore provision.

Nevertheless, within a month of the passing of the Foreign Assistance Act came the first authorization by the Americans for payment from ERP funds for United Kingdom purchases in Canada. In a short time it was revealed, at least in the opinion of the Canadian ambassador in Washington, that provisions for Canada were 'as generous ... as I think we could possibly hope for.'[47] The American officials had proved most co-operative but they had to keep quiet about their intentions. The Canadian ambassador advised Ottawa strongly against any tendency to open gloating or undue satisfaction in Ottawa about the provisions. He hoped that the press might be educated 'to look upon the ERP as something other than a large pie from which we may expect our cut.'[48] By 24 June 22 per cent of the ECA authorization had been for Canadian goods. This was a situation which Canada owed to its friends in Washington – a notable success for quiet diplomacy – but it put the latter in a difficult position vis-à-vis Congress. Those Congressional leaders who had been persuaded to support the Marshall Plan in the belief it would provide markets for their own produce would not like these funds being used to purchase foodstuffs from their Canadian rivals.

It looked as if the Canadians were importunately demanding favours from the Americans. However, the Canadian way of looking at it was different. As the minister of finance put it: 'All we ask and expect, is that Canada be used as a normal source of supply for European trade under ERP, where and to the extent that we can supply on competitive terms or better.'[49] For this and other reasons the Canadian balance of payments began to improve in 1948. That very improvement, however, undermined Canada's stance on European recovery and led to embarrassing proposals from Washington. In February 1949 Wrong warned that Congress was attacking large ECA purchases of wheat. Mid-western senators were asking why $55 million had been authorized in January for the purchase of Canadian wheat. On 12 February St Laurent in Washington told Truman that if Canada's wheat exports overseas were seriously threatened, Canada's whole foreign economic policy would have to be changed. This would mean a new form of economic rivalry between Canada and the United States that would have wide ramifications and serious results in the political as well as the economic field. The president, needless to say, was quite unaware of Canada's problem.[50]

The story of Canada's association or non-association with the Marshall Plan is interesting in that it initiated a new series of problems arising out of changed transatlantic relations. The fact that the Europeans were alike in their helplessness and the North Americans were alike in their unique capacity to help forced a functional alignment of the Europeans on the one hand and the North Americans on the other in the economic as in the defence sphere. In the face of this implied 'continentalism' on both sides of the Atlantic, Canada would have to be wary. The concept Canada preferred, that of community, was described by Douglas LePan in a perceptive memorandum of 25 September 1947: 'Canadian cooperation in the Marshall Plan would tend to show that the western world is not to be pictured as a single giant towering above a cluster of mendicant clients, each holding out a begging bowl, but rather as a group of freely associated states, differing widely to be sure in their resources and needs, but also held together by a great number of ligaments both of interest and of sentiment.'[51] That was very much like James Reston's argument in the *New York Times* that Canada's presence in NATO turned the whole affair from an aid to Europe scheme into an Atlantic community.[52] The problem for Canadians was threefold. They did not want to be drawn into a junior partner relationship in the North American responsibility for relief. They were concerned over the tendency on the part of the Europeans to form their own self-help group. Furthermore, in the critical balance-of-payments position of 1947, they looked more like the mendicant client than the generous giant.

The challenge from the Americans came in the form of pressure on Canadians to associate themselves formally with the Marshall Plan. This was an embarrassment because in the earlier stages Canadians had shown some anxiety to be involved in the planning, fearing that if they were not, they would lose the chance to have Canadian produce included and be excluded by the Americans from getting their foot in European markets. The Americans took a generous view of the use of funds by the Europeans to buy Canadian goods, but they were not prepared to let Canadians off the hook. Without being too formally specific, Washington gave the Canadian ambassador a strong impression that the price for this concession was the kind of participation in the ECA programme that would tie Canadians to fixed obligations to European recovery. Wrong reported that he had headed off a draft letter he had seen which envisaged Canada joining in a 'permanent concurring partnership' in the ERP which read like 'a gratuitous letter from our neighbours on what was important to Canada.' His tack was to argue for discussion of ERP 'problems of mutual concern.' He described the Canadian dilemma as 'whether we would get more burned by going in than frozen by staying out.'[53] The objections were considerably more than just a dislike of being forced to give more money. There was an instinctive reaction against this kind of continentalism. ERP was not a joint programme, and it would be dependent for its policies and for its very continuance on internal American problems. Canada would have to adjust its timing to its own balance of payments. Finance officials were alarmed at any further commitments to European recovery until the improvements in the Canadian position could be more securely assessed.

Sydney Pierce, who had been sent to Paris to deal with Canadian interests vis-à-vis the ERP, was coping with a similar proposal for 'joint operation.' He told the head of the American ECA office that he saw serious difficulties in a formal partnership, such as the fact that Congress had already dictated the terms of the programme. To Ottawa he reported another canny consideration: 'We might not want to be considered by ERP countries as in the same kennel with the ECA watchdogs throughout Europe, or to change the metaphor, "the horse could do with more hay but there are enough hands on the whip."' He thought the rest of the world would regard the arrangement not as a partnership, but 'at the very least as a subordination of Canadian external interests in the United States, if not as a loss of our independent status.' His preference was for a joint committee along the lines of those that had been worked out during the war for the Mutual Aid and Lend-Lease operations. Such a committee would be formal enough to suit the United States and loose enough to reassure Canadians.[54] Ottawa was in entire agreement with these views.

For Americans it is difficult to understand why Canadians are hesitant to take their fair part in continental institutions or programmes, whereas Canadians recognize these are bound to be American designed and dominated, whatever the good intentions of the Americans to consider the needs of the northern half. The offer to share direction with a great power can be alluring. It is interesting to speculate on the consequences if such a precedent had been established while a whole new set of transatlantic relationships was being created. On functional grounds the arrangement could have been described as unique, but a pattern set at a formative stage is hard to abandon. The image of Canada held by others would have been fixed. Indeed, the whole experiment could well have proved such a disastrous error for Canada as to discourage any form of further collaboration with the United States. The Americans, however, backed away from the proposal for formal association. Instead there was constant consultation and constant argument – all very healthy and normal – among the American and Canadian officials about the amount both of Canadian assistance and of the offshore purchases in Canada. It perhaps became obvious during these discussions that the economic and political situations in the two countries differed sufficiently to make single policies unworkable, although they did not rule out co-ordination, co-operation, or jostling.

In their attitude towards intra-European co-operation Canadians displayed the ambivalence which was to characterize their attitude for the next two decades. As good internationalists they could not in principle object to efforts by countries to co-operate with each other and remove barriers. On the other hand, what to participants seems like the removal of barriers looks to outsiders like the creation of an economic bloc, and to that Canada was opposed in principle. The Americans were inconsistent. Whereas they took hysterical objection to a vestigial system of Commonwealth preferences, they were actively encouraging European co-operation in the belief that this was the formula to take the load off the rich uncle. During the gloomiest days of early 1948 Sir Stafford Cripps told the Canadian high commissioner that he was thinking more and more of 'developing the resources of Western Europe plus Africa on a hemispheric basis' as a long-term way to reduce dependence on the Americans. Robertson cautioned him about drying up the springs of American generosity which fed the Marshall Plan and gave also a 'gentle warning' that too vigorous a hemispheric policy would probably force Canadians 'into a parallel hemispheric grouping with the United States and might destroy the special trading relations which had existed for so long between the United Kingdom and ourselves.'[55] In the autumn of 1947 the possibility of a European customs union was examined by states in the Marshall Plan. Robertson was told by Ottawa: 'We would not oppose any plan which would result in a closer integration of the economies of the European countries and which would assist in their recovery,' but Canada could not overlook the United Kingdom as a valuable market for many Canadian agricultural products and exports would be seriously affected 'if the participation of that country in a European Customs Union meant that preferential treatment for Canadian products would disappear or that European products would receive better treatment.'[56]

There were, however, voices pointing out that basing the hope of a balanced international trade position on the recovery of Europe could prove an illusion and that Canada might have no alternative in those circumstances to looking for prosperity in a greatly increased continental market. There was reluctance among officials to accept this conclusion lest it jeopardize their hopes for Canada as a political entity on the world scene. Nevertheless, facts, it was thought, had to be faced. During the worst of the balance-of-payments crisis of 1947 some of the more suspicious officials in Ottawa thought the British were seeking to lure Canada into a Commonwealth association. Whereas the sterling bloc was a reality, however troubled, the idea of a revived Commonwealth economic bloc including Canada could not be given serious consideration – although it sometimes appeared to Western Canadian producers and politicians as an answer. Bevin and other British Labour leaders, usually sensible on Commonwealth affairs, were inclined in certain situations to use old-fashioned rhetoric. They had a habit of summoning meetings of Commonwealth ministers when they were in trouble, even though the solution was not to be found in Commonwealth action. Canadians were irked by the casual way in which the debtor would summon the creditor to meet in London. They were worried also because of sensitivity in Washington about the Commonwealth 'ganging up' on them. When Bevin made one loose reference in a speech to the Trades Union Congress to a customs and defence union of the empire, Pearson reported 'personally' from Ottawa that 'all the old skeletons are rattling furiously in the cupboard.' Cabinet discussed the matter, and Canada House was informed that: 'If the United Kingdom authorities think ... that our financial difficulties with the United States might make us more receptive to the Commonwealth scheme, they are making a great mistake, and the sooner they can be disabused of this idea the better.'[57] Canada House constantly sought to get the Ottawans to take a more relaxed view of these atavistic flights of fancy by the British, but Mackenzie King enjoyed horrifying himself with the old familiar spectre.

That Canada should make every effort to avoid a policy of discrimination directed at the United States was the strong advice in 1947 of Dana Wilgress, Canada's principal negotiator in international trade talks, in the context of the negotiations in Geneva for the International Trade Organization, and of Norman Robertson, the high commissioner in London. Robertson did not want to see the Canadian economy pushed 'into an impoverished sterling area held together by policies of discrimination against United States exports and not much more,' and admitted that 'if he had to make a choice' he would favour the other 'polar extreme' of closer continental integration with the United States.[58] In September 1948 the undersecretary, Lester Pearson, commented on a memo of the deputy minister of finance concerning the bleak prospects for Canadian exports to the United Kingdom: '... we should consider more seriously the possibility of some pretty far reaching agreement with our neighbours to the south which might become not a matter of choice but of dire necessity.'[59] He and his colleagues, however, continued their efforts to forestall this 'dire necessity.'

The wonder is that relations among the British, Canadians, and Americans did not suffer even greater damage in the reconstruction period. It was humiliating for the British, after their great contribution to victory, to have to act as importunate beggar to a former colony. They were in no position to be generous as a mother country should be. Canadians had their own serious problems and at times it was almost a question of two bankrupts trying to make deals with each other. The inability of British officials to adjust to a new relationship with the senior dominion is illustrated in an incident when Bryce and Rasminsky went to London, at a time when the British were drawing heavily on the postwar loan and Canada was losing its United States dollar reserve alarmingly. The Canadians gave a mild but closely reasoned analysis of the reasons why, though they were very sympathetic to British difficulties, they found it necessary to ask that Britain draw more moderately on the Canadian credit. The senior British Treasury official said they would think over what had been said 'and see whether there is some way that we can help you out.' To which the courteous Rasminsky replied, 'It seems to me that there is a very serious confusion here as to who is helping whom.'[60]

It was fortunate that Canadian relations were with a Labour government, even though Canadian cabinet ministers, more so than civil servants, were sceptical about socialism. Attlee was sensitive about Commonwealth relations, and although Bevin occasionally offended by assuming to be a spokesman of the Commonwealth, his gaffes appeared not as calculated misdemeanors but the oversimplifications of a man whose speech was rarely precise. The credit belongs most of all, however, to a group of dedicated civil servants in London and Ottawa, and in particular to Norman Robertson, whose capacity for understanding, interpretation, and the spinning of apt formulas saved the day on many occasions. He was trusted implicitly in Ottawa as a defender of Canadian interests and looked upon by the British as the most sympathetic of friends. The chancellor of the exchequer, Sir Stafford Cripps, although he had to bargain hard, understood the Canadian dilemma. In a memorandum to C.D. Howe in the spring of 1949 he expressed the hope that the Canadian government would do all it could '... to prevent their public opinion from forming an impression that what is in reality an inescapable choice for the non-dollar world and the United Kingdom in particular arises only because of doctrinaire attitudes, unwillingness to understand the Canadian point of view, or plain ingratitude for what Canada has done in the past.'[61] Canada House also understood. When suspicion was voiced in Ottawa that the United Kingdom was exaggerating the crisis to justify its measures, Canada House replied that 'an animal caught in a trap has very little room for tactics or manoeuvre.'[62] The intimacies of the wartime association and the common cause were paying off.

The same was true in relations between Canadians and Americans. In Washington also Canada had a superb representative, Hume Wrong, who knew how to make himself listened to even by the busiest of civil servants and could lead Canadian officials to the centres of power. Dana Wilgress, both as a leading architect of GATT in Geneva and Havana and as high commissioner in London after Robertson, acquired wide international respect for his tireless efforts to bring and keep the United States and United Kingdom together. On the American side there were men like Dean Acheson and Jack Hickerson whose vision of the postwar world that Americans and Canadians were jointly involved in creating overcame the petulances of the moment – and Dean Acheson could be exceedingly petulant about Canada, his parents having come from Toronto. They showed courage in getting relief for Canada in its exchange problems by the offshore provisions of the Marshall Plan in the face of Congressional ill-will and thereby saved Canada from desperate measures. Paul Hoffman, the head of ECA, was especially aware of Canada's deserts because of its earlier contributions to European recovery. The only desperate measures available to Canada at that time would have been to ask for special favours of Congress, thereby incurring obligations, either specific or moral. It would surely have been apparent to shrewd men in the State Department that they were, in what they did, serving to strengthen Canada's ability to stand on its own feet and that this made for a healthier relationship than encouraging Canadian dependence. It was experiences of this kind which encouraged Canadian officials and politicians to see the value of 'quiet diplomacy' – and possibly to place too much confidence in it as a plan for all seasons.

In these particular issues the Canadian stake was sufficiently significant and intermediate to make the linchpin role inescapable – and quite unselfconscious. This was particularly notable during tripartite talks in London in July 1949. Canada had assisted in engineering the meeting, partly to steer the British away from seeking to take a Commonwealth stance. It suited the postwar Canadian personality, furthermore, to keep this kind of élite company. The American ambassador told the Canadian high commissioner before the meeting he welcomed Canada's participation because they could say things to the British the Americans could not. Wilgress could agree to that, but he and his team dined the evening before the meeting with the senior British officials to consider 'points which the Canadians might consider making to the United States.'[63]

DIPLOMACY

In diplomacy, as in defence, we are dealing with an entirely new historic phase in North America. Economic issues differed in scale from anything previous, but there was continuity in the themes. Before the war Canadian diplomacy had been concerned to a considerable extent with the United States, but the subjects of preoccupation were rum-runners, tariffs, or pollution by the Trail Smelter. Exchanges on world issues were minimal, although there were a few enquiries over the state of the world and the League, and some consultation on serious issues such as the proposed sanctions against Japan and Italy. The United States was out of the League and Canada was in, but the United States, as a giant economic and naval power, was a good deal more involved in world politics, whether it liked it or not, than was Canada. Until the war began there was little sense of common commitment or the need to work together or even to persuade or dissuade each other. Such attitudes were entirely changed long before the war ended. Relations with the United States acquired an overwhelmingly important international dimension they had not had before. Relations became warmer, more cooperative, busier, and a great deal more difficult. In spite of the prestige attached to the great international issues, however, far more diplomatic man hours would still be consumed on fisheries in the Great Lakes or trucking in bond across southern Ontario.

The war unleashed Canadian diplomacy. It still had an establishment far less than that of the United States, but it was learning how to exploit functionally the limited strength it had. Fencing with the British remained a diversion in the immediate postwar period, but the great challenge was the new and exhilarating game of one-upmanship and team-manship with the world's greatest power, who was also that friendly neighbour, Uncle Sam. The Canadian tone was accommodating but by no means docile. On 13 February 1945, for example, a very abrupt note was sent to say that Canada would accept no further responsibility for financing procurement of relief supplies in the absence of assurances that Canada would not have to pay more than its agreed figure. The United States gave in.[64] It did not, of course, always do so.

It was a time when diplomacy, for good or ill, was highly classified and largely quiet. Being privy to the secrets of American policy in its formative stage, as Canada often was – and frequently from British sources – there was no alternative to quiet diplomacy if one was to have any impact at all. Betraying one's sources dries them up. There were enough successes during a period when Canada, as probably never again, was in the centre of things to warrant confidence in private armtwisting as more effective than public demanding. As the agenda multiplied the simple appeal of prime minister to president, which had worked well up to Hyde Park in 1941, was inadequate and had to be saved for crucial occasions. The development of greater technical virtuosity as the expanded Canadian diplomatic team fanned out even wider at the end of the war was enormously aided by the process of establishing the United Nations. Canadians took to multilateral diplomacy enthusiastically and began to discover the value of combinations in coping with the great power.

What of the role of linchpin, of intermediary between Britain and the United States celebrated so often in the rhetorical flourishes after dinner? Was this vocation strengthened by the wartime experience? First the question has to be asked whether there was ever much substance to this neat formula? In its history Canada had probably been more often a cause of dissension than a bridge between the great Anglophone powers, and they had, according to Canadian tradition, reached accord all too frequently by sacrificing a Canadian interest. Washington and London had been dealing with each other for so many years they did not need a youthful interlocutor. At the same time there were no doubt many times when Canadians, because of their understanding of, and even affection for both parties, had assisted Anglo-American agreement on one or other of the hundreds of issues in which they were all involved. The effort to do so had been stimulated by the long-standing conviction that such agreement was a foremost national interest of Canada. This need was never felt so strongly as during the period between Munich and Pearl Harbor, and Canadian diplomats and statesmen worked hard at it. Mackenzie King took advantage of his association with Roosevelt to this end, although it may have been rather a question of Roosevelt shrewdly using Canada, a belligerent state for whose security American voters were more likely to be concerned than for that of Britain. The mediatory function for Canada was quite valid and still is, provided it is seen as habitual diplomacy rather than as a national vocation.

Such a function may have been appropriate when the British and Americans were more nearly equal. It was not necessarily promoted by the rise to dominance of the United States. There was a clear warning in the extent to which Canadian influence in Washington declined after Pearl Harbor. During the period when Roosevelt was moving his countrymen closer to the allied cause, he had found Canada useful. With the declaration of war, however, there was no longer any need for him to be devious. The United States moved swiftly to take command of the operation and assert its will directly with both Britain and Canada. The previous American interest in fitting Canada into a hemispheric defence system became secondary when the United States itself was spilling out of the hemisphere to win a world war. In a memorandum for the prime minister in December 1941 Norman Robertson noted this change already: 'Canada naturally loomed much larger in the

American scheme of things when the President and both political parties in the United States were thinking primarily in terms of continental and hemispheric defence. Now that the world war is joined on both oceans, the United States is, not unnaturally, inclined to take Canadian concurrence and support entirely for granted.' He feared the loss 'of the preferred position Canada had gradually consolidated through long years of close and friendly collaboration with the President and the Department of State.'[65]

The Americans did move into the driver's seat in the conviction, dating back to the Founding Fathers, that the United States itself was not just a nation but a cause, that although it must work with allies it alone had the moral qualities to lead the flock. King never recovered the influence in Washington he had had at Hyde Park just before Pearl Harbor. Although he could still press with success a particular Canadian case, and Quebec could be an apt meeting ground for the great, he was far from the grand strategy. Canadian officials and ministers did, however, manage to maintain a special position with the State Department and officialdom in general because they were able to continue proving that they could produce good ideas, set examples, and in many ways help the cause. They could be stubborn but, on the whole, they made more headway by being reasonable than unreasonable – a lesson which persisted. As they were well aware, the Americans would hope to use them as they in turn would use the American diplomats. Pearson noted, in discussing his efforts to persuade the Americans to support Canadian representation in UNRRA, 'their confidence that ... when the decision had to be made we would be "good boys" and help them in their difficulties with Moscow and with Latin America.'[66] The Americans did get a good deal of help when the Canadians agreed with them, but otherwise only when Canadians considered the issue so serious as to warrant a priority for solidarity.

Judgments on how successful Canada was in influencing the United States during 'the creation' depend on the judge's view of what was possible. Insofar as the new international order was the shift in the balance of power to the United States, that was an historic event that no one, not even the Americans, could do much to alter. It behooved every country to calculate how to cut its losses and increase its benefits from this new situation. The new order, it needs to be emphasized, was not imposed by the Americans. It was encouraged and to a considerable extent designed by Europeans and Canadians. The American will could be decisive, of course. It could not be forced, but it could be bent. In spite of the variations in power, the designing was essentially collaborative. One could add up a list of Canadian successes in bending the Americans – at San Francisco or even more so at Chicago or

Bretton Woods – and compute percentage results without learning much. Multilateral diplomacy cannot be disentangled and coded. It might be wiser simply to acknowledge that United States policies and the position occupied by the United States in the new world order were different from what they would otherwise have been, and less hegemonial, because they were encased in international structures. To achieve this end the system required a number of diplomatically lively and effective states, of which Canada was certainly one. Confronting the United States single-handedly, except on a sub-paragraph, was not likely to be successful. Confrontation, however, was not the normal policy because Canada and its allies did not want to oppose flatly what has been called 'the new American order.'[67] By and large they liked it.

It is easier to talk of Canada's policy towards the United States than vice versa because there is always an element of sleep-walking in American policy vis-à-vis Canada. Certain people and departments in Washington had ideas of what they wanted, but policy on the higher level was spasmodic and uncoordinated. There were, of course, variations in attitude among Canadian cabinet ministers and officials towards the United States, and one must avoid too categorical definitions of government policy, which was humanly inconsistent. However, there was in Ottawa a good deal more concentration, at the higher and lower levels, on the broader picture, on trends, and on long-range implications of short-range decisions than there was in Washington. It was often contradictory. Like the prime minister, the cabinet could shift from a consensus that the Americans were Canada's best friends (and customers) to fierce resistance to American 'arrogance.' Generalizations from specific occasions or comments – spasmodic outbursts in King's diary, for example – are hazardous.

CONCLUSIONS

Canada is not, as its frustrated citizens would often like to assume, a philosophers' kingdom. It is anchored in time and place. It is and always has been the northern half of North America which the Canadian forefathers, regardless of the doubts of London and Washington, wanted to run as an independent American country, making the best of the circumstances. It is a product of heredity and environment. The central theme of its foreign policy from the beginning has been the juggling in shifting circumstances of the advantages and disadvantages of its location. Policy planners at the end of the war saw plenty of both, and policy was an effort to manipulate the situation as skilfully as possible – with the resources available. It was not a new game, for that is how Canadians had been living for two centuries. The issue was not immaculate independence, but, as it always has been, the best mix of prosperity and independence obtainable, and as free a hand in policy as a middle power could expect. As Warren James noted about the issues which had arisen between Canada and the United States during the war: 'Ever since the emergence of national states, the existence of large and small nations side by side has necessitated some definition of the terms on which they shall co-operate, for co-operation in some degree is unavoidable.'[68]

The Americans had become more powerful and assumed the role of a world power, but their pretensions and extensions also made them more vulnerable, more in need of allies, customers, and suppliers. They were certainly not dependent on Canadian co-operation, but Canada also had become stronger and better endowed to resist or to offer co-operation. Assessing the profit and loss is a treacherous endeavour, and the conclusions are false if they ignore the significance of broadening the common or mutual interests. It is hard to say whether Canada, on balance, became more or less independent in the forties because the meaning of independence changed. Independence was regarded less as an end in itself than it came to be when, partly because of the Vietnam War, some Canadians developed ideological reasons for dissociating Canada from its large neighbour. The Second World War had been a forceful reminder of Canada's dependence on the state of the world at large. Pursuit of the national interest had a priority over mere independence, and independence, in any case, was seen as the right to sit with the major powers and assert the Canadian right to agree as well as to disagree with them.

Although this study is primarily about government policy, the actions of government may have been less decisive than is often assumed. The economies of the United States and Canada were certainly intermeshed during the war and postwar periods. 'Intermeshed' is a deliberately crude way of describing what happened, as 'integrated' is a question-begging term. Government action was directed more to controlling than encouraging the flow. Encouragement was not needed; the Canadian public, coming out of wartime austerity and, having no other place to turn, rushed to the American supermarket, heedless of consequences. The government watched those consequences with some dismay as a surplus turned to an alarming deficit. Eventually they had to threaten stiff export controls, although they were themselves trying to lead the world away from such bad old ways. They were Liberals with a thin majority and could probably not have survived an effort to check this kind of 'continentalism' by draconian methods. They had, moreover, an electorate conditioned to think in terms of an alliance, to identify its interests with those of the United States and Britain and the leadership of the Western powers in the new United Nations.

The electorate were pliant, reasonably nationalist when it came to Canada's rights, but unlikely to endorse a really deviant course for Canada. Standing up to the Yanks on a specific issue was, as always, good politics, but the popular mood of the day was certainly not anti-American. Harold Innis, one of the few Canadians to express concern at that time about the danger of United States 'imperialism,' said that although Canadians had complained often about British interference, 'no questions are asked as to the implications of joint defence schemes with the United States.'[69] Innis disliked Ottawa so much he was never really in touch with what went on there. Concern was loudly expressed in the debate in the House in June 1947 on the legal provisions for American forces in Canada. Even though the government won an easy victory,[70] the debate did reveal that questions were being asked about the implications of joint defence and economic dependence. They were being asked in the House, in External Affairs, and by the prime minister in his diary. Misgivings, however, did not add up to outright opposition.

While Canadians were busily helping to formalize relations among states, there was no inclination to do the same for the continent. The argument about the virtue of surrendering sovereignty to a higher authority was all right so long as the authority was multilateral. There was no escaping, however, the prevalence of the United States. Some committees had to be established and some understandings put in writing. These, however, were not necessarily evidence of a desire to create a continental framework. Usually they indicated the need perceived by Canadians to check the force of 'continentalism' by establishing rules to control it. They were inspired by a will to co-operate in the mutual interest but at the same time to stake out and thereby protect a Canadian interest or assure a Canadian right to be heard. The International Joint Commission had been the classic case of such an intention realized.

The Permanent Joint Board on Defence, set up during the war, may have been in American eyes a means by which Canadian co-operation could be obtained in hemisphere defence. From the Canadian point of view it was based on a realization that there were mutual advantages in the continental defence concept but also pitfalls and that an institution like the PJBD could, as it did, provide Canadians with a chance to state their concerns where they might best be heard. They could not escape the consequences of the United States determination to defend the continent, and it was better to put continental defence on a rational basis when rational thought was still possible.

Such arrangements did not always work out as intended, but a rejection of co-operation would have impaired Canadian sovereignty by default.

Both the Ogdensburg and Hyde Park agreements had proved, on balance, of great advantage to Canada. They secured to begin with the help of the powerful neutral in Canada's war and protected Canada's military and especially economic interests in ways that would not otherwise have been possible. If Roosevelt had not seen them as being in the American interest as well, they would never have been reached. He and, to a great extent, his associates may have had dreams of Canada's place in a continental, hemispheric, or global benevolent imperium which these arguments might serve. Canadians knew how they could take advantage of a common interest without sharing fully the American intention. Mackenzie King, who led Roosevelt into the Hyde Park Agreement, could talk about it aloud in lofty terms, seeming to suggest that it was preliminary to the dawn of a great union, but his diary notes make clear his intention not to be led along that path. His vigilance had been alert since early in the war, particularly in connection with the American operations in the northwest. On 9 May 1946 he warned cabinet that 'the long range policy of the Americans was to absorb Canada. They would seek to get this hemisphere as completely one as possible'[71] – undoubtedly an over-statement of his real concern.

There were certainly short-range advantages in a co-operative stance. The minister of finance told the House of Commons in 1948 that 'Export permits and export controls have never been enforced by the United States against Canada, as they have been against every other country. When hon. members stop to reflect for a moment on some of the essential raw materials we have to obtain from the United States, such as oil, steel and so on, I think they will agree it is important that the United States should continue to treat us in that way. That is something we might well bear in mind.'[72] On the other hand concern has been expressed in later years over a tradition of seeking special concessions in Washington, a habit sometimes dated from Hyde Park, a policy labelled 'exemptionalism' which, as critics see it, served to confirm the idea of Canada as part of a continental economy. An interesting exception that should be noted was atomic energy where the special relationship was denied by the United States for security reasons[73] and Canada stood very successfully on its own feet. There were some advantages in a little ill will on the American side. The response made to the critics is that Canada was not at Hyde Park or on later occasions, as for example when it obtained the right for Marshall Plan funds to be spent in Canada, seeking favours or 'exemptions' but was rather proposing functional arrangements to cover features particular to the Canada-United States situation and therefore to serve

United States as well as Canadian interests. In the case of Hyde Park and the Marshall Plan Canada was, like the United States, a provider, not a recipient of economic assistance, and these were essentially plans to co-ordinate terms for the benefit of all concerned.[74]

The changes in the relationship were more in texture than in form. Attitudes and habits were altered. Most important of all perhaps was a sense of common purpose and responsibility in the world at large. Canadians and Americans were working together more closely than they ever had before. They had done so, for example, in defence production, and although little was left of that but a declaration of intention, the recollection of something that had worked and might work again if necessary remained. Canadian leaders had liked to think of it as part of the pattern of a new free-trading world, but its implications, like that of the auto pact later, were more mercantilist than liberal internationalist. It was not a scheme for all seasons, especially not the postwar season of reciprocity, but it would not be readily forgotten.

Canada was not set by choice on the path of continental integration in 1945. World War II and later the Cold War did give an impetus to the creation of institutions, mostly for defence, but these, according to Professors Holsti and Levy, 'contain few integrative features, and decision making tends to be based on bargaining between national teams of negotiators or just consultation.'[75] The important function was the avoidance, prevention, or resolution of conflict. The Canadian perception was perhaps best expressed in the homely words of Louis St Laurent in his Gray Lecture of 13 January 1947 in which he set out the authorized version of postwar foreign policy. He referred to the United States as 'a state with purposes and ambitions parallel to ours.' As for the relationship: 'Like farmers whose lands have a common concession line, we think of ourselves as settling, from day to day, questions that arise between us, without dignifying the process by the word "policy." ' It was a quite different philosophy from that already being proclaimed in Europe and which took form later in the Treaty of Rome.

7

The Atomic Triad

One of the shrewdest observations on Canadian foreign policy by an outsider was made in Quebec in 1953 by the British historian Denis Brogan: 'What I am more concerned to point out is that the basic Canadian relationship is not either with the United States or with the United Kingdom but with the world of the hydrogen bomb. The very fact that Canada is now one of the treasure houses of the world makes the naïve isolationship of the inter-war years ... impossible. A uranium producing country cannot be neutral.'[1] The Canadian experience as an 'atomic power' during and for a decade after the war, until the term 'atomic power' was lost in the new term 'nuclear power' with a quite different significance, matured Canada as a participant in world politics. Canada was willingly and unwillingly drawn into the most desperately serious aspect of international politics for reasons that continue to be relevant. In the first place it was because Canada possessed the essential resource – in this case, uranium. Secondly, it was because Canada had enormous space and provided sanctuary for experiment in a world at war. Thirdly, Canada had the nucleus of an industrial and technological capacity.

As a partner – of sorts – with the United States and the United Kingdom in the achievement of atomic fission Canada was regarded as one of the three 'atomic powers.' The event which symbolized its initiation into the world of high policy was the meeting in Washington in November 1945 at which Truman, Attlee, and King produced the communiqué that invited all powers to consider an international control system for this devastating new force. Although it was not realized outside a small circle, a major purpose of this gathering in Washington was to consider in utter secrecy what the three countries might do about the revelations of a defector from the Soviet embassy in Ottawa, Igor Gouzenko, concerning Soviet espionage not only in Canada but in the other two countries as well. In more than one way Canada was being drawn into the nasty and brutish world from which it had recoiled in peacetime.

There was a price to be paid for status. Serving as a linchpin between the two great powers was an attractive idea for some Canadian statesmen, but when the stakes were this high they could get caught. Canada was sometimes forced to make choices that one or both of its major partners would not like, or to sit on the fence, which they both resented. For Canada there were conflicts among its strictly national interest, its interest in the Anglo-American-Canadian entente, and its zealous interest in the wider new world of the United Nations. When the larger powers have not only the most to gain, but also the most to lose, and to gamble, the obligation on the lesser power to defer is compelling, and its initiative is severely limited. Because the common interest was in winning a war and maintaining peace, the argument for deference was strong.

Nevertheless, for lesser and greater powers, the higher aim could not be divorced from the calculation of economic and military advantage in the postwar period. For Canada the economic, industrial, and scientific gains were enormous. The postwar position acquired gave the Canadian launching in international diplomacy a powerful shove. There was, however, a certain falseness and transience about it, and the disgruntling suffered when Canada retired from these high politics distorted the national assessment of Canada's normal role in the world. 'If Canada were a great power,' Charles Ritchie commented in a memorandum a month after Hiroshima, 'its monopoly of the indispensable component of the atomic bomb might put this country in a position to determine decisions as to the future use and control of the bomb; but as Canada is not a Great Power, her possession of uranium is perhaps more likely to expose her to embarrassment and difficulties.'[2] The seat at high table, while it lasted, was as embarrassing as it was profitable and it was occupied with cunning reticence.

WARTIME COLLABORATION[3]

Each of the three countries had started independently on atomic research. Dr George Laurence's work at the National Research Council in Ottawa was on a smaller scale, but it meant that Canada did have some competence to put into the pot in addition to raw material. The British, because of the wartime pressures and the fear of the Nazis getting a bomb first, had a brief headstart. It was the so-called Maud Report in Britain in 1941 that galvanized scientists both in Britain and the United States into action. Unfortunately, the British were reluctant to accept American suggestions for co-operation in 1941 when they had a slight lead. By the time they realized the grave limitations on what they could do on a beleaguered island the Americans were at war and throwing all they had into the effort. The Americans owed an enormous debt to the British and European scientists who had contributed crucially to the scientific breakthrough, a fact better appreciated by scientists than politicians. The British, realizing full well that the atomic secret had significance for their postwar economy and their military status, nevertheless offered almost total collaboration with the Americans and sent many of their good scientists there. When the Americans were mobilized, they perceived only marginal need of British assistance, as well as Canadian. Desperate pressure to beat the enemy to an atomic bomb persuaded them, and also gave them an excuse, to reduce co-operation to what they considered essential for their own purposes.

It is true that the British-Canadian operation during the last couple of years of the war had no serious prospect of contributing to the bomb, but the possibility was foreseen that it might produce the element, later called plutonium, which was another potential explosive for bombs. Those engaged in day-to-day operation found collaboration difficult because of imposed restrictions, although as good scientists they managed on the whole to subordinate national grievances to a sense of common cause. Many American officials were aware of the significance of the British decision to pool their resources and worked for fair partnership. It was only, however, at the highest level when Roosevelt and Churchill, and sometimes also Mackenzie King, got together that the basic interest was reaffirmed and co-operation would have a new spurt. The problem was not so much American arrogance, although there was plenty of that. It was the disparity in power and consequence. During the war there was a lack of sensitivity and in the postwar period a deplorable lack of magnanimity to their war-ravaged partner, Britain, but on the United States rested the responsibility of winning the wartime battle for atomic control. After the war crucial decisions could be taken only by the country that for five years remained the unique possessor of the weapon. If the Canadians recognized this fact of life somewhat more easily than the British, they had less to lose by doing so.

Canada was involved in the first place as a partner or at least collaborator with the British. When it was recognized in Britain in 1942 that it would be impossible to develop in wartime England the necessary plant, Canada was looked to for help and sanctuary. The British first asked to move their teams to the United States, but the Americans refused. So Canada, which was close to the centre of action, looked like a good alternative. Canada had the uranium. It had a nucleus of scientists and adequate industrial capacity with assistance from across the border. The very few Canadians in on the secret responded enthusiastically to an invitation to share with a major scientific power the development of this revolutionary force. The pioneer scientists in this field at Cambridge were regarded with awe. Canada put a good deal of effort and expense into the establishment in Montreal of a laboratory where British, Canadian, Free French, and other scientists worked on the atomic process, and later into the building of a reactor at Chalk River.

The great problem was to get American assistance, to keep in touch with research in their laboratories, without which progress would be limited. The wartime story is a long account of the often frustrating effort to do so. The Americans never felt the British-Canadian effort in Canada to be vital, but as it might be helpful they were willing to provide some materials and some secrets. Some obligation was fitfully recognized because British scientists were doing essential work in the United States. Nothing, however, was to interfere with what the Americans needed for their own experiments – including access to Canadian uranium. Before the British had approached the Canadians about a co-operative enterprise, the Americans had been in negotiation directly with Eldorado Gold Mines, the Canadian company which was the largest source of uranium outside the Belgian Congo, to secure supplies and had acquired thereby some claim to a priority.

Although in the end British and Canadians had reasons to be grateful to each other for the contribution this co-operative endeavour made to their atomic capability after the war,[4] it was dogged with irritations and suspicions. The British were bossy and the Canadians thin-skinned. Both had frequent reasons to be upset by the ruthlessness of the Americans, but the Canadians always insisted that a *sine qua non* of the operation on their part was American co-operation, and they rejected the occasional British suggestion *in extremis* that they and the Canadians might go it alone. There was the Canadian instinct for a triangle. There was also the horse-sense of Dr C.J. Mackenzie of the National Research Council and of C.D. Howe, the minister of munitions and supply, in recognizing that the Americans were in the driver's seat and there was a war on. There was perhaps also a canny recognition that the national interest lay in keeping on as good terms as possible with the country that was going to set the pace.

The Anglo-Canadian operation got off to a bad start. The Canadian government had agreed with the British to see that they got a fair share of uranium but the British were unhappy over the amounts that Gilbert LaBine, the owner of Eldorado, had committed to the Americans. It was a slip-up under wartime pressure, but the British were furious and, unfortunately, Churchill's intemperate comment that Howe had 'sold the British Empire down the river' got back to Howe. Howe was irritated with the British, but he did not favour the Americans; he was always looking for the Canadian advantage. Mackenzie took on the role of interpreter by going off to talk to the Americans himself. The British respected him but were never happy about the Canadian reluctance to stand up in a joint front when this seemed called for. The friction can, of course, be seen out of proportion. Sir John Cockcroft, who was called in to put the Montreal laboratory on its feet, and other British scientists who worked with the Canadians to develop Chalk River were highly regarded and liked by the Canadians. These were the British who also got along best with the Americans. It is doubtful if the people in London saw Canada as a partner in a joint enterprise. There was a tendency to look on it as Commonwealth territory and somewhat, therefore, at their disposal. The idea of partnership with a dominion was not one to which Sir John Anderson, who was in charge of British atomic affairs, could easily adjust. The retreat to Canada was regarded as a regrettable wartime necessity rather than an opportunity for a great Anglo-Canadian enterprise. The British, as the official historian of their operation, Margaret Gowing, states, were always clear on the central point: 'The control of policy ... should be retained in this country.'[5] Much of the controversy, after as well as during the war, was the inevitable consequence of harried people with reconcilable objectives but irreconcilable perspectives.

A typical explosion was set off by American anger over the willingness of the British to endanger security by allowing the French scientist who was in charge at Montreal to make a trip to liberated Paris. The Americans tried protesting to the Canadians. The Canadians might well have supported the British position but they had never been consulted in the first place, even though the man involved, Halban, was associated with a joint Canadian-British enterprise in Canada. Tempers flared, but there were always enough men of good will and dedication in each camp to get the lid back on. The flames were never fanned by the public because for this performance there was no public.

The Canadian position was ambiguous. It was not clear whether Canada was one of a partnership of three or a junior partner on the British team. It is obvious from the numerous American accounts of these events that they linked the British and Canadians as a team to be treated as such. By habit they regarded the British as the spokesmen. For the Americans as well as the British, bilateral discussion was simpler, unless Canada on special occasions looked to one like a potential ally against the other. The atomic 'partnership,' such as it was, had been initiated by British-American discussion and understandings. That was how the war was being run in general. And in this case, the Canadians seemed to prefer it that way. Canada had membership, on the basis of one member to two each from the major powers, on the Combined Policy Committee and the Combined Development Trust, which guided the operation, but these were set up largely as a result of Anglo-American negotiation. King and Howe seemed happy to accept the 3-2-1 ratio on the committees and recognize in practice that these were basically Anglo-American bodies in which they had the right to speak. They were content to recognize as a bilateral document the Quebec Agreement of 1943, which set the terms for continuing Anglo-American co-operation, and did not ask to be associated with the Declaration of Trust which came out of it.

Why not? Canadians were quick to resist unfair treatment and to defend their position as the country with the resources. They were not going to let the others dispose of those resources. What they wanted was a chance to state their requirements, not the responsibility of the grand decisions. The number of Canadians involved in policy was extremely small, and External Affairs was out of the picture. King's reluctance to get involved in Anglo-American disputes was to be expected. Howe's interest was in protecting the Canadian side of a working operation, not in high policy. He wanted to win the war and give Canada a head start in a new industry. That required British and American help and a self-confident playing of the strong Canadian hand with both. Keeping clear of British-American disputes would be wise. The Americans, of course, needed some stubborn resistance, but the Canadians were better able to do that on their own. They had more to bargain with than the British although the Americans needed some lessons on Canadian sovereignty. The United States government, for example, negotiated directly with the Trail Smelter in British Columbia to construct facilities for heavy water without any notification to the Canadian authorities. Later, when Canada and Britain needed heavy water from Trail for their own operation, they were told by the United States that they would allow no sharing of information, that the Canadian team could have the Trail output for a while if in effect they did fundamental scientific work for Du Pont, and that was that.[6] In the early stages fear by Americans that the Canadian government could stop shipments of uranium and heavy water from the Trail plant was an argument used in Washington against restricting information to the British and Canadians.[7] The Canadian hand was tied by the constant danger that any kind of row would threaten disclosure, simply by attracting attention to the industries involved. Nevertheless, the Americans were led by Howe and Mackenzie to a better appreciation of Canadian rights.

Not much of the Canadian or the Canadian-British experiments contributed to the actual fabrication of the atomic bomb. Nevertheless, those Canadians involved accepted the fact that the production of a bomb was the most important immediate result of what they were setting out to do. There is not much evidence, furthermore, that the Canadians involved objected to the idea that an end result of their work might be the production of this hideous weapon – although, like the British and American scientists, they seem to have thought of an atom bomb as a super-explosive, which might, in fact, not come off, and only dimly perceived what it would do to a Japanese city. The desperate need to produce such a weapon to forestall the Nazis doing the same was certainly the basic motive. There was no disposition to deny Canadian uranium on moral grounds. It was a time when people were less squeamish about bombing a 'barbaric' enemy. Canadians and Britons participated in the annihilation of Dresden.

Canada was not involved in the decision to use the bomb in the way in which it was used. King did have some months' intimation that a bomb was probably going to be produced and was probably going to be used. Howe was present at the meeting of the Combined Policy Committee on 4 July 1945 at which Field Marshal Maitland-Wilson gave what was regarded as the British assent to the use of the bomb against Japan. The Canadian government could presumably have dissociated itself from the decision if it had wanted to do so. Howe regarded the CPC as a bilateral body with a Canadian specialist looking after particular Canadian interests. Ottawa asked no more questions and gave no advice. The prime minister of South Africa, Jan Smuts, was told slightly in advance and, being more interested in grand strategy than King and less modest about it, he immediately raised with Churchill the formidable issues of how to control this genie. The people in Ottawa who would have worried most and who were busy working on the structure of a postwar security organization were in the dark. That they would have recommended using the bomb less painfully is a reasonable conjecture, but it is doubtful if they would have convinced their prime minister. It would probably not have been difficult to persuade him that the bomb should not be dropped on a crowded city but more difficult to persuade him to intervene, although he does seem to have indicated to Roosevelt that it might be a good idea to give the Russians some advance warning that a secret weapon was to be used.[8] If the bomb had been destined for Europe it might have been a different matter.[9] However, it was to be used after the European war was over, and the preference for leaving Pacific strategy to the Americans had been strengthened by the anxiety not to increase commitments in that area. The record then does not provide solid grounds for arguing Canadian innocence of 'complicity.' There is not a good case either for arguing that Canada could have done anything to prevent Hiroshima or Nagasaki. This was an instance in which Canada, on functionalist grounds, might have claimed a voice but preferred silence.

POSTWAR PROSPECT

During the war the triangular partnership, in spite of recurring bouts of suspicion, had survived because of the common goal and the common fear. There were too many divergent interests in a peacetime world, however, for it to last long. The clash was chiefly between the British and Americans, but there was a Canadian perception of particular interest that limited enthusiasm for too tight a triangle. The wartime urgency was succeeded by a common concern for international control of the devastating force which had been unleashed, an anxiety to exploit the industrial potential, and a recognition of the obligation to share this potential with the rest of the world. There was still, however, no equality because the United States alone had decisive control of the atomic weapon. The British and Canadians, although they did not regard this as an ideal situation, were too nervous of uncontrolled atomic proliferation to want the monopoly to slip out of the hands of the country which, in spite of differences, remained their champion. For Canadians the problems in the immediate postwar period were of three kinds: their part in the maintenance or alteration of a tripartite relationship; their own relationship to the United Kingdom in the continuation of wartime collaboration; and the question of international control.

First of all External Affairs had to find out what had been going on in atomic research, how Canada was involved, and what the consequences were for Canada's position in the world. A series of direct questions was put to C.J. Mackenzie,[10] president of the National Research Council, to which he replied at some length on 26 October. Among the points he made in his letter were the following: the American project was not entirely dependent on Canadian ore; they had stockpiled a great deal of Congo material. Canada's development work was not a major factor in the production of the atomic bomb dropped on Japan but might have a great effect on future plans in which Canada's raw material was a significant aspect. Canada had, of course, no advantage over the United States or Britain in knowledge of relevant scientific, technical, and industrial know-how but certainly had over the rest of the countries of the world. Its scientific knowledge was greater than its industrial know-how, but this would change within the next year. As owner and operator of the only plant in the British empire Canada had a strong position as far as everyone else except the United States was concerned. 'While I think the United States welcomes the Canadian contacts I also think they feel, as they do in the matter of military defence, that they are quite competent to look after themselves.' The question of where and how much raw material there was in the world was not certain, but Mackenzie did not think that the control of the raw materials in Canada, the United Kingdom, and the United States would prevent for any length of time developments in other countries. He cited the 'more experienced engineer industrialists' in his estimate of a minimum of five, with a probable ten, years as the time it would take countries like Britain, the Soviet Union, Germany, or Japan to produce the bomb if they were working under prewar conditions.

THE WASHINGTON CONFERENCE, NOVEMBER 1945

In the meantime there were expectations that the 'three atomic powers' would take some initiative. Ottawa was being kept well-informed on British thinking, but even a few weeks before the Washington Conference of Truman, Attlee, and King in November 1945 they were able only to speculate on American intentions, based on Truman's enigmatic public statements. In Washington their contacts were coping with wide differences among policy-makers and reluctance to consult the Canadians and British. Scientists like Vannevar Bush and James B. Conant urged Truman to go slow on special tripartite relations lest these alienate the Russians and risk the possiblity of United Nations action.

King was in London a good deal of this time in close consultation with Attlee and anxious for a tripartite meeting. What was mostly on his mind, however, was the way the three powers would treat the Gouzenko revelations. Gouzenko had revealed the names of Canadians in an intelligence network, as well as a scientist in London who had worked at the Montreal laboratory, and suggested American contacts as well. Those few participants in the know recognized the relationship between the two issues. The British security people had practical reasons for wanting to arrest their man quickly, but the Americans wanted to put off revelations until they had tracked down further leads in Washington. On the political level, however, there was agreement that a disclosure of Soviet espionage before an invitation had been issued for Soviet co-operation on the control of atomic energy would be widely regarded as deliberate provocation intended to frustrate Soviet participation and justify a Western monopoly. In Ottawa the desperate need for international control in which all the great powers would participate overrode in these fearful and anxious months the alarm and anger over Soviet behaviour in Canada. In any case Mackenzie King wanted the announcement about espionage to be tripartite, and it could not therefore be issued until after he had had his talks with Truman and Attlee.

However baffling the problems, it was recognized that Canada now had a considerably enhanced – or exposed – position in the international hierarchy. An internal memorandum in DEA of 6 November[11] calculated as follows: 'So far as the United States is concerned the fact that we control an important source of potential raw material, combined with our geographical position, must give Canada a new importance from the stand-point of United States interest. While it has always been true that the United States could not look with indifference on any major development of Canadian foreign policy this will be much more the case in the future.' The position was regarded as even stronger vis-à-vis the United Kingdom, for whereas the United States was not dependent on Canada for the continued production of atomic weapons or experimentation, the United Kingdom was dependent. Most significant was Canada's new vulnerability. 'The unique position of Canada in relation both to the United States and the United Kingdom will certainly not fail to attract the attention of the Soviet Union and may have important though unforeseeable effects on the relations with that country.' This feeling that the lid was now off the Arctic was one of the strongest public reactions in Canada to the atomic bomb. There was some disposition in Ottawa and in Washington to see North America as the continent more exposed than Europe to the Soviet threat and to complain of European myopia on the subject. Mackenzie King reported that Dean Acheson told him in Washington 'that the United States and Canada would be more immediately affected by the consequences of any action which severed relations with Russia, than even the U.K.'[12] The External Affairs memorandum concluded that the principal interest of Canada was the avoidance of a situation in which the nations of the world would be conducting a desperate race in the production of new forms of atomic destruction and, in particular, that the world should not split up into great blocs of power, one headed by the United States and the other by the Soviet Union. 'Such a development would offer particular danger for Canada since, should a final atomic struggle break out between these two power blocs, Canada on account of her geographical situation, her control of the principal source of raw material, and the location in this country of an important plant, would become a target for attack.'

There was no doubt in Ottawa that the answer had to be international control. The bomb had swiftly radicalized the Canadian view of world order. What was envisaged to control atomic energy was a supranational régime with much greater authority than had been considered feasible a few months earlier at San Francisco. External Affairs memoranda recognized, however, that it was enough to state such objectives to appreciate the formidable obstacles. The United States would almost certainly be unwilling in the interim period, before a system of control was set up, to share with the Soviet Union information about the manufacture of the bomb. There would be, therefore, a period of accumulating mutual suspicions that would certainly not be laid to rest by signatures affixed to a pact of renunciation of the atomic bomb. 'It remains to be seen whether in this atmosphere of suspicion it will be possible to achieve any progress towards the solution of the problems raised by the discovery of atomic energy, but at least it is to be hoped that the facts of the situation will be squarely faced at the forthcoming Washington meeting. Even if the United States is only prepared to move slowly it should move in the right direction – that of eventual international control – and it is to be hoped that the discussion will not be obscured by proposals which sidestep the central issue.'[13]

The Canadian memoranda prepared for possible presentation at the Washington Conference were somewhat more resolute. It was not the occasion to dwell on doubts about the practicality of international control. The memoranda were based firmly on the assumption that the atomic bomb was not just a new weapon but something revolutionary and unprecedented, that the atomic bomb was only the beginning of something far more destructive, that the secret of the bomb could not be kept for more than five years, the manufacture of the bomb was possible in any industrial state that knew the secret, and the projection by rockets with accuracy over great distances was or would shortly be possible. The memoranda boldly countered the assumption held by some in the United States that any government had the right to give its people a feeling of security 'which can only be false, by basing its policy on the opposite assumption, that a national or three country monopoly of development and production is possible.' The memoranda reflected the current feeling that the bomb was particularly dangerous in the hands of a totalitarian government because no parliamentary democracy would be capable of taking the decision to use it. (The fact that one democracy, with the passive assent of two others, had just done precisely that was ignored, presumably because what they had in mind was Pearl Harbor-type aggression.) Any constructive solution to the problem must be international. 'There is, in fact, no national solution.' It would be folly, however, for the three countries concerned to make a gift of their atomic knowledge to other countries without conditions.

... they should exploit the temporary advantage they now possess in order to bring this weapon under international control, so that it can never be used by anyone. This can be attempted by trading the knowledge of invention and manufacture they alone possess at present, for renunciation by all nations of the right of production or use, except, possibly, on orders from the United Nations. This in its turn means international supervision and control of the development and use of atomic energy. If an honest offer of this kind, made by the United States, United Kingdom, and Canada, were refused by any other state, that refusal would certainly disclose which nations were to be trusted and which feared.

The outlawing of atomic warfare was considered desirable as one of a number of steps but dangerous as a single step. External Affairs favoured destruction of all existing weapons or their transfer to the United Nations as trustee, the pooling of all the basic scientific knowledge so that secret development of new weapons would be impossible, establishment under the United Nations of an international commission of scientists with authority to make periodic investigations of national laboratories and industries. A sceptical view was taken of the 'sacred trust' approach contained in President Truman's statement of 27 October. That was no substitute for international agreement. 'The USA simply cannot remove fears concerning atomic warfare, or prevent the inevitable and fateful competition that would follow, merely by sitting on the bomb as a self-appointed sacred trustee.'[14] As Canada had clearly accepted the idea of temporary trusteeship by the three powers until the United Nations could take it over, the opposition in the memorandum was presumably to those Americans who wanted to be 'trustees' permanently.

In fact, there was considerable meeting of minds at the Washington meeting and no particular need for the Canadians to carry the torch for international control. There were British and American drafts and in the early stages, confusion. No Canadian draft was submitted, but King secured several revisions of the American draft. He argued that the reference to the appointment of a United Nations commission should be subordinated to the recommendations of the three signatories as to immediate action. What may look like an effort to downgrade the role of the United Nations in fact reflected the Canadian fear during this period that the great powers, and especially the United States, would develop a 'leave it to the UN' attitude, failing to recognize their responsibility for initiative. Another change King obtained reflected a Canadian anxiety to emphasize not just the negative aspect of limitation but the positive opportunities for sharing information on the industrial application of atomic energy.

The final agreement, on which the president and two prime ministers rested their plea to the world, was the work of a small drafting committee consisting of Dr Vannevar Bush, Sir John Anderson, and Lester Pearson.

In this declaration the three heads of government expressed their willing-ness, as a first contribution, to proceed with the exchange of fundamental scientific information for peaceful ends with any nation that would fully re-ciprocate. They did not think that the spreading of specialized information regarding the practical application of atomic energy was advisable at that point, but they were prepared to share on a reciprocal basis as soon as effec-tive and forcible safeguards could be devised. They advocated the creation at the earliest practicable date of a commission under the United Nations to prepare recommendations for submission to the United Nations. The commission should make specific proposals for extending the exchange of scientific information for peaceful ends, the control of atomic energy, the elimination from national armaments of atomic weapons and all other wea-pons of mass destruction, and effective safeguards by way of inspection and other means. It was recommended that the work of the commission proceed by separate stages, the successful completion of each one developing the necessary confidence before the next stage was undertaken.[15]

The Washington Conference has been regarded by some historians as a set-back to the cause of Soviet collaboration and international control be-cause it emphasized the solidarity of the Anglo-Saxon powers.[16] This worry had been in the minds of many Americans in resisting the British pressure for a tripartite meeting. The same concern is not evident in Canadian think-ing. The conference in fact took the direction proposed in a Canadian pre-liminary memorandum which looked upon the meeting not as an occasion to consolidate a triumvirate but as one on which those who had launched the bomb would offer to the Russians and the world at large the opportunity to control the new force internationally and to share in its blessings. The Brit-ish, more sceptical of international control and much more anxious to be reassured on partnership, may have had a somewhat different perspective. Pearson had even suggested, in a memorandum in which he said 'it was unlikely that the world would be reassured by Truman's promise to regard the bomb as a sacred trust,' that the air channels of the world should be cleared for broadcast statements by the three heads of government.[17] It was to be a celebration of internationalism rather than restrictionism.

A month after the Washington Conference the four powers in Moscow approved the setting up of a United Nations Atomic Energy Commission. Canada became the only country not a great power to have permanent membership – a role to be taken seriously. Intensive preparation began in Ottawa, and participation on the most senior level was guaranteed by the appointment of General A.G.L. McNaughton as Canadian representative, with strong scientific and diplomatic support. The commission got to work in mid-1946 on the basis of a far-reaching United States plan for control by an international authority. Canada gave general support to this proposal, and McNaughton, with the subtle professional advice of George Ignatieff from External Affairs, further enhanced Canada's status in atomic affairs by his skilful diplomacy, his mastery of the subject, and his willingness to stand up to the American representative, the fearsome Bernard Baruch. However well intentioned – and however necessary it was to explore the possiblity of drastic international control – the Russians would not accept it, certainly not before they too knew how to make a bomb. Whether the other major powers would have accepted it in practice is doubtful.

A detailed account of the work of the UNAEC will be included in the second volume with a discussion of the general effort at collective security within the United Nations.[18] Attention in this chapter is directed only to the tangled history of the ABC relationship, which took on a different aspect as the effort to achieve a broader international control was gradually abandoned – with relief in some quarters, but great reluctance in others. Canadians had less to venture and more to gain and were perhaps the most reluctant of the three to abandon the effort. International control, among other things, might have delivered them from the travails of the triangle.

ABC RELATIONS

When the British minister of aircraft production, Colonel Moore-Brabazon, had in 1941 officially passed on the Maud Reports, he urged a long-term view. He asked if the atomic projects did not present the world at last with the real possiblity of an international police force. 'America and Britain, policing and controlling the world, would have an overwhelming superiority of striking power without needing to keep up an overwhelming air force.'[19] Whether cloaked in such imperial language or not, Churchill, King, and Roosevelt all in their own way saw a strong Anglo-American base as the core of a new effort at international collective security. It was a rhetorical idea sincerely enough held but difficult for the practitioners to cling to. Economic considerations on the part of each of the three countries may have been sordid, but they were also inescapable. Because the United States alone had been able to make the investment in production as distinct from the theory of atomic energy, they were disposed to forget their debt not only to the British but to French and refugee European scientists who had been largely responsible for the theoretical basis. The United States, they were confident, would be a custodian for mankind and see that the benefits were distributed.[20] The tight security established by the United States during wartime was understandable, even when it excluded the British and Canadians from sharing their production secrets, but it was also a good way to protect the economic advantage.

Security bedevilled the issue. Both Canadians and British resented American suspicions of the international band working in Montreal, but two of them were discovered to have been passing secrets to the Soviet Union. The fact that the Americans too had spies in their atomic apparatus was not revealed until later. None of these scientists was passing information to the wartime enemy. After the war, however, security had a different orientation. There was a panic reaction to Hiroshima; some deadly poison had been let loose and must not spread. The genie must be put back in the bottle. As this was accompanied by predictions of scientists in all three countries that the secret could not be kept and the Russians should be able to produce a bomb in about five years, the policy of extreme secrecy looks in retrospect either irrational or hypocritical. Sharing the secret with the Russians was seriously considered in Washington. It was debated in Ottawa and London as well, but neither government urged such a course on the United States. It was rejected not so much because the logic was unacceptable as because of a general instinct in that unnerving situation to play safe. The disposition to share, strong at first, diminished rapidly because of increasing evidence of Soviet hostility in 1945-6 and Soviet secretiveness which discouraged even the optimists from their faith in free scientific exchange.

What to begin with was a blind instinct to keep the secret from everyone, including Americans, was directed increasingly to Soviet 'spies.' That did not mean, however, any relaxation in the opposition of Congress to sharing with allies. Among the American policy-makers were those who said the United States should share no secrets because it had a right to reap industrial advantage from its own scientific and technical genius and those who believed that it was essential to withhold secrets from any other country until a system of international control had been established. Canada agreed with the latter argument. Both arguments, however, reinforced the case for unilateralism and paranoiac security, the manifestations of which Canadians did not like.

The basic principles for transatlantic co-operation had been laid down in the Quebec Agreement of 1943. It was clear that this agreement, which was ambiguous about its duration, would have to be revised after the war was over. Whereas the British clung to the American commitment to the sharing of resources and secrets agreed upon at Quebec, the Americans were anxious to minimize it. The actual agreement at Quebec remained secret, and Congressmen had little idea of the British and Canadian part in the enterprise or the commitments made to them. With considerable pressure from

London, and with many reservations among American scientists and soldiers, the basic commitment to collaboration, with some reservations, was reaffirmed on the highest level when Truman, Attlee, and King met in Washington in November 1945. That agreement gave Canada clear status as one of three partners on its own.

There followed many efforts over the next few years by diplomats of the three countries to work out arrangements by which the British and Canadians might get some at least of the useful information they thought they were entitled to. The British were more dissatisfied and put on the pressure. In the State Department there was anxiety to foster Anglo-American co-operation in general as the basis of postwar security, but their efforts to reach compromise agreements with the British and Canadians were smothered by the nationalist attitudes growing in Congress. 'The American attitude,' according to Andrew Pierre, 'was a curious mixture of monopolism, insecurity, and idealism.'[21] The idealism was the conviction that the continuation of the tripartite wartime collaboration would or would at least seem to be in contradiction to the aim of a genuine United Nations direction of atomic policy. So the isolationist Anglophobes and the one world internationalists were linked in their aims.

One of the American arguments least acceptable to the British was that there should be neither atomic bombs nor even nuclear power stations in Britain because the country was too vulnerable to communist occupation. The view of Britain and Western Europe as a glacis of the heartland of the 'free world' seemed logical enough in the American mood between victory and NATO. Even General Eisenhower, the staunchest defender of British rights in subsequent debates,[22] argued early in 1946 that on grounds of security British piles should be in Canada.[23] In the CPC Pearson agreed because Howe at that time wanted the piles in Canada. So did Sir John Cockcroft. The chancellor of the exchequer, however, feared the cost in dollars, and London turned it down because, as Attlee told his ambassador in Washington: 'If the pile is to be built and paid for by the Canadian Government it becomes a Canadian enterprise, and even though we might be ready to help by lending staff, the plant would necessarily be owned and to a large extent controlled by the Canadian Government.'[24]

The disadvantages of Canada's exposed position were apparent to the diplomatists. Howe also had reservations. External Affairs was having the difficult experience of moving into an exercise of which they had been ignorant. It was hard for them to get the feel of it, very hard even to find out the facts about Canadian participation. It was not until December 1945 that they even saw King's communications with Churchill at the time of the Quebec Agreement, and Pearson was embarrassed that month at a CPC meeting to consider the Combined Development Trust, as he had never seen the document setting up that body. The Eldorado records were a mess and External Affairs could not get any accurate information on what they had been or were producing. Nevertheless, they had to plunge into the very difficult discussions after the Washington agreement on the re-establishment of the CPC and the CDT.[25]

The Canadian attitude on tripartite control was revealed in discussions between Howe and External Affairs on Canada's position in the CDT. Canada was not as desperately anxious as Britain to maintain American co-operation. They wanted to share as many secrets as possible but they were not interested in producing a bomb. Unlike the British, they had a plant established and under way. Still, Anglo-American co-operation as a general principle was an article of faith in Ottawa. Canadians were able to understand the perspectives of both London and Washington. Nevertheless, they had their own as well. Canada was a supplier of uranium whereas the British and Americans were scrounging hard to control all supplies of uranium and thorium, in the interest both of their own economies and of world security as they saw it. The Congo was still the largest source of uranium and the British were busy with the Belgians trying to tie this up. Canada was the second largest developed source, but its importance lay in the prospect of much wider discoveries and in its proximity to the United States. At this crucial period Americans did not feel dependent upon Canadian supplies but they could not ignore Canada. It was not the kind of leverage that alone would enable Canada to coerce the Americans on matters of policy. The latter assumed no doubt that Canadian resources were something they could confidently count on; Canadians always wanted to sell things, and they would recognize their own security interest in seeing that the Americans had the raw material for bombs.

So Howe looked at membership in the CPC and CDT with a cool calculation of Canadian interest. 'The Prime Minister feels that we should try to be as independent as possible in all these matters,' he wrote to George Bateman, the Canadian representative.[26] If participation in the CDT meant that Canadian resources would be disposed of by a tripartite body dominated by two larger powers, then he was against it. At the same time he wanted to develop the uranium industry but had to be prepared for a drop in demand. If the trust would make some kind of commitments to take Canadian uranium regardless, that was a different matter. If pulling out of the CDT meant also pulling out of the Policy Committee, that was all right with him. His notices of meetings often arrived late and he could not attend.[27] He assumed the international issues were now the responsibility of diplomats and preferred that Pearson attend with Bateman. He even took the position that Canada was not a member of the CDT, that the Canadian director, George Bateman, was there representing the United Kingdom, although Bateman himself said he had always been recognized as the Canadian representative. Pearson did not like this way of handling things, although he had doubts about the advantages of staying on the Policy Committee. 'Frankly,' he wrote to Norman Robertson, 'I feel that, as a junior third party in this Committee, we may be dragged along in directions where we might not desire to go but over which we would have little control.'[28] He wondered about leaving the Policy Committee to the two governments chiefly concerned and regulating the Canadian association with it on the basis of being called into consultation when they desired, an association which he compared with that with the Combined Chiefs of Staff in Washington. He foresaw the old dilemma: what looked like a means of gaining a voice in policy-making could prove to be merely sacrificing the greater flexibility of independence.

In spite of the temptation to withdraw, however, Canadians were reluctant to appear to be walking out at this particular time, and Howe came to see some advantage in remaining on the Policy Committee if that would help in the sharing of information. When differences between the British and Americans got worse by the spring of 1946, the Canadians lay low. Disagreement between the United States and the United Kingdom on the sharing of information and of raw materials might be fraught with serious embarrassment for Canada, but when a working group was set up to find a solution Canada did not seek representation on it. According to a memorandum for the prime minister of 20 April 1946 from Arnold Heeney: 'Mr. Howe feels that we should "keep out" of this dispute so far as possible.' It was difficult, however, to refuse a reply when Attlee asked King to contribute to the discussion his interpretation of the meaning of 'full and effective co-operation in the field of atomic energy' as contained in the Washington Agreement of 16 November. It was a crucial question and the British would expect support from the Canadians for their interpretation. The Canadian response was to avoid the apparent taking of sides by providing the following answer: 'Mr. Mackenzie King's understanding of the Agreement in this respect is indicated by the fact that we have, both during the War and in the post-War period, provided United States authorities with full information on all Canadian activities in this field. In particular, they have had access to full information as to developments at Chalk River. In fact, a United States official is stationed there permanently and is in a position to secure a complete picture of the work going forward in the plant.'[29] Acheson expressed to Pearson his admiration for the 'ingenuity' of that reply.[30]

One aspect of the problem concerned the United Nations. If what was reached between the British and Americans was a new agreement, then, according to the terms of Article 102 of the Charter, it would have to be registered with the United Nations. When the British tried to find some way around this, Byrnes regarded it as a legal subterfuge and Pearson, ever sensitive about the obligations of the Charter, agreed with him. The disposition of the Americans to minimize the ABC relationship lest it interfere with genuine United Nations control provided a dilemma for Ottawa. They did not want to provoke the Russians or offend the United Nations community, but at the same time they saw Anglo-American collaboration as indispensable for the United Nations. The answer therefore was piously to say: 'We are, of course hopeful that the United Nations Atomic Energy Commission will be able to make progress toward eventual international control and we are at present examining the various proposals which have been advanced in this connection. In the meantime, we feel that continued co-operation between our three countries need not prejudice the success of the Commission and indeed may assist toward that end.'[31]

Matters concerning tripartite co-operation remained in limbo for several years. Ottawa was not worried on its own account by the stalemate. '... while the present situation is in some ways unsatisfactory, it is questionable whether more precise definition along the lines of the new Trust agreement would not create more problems than it would solve,' Heeney noted in a memorandum to Howe. The initiative lay with the United States and they were not moving, and 'Unless there are any pressing difficulties in the present Canadian situation as a supplier of raw material, or otherwise in our relation to the Trust, it does not seem to be in our interest to urge any immediate conclusion of the proposed revised agreements.'[32] The McMahon Act of June 1946, which restricted the sharing of atomic information by the United States, made it clear that co-operation would be extremely limited. Because Canada was not a signatory to the Quebec Agreement and was not developing atomic weapons, Canada did not protest, and Pearson later said that the United States were, 'perfectly within their rights' in passing the bill.[33] The British decided to go their own way constructing nuclear power and a bomb.

The revelations in March from Ottawa about Soviet espionage hardened the American Congress and public against any exchanges with Britain and Canada and the Washington agreements in this respect were not implemented. The historians of the United States Atomic Energy Commission attribute a decisive role to the news from Ottawa, citing a report that the steady flow of correspondence supporting more flexible provisions for control ceased the day 'the spy story' broke. 'Disillusionment with the Russians, the impulse to protect even more carefully what secrets might remain, and elemental fear seemed in a moment to drown the sort of postwar idealism that prompted scientists to advocate the free exchange of scientific information.'[34] It was not an interpretation of the Gouzenko affair pressed by Ottawa. It was a consequence they had hoped to avoid when they made their inevitable revelation.

An indication of a new look in Washington came in September 1947, in a proposal for a public tripartite declaration of atomic collaboration, just what the Americans had resisted a year earlier. The British saw their chance at last for opening the exchange flow. By this time the interest in information had become a stronger motive for the Canadians. In the guidance sent to Wrong with approval of Howe and St Laurent, it was stated: 'In our view, the real Canadian interest in these discussions lies in the possibility that they may result in really useful information being made available to us and to the United Kingdom. We appreciate the difficult position of U.S. authorities under U.S. legislation and in relation to Congress but, as Dr. Mackenzie has reported, there is a good deal that the United States can make available to us through cooperation in specific fields. General McNaughton agrees that our chief interest is in widening to the maximum extent these "areas of collaboration" and every opportunity should be taken to secure U.S. consent to such arrangements.'[35] The Canadians consistently differed with the British on the best way to get American information. They were less anxious to get some new formal arrangement that might prove no more valid in practice than that solemly agreed to in Washington in November 1945. They had had more success with informal contacts. Furthermore, they did not like this new proposal which, they thought, would probably destroy the United Nations Atomic Energy Commission, and they were not ready for that. From Washington Wrong estimated that the United States had abandoned all hope of reaching agreement in the United Nations commission. Although he shared this view of its prospects, he thought it rash and unwise to take such a stand in the present international situation.[36] The government saw it the same way. Wrong was sent for his guidance the text of the instruction just approved by St Laurent for the General Assembly delegation: 'You should endeavour to avoid the premature development of any issue to the point where it is likely to destroy the United Nations or to drive any of its members to withdraw immediately' and '... at this Assembly the emphasis should be on warning what *may* happen rather than of forcing issues to the point where things *will* happen.'[37]

By late 1947 the United States was discovering a considerable need for uranium, inducing a more companionable attitude towards Canada and towards Britain, which had some control over Belgian and Commonwealth sources. NATO was being formed and there was a new spirit of alliance. The internationalist officials in Washington were gaining strength. In December 1947 the Americans indicated that they would like an early meeting of the CPC to discuss renewed co-operation. The Marshall Plan was coming up for Congressional discussion and there was a possible tie up, as countries receiving aid might supply uranium as a *quid pro quo*.[38] George Kennan of the State Department told the Canadian ambassador he had succeeded in securing a liberal construction of the McMahon Act under which they thought they could exchange atomic information on the grounds that it was in the national interest. Wrong was surprised by 'the frankness with which the U.S. representatives had taken us into their confidence.' He stressed the United States concern over raw materials but was himself concerned over the view of experts that by 1951 Canada would drop from being a poor second to fourth as a source of supply behind the Congo, South Africa, and the United States.[39]

The Canadian government played it very cool. Wrong was told that Canada's position would continue to be secondary to that of the major powers and that would condition Canadian participation in the current discussions. They understood United States political problems but were not going to be rushed unless the connection with the Marshall Plan proved a unique opportunity to get better United States co-operation. He was reminded of the view of the Canadian Advisory Panel on Atomic Energy that 'efforts should continue to be made to reach agreement upon an acceptable system of international control and that it was in the Canadian interest that the Commission be kept viable for this reason.' Canada's limited part in the trust was affirmed and Howe's insistence that Canadian production should remain under the sole control of Canada, although they would consider a pledge to sell excess supplies of uranium only to the United States and the United Kingdom and consult them about any other sales. As for the proposal that the United States would agree on freer exchange to the United Kingdom if the United Kingdom transferred its stockpiles and facilities to less exposed territory, that was up to the two countries to decide, but, 'It certainly cannot be assumed that we would be prepared to accede to any such proposal involving Canada.'[40]

In January 1948 the CPC agreed to proceed on the basis of a modus vivendi, with the trust to continue as the 'Combined Development Agency.'

After a while it became clear, however, that this effort by internationalist officials was up against the same old obstacles. These moves were criticized in the United States by the Congressional Committee and the Joint Chiefs of Staff. The revelation in Britain that Klaus Fuchs, who had had access to secrets of the bomb, had been providing information to Moscow had a disastrous effect. The baleful influence of the House Committee on un-American Activities was growing. The Soviet explosion of an atomic bomb in September 1949 did not help either, as it was assumed that lax security of the Canadians and the British had helped this along. Tripartite talks continued in an effort to replace the modus vivendi, but they were eventually adjourned. Moscow papers gloated over Anglo-American discord. Canada maintained its attitude of 'interested neutrality,' as Heeney described it in a memorandum of 13 December for the minister: 'Our major interest is to see that the negotiations do not break down, as we stand to gain a great deal from any sort of agreement within the framework of the discussions which have been proceeding.'

THE ANGLO-CANADIAN RELATIONSHIP

In the meantime the Canadian-British partnership had been considerably transformed. Faced with the unco-operative attitude of the American ally, the British were disposed to concentrate their resources in the United Kingdom and push ahead on their own. They had provided one of their best men, Sir John Cockcroft, to head the Anglo-Canadian development and under his inspired direction remarkable progress was made at Chalk River. In a letter of 26 October 1945 to Hume Wrong, C.J. Mackenzie summarized the situation as follows:

As far as the United Kingdom is concerned it is my conviction that we hold very strong cards at the moment as they have no atomic energy plant whatsoever in England, and it will take them some time to build even an experimental pile. So, for the moment and for the next year or so they will be dependent entirely on our development in Canada for experience in piles and it will be from our plant that they must obtain any of the by-products which look so promising in the field of medical research. At the present moment there is much discussion in England as to future plans. One school apparently would like to build large scale plants there and they are talking of capital expenditures in the order of 80 million pounds. The other school of thought, which in my opinion is by far the better informed, feels that the wiser plan would be to establish a large Commonwealth plant in Canada, which could supply the material for the other parts of the Empire, and to the research laboratories of which teams from the various Dominions and Britain could come for research work. Personally I think this latter is by far the wiser scheme unless there are some higher policy considerations unknown to me.

A few days after that memorandum Howe was informed that United Kingdom personnel, including Cockcroft, would be withdrawn. Howe complained of the abruptness of the decision. When the British, at the CPC meeting on 16 February 1946, made a statement about their intentions, the Canadian reply was that Canada offered no objection to the proposed programme but since it involved withdrawal from Canada of scientists at present directing the Chalk River project Canada considered that the partnership arrangement previously recorded in the minutes of the CPC would be ended. There were, however, arrangements made for a good deal of co-operation and exchange. Another able scientist, W.B. Lewis, was obtained from Britain to take Cockcroft's place. He proved a great success and remained in Canada. Although Howe claimed that Cockcroft had been recalled without consultation, Mackenzie had learned of the possibility during the summer and had argued vigorously both to Malcolm MacDonald and Sir John Anderson that the withdrawal of Cockcroft would give Canada no alternative but to go in with the United States.[41] It was an idle threat. The Americans were sharing with nobody. Howe continued to nurse his grievance, and when the Americans in 1947 showed an interest in renewing co-operation he wrote to the chairman of the Atomic Energy Advisory Panel,[42] Arnold Heeney, that the position of the United Kingdom was that it insisted on a United Kingdom programme with a great deal of help from 'this continent.' To date Canada had been furnishing that help without getting much in return. 'Although Canada is now in complete control, there is constantly a large group of U.K. scientists at Chalk River for the purpose of obtaining information for the U.K. development.' He suggested that the ambassador keep in mind that a bilateral arrangement between Canada and the United States providing for a complete interchange of information would be more advantageous for Canada than the tripartite arrangement.

From the time the British had first approached the Canadians during the war, C.J. Mackenzie had envisioned great things for Canada from this collaboration. For Canadian scientists and engineers to collaborate with the distinguished Cambridge laboratory would enable Canada to be on the ground floor of most important developments. Americans were, of course, regarded as part of the venture. Now, however, they were rejecting their partners, and there was a new argument for Anglo-Canadian collusion. Cockcroft and some of the scientists may have seen the possibilities of a joint enterprise, but no one in London seemed to have grasped that vision. The British made use of Canada when they had to, but when they were jilted by the Americans there was little awareness – on the political level at least – of the consideration that might be due to their erstwhile partner or, what was more tangible, the opportunities. Perhaps they had been offended by the failure of the Canadians to stand up with them against the Americans. Perhaps they were over-confident of their own capacity without help from the colonies. The judgment of Margaret Gowing, the scrupulously fair-minded British historian of the project, on the withdrawal of Cockcroft is that: 'It was a sorry business, badly handled, but even now the British had not learned their lesson about the need for the fullest possible consultation with Canada.'[43]

There is an interesting contrast in the way the British and Canadians moved on the question of the bomb after their wartime partnership. The British developed their own reactor for peacetime purposes but they also went ahead to produce their own nuclear bombs. They seem never to have taken an agonizing decision to produce a bomb because it was taken for granted that a country of Britain's assumed stature in the world would have one. The Canadian situation was the reverse. At no time was serious consideration given to producing Canada's own bomb. In the earlier stages there were vague ideas that the tripartite partnership would mean some kind of combined trust for the bomb, but there is no evidence of Canadian anxiety to have a finger on the control of such a weapon. Canadians were beginning to refer to themselves as a middle power, but few had ambitions for the responsibilities of great-power status. It hardly seemed necessary to get an American pledge to protect Canada from atomic attack; there was President Roosevelt's promise given in Kingston in 1938 not to stand idly by if Canada were the victim of overseas aggression. It was not to be expected that a Mackenzie King government would opt for independent Canadian possession of a bomb and there is no evidence that the Canadian military pressed for such a capability. Howe said to the Commons in December 1945: 'We have not manufactured atomic bombs, we have no intention of manufacturing atomic bombs.'[44]

It should be recorded that after the postwar controversies settled, the Canada-United Kingdom relationship on the technical side improved notably. A month after the notification to the CPC that the partnership was ended, Howe wrote to the United Kingdom high commissioner: 'We have discussed the relative position of atomic energy developments in the United Kingdom and in Canada, and have had the advice of Dr. C.J. Mackenzie, Sir James Chadwick and Dr. Cockcroft and have, in my opinion, reached a complete understanding of the matter.'[45] So long as there was an ambiguous relationship with an assumption of ultimate authority in London, there was bound to be trouble. When the Commonwealth principle of equal powers in no way subordinate one to another was implemented, partnership could become easy and productive.

INTERESTED NEUTRALITY

Did the Canadians support the Americans in their postwar atomic policy, or the British, or was their's really an attitude of 'interested neutrality' as Heeney had described it? Margaret Gowing's comment is that: 'On both the main issues of the Anglo-American-Canadian negotiations – the international aspect and the location of the British plants – the Canadians sympathised much more with the Americans than with the British.'[46] That is a fair comment as far as those specific issues were concerned. The Canadians also, as she notes, were reluctant to support strong British complaints about the release of information by the United States. The Canadians were much less dissatisfied on this score, but their difference was also tactical. They thought the British were unwise to press this case as vigorously and as often as they did, that they were threatening the vital Anglo-American front in a vain cause. The British accused the Canadians also of joining the Americans in opposing atomic development in the United Kingdom. When the British ambassador in Washington told Howe that Byrnes had said this to Bevin, 'Mr. Howe said that we had never taken this line.' Canada's objection, he said, had been to the embarrassment of the Canadian project by the withdrawal of personnel.[47] Although Howe and others did want Chalk River to serve a major purpose in British plans, the Canadians were careful not to argue the case against British atomic development at home, to which the Americans took such strong objection. The British, it was recognized, had dominion status.

The Canadian belief was that it was better to work away quietly and ad hoc to get as much information as the scientists could extract from their American counterparts than confront their friends in Washington with formal declarations Congress would never accept. The attitude of Congress was a fact of life, not a point of view Canadians agreed with. The strategy worked for the Canadians and would probably have been wiser for the British, although the American attitude to Canada was a little less vigorous, partly because they did want something from Chalk River, they did not regard Canada as vulnerable, and perhaps also because they had not been made stubborn by the importuning of Canadians as they had been by the British. Canada could probably have got more information from the Americans if they had cut themselves off entirely from the British, but that would have been self-defeating. Whereas they could co-operate with the British, they could only be swallowed up by the Americans. Mrs Gowing's comment on Canada's happy position at about that time implies her respect for Canadian tactics. After the anxiety in Canada in 1945, she says, there was now 'great and justifiable confidence in Canada's ability to run an independent project successfully.' The NRX reactor, in her opinion, was the most successful experimental pile in the world. 'In these circumstances Canada was relaxed and generous, ready to help the British and the Americans without bothering too much whether she got back as much as she gave. An odd twist of wartime fate had made her into an important country atomically speaking. She wanted full collaboration, but she now valued her independence as well.'[48] It is a comment to remember. Canadian foreign policy may have been most successful when the national mood was 'relaxed and generous.'

The essential question is not whether Canadians supported the Americans but which Americans they supported. There was little affection in Canada for General Groves, the nationalist, militarist director of the United States project, nor for the likes of Senators Hickenlooper and McKellar. Of the latter Wrong once reported that 'the Senator is unfortunately recovering from a recent illness.'[49] Working with the internationalists like Kennan and Acheson in the State Department or David Lilienthal, chairman of the JCAE, was a different matter. Pearson and Wrong in Washington, as well as British ambassadors like Roger Makins and Oliver Franks, seemed at times to be working in concert with their American friends to thwart the wild men. If they did not share the same perspective they could at least see each other's. Canadians often supported the State Department not because they were pro-American but because they were anti-Hickenlooper. United States policy was not monolithic. It was being constantly shaped by the contest of powerful forces. Canadian, as well as British, officials were inevitably but discreetly engaged in supporting those in the United States apparatus whose approach was in their interest. After a CPC meeting in July 1948, Wrong and the British ambassador suggested to Lilienthal he might make a speech explaining the extent of United States-United Kingdom-Canadian co-operation now going on with such benefit 'to avoid the criticism that it was something clandestine and therefore evil.' Lilienthal got approval for his plan to visit Chalk River and then make that kind of speech in Ottawa. This could not be worked out and in the end he made the speech on 21 August at the Waldorf Astoria on the occasion of the New York Golden Jubilee. The speech was followed by a torch-light parade down Lexington Avenue and a good deal more press coverage where it mattered than it would have received from Parliament Hill.[50]

Part of the game was, of course, not appearing to intervene in United States domestic affairs. Sometimes public support was expressed for United States policies which were merely less offensive than the alternatives. Senator Vandenberg, for example, was an American nationalist who could write: 'America must behave like the *Number One World Power* which she is. Ours must be the world's moral leadership – or the world won't have any!'[51] – a conviction hard for a Canadian to swallow whole. On the other hand he was the strongest political force behind the United Nations in his country, the best guarantee against the tragedy of Woodrow Wilson. He was woolly and lop-sided in his conception of international control, but he was a true convert to the belief that the United States should avoid going it alone. The Canadians could not let him down. Canada was 'supporting' American policy in order to push it in the directions Canada favoured. It is usually, although not always, a more effective way of getting at least some of what a middle power wants than to oppose, confront, and denounce, although it may not be as satisfying to the national ego.

PUBLIC ATTITUDES

The question of public opinion on atomic issues throughout this period requires attention as it casts some light on popular and parliamentary attitudes to United Nations policy in general. The decision to take part, however vicariously, in the production of the dreadful weapon was undertaken, of course, without any public opinion whatsoever. The circumstances were unique. King was always a good barometer of public opinion and it may be doubted whether there would have been much, if any, public objection if the whole thing had been debated in the House of Commons. King assumed that he knew best what the citizenry wanted, and the infuriating conclusion has to be that the assumption was largely justified. The discussions in the House of Commons and in the press after the Canadian announcement in August 1945 of its participation and after the Washington declaration later in that year suggest that the public was bewildered but not critical of what had been done.

Even after the war Howe managed the subject through crown agencies that were similar to his wartime creations. That in itself encouraged a continuing wartime attitude by parliament and the public. As in the United Kingdom the hot subject was handled by a small group of officials and ministers. The fact that they were able and conscientious made the secrecy less controversial. The heavy emphasis on secrecy over technical aspects and the fact that the tripartite discussions described above had to be carried on without even disclosing the basis of their existence certainly encouraged and excused privacy. It was not just the public that was in the dark. As J.E. Hodgetts noted: 'The most significant organizational gap seems to be at the top of the structure, where ministerial guidance and collective cabinet consideration of the nation's total scientific program are far from adequate.'[52] On 31 January 1946 Heeney wrote to Pearson, à propos of cabinet's consideration of the new agreements on the CPC and CDT, that he was worried because 'apart from Mr. Howe none of the Ministers (including the Prime Minister) has any understanding of what is involved.'

Parliament accepted that atomic matters had to be left in the hands of the prime minister with little protest – in great contrast to the rumblings of Congress. King reported to the House on the atomic situation after he had signed the agreement in 1945 (15 November), but it was not until 27 March 1946 that cabinet set up the 'Advisory Panel on Atomic Energy,' an interdepartmental committee whose terms of reference were 'to consider and advise the government upon problems arising out of the development and uses both international and domestic of atomic energy.' However, no parliamentary committee was set up. When pressed in 1947 for some committee similar to the American Joint Committee on Atomic Energy, Howe doubted the advisability of doing so and said: 'The world is very sensitive to atomic energy matters, and any publicity that would come from the committee would be disturbing perhaps in a good many quarters.'[53] On 1 February 1949 Howard Green asked again about the possibility of setting up a House Committee to consider atomic matters. He compared the Canadian situation with that in the States where there were three Congressional committees. Nearly four years after King's first report to the House, Howe finally, on 25 October 1949, moved the establishment of a House Committee on Atomic Energy, and Green was on it. But as Professor Hodgetts commented, 'one has the impression that apart from the salutary educational service rendered the members, officials actually use the opportunity to obtain a rather uncritical stamp of approval for the results of their stewardship.'[54]

There was in Canada, unlike the United States, almost no objection to the principle of government control of atomic energy. Government control of a great natural resource was a more normal phenomenon in Canada. The Atomic Energy Control Board of Canada was set up in August 1946 with power to acquire 'prescribed substances' or any mines and works for production of or research into atomic energy and to regulate the industry. No opposition party in the House objected. In presenting the proposal, Howe put it in the context of similar action by Britain and the United States to acquire national control as a preliminary to international control. The Canadian representative on the UNAEC, it was provided, would be a member of the AECB of Canada. The National Research Council took over the operating and research functions under the supervision of the board. Whereas there was great controversy in Congress and at Westminster over similar legislation, it passed quickly in Ottawa after a constructive discussion and only minor amendment.[55]

There has rarely been such evidence of the docility of the Canadian public as during that period on atomic questions. It may have been that, as in the question of government control through the AECB, there were no plausible alternatives. At the end of 1945 in a poll by the CIPO asking whether Britain and Canada and the United States should tell the Russians that they were ready to join a world government and give that government all the secrets of the atom bomb or continue to try to keep the secret, 58 per cent replied 'Keep the secret' and only 32 per cent 'Give to world government.' Among other attitudes revealed by polls in the year after Hiroshima were strong approval of the use of the bomb against Japan, doubt that Soviet attitudes were attributable to withholding the atomic secret, and a notable confidence in the benefits of atomic energy.[56] This was a subject on which the public seemed to accept government leadership with little questioning. A poll in July 1946 showed that nearly 60 per cent of Canadians would be willing to have Canada turn over control of all its armed forces and munitions, including its atomic bomb materials, to a world parliament provided leading countries did the same. Although that was certainly not what official planners were seriously contemplating a year after the war ended, it was the impression the public might get from the oratory. Neither the questions nor the answers were well disciplined, but they reflect the simplicity of public comprehension at the time.

It should not be taken for granted that the answers meant the forward-looking internationalist policy of the government represented a Canadian consensus. Perhaps Canadians were so much preoccupied with rehabilitation and domestic economic questions that they had not time to care much what the government did. Indeed, the CIPO poll taken in later 1945 on the greatest single problem facing the government produced the following results: 40 per cent full employment, 27 per cent rehabilitation, 8 per cent reconversion, 1 per cent 'peace problems, maintaining world power.' At any rate there was not the same evidence of reaction against participation that was notable after the First World War. There was certainly little will to send the boys abroad again – or to keep them in uniform at all – but not the resentful abstention that had been policy towards the League in its early stages. Whereas in the twenties Canadian governments, both Conservative and Liberal, had been seeking to emasculate the collective security provisions of the League, in the late forties Canadians were eagerly assuming a position well out in front, demanding international control of atomic energy of a kind that would have been anathema to the political leaders of the twenties. The reasons for this change were a long and bitter experience, the fact that the most powerful and the most involved nation on earth was right alongside a lengthy border, and the emergence of a revolutionary new force in international affairs from which Canada, as a producer, could not remain neutral.

PART IV: ESTABLISHMENT OF THE UNITED NATIONS

8

Drafting the Charter

The creation of the United Nations was under way long before the war was over. It was spasmodic and decentralized. The great ad hoc conferences at Hot Springs or Bretton Woods which created specialized agencies were as important in the long run as the preparation of the Charter by the great powers at Dumbarton Oaks and by all the allies at San Francisco. These events, as described in chapter 2, largely predated the Charter and largely predetermined what kind of United Nations there would be, even though it was the drafting of the Charter that attracted public attention as 'the birth of the United Nations.'

At Dumbarton Oaks, Washington, in August 1944 the great powers came together to design a United Nations considerably more restricted in its authority and in the scope for lesser powers than what most Canadian had been loosely talking about. The Charter that emerged at San Francisco in June 1945 is often regarded as a descent from the ideal to the cynical, but it can also be regarded as an advance from the romantic to the practical. The great powers, who were largely responsible, are an easy target, but their citizens were arguing their way through the same contradictions as were Canadians – the relationship between power and responsibility, order and equality. Tradition has encouraged the legend that 'power politics' denied the little people the peaceful world they planned, but the record does not sustain the view that, but for the rapacity of those in the major league, more high-minded lesser powers would have created an international structure in which all would submit to the wise collective will. O.D. Skelton had written of the pursuit by the great powers of 'their own vital and highly pervasive interests' so that the lesser powers had to protect 'their peoples' less ubiquitous and mystical but still equally vital concerns.'[1] In the process of creating and perpetuating the United Nations the rights of lesser powers became a theme quite as mystical as those of their betters, and their claim to jurisdiction in the affairs of the universe almost as ubiquitous. From Ottawa there came a good deal of the rhetoric of injured innocence, and many of its protests against the great powers were justified. The job of External Affairs, however, was to find ways and means of accommodating the rights and responsibilities of large and small powers rather than simply to rage against those who, while they were often antagonists, had to be seen, by the illumination of the war, as partners and protectors as well.

Canadian association with the preparation of the United Nations Charter was in summary as follows. In 1943 the Department of External Affairs began to sort out proposals for an international organization. On 9 July of that year the prime minister made his statement on the functionalist approach to the House of Commons, but the effort to promote debate on the general subject was frustrated by its coinciding with the invasion of Sicily, which diverted the attention of press and public. When in November the four major powers in their Moscow Declaration agreed to set up a general international organization, the main issue was settled and everyone could get down to details. The Throne Speech at the beginning of 1944 announced the government's intention of seeking parliamentary approval of Canadian participation, and the officials started planning. A Working Committee on Post-Hostilities Problems was set up and scrutiny was given to a British PHP paper on 'military aspects of any postwar security organization.'[2] This committee concerned itself more with postwar occupation questions and long-range strategic issues than with plans for a new world organization, but its perspectives conditioned the thinking of the Department of External Affairs members who were at the same time studying British and American plans for a United Nations.

In May 1944 Mackenzie King attended the Commonwealth Prime Ministers Conference in London where British views on a postwar order were fully discussed. In the light of Commonwealth opinion these views were revised and submitted to the other great powers. There was no question of any but the great powers attending the meetings at Dumbarton Oaks but the Commonwealth representatives in Washington were briefed regularly by the British. Close contact was also maintained by the Canadian embassy with the United States State Department and with other interested lesser powers, particularly the Australians, New Zealanders, Dutch, Belgians, and Brazilians. Consideration was even given to something like middle-power bloc tactics.[3] Although the ambassador, Lester Pearson, and his staff talked to their State Department friends, he reported in October that the Americans knew of the Canadian views largely through the British and, now that the State Department had presented them with a draft charter, he thought it time for direct talks with the Americans. He kept Ottawa closely informed on the great-power bargaining, even noting at one point: 'Tonight the Russians are taking the British to a baseball game. This represents concessions on both sides.'[4]

Canadian views on the Dumbarton Oaks proposals were then consolidated in a formal memorandum of 12 January 1945 and presented to the governments of the five great powers, including China and France.[5] There was a preliminary run through the Charter at a Commonwealth meeting in London on the eve of San Francisco. In March 1945 the House of Commons discussed and then approved by a vote of 202 to 5 the Dumbarton Oaks proposals as a basis for discussion. Canada, the resolution said, should become a member of the organization, but the Charter should, before ratification, be submitted to Parliament for approval. An all-party delegation was sent to San Francisco, led at first by the prime minister. After the Charter had been agreed upon, the Executive Committee, on which Canada sat, began meetings in London in August 1945, and the Canadian representatives were active here and in the Preparatory Commission which gathered in November to make plans for the procedures and agendas of the First Session of the General Assembly. In October 1945 the House of Commons unanimously approved the Charter. In the meantime, the first atomic bomb had gone off, four-power unanimity was cracking, and the parliamentarians were more worried about the strength of the international organization to cope with the terrifying situation than in the particular Canadian grievances. The prime minister did not go with the Canadian delegation to London for the opening session of the General Assembly. The leader was the minister of justice, Louis St Laurent, who was accompanied by two other cabinet ministers and a strong group of officials. As at San Francisco and in the Preparatory Commission, there were representatives of opposition parties.

THE OFFICIALS

Planning for the United Nations was in the first place the responsibility of officials. They operated without much guidance from cabinet, but they were experienced in calculating what the traffic would bear. The initiative rested in External Affairs, but the military were closely involved in the PHP exercise, as was the secretary of the cabinet, A.D.P. Heeney. In fact, the whole remarkable mandarinate of the period was a more integral part of the process than the formal records reveal. Ottawa was a small, closely-knit capital, and policy proposals germinated or were adjusted in the Chateau Laurier cafeteria or on the banks of the Gatineau. Notable among those outside External who made contributions were General Maurice Pope of the Privy Council Office, W.A. Mackintosh and R.B. Bryce of Finance, Graham Towers and Louis Rasminsky of the Bank of Canada. Rasminsky was an old Geneva hand and a member of the delegation at San Francisco. Contrary opinions were melded into something that might be called a Canadian approach, although not even in External Affairs was the attitude monolithic.

The presiding officer was Hume Wrong, associate undersecretary of state for external affairs. Mackenzie King said that Wrong 'more than any other man in this country, has from the beginning of its consideration to this hour followed every move in connection with the formation of this world organization, so far as it has been humanly possible for anyone to do so.' He added that 'Mr. Wrong has been present at meetings of the cabinet when we have been discussing these matters. We have benefited by his expert opinions and suggestions, and he has full knowledge of our attitude.'[6] That was no exaggeration, although King had his reasons at that moment for persuading the opposition that they should be satisfied with Wrong rather than the prime minister himself as custodian of the Canadian interest at the Commonwealth conference. King respected Wrong but never felt comfortable with his sharp intelligence. Wrong was a descendant of Edward Blake. He suffered politicians less gladly than did Norman Robertson, but his genius lay in his capacity to reconcile the ideal with the politically and tactically possible. He was impatient of human folly but never daunted by it. He shrewdly reckoned not only with the limitations imposed by Canadian politics but also those imposed by the harsh world in which Canadians had to live and hew their place.

It was Wrong who early perceived the need to get a Canadian perspective on the plans for the end of the war, for a postwar order, and strategic issues of the future. In addition to questions directly related to security, he urged that thought be given to broad political and economic problems. He advocated intellectual preparedness rather than rash initiative, having a shrewd sense of how Canadian pressure could most effectively be applied.[7] His capacity to foresee how situations would develop was extraordinary. 'What is agreed upon before the end of the war is likely to determine the course of history for many years to come. The problems mentioned in this note are mainly long-range problems. Nevertheless, the answers to them will grow out of wartime decisions, reached often in a hurry so as to take advantage of personal conferences of leading statesmen or of an opportune moment to secure a firm reply from one of the leading powers. To pay attention now to these problems is, therefore, a necessary complement to meeting the problems of the conduct of the war.'[8]

Although they knew they would have to trim their views to accommodate the predilections of the all-powerful, most Canadian officials began with a hope that the new United Nations could be more boldly innovative than the League. External Affairs regarded the first British PHP paper as too conservative. It had dismissed the idea of an international police force on the grounds that that implied the existence of a world state. The department was still at the drafting board. Although the officials' utopian inclinations were restrained by a recognition that there was no possibility of abolishing national armies in favour of an international force with full responsibility for the preservation of peace, they were interested in experiments with international forces which might at least guard international bases. That would not require a world state. Wrong saw an encouraging precedent in the polyglot air force then operating out of Britain. Robertson also stressed Canadian wartime involvement in allied forces, typically seeing the need to anchor experimentation in historical experience. He wondered also if such a police force might not provide for the restless young a release comparable to that of the RCMP or the Foreign Legion.[9] Others like Lester Pearson and Escott Reid, operating from the Washington embassy, were inclined to go further. Reid formed the more utopian wing of officialdom, Pearson remained strongly conditioned by the failure of collective security in the thirties and stubbornly reluctant to bow to the 'wisdom' of the great powers. Wrong was often impatient of Reid's ideas as being 'pushed too far.' When Reid pressed after Dumbarton Oaks for a strong statement of Canadian positions by the prime minister, Wrong typically warned against getting publicly committed to amendments 'the inclusion of which we may not be able to secure.'[10] Differences between Wrong and Reid, which became more pronounced later over the North Atlantic Treaty, were less ideological than temperamental. In that their dispute reflected the continuing dilemma of Canadian foreign policy, it was an extraordinarily creative dialogue which prevented Canadian positions at this crucial phase from becoming engraved.[11]

In 1944-5 the divergence was more of emphasis than a cleavage between the Ottawa and Washington offices. The Ottawans, however, were, if not in the driver's seat, at least sitting behind the driver. The undersecretary, Norman Robertson, realized that although King was paying lip service to a strong United Nations, he was unlikely to approve of one which could order Canadian troops into battle. In a sense, Robertson and Wrong were the philosophers of Canada's UN policy; Pearson was the creative operator. Pearson was the supreme strategist who could take a philosophy even if it was not quite his and make a success of it. By making himself indispensable to UNRRA, at Bretton Woods, or at San Francisco he created respect for Canadian positions, but his part in the formulation of these positions in 1944-5 was not decisive. At San Francisco Robertson was the senior civil servant in his position as 'alternate and adviser' to the prime minister in the Steering

Committee and the channel from King after the latter returned to Ottawa. His unique authority was attributable to his own high intelligence and his proximity to the throne. Robertson was the first choice of Acheson and others in the State Department as secretary-general of the United Nations. They showed a slight preference for him over Pearson although they recognized that the latter was a superb 'conference man.'[12]

The planning in External Affairs and in the interdepartmental PHP Committee went on without much reference to the prime minister, except when he had to be briefed for speeches or for meetings abroad. His own conceptions of a new world order, as revealed in his diary records of talks with Churchill and Roosevelt, were mostly platitudinous and often determined by his preoccupation with Canadian issues. His views on an international force, for example, were those of a man involved with a conscription crisis at home. On the whole, however, he seemed reasonably content with the proposals of the officials as filtered to him by Robertson. Some of their earlier ideas about an international force would no doubt have upset him if he had read their papers very seriously. By the time he became involved in actual discussions of the United Nations with the Commonwealth and other leaders, the Canadian emphasis had shifted from abstractions about collective security to the injustices for a responsible middle power of the great powers' plans for them. Canadian grievances of that kind were King's stock in trade. Consideration of a security system with teeth had to be suspended until the rights of the lesser powers were cleared up. By the time that was done at San Francisco, great-power divisions were making any utopian concepts of security irrelevant.

Pearson and Reid continued to regret the failure of the great powers to go beyond the League in providing for collective security. In a letter to Robertson as early as 14 March 1943 Pearson said: 'We are hearing far too much these days that there is no use of the World Organization even contemplating the imposition of sanctions against a Great Power.' He recognized political reason for this line in certain countries, 'but I see no reason why we should encourage it in Canada.' Robertson and Wrong recognized that neither the great powers nor the Canadian government were going to accept that kind of world authority. Nevertheless, Wrong told Pearson he fully agreed with his criticism of the outright rejection by the British and Americans of a Soviet suggestion for an international air force and thought this position would be supported by the government,[13] but such ideas never reached the stage when the Canadian government had to look at the implications for Canada.

Robertson and Wrong were more disposed than their Washington colleagues to temper their conceptions of an ideal world order with a recognition that the willingness of all great powers to participate was of over-riding importance. Robertson, in the latter stages at San Francisco, got King's agreement to a position which he set out as follows:

It seems clear to us that, in this year of grace, there cannot be a World Organization established, with Russia a member, unless it provides for voting rights in the Security Council substantially as set forth in the Great Power memorandum ... The effective choice appears, therefore, to be between such an Organization and an Organization from which the Soviet Union and those countries which feel their security most closely dependent on their relations with it are excluded. Our view is that it is better to take the Organization that we can get and, having come to that decision, to refrain from further efforts to pry apart the difficult unity which the Great Powers have attained. This means foregoing the luxury of making any more perfectionist speeches either on the voting procedure itself or on the general amendment procedure, which is very closely linked with it. We can continue to oppose the Soviet Union and other Great Powers on ... essentially secondary questions, but we should not insist on forcing decisions on such central questions as veto and amendment to a vote in which our association with the other middle and smaller Powers might well result in the rejection of the Dumbarton Oaks proposals.[14]

The position was directed ostensibly against the Australian external affairs minister, but Robertson probably had in mind a tendency to 'perfectionism' in the Canadian ranks as well.

FUNCTIONALISM AS A PRECEPT

It would be misleading to identify the exact prescription Canada advanced for the new world order. The earlier projections had to be modified rapidly in 1944 to take into consideration the compromise the great powers were reaching, the functional institutions which were already under construction, and the chaotic state of the world. One can, however, identify an approach, a creed perhaps, certain principles which could be applied to the structure as it came together. When it became clear that the earlier vision was unattainable, the Canadians kept working to make the best of what was left. By moving with the tide they avoided the danger of splendid isolation and were of some consequence in the creation of structures which were not really what any of the powers had intended – and probably the better for that. What was set out in various charters and then shaped in use may have been a United Nations system more consistent with the Canadians' functionalism than the somewhat authoritarian blueprint with which they tentatively set out in 1943.

The Canadian theory of functionalism was more than an argument for a larger Canadian role. It was a philosophy for world self-government. It accepted a special role for the great powers in matters of security, and therefore the veto, not simply because of political necessity but because security was the appropriate function of the great powers. But security wasn't everything, and those who had major military responsibilities could not claim on that basis to dominate other international matters. The hierarchy of economic powers was different. The four major military powers – although not necessarily at that moment – happened also to be the four major economic powers and they might have special places in economic bodies but on the grounds of their economic qualifications. This was a theory of world governance, but it was intended to avoid centralized world government. It was not a scheme of world federalism, although spokesmen about any kind of international institutions had a habit of implying that the eventual goal was a kind of BNA Act for the world. Canadian functionalists sought to put the function of security in its place and not allow it to dominate all others. The theory was designed to prevent the Security Council from becoming an executive committee or cabinet of the United Nations. The great powers were not going to be allowed to run everything through the 'World Council' as it was called in earlier drafts. The General Assembly would not be subordinate to the council. Although the linkage of various functional bodies, especially the Economic and Social Council, was stressed in the interests of co-ordination, nevertheless the domination of the great powers and the exercise of the veto would be limited. The functionalist thesis was intended to deal with the dilemma that if every country demanded representation on every body, then international government became impossible.

If there was to be a special place for great powers in matters of security, then there should also be a special place for secondary powers – a term Canadian officials used until the end of the war when they gradually adopted 'middle power,' which was coming into wider usage. In his statement to the Commonwealth prime ministers on 11 May 1944 King referred to Canada 'as a power of middle size.' Canada was as anxious to distinguish its position from that of the small powers as it was to acknowledge the position of the great powers. At first Ottawa played with the idea that there might be some special position in the Charter reserved for semi-permanent members of the Security Council based on military capacity. During the Dumbarton Oaks meetings they pressed the case for tying eligibility for the Security Council to a commitment to provide forces for UN service.[15] These ideas had no future. There were middle powers without military capacity, especially in Latin America, who would vote down any such proposal. Whatever sympathy some Americans had with the Canadian attitude, the United States was determined not to oppose the Latins.

The emphasis on the relation between power and responsibility made good sense, but a somewhat Presbyterian view was taken in Ottawa of responsibility. Countries which qualified as middle powers had to be very, very responsible and being responsible meant paying one's dues and not being irresponsible in word or deed. There were no doubts about Canadian worthiness or of the price Canada had paid for due representation. In retrospect Canada's contribution to the victories of 1945 may not look as handsome as it did to those who felt that Canada was one of a very few allies that had gone to war without being attacked. The particular selflessness of the Canadian contribution made up for the unavoidable lack of suffering on the home front. In its attitude to the League, Canada had been afraid of commitments that would take it to war. Now it had been taken to war, had done a good job, and seemed to hope that that one contribution could justify a permanent status based on past effort. In fact, it was probably the potential Canadian contribution to relief and rehabilitation rather than its past military effort that made this Canadian self-image more acceptable to allied countries.

The avoidance of rigidity was a Canadian aim throughout the debate on the new organization – even though the Canadian delegations did press in certain places for more precision in the Charter. Canadian views were by no means always entirely consistent with each other, the emphasis often depending on the drafters of the message. It was accepted that the fears of the great powers for their security would have to be accommodated by special rights on security questions and, that being the case, the lesser powers were better off in a loose structure than in one based on a formally defined hierarchy. When in September 1944 there was deadlock at Dumbarton Oaks over security arrangements a message went from Ottawa to Churchill which was designed to avoid a confrontation with the Russians by not meeting this problem head on. King's telegram said: 'In actual practice it seems to me that this matter of individual veto is likely to be more formal than real. It is unlikely that important questions directly interesting the Soviet government would be pressed to a vote in the Council over Soviet opposition. If they were so pressed, it is still more unlikely that they would secure requisite support from other Council members. If the Soviet government were fully conscious of the respect which other nations have for their strength, they would realize that, even without being assured a right of veto, their own power is a safeguard against the adoption of decisions which they are unwilling to accept.'

The telegram, which reflects Robertson-Wrong pragmatism, stressed the practical importance of the organization's having the support of smaller powers. 'From the point of view of countries without permanent seats on the Council, especially those which are expected to make a substantial contribution to the maintenance of security, the problem is not fundamentally one of status but of the degree to which their people will accept a permanent delegation of control over their own policies and actions to a body on which they may not be represented.' These proposals, King said, raised more than theoretical issues of sovereignty. 'I am conscious of the potential political difficulties in Canada if such pledges were sought and it seems to me that these difficulties will present themselves more acutely in European secondary states.' Ottawa saw a possible solution as follows:

While Soviet participation in the Organization is vital for its success, it is also most important that public opinion throughout the United Nations should warmly support the plan, not only now but for many years to come. If the Organization is intended to be mainly an alliance between the United States, the United Kingdom and Soviet governments (which is, of course, one of its purposes) it would be logical now to accept the Russian view on the question of the veto. It would, however, be more realistic and probably more acceptable to other countries if such an alliance were represented as a necessary transitional stage in the organization of world security, and not as part of a general and permanent system based on 'the sovereign equality of peace loving states.'[16]

THE TRANSITION FROM WAR TO PEACE

The concept of a transitional stage on the way from the wartime alliance to a peacetime international structure was important in Canadian thinking during the months before San Francisco. It was, for one thing, a means of reconciling present exigencies with the persistent vision of what a new league of nations should be. Wrong saw clearly the risks in the Dumbarton Oaks discussions, which, he said, 'involves an egg-dance because there is too much make-believe.' Among the illusions he noted was the assumption that China and the United Kingdom were great powers; that France did not exist; that no new great powers would arise; that the great powers would never quarrel or if they did it was no concern of the others, even though they might be sacrificed to avoid a conflict, as were Czechoslovakia, Finland, and Poland. There were, he recognized, more or less valid reasons for all of this evasion and make-believe. 'But is not its magnitude so great as to render constitution-making premature? Of course something must be done now but might it not be better to have a temporary device? In this context he suggested looking at 'the possibility of amendment' and 'the promise of overhaul.'[17]

If one judged by published statements alone, one would assume that Canadian planners were naïve in their assumption that quarrels among the great powers did not pose a serious threat to the United Nations. Internal memoranda make clear that there were few illusions. R.A. MacKay, for example, in a comment dated 29 February 1944 on a PHP paper, noted that the dangers, rather than from Germany or Japan, came from the conflicting interests among the Big Three. They were likely to reassert themselves, and it was doubtful if the coalition could be maintained by conjuring up hypothetical foes. Wrong recognized that the Security Council could never handle a serious dispute between the great powers.[18] The problem was that public acknowledgment of this fear threatened the allied unity necessary for the last thrust to victory and whatever possiblity there was of maintaining the great power coalition at the heart of the United Nations.

At the same time as they were planning the new international organization External Affairs officers were contemplating proposals for the occupation of Germany and Japan, both of which were expected to be more turbulent than they turned out to be. The struggle for a voice in the international organization could not be divorced from the difficult questions concerning a role in the occupation régimes and the relationship to that issue of a commitment of forces.[19] Canadian attitudes were ambivalent. On the one hand there was the argument for regarding the postwar arrangements for enemy states as interim, divorced from a more 'democratic' régime for a lasting United Nations. There was the persuasive argument that the League had been handicapped by its too close connection with a punitive peace treaty. Nevertheless, there was a case for mobilizing wartime attitudes to strengthen the peacetime crusade. The United Nations had been established as an allied struggle against aggression and this spirit must be continued. If the United Nations were to prosper on the basis of precedents there must be successful precedents. Great-power unity vis-à-vis the defeated states could well be the most effective precedent. In King's telegram to Churchill mentioned above[20] he suggested that 'in the United States and in nearly all the other allied countries public opinion would accept far-reaching obligations designed to prevent a further outbreak from Germany or Japan. This would be regarded in quite a different light from the assumption of permanent and indefinite obligations to assist in all circumstances in the enforcement of settlements prescribed by the Council.' In a statement of questions arising from the Dumbarton Oaks proposals put forward for discussion by the Canadian delegation to the Commonwealth meeting of April 1945,[21] it was stated:

The first stage of the control of Germany by a Military Control Commission will, of course, be in many respects the final stage of military operations against that enemy. Full military occupation and government is expected, however, to give way before very long to other methods of supervision. If the Security Council is not associated with this long-term supervision, its importance may in fact be small during the years when it is most desirable for it to acquire prestige in respect of all nations.

'This conception of the organization in its initial stage as a transitional arrangement' was recommended to the Commonwealth meeting as 'realistic in view of the impossibility of long-range planning during the final stages of the war before the peace terms are agreed upon. Furthermore, the knowledge that a member would have the opportunity of reviewing the question of membership after a term of years would help to make palatable the initial acceptance of the Charter which doubtless will incorporate a number of provisions open to valid and serious criticism.' For this reason importance was attached to an easier arrangement for amending the Charter and also for withdrawal. The United Nations ought not to be paralyzed by withdrawal as the League had been, but at the same time it was recognized that the United Nations might quickly be transformed into something rather different from what its members had thought they were joining and they should have a clearly specified right to get out. As it was obvious in the last months of the war that the great powers were planning their treatment of the enemy among themselves alone and intended to make clear in the Charter that there would be no interference from the United Nations, Canadian attention moved from advocating the concept of a transitional arrangement to providing for amendment of the Charter after a fixed period and by as flexible a process as possible.

THE PRIORITY ISSUES

Up to the spring of 1945 Canadian attention was increasingly fixed on two related aspects of the new organization that seemed directly to affect the Canadian interest. One might be described as the right of consent, the participation of lesser powers in decisions that would commit them to provide forces or engage in sanctions, a demand rooted deep in Canadian history. The other was the recognition of 'responsible' powers with medium military capacity in the selection for non-permanent seats on the Security Council. Much effort went into finding formulas to avert an obligation by lesser powers to enforce decisions of the Security Council in which they had played no part. It was the blatant inequity of the great-powers proposals which riled.

Whereas they would be protected by their vetoes from enforcing decisions they disliked, other members were regarded as obligated to do what they were told. Although the latter's military obligations would be determined by special agreement separately ratified by each member, once consent had been given the Security Council could presumably call upon the member to act. Much was made in Canadian memoranda of the argument that no state can really represent another and that it was not in the Canadian tradition to delegate.[22] There were various Canadian suggestions to meet this situation: by securing Assembly approval of such Security Council decisions or by giving temporary membership on the Council to states whose co-operation was needed.

On the eligibility of middle powers for special consideration in appointments to the Security Council, the Canadians from the beginning pressed their case hard with the British who gave them some heed. It was proof of British loyalty that they did what they could to help, although in their exchanges with the Canadians they produced some dismaying questions. In a telegram of 21 August 1944 from the secretary of state for dominion affairs to the secretary of state for external affairs, agreement was expressed in principle that weight should be given to difference in power, status, and functional importance as well as to the need for representation from the different regions.

But we feel that any system which attempted to classify secondary powers in different categories might arouse antagonism to the organization at the outset. Moreover ... it is questionable whether any special weight should be given to military power as a qualification for election. It is by no means certain that it would operate to the advantage of British Commonwealth countries. As regards the suggestion that the part played in the present war by candidates for the Council should be a relevant criterion, this will no doubt be the case to some extent in the early postwar years, but it will be impossible to ignore the claim of European countries whose co-operation will be essential, though their contribution to victory may have been limited because, owing to their geographical situation, they have been over-run by the enemy.

Subsequent Canadian communications failed to grapple with the British arguments but merely stated again the injustice of it all and the political difficulty it involved for Canada.

This preoccupation during the Dumbarton Oaks phase with special grievances perhaps distracted officials from the broader issues they had contemplated in the beginning. They justified their concern, however, on the grounds that no international institution could be strong and stable without the willing support of the lesser powers. They were also convinced that Canadians would reject a charter that would obligate them unjustly. In retrospect their nervousness about parliamentary reaction seems exaggerated, as the Canadian government and parliament were by 1945 too far committed to a United Nations to reject anything the British and Americans would join. Public opinion polls of the time suggest that Canadians, particularly those who spoke English, favoured a United Nations with forces at its command and were not especially sensitive about whether Canada was represented on the body that called them in to action.[23] Warnings that parliament 'would not understand' are, of course, the instinctive weapons of diplomats. The Americans could get almost anything by warning that the Senate might again walk out. Canadian diplomats were encouraged by their prime minister to take a cautious view of the international dedication of the Canadian people. Some of them realized, furthermore, that it would help the Canadian people to swallow certain inevitable provisions if they knew that their representatives had put up the best possible fight against them. In a realistic assessment of the prospects for the military provisions of the Charter in early 1945, Hume Wrong concluded:

The proposals looked at by themselves appear more formidable than they are likely to be in reality, at any rate for a number of years. The Security Council will control military power less extensive than one would expect from the text of the proposals. The chief organization of power will probably arise from the commitments made between the major allies to enforce the execution of the peace terms.

There are, nevertheless, serious objections from the Canadian point of view to the acceptance without change of those parts of the draft which define the authority of the Security Council to call upon all members to assist in enforcing its decisions. These objections are likely to be less important in practice than in securing public support for the plan.[24]

It is of interest also to note the subjects which did not get much attention in the preparatory studies, including some which were to prove controversial and to occupy priority attention on the agenda of the evolving United Nations system. There is little in the working papers about human rights,[25] partly because of the wariness of the federal government on the subject and partly because of the conviction that there were too many honest but diverse national interpretations to permit much useful initiative by an international organization. On the question of interference in the internal affairs of a country the Canadian view was also cautious. Support was given to the British opinion that the only valid reason for interference was to forestall conditions that endangered international peace and security. Even more surprising is the lack of attention in the position papers to the economic and social functions. One reason was that they were not given much attention in the great-power proposals on which comments were being made. It was the security issues which mattered to them, and the Russians discouraged consideration of other functions. Canada did at least let the powers know that they planned to rectify this situation at San Francisco.[26]

There was little mention of disarmament either, a subject regarded of great importance in the League and one in which Canada was to be much involved in the United Nations. The planners in Ottawa were, of course, unaware of the atomic bomb to be unleashed in August 1945, an event which would have upset any previous calculations on the regulation of armaments. On this question Canadian thinking reflected that of others. Everyone's mind was on collective security rather than disarmament. A wartime poll (20 January 1943) found 80 per cent favouring the maintenance of strong armed force after the war. One of the few mentions of disarmament was in the memorandum entitled 'Military Aspects of the Dumbarton Oaks Proposals' by Hume Wrong.[27] Under the heading 'Regulation of Armaments' he noted that in contrast with the League Covenant the draft Charter had little to say on the control of armaments, except for a brief statement that in order to promote peace and security with the least diversion of human and economic resources for armaments, the Security Council should formulate plans for a system of regulation of armaments to be submitted to members of the organization. Wrong's comment was as follows: 'The word "regulation" has been deliberately adopted in place of the word "limitation" with the idea that it might prove desirable to agree on the minimum as well as the maximum armaments which should be maintained by members. The regulation of armaments has a low priority in the minds of the framers of the proposals and consideration of it is put off until the Military Staff Committee is in a position to advise the Security Council on a general system of regulation for submission to members of the organization.' Disarmament got scant attention at San Francisco and only a brief reference in the Charter.

THE COMMONWEALTH AND THE UNITED NATIONS

There had been those who regarded Canada's association with the League of Nations as a threat to Commonwealth loyalty, but by 1945 there was little opposition to the view that each had its function and they were compatible. Among those notions which did not survive the brass-tacks stage of negotiation was that of designating the British Commonwealth, rather than the

United Kingdom, as one of the great-power members of the Security Council.[28] In the Foreign Office they laughed at the idea.[29] Although King assumed that Churchill favoured it, Churchill does not seem to have raised it with him personally and specifically. Speakers continued carelessly to refer to the Commonwealth as a great power, but it did not appear in any of the British proposals discussed at or after Dumbarton Oaks. The British, in fact, were seeking to get an assured seat on the Security Council for a Commonwealth country in addition to the United Kingdom. This was a proposal about which the Canadians were unwisely cool. Miscalculating, as they were inclined to do at this time, the continuing importance of Canadian power, they thought such an arrangement would give Canada inadequate opportunities to serve on the Security Council. When United Nations politics started to work, however, they realized it was a considerable advantage to be a member of the most exclusive of all the groupings.

On the eve of the San Francisco Conference there was a demonstration in London of the value of Commonwealth consultation when the representatives had what Lord Cranborne described as 'a sort of dress rehearsal for San Francisco.' As Massey pointed out in a report to Norman Robertson dated 23 April, the question of a 'single voice' was irrelevant. He thought it unfortunate that advocates of such a policy could not see the Commonwealth consulting together in this way so that they might realize the impracticability of the single voice in real situations.[30] If the delegations had in fact cast votes on each issue, the United Kingdom would have found itself out-voted on several matters in which it had at least tacit commitments to the Soviet Union and the United States. It was the stronger opponents of a collective voice, Canada and South Africa, who were in fact closest to the United Kingdom in their views on major United Nations issues. Messrs Fraser of New Zealand and Evatt of Australia, already preparing for obstreperous roles at San Francisco, took vehement issue with the British even on matters which the British considered of critical importance – the question of mandates and dependent territories. Massey called Fraser 'the only Wilsonian present.'[31] He was not even prepared to compromise by accepting the Yalta voting formula. He got some Canadian support for his stand against admitting to San Francisco what he called 'the bandwagon states,' those who had made death-bed repentances by declaring war at the last minute. The Commonwealth members had all been upset by the bloc tactics of the Latin Americans at the Philadelphia ILO conference, Bretton Woods, and particularly the International Civil Aviation Conference in Chicago[32] and wanted to prevent such activities from frustrating the purposes of the new organization.

Although Canada got broad support for its views on the rights of secondary powers, the amendment of the Charter, and the right of withdrawal, they did less well on the obligations of non-member states to enforce sanctions. Smuts agreed with them, but there was opposition from the United Kingdom, Australia, and India. Here they ran into the strong prejudice against anything which would seem to weaken the credibility of the United Nations as an instrument of collective security. Smuts and the British clashed with Fraser and Evatt on the anti-colonialist ideology of the Labour governments in Australia and New Zealand. It was undoubtedly useful for the British to have this preview of what they would encounter at San Francisco, and later in the United Nations itself, and no doubt their positions were modified to some extent. Although there were some vigorous anti-colonialists in the East Block, Ottawa did not share the more extreme views of Canberra and Wellington at that time. They did think it in the interests of Britain and the other imperial powers to co-operate in a reasonable system of mandates and they were worried about friction with the doctrinaire views of the Americans on colonialism.

THE SAN FRANCISCO CONFERENCE

An interesting aspect of the preparations for San Francisco was a determined effort to engage the public in the discussion – an effort at participatory democracy hardly equalled by those who some years later invented the principle. King discouraged discussion. It would have been contrary to his instinct about the special nature of foreign policy actually to want advice from the public. Nevertheless, the Wartime Information Board put out a pamphlet on the Dumbarton Oaks proposals in the autumn of 1944 and distributed over 40,000 copies. The illustrative charts were sent to newspapers and other periodicals, discussion groups were encouraged, speakers notes were provided for radio in co-operation with the Canadian Council for Education for Citizenship. The prime minister tabled a copy of the Dumbarton Oaks proposal and had it distributed to every MP. Behind this effort were some enthusiastic officials who felt strongly the need for broad public support if Canada were to play the active role they wanted in a new international organization.[33]

King concealed his doubts about the whole project and went off to San Francisco at the head of the delegation. He had no alternative. He liked the sense of historic occasion but had not worked up much interest in the major issues. He was preoccupied with the June election and was absent from San Francisco for about six crucial weeks. For the same reason the other parliamentary delegates were present only for the first month or so. The officials on the delegation were a remarkable group. For the infighting in committees they had the knowledge required. Lacking the political clout which only ministers can bring to bear, they had to use their wits. They could not cut the figure of politicians like Evatt or Fraser or play the kind of role Smuts did in the drafting of the Preamble to the Charter. Professional diplomats, however, knew they were there. The Canadian position was perhaps helped by the rudeness of the Australians and New Zealanders. In the critical late stages Pearson was asked by Halifax, Dulles, and Vandenberg if he would caution Evatt about carrying too far his demands on powers being accorded the Assembly, and Pearson was able to do so. The Canadians had a more sympathetic awareness of the political problems of the five powers and this was appreciated. Their expertise at drafting compromises (both because they were good drafters and good compromisers) firmly established the reputation which had been growing at Bretton Woods, Atlantic City, and Chicago. It is ironic that Pearson's reputation for mediation owed something to a much noted intervention to relieve with humour the tension created by an unpleasant public row on the part of the Australians and New Zealanders with the British at San Francisco.[34]

Although the parliamentary representatives had to leave most of the negotiation to the professionals they were by no means cyphers. The presence on the delegation of members of the opposition, made particularly necessary by the fact that there would be an election before any United Nations Charter could be considered for approval, reflected the collective will of parliament to pledge non-partisan support for the new organization. King said the government would have to take ultimate responsibility for positions adopted and also for appointing the delegation, but he would not prevent any member, if that member found it impossible to agree, from making his views known. He preferred to have the members go as one delegation rather than have those from the opposition present as associates or advisers.[35] He had been somewhat reluctant at first to have an all-party delegation but his hand was forced by the British and Australian announcements that they planned to do so. King did not, however, allow the parties to choose their own representatives. The Conservatives protested the failure to include their leader, John Bracken, but the government's choice of Gordon Graydon was a happier one. Bracken subsequently proved at United Nations assemblies his innocence of international affairs whereas Graydon worked hard and effectively. That his views on some controversial issues, such as those having to do with the Commonwealth, were closer to those of the government than were the positions of some Tories was undoubtedly a consideration in King's mind. M.J. Coldwell for the CCF was one of the best-informed parliamentarians and conscientiously interested in all aspects of the subject. Partisan differences did not in fact arise, but there was no doubt who was in charge. As Pearson commented: 'For a few weeks at least, Canada will probably have a national government – at San Francisco!'[36]

The opposition members from the beginning accepted the principal emphases of the delegation. When the prime minister outlined the position he would take on the commitment of Canadian forces by the Security Council, Coldwell said that so long as the great power veto remained, the policy suggested was the only one that could be taken by Canada. Graydon suggested that, while it was implicit in the statement, it might be made clear that Canada was anxious to meet its full obligations for security and was making its suggestions, not to evade those obligations, but in reality to increase the capacity for ready and effective action – a position which was closer to the hearts of the officials than to the prime minister, although he could not have denied it.[37] The government was influenced by a general anxiety to raise Canada's part in the international organization above domestic politics and, with the helpful collaboration of the opposition, the United Nations did not become an issue of any consequence in the elections which took place while it was being created.[38]

Mackenzie King, reaching for the historic moment, put a great deal into his opening speech at San Francisco. A little too much of himself perhaps went into it. There was a lot about nations uniting to save and to serve humanity, forging and fashioning from the fires of war an institution for world security, and giving hope to grief-stricken humanity. The Canadian aim was 'to help to bring into being a world community in which social security and human welfare will become a part of the inheritance of mankind.' King's excessive modesty about what the Canadian delegation would do proved to be wishful thinking. 'We shall not,' he said, 'be guided by considerations of national pride or prestige and shall not seek to have changes made for reasons such as these.'[39] Although this kind of holiness was peculiarly Mr King's, the business about prestige was echoed in the solemn insistence in the official papers that countries should not seek seats on the Security Council for reasons of prestige. Such low-mindedness was constantly deplored.

At San Francisco the Canadian delegation ably argued its favourite causes and managed to get some revisions of the Charter. Much of the effort was directed against the great powers, but the British, and sometimes the Americans, tried to be helpful. On a few issues Canada had prejudices which were more North American than middlepower. It opposed the movement led by

New Zealand to get a guarantee of the territorial integrity of states. It would approve a general principle of respect for the sovereign equality of states, but a sweeping guarantee of the status quo territory of every member had been what Canadians disliked in the League. The United States Senate had maintained a similar bias, and US opposition was such that Canada was not required to put up much of a struggle. Altogether, the great powers did bend somewhat more than might have been expected, although no great dent was made in the Dumbarton Oaks or Yalta frameworks. In the process of a good energetic conference the Charter was made more attractive to the lesser powers and could be accepted as something they had helped create rather than something that had been entirely imposed upon them. In their anxiety to make the Charter widely acceptable to the Canadian parliament and people official spokesmen perhaps exaggerated the success of the Canadian delegation but, given the odds, it was creditable.

Like the other lesser powers the Canadian delegation favoured widening the scope of the General Assembly, but this purpose was conditioned by concern that the great powers accept rather than run away from their security obligations. According to the delegation's report, 'in order to place responsibility where it belongs and to avoid divided or concurrent jurisdiction and jurisdictional disputes which will play into the hands of trouble-making states,'[40] the General Assembly must not be able to act on matters of peace and security when the Security Council is dealing with them actively and effectively. However, the General Assembly should be able to take over responsibility if a veto in the Security Council made action impossible. The delegation opposed some of the more extreme claims for the General Assembly, as for instance those put forward by New Zealand. They favoured the granting of power to the Assembly to take initiatives in securing peaceful change (Article 14) but recognized the danger of being too specific. For example, referring to treaty revision might inspire disrespect for existing treaties. The Canadian view was that the Security Council was not a creature of the General Assembly. It was not responsible to the General Assembly, but at the same time it was not an executive committee of the General Assembly. It was a body whose powers, like those of the General Assembly, stemmed from the Charter. Canada favoured reports from the Security Council to the General Assembly but denied that this empowered the General Assembly to subject Security Council actions to inquisition.

There was, of course, much opposition to the veto from middle powers. Canada defended it on functional grounds but joined other middle powers in opposing the application of the veto to peaceful settlement as distinct from breaches of the peace. They had hoped also to limit its use over membership.

From the beginning the delegation recognized that the case against the veto over peaceful settlement was one they must support – but with the proviso that it would not drive the Russians out of the UN. Within the delegation, Wilgress, the Canadian ambassador in Moscow, argued that although it would be a mistake to be 'tough' all down the line with the Russians, it was necessary to stand firm on important issues like this one that could be defended.[41] The Western great powers agreed that the lesser powers had a good case and tried to get a compromise agreement with the Russians. When they failed, it looked as if the conference might break up, and desperate measures were being considered.

At this point Norman Robertson asserted his authority. The ministers were all back in Ottawa. Fraser and Evatt accused the British of duplicity for abandoning the position they had taken with Commonwealth countries on the veto. Robertson said the British position was understandable in the light of their obligation to maintain great-power unanimity. Robertson and Pearson talked to Evatt who said he had in mind both the possibility that the great powers were bluffing and the probability that if he pressed his stand to an ultimate vote he would not get enough support but would be in a stronger position in dealing with domestic criticism. Robertson said there were many things on which it would be desirable to point to a firm stand on principle but it was a luxury which could not be enjoyed by many delegations without running the risk of upsetting the entire conference. At this point Robertson thought that if Canada threw its weight energetically behind Evatt, they could probably defeat the great powers on the veto question, but he got the agreement of the prime minister to a policy of not forcing the question to a vote.[42] In the end the Russians took a more flexible position on the right of the Council to discuss an issue without the veto, but there was no compromise on the veto right over any action or decisions. Canada did not vote with Australia and the other intransigents on this issue although they tried unsuccessfully a couple of compromise suggestions.[43]

The guiding Canadian attitude was summed up in the statement of St Laurent to the House of Commons on 16 October 1945 when he said: 'It was apparent that the joint interpretation of the Yalta voting formula represented the greatest possible measure of agreement which could be obtained among the great powers themselves at this time on this subject.'[44] He said he had been influenced by the combined statements of the representatives of the great powers that they would use their special voting position with a sense of responsibility, consideration for the interests of smaller states, and, therefore, sparingly. Getting this pledge out of the great powers was properly regarded as an achievement by the lesser powers. Western powers did use the veto sparingly, although it may be argued that they were guided less by their pledge than by the realization in the early years of the United Nations that they could normally count on majority support in the Security Council in any case. The Canadian delegation's report recognized that the United Nations was going to be a highly political organization and its practices would be determined more by the art of the possible in varying circumstances than by legalistic provisions. 'There was the further consideration that it is possible to exaggerate the importance of voting arrangements in the Council. For example, during the whole course of the Conference the Great Powers had been able to work together without taking formal votes.'[45]

In the Canadian view the Charter to be constructed on the basis of the Dumbarton Oaks proposals was to be a beginning and not an end. 'It was to be the foundation of a new structure to create and preserve peace, not the whole vast completed edifice. If the Organization is to free the peoples of the world from the fear of war, it would eventually have to be given the right and the power to restrain any disturber of the world's peace.'[46] In spite of this belief, however, in the need for an instrument of collective security, Canadian boys were not going to be sent to war by external bodies. Not only the Russians, however, but also some vulnerable middle powers feared that any provision for special representation in the Security Council would raise doubts about the credibility of that body as a deterrent to aggression. It was the kind of opposition Canada had roused when it opposed Article 10 of the League. The British, French, and Chinese agreed with a proposed Canadian amendment to the effect that any member not represented on the Security Council could participate in the decisions concerning the employment of contingents of its armed forces. The Americans came round, but the Russians were very dubious. Privately the Russians said they accepted the reasonableness of the proposal so far as it concerned Canada but could not agree to the generalization of the principle. Novikov of the USSR told the Canadians in confidence that there were only four countries that had really fought the war, the USSR, the United States, the United Kingdom, and Canada[47] – a gross misrepresentation but calculated to appeal to Canadian prejudice. Eventually the Russians agreed to accept a wording that applied only to situations in which the use of the member's forces was under consideration if Canada would drop two other amendments concerning temporary membership on the Council. As these latter had little chance of adoption, Canada agreed to get what it could and Article 44, providing for participation as Canada wanted, was enshrined in the Charter.

The effort may have been worth while to appease the Canadian sense of grievance, but as the special agreements called for in Article 43 have never been reached, there has been no occasion to apply Article 44. When Canada eventually did provide forces for peacekeeping operations, an entirely different kind of operation from what was envisaged in 1945, this was done on a voluntary basis. In the kind of United Nations which developed there could be no question of conscripting the forces of any member state. What was achieved in getting Article 32 into the Charter may have been of more lasting importance. This article provides that a party to a dispute which is not a member of the Council should be invited to participate in the discussions. The Canadian and Dutch delegations were unsuccessful in their effort to see that both parties to the dispute would have equal voting privileges, even if one was a member and one was not, but, in spite of the apparent logic of the demand, it was clear to a majority that voting privileges for ad hoc participants in Council sessions would introduce a chaotic element.

Canadians might have taken more credit for the role they played in emphasizing the Security Council's function to promote peaceful settlements of disputes under Chapter VI. There was some general nervousness, shared by the United States, about the Council's seeming to 'impose' peaceful settlement. The Commonwealth members in April had argued that the Council should be empowered to recommend appropriate terms of settlement whenever it thought fit to do so in serious disputes. Both France and Canada made proposals to this effect at San Francisco, but their suggestions were not adopted. On this move Ruth Russell in her authoritative *History of the United Nations Charter*, commented: 'The two delegations, it will be noted, had suggested changes that would have altered the Dumbarton Oaks concept of the Council as primarily policeman, rather than as an arbiter or mediator concerned with the merits of the disputes or situations.'[48] Eventually, however, the latter is the way the Security Council moved.

In the mood of 1945 the mediatory functions as stressed in the League were considered inadequate; the new body must have the powers of a police force. Canadians shared that view to a point, but they had always considered the mediatory functions as important also. In his report to parliament St Laurent modestly said: 'It is, I think, satisfactory that the charter dealing with the peaceful settlement of disputes has been enlarged and improved, because it is before violence has broken out that the organization can do its most useful work in preventing aggression.'[49] This was beginning to sound more like the prewar views on the functions of an international organization.

The much heralded triumph of Canadian functionalism was the insertion in the Charter of Article 23 concerning the qualifications for non-permanent members of the Security Council. This also proved a hollow victory. Article 23 directs that in the election of the members of the Security Council due regard should be 'specially paid, in the first instance to the contribution of Members of the United Nations to the maintenance of international peace and security and to the other purposes of the Organization.' At San Francisco there were pressures for various criteria. The Latin American bloc sought a permanent seat for the region or a specified allocation. India wanted due regard paid to population and economic capacity. The Dutch wanted middle-power membership formally specified in the Charter. Canada wanted to require the Assembly to adopt rules governing selection, but this was defeated. When the British proposed adding 'equitable geographic distribution' as a second criterion, this was adopted as a 'sponsors' amendment.' In spite of Canadian insistence that the second criterion was intended to be subordinate to the first, it could not be said that this interpretation was affirmed by the conference. In fact this question, to which Canada had attached primary importance in the early stages of preparing the Charter, fizzled out as a major issue at San Francisco. Perhaps the Canadian attachment to a logical case, based on an impeccable principle of functionalism, obscured from them the political unreality of what they sought. It is difficult to avoid the conclusion that the Soviet Union, the United States, the Latin Americans, and others considered the best tactic was to accept the amendment and ignore it – as they did.

On regionalism[50] the Canadian attitude was decidedly sceptical. At the Commonwealth Prime Ministers meeting in 1944 King had successfully shot down some impractical views of Churchill on this subject, views which were not shared in the Foreign Office. These provided for regional councils on a continental basis. What King especially disliked was that the Commonwealth would be represented by one of its members on each council – Canada on the North American Council, for example.[51] When Churchill realized that the other prime ministers were dubious, he withdrew his paper, saying that he had himself wondered how the representation would be worked out.[52] The basic Canadian premise was that world security could not be trusted in the first place to regional organizations, although certain functions, both economic and strategic, might be handled by ad hoc regional bodies strictly within the authority of the world organization. It had been continental isolationism, they believed, that had allowed the two great wars to happen. They had not liked the early proposals by which regional organizations would have the authority to settle local disputes because they preferred that regional organizations have no political authority. They realized, of course, that it would be difficult to secure United States consent to an agreement that did not allow the settlement of inter-American disputes by inter-American bodies. It was important, however, that no enforcement action be taken without approval by the Security Council. It was recognized that there were likely to be regional agreements in Western Europe to prevent the resurgence of Germany, but these could be treated as part of the special arrangements to enforce the peace.

At San Francisco Canada's attitude on regionalism was muted. Although the official delegation report describes in detail the discussion of regional arrangements, it is curiously silent about any Canadian position, probably because an energetic Canadian position was unnecessary. The British had views which Canada had approved and they were very effective in securing the necessary compromise. The Canadian delegation considered it tactically wise to direct its resources where they were needed and avoid wasting credit.

In view of their importance later, at the time when NATO was established, Canadian attitudes towards Article 51, which provided for the right of individual or collective self-defence, and Article 53, on the rights of regional agencies for peace and security, are of interest. Canada favoured the assertion of the authority of the universal body over the regional body when it came to enforcement. The problem was that the zealous desire of the Latin Americans to preserve the autonomy of their inter-American system got mixed up with the concern of the European states that they be free to take action against Germany, or Japan, or unspecified aggressors in the confused post-hostilities situations expected before the Security Council had achieved the power and authority to assume responsibility. The Latins did not want the European powers with vetoes to be able to interfere with their holy right to settle their own affairs. This view was supported by some American politicians but the wiser heads in Washington recognized that such a precedent would rule out American exercise of its great-power rights in other hemispheres. The question was how to provide for the Europeans to act in accordance with their mutual defence treaties during the perilous time of transition without making exceptions which would enable a regional group like the pan-Americans to act indefinitely without the authority of the Security Council. The solution finally agreed upon was the provision of both Articles 51 and 53.[53] Article 51, which authorized collective self-defence, was designed to allow the Europeans to do what they felt was needed in their uncertain situation and also to justify action by the western hemisphere powers in the event that non-American powers in the Security Council tried to obstruct their activities. Article 53 provided for enforcement by regional agencies provided it was authorized by the Security Council.

It could not have been clearly foreseen at the time that within a couple of years Article 51 would be what Canada and its allies needed to justify a North Atlantic Treaty Organization because lack of unanimity had paralyzed the

Security Council. Nevertheless, a Canadian PHP paper, dated 21 April 1944, had pointed out the important difference between regional security and regional defence organizations, regarding the latter as essential and the former as dubious. In Hume Wrong's frequent considerations of the need for transitional or fall-back positions to allow for collective defence there was a clear distinction between the action provided for in Article 51, by which countries could combine forces against an external threat, and arrangements by which regional groups, possibly dominated by a great power, could impose security upon their own members. NATO, it should be borne in mind, is a collective defence organization under Article 51, not a regional collective security organization under Article 53.

In the latter days of the conference Canada actively sought fixed provisions for amendment of the Charter. Although Canada was willing to recognize the exigencies of postwar stresses and great-power collaboration, nevertheless, what was being produced at San Francisco was regarded as a lowest-common-denominator United Nations. In the interest of stability amendments should not be too easy, but they should certainly be possible. Canada did not like the right of veto over amendments but recognized that there could be no absolute dispensing with it. The delegation tried to ease the process somewhat. With majority support from the middle powers, they sought to provide for a revisionary conference after ten years. By the time this item was discussed at San Francisco everyone was tired and the issues of amendment and the right of withdrawal became badly confused. The Russians were suspicious, and the Americans were sure the Senate would not accept a Charter unless the United States maintained the right of veto over any amendments. Pearson, Robertson, and Wrong argued with the Americans that provision for a constitutional conference at an appointed time, without reference to procedure at that conference, would not oblige them in advance to accept amendments which they did not approve. Pearson was inclined to call what he regarded as an American bluff, but Wrong felt obliged to remind the delegation that 'our instructions were not to push our opposition to a point where it might endanger participation by the United States in the Organization.'[54]

A Canadian proposal did play a part in getting the sponsoring powers, at United States urging, to propose a general conference to review the Charter. Such a provision was essential to the Canadian conception of a transitional phase of the UN. After much proposing and counterproposing, however, with the fight gone out of the lesser powers, Article 109 was adopted. It provided for a review conference to be considered at the Tenth General Assembly at the latest, but the veto would apply to any amendments. Again, the fight was probably worth putting up to register a point, but as Goodrich and Hambro point out: 'In reality, the "concessions" incorporated into Article 109 were of no great significance.' The great powers could block recommendations of the conference and, as any member could at any time propose that the Assembly call a Charter-review conference, the special provision for the Tenth Session was of minor importance.[55]

Canadian ideas on membership were liberal. On the designation of great powers Canada not only supported a permanent seat for France, but had argued for conferring this without delay. It was cooler about China. Canada feared that the Americans, because of their hostility to de Gaulle and deference to Chiang, would put off recognition of the French right as long as possible. The British thought China was not really a great power and suggested that if it were given a permanent seat it should not be given the veto powers. There was little hope, however, of any such provision securing United States approval.[56] In general, it was held in Ottawa that membership in the UN should be as comprehensive as possible, except that the cases of Germany and Japan should be left for consideration after a period of years. Canada did not like the agreement reached at Yalta to accept separate membership for the Ukrainian and Byelorussian Soviet Republics, especially as there had been hints of an analogy with the Commonwealth, but if this was to be the price of Soviet adhesion – or at least the price of Soviet consent for the admission of India – it might be necessary to pay it, without, however, going publicly on record in support. Canada did not favour the exclusion of neutrals and especially wanted Ireland admitted soon, as well as Switzerland and Sweden. It was privately recognized, however, that one advantage of confining membership at the start to fighting allies was that it would reduce the strength of the Latin American bloc.

Membership was not in itself a serious issue at San Francisco in spite of a row over inviting neutrals to the conference. There were disputes over suspension, expulsion, and withdrawal. Canada joined unsuccessfully with Australia in seeking to remove the veto power over membership and restricting it only to the membership of enemy states and Spain. While not accepting the view that any state, simply by reason of its existence, had a right to membership, Canada supported proposals 'that tended towards the principle of universality.'[57] Canada did not like, however, the great powers' proposals for expulsion of persistent violators of the Charter, arguing that this would release the violator from his obligations whereas suspension would not. This case was almost won, but at Soviet insistence the Dumbarton Oaks provision for expulsion (Articles 5 and 6) was finally put into the Charter. In accordance with its belief in keeping as many states as possible within the UN discipline, Canada was not enthusiastic about providing for a right of withdrawal. However, when this question came up at a late stage, in the context of the great-powers' insistence on maintaining their veto over amendments to the Charter, Canada and other small powers could not agree to being locked into membership of an organization which could alter its constitution without their consent. Canada did not want withdrawal provided for in the Charter and proposed that it be restricted to those who were still dissatisfied after a revisionary conference. In the end a restricted right of withdrawal was conceded in the Rapporteur's report, the legal status of which has been a subject of some difference of opinion.

On domestic jurisdiction, which was to loom large in the history of the United Nations, Canada did not take a strong public stand. Article 2(7) prevents the United Nations from intervening in matters which are essentially within the domestic jurisdiction of any state and has been at times denounced and defended by almost all members of the Assembly, depending on whether a friendly or unfriendly state was involved. At San Francisco practically everybody was really in favour of it, but most were shy about saying so categorically. The Russians naturally opposed any interference and the Americans wanted such protection for the sake of Congress. Latin Americans insisted upon it out of their traditional fear of intervention, and Australia led the lesser powers in insisting that it was unfair for the great powers to have this protection in the Security Council through their veto while the lesser powers had no such defence. The Australians wanted no interference with their immigration policies. Neither did Canada, but Wrong advised King that these fears were unfounded, as a dispute over immigration policy could not come before the UN unless it was leading to war. 'In that event it is not a domestic dispute but an international dispute which the Council should be able to deal with as threatening the peace of the world.'[58]

The only reason there was any argument over 2(7) was that everyone knew wars could arise from domestic situations – the oppression of minorities, for example. Some European countries, Norway in particular, were anxious that the Security Council not be hamstrung. The great powers at Dumbarton Oaks had included a domestic jurisdiction provision to apply only to peaceful settlement of disputes by the Security Council, but at San Francisco they proposed an amendment extending it to all the functions of the organization, the reason being the broadening of these functions in the economic, social, and cultural fields. However, to make clear that the security role would not be weakened the qualification was added that this limitation would not prejudice the application of the chapter on 'Threats to the Peace.' Although they recognized the argument put forward, for instance, by the World Jewish Congress that the amendment would exclude many questions of human rights from UN jurisdiction, the Canadian delegation regarded the sponsors' amendment as a compromise they might appropriately support. Evatt led a successful move to have the amendment altered to refer specifically to the application of enforcement measures under Chapter VII. His fear was that all a great power needed to do otherwise was to threaten a breach of the peace in order to claim that a question involving a lesser power was not a matter of domestic jurisdiction.

Given Canada's concern with enforcement action, the delegation might have been expected to play an active role. At an early meeting of the delegation, however, the prime minister had mentioned, according to the report of a delegation meeting on 14 May, 'that in any general clause concerning human rights, it would be necessary to bear in mind the related clause about no intervention in matters of domestic jurisdiction. He felt that, so far as Canada was concerned, the provinces would want to be sure there would be no intervention in matters such as education which fell within their jurisdiction.' St Laurent and many provincial premiers had stern attitudes on the subject. It was an area of the Charter in which it was obviously better to lie low while the prime minister was in Ottawa – even though this concern for domestic jurisdiction ran counter to the aspirations for the UN of some members of the delegation. The report on San Francisco notes that the Australian position was supported and expresses satisfaction that 'the protection accorded to the domestic jurisdiction of member states is now very complete as it is clear that there can be no interference in the domestic economy or internal legislation of Members.'[59] Whereas some members of the delegation were eager to strengthen the powers of the Assembly, Wrong warned against supporting proposals 'which had the objective of making the Assembly a legislative body.' Rasminsky cautioned against the same temptation in dealing with ECOSOC.[60]

INTERNATIONAL COURT OF JUSTICE

The creation of the International Court of Justice was another subject on which Canada had convictions but on which a quietly constructive rather than a spectacular role was required. At the preliminary meeting of a Committee of Jurists in Washington in early April Canada had been well represented not only by J.E. Read, legal adviser to the Department of External Affairs, but also by the president of the Canadian Bar Association and the chief justice of British Columbia. This body produced a draft chapter for the Charter and a draft statute for the court. It was the only case in which representatives of all members and not just the great powers had produced the draft, and controversy at San Francisco was thereby reduced. Read was appointed chairman of the Drafting Committee and took no strong positions on the issues discussed. He reported that he had been in a minority of one on a point 'but I have some doubt as to whether the other 39 representatives understood what they were doing.' The main point of difference was on the basic question of the 'optional clause.' Read reported that that committee would have voted 3 to 1 for some form of compulsory jurisdiction, but 'I think there is a good deal of danger that insistence upon compulsory jurisdiction would make it difficult, if not impossible, for Moscow and Washington to accept the Statute ... I should be somewhat concerned about the possibility of breaking the whole San Francisco Conference on this issue, or of reviving the isolationist movement on this Continent, in the event of acceptance of compulsory jurisdiction followed by a fight in the Senate of Washington on ratification.' It was a typical Canadian response to the American problem. So also was the following: 'Language question is being settled by preparing reports in American, French, Russian, Spanish and Chinese, but with no English text.'[61] Canadian officials had a low opinion of American drafting.

One major issue was whether to continue the old Permanent Court or create a new one. Canada favoured the maintenance of the established court in the interest of strength through continuity, but, because of the objection of the Soviet Union, the United States, and others, submitted to a decision which, in Article 92, did at least recognize that the statute of the new court would be based on that of the old. Strengthening the court's prestige and authority was an essential element in the Canadian conception of the new world order based on the rule of law – at least a conception of officials and politicians who made speeches on the subject. The Canadian delegation sought with other like-minded delegations not only to affirm the court's right to give advisory opinions but to extend the right to seek such opinions to organs other than the Assembly and Security Council and, in particular, to move towards compulsory jurisdiction. They had limited success in the former aim; the latter proved to be as difficult as Read had foreseen.

Possibly because of the prevalence of lawyers in this committee, there was a widespread conviction that the time had come to take the important step by which states would bind themselves to submit their disputes to the court by mere adherence to the statute or as a result of their signing a special declaration known as the 'optional clause.' When Canada had adhered in 1929 to the 'optional clause' it had reserved from the court's jurisdiction disputes with members of the Commonwealth and those which fell within the domestic jurisdiction of Canada. Other states had similar reservations.

The difference between the 'optional clause' procedure and what was called 'compulsory jurisdiction' was not great, especially as no country intended to give up its reservations. The latter, however, sounded better in the ears of those who wanted to move to 'a world rule of law.' Canada, however, again gave way to the views of the minority which would not otherwise have supported the court at all.

In spite of their anxiety to put teeth in the law, the delegation was more cautious in its attitudes to a move led by New Zealand to give the Security Council the responsibility of taking action if one party to a dispute failed to comply with a decision of the court. A compromise was reached by which the Security Council might make recommendations or decisions in such circumstances. It should be noted, however, that the election of judges was one case in which the lesser powers, with Canada in the forefront, were able to eliminate the veto.

NON-SELF-GOVERNING TERRITORIES

In the discussions on non-self-governing territories and trusteeship the Canadian delegation was ostentatiously silent. One can detect an anxiety to prove the Canadian dedication to functionalism by an act of renunciation and also perhaps some trace of that smugness Canadians cannot seem to escape when questions of other peoples' imperialism are raised. This silence did not mean that the subject was not taken seriously. Politicians and officials in Ottawa did believe in the liberating force of self-government, from their own experience, and favoured an orderly and peaceful progress in the British pattern. They did regard imperial competition as a cause of war, and most important of all a cause of friction at that time between the British and American peoples. The importance attached to the subject is reflected in the attention given to it in the report on San Francisco, all with a studied neutrality. The only references to Canadian positions, however, are to note, under 'Dependent Territories,' that, 'The Canadian Delegation, because of the lack of any direct responsibility on the part of the Canadian Government for the administration of colonial dependencies, took no active part in the discussions, but followed them with close attention'; and that the 'delegation opposed the principle that the permanent members of the Security Council, whether or not they were trustee powers, should be permanent members of the Trusteeship Council.'[62] Needless to say, this opposition was unsuccessful. They argued also for a respectful assumption by the UN of mandates and other responsibilities of the League rather than ignoring that body as the Russians and Americans preferred.

THE SECRETARIAT

Canada's strait-laced attitude was noticeable when it came to the Secretariat. Considerable satisfaction was taken in the report over the prevalence of the view supported by Canada that the UN should be served by a genuinely international civil service whose members were responsible not to their governments but to the organization itself. The conviction was based on the experience at the League and also of course on fundamental attitudes of the British and Canadian civil service. There were examples of Canadians who at Geneva had become truly international men, and it was possible for those with the Canadian experience of government to believe in the immaculate civil servant. There was little attention given to this aspect of the UN in early Ottawa papers, possibly because the desirable principle seemed so obvious. However, there were always those Latin Americans to worry about, and the delegation arrived in San Francisco with three draft paragraphs for Chapter X on the Secretariat. The first two amendments provided for the complete neutrality of members of the Secretariat, their appointment by the Secretary-General, not by governments, on the basis of competence, with only 'due regard' to the need for recruiting on as wide a geographical basis as possible. The third amendment provided for the legal status and immunity of personnel of the UN and associated agencies. The first two amendments were used as a basis of discussion by the committee along with the sponsors' drafts on the same subject, and, with a few omissions in the interests of brevity, became Articles 100 and 101 of the Charter. Article 101 was carried in committee against the objection of the Soviet bloc who argued that such details should not appear in the Charter. The points raised in the third amendment were largely covered in Articles 104 and 105 of the Charter.

The selection of the secretary-general and his deputies was a more controversial issue. In accordance with its general wish to limit the veto, Canada argued that the Security Council should make its nomination for secretary-general on a vote by any seven of its members. Along with other lesser powers it successfully opposed the sponsors' proposition that not only the secretary-general but his four deputies be elected by the Assembly on recommendation of the Security Council for a period of three years.[63] This was regarded as a blatant attempt by the great powers to extend their domination to the Secretariat, the assumption being that each of the deputies would be a citizen of one of the great powers, with another citizen rotating as secretary-general. Canada argued that the secretary-general must have authority over his deputies whereas the great-power proposal would mean in practice administration by a committee of five. On the veto power over selection of the secretary-general Canada had a victory in committee by a typical ploy, omitting a reference to the veto and putting into the Rapporteur's report that concurrence of the permanent members would be unnecessary. This was overruled, however, by the acceptance of the whole Yalta voting formula by the conference. This defeat was not really consequential because in practice it would be essential for any secretary-general to have the support of the great powers.

What proved far more important for the development of the secretary-general as a strong and influential force in the system, a counter-balance to the hegemony of the great powers and a critical element in Canada's UN diplomacy during the fifties, was the success of Canada and its friends in preventing election of the deputies and removing the drastic limitations proposed for the secretary-general's term of office. No term of office was specified in the Charter. The first secretary-general was appointed for five years and that was accepted as a norm, thereby permitting men like Hammarskjöld to make their extraordinary contribution to the institution. His authority was greatly reinforced by the omission of any provision for deputies in the Charter, thereby giving him a free hand – with due regard, of course, to the expectations of the great powers. This latter was one of the few cases of a clear-cut victory over an intransigent Soviet Union by the lesser powers, with assistance from other great powers less convinced of the wisdom of their own agreed proposition. A good deal of the success both in drafting and negotiating is attributable to Escott Reid, who carried on the efforts in the Preparatory Commission in London against pressure from the Russians and Yugoslavs.

The Canadian government refused to have anything to do with the appointment of its own nationals. Because so many Canadians had been involved in the establishment, the Canadian content of the Secretariat remained for many years out of proportion. This view of the Secretariat, however, was not observed by others, and as Canadian numbers dwindled the government was obliged to intervene to protect the rights of its nationals. The Russians were, of course, quite honest from the beginning in stating their disbelief in the international man. Although Lester Pearson was in 1945 and again in 1951 supported for the office of secretary-general, it was clear that the Russians, who rarely showed a personal dislike for him, believed that he could not help being a 'western man' and was, therefore, unacceptable.

THE PREPARATORY COMMISSION

At the end of the San Francisco Conference a good deal of gratification was expressed in parliament and the press. Much hard thinking and effective diplomacy had gone into achieving certain ends that proved, however, to be of less significance than had been anticipated. The points were well taken, but they were based on a mistaken premise about the way in which the UN would in fact operate. The concern over having a voice in the Security Council when Canadian troops were to be called upon proved irrelevant, and the principal reason for having countries of some military consequence as non-permanent members disappeared when the Council became a body concerned with the settlement of disputes rather than the enforcement of sanctions. The preoccupation with the legitimate struggle for the rights of middle powers seemed to divert too much of the Canadian effort away from the less spectacular issues which were of greater consequence in the long run – setting up the infrastructure for a flexible and practical intergovernmental organization. To some extent the diversion was inevitable because these issues of 'collective security,' of vetoes and sovereignty, were central in the eyes of other powers and other peoples, large and small. The structure which emerged was not all that Canada had hoped for, but in the process of international negotiation its hopes were being constantly adapted. It was not a question of hopes disappointed; it was an exploratory and a learning process, involving the revision of preconceptions. There was cause for gratification in the constructive attention to detail of Canadian delegates, in their willingness to compromise and their demonstrated inventiveness. The respect which Canada acquired in the UN was not so much because of its support of any particular causes but rather because its representatives could be counted on for common sense – although at times the devotion to common sense in a world of emotions was a little lacking in common sense.

It was this kind of contribution that Canadians made most effectively during the summer and autumn of 1945 when the Preparatory Commission and its Executive Committee were meeting in Westminster. Canada had been a member of the Executive Committee at San Francisco and as such served on the Executive Committee for the Preparatory Commission, which was intended to prepare plans for the first Assembly. Although Escott Reid was only the alternate delegate on these preparatory bodies, he stayed in London throughout and was a major dynamic force during this period. Reid was a superb and a compulsive draftsman, with a zealous sense of mission about international organization.[64] Lester Pearson once said, 'Escott would bring the Archangel Gabriel to the mat for a comma.'

Under Reid's influence the delegation concentrated much of its attention on rules of procedure for the Assembly and other organs. In company with the Australians the Canadians urged the necessity of providing a set of provisional rules of procedure even for the Security Council. The great powers did not much like this presumptuous attitude and permitted only an inadequate compromise to be drawn up. In one case amendments submitted by Canada for the Security Council were rejected at the same time as they were being accepted by another committee for ECOSOC. Its two working papers embodying a complete revision of the rules for ECOSOC were regarded as evidence that a middle power knew its place. When the United Nations became not an ideal constitution but a turbulent political body, these good intentions may seem to have been in vain, but in fact UN politics would have been far worse if there had not been this notable effort to devise procedures in the reasonably calm atmosphere of Westminster during the summer of victory.

The solid Canadian contribution in London to the nuts and bolts lends itself to few generalizations except to say that it was constructive and prudent and, on the whole, aimed in the same directions as at San Francisco: wary of the excessive claims of the great powers and jealous of the rights of the Assembly. Compromises were put forward. When the USSR, for example, wanted a separate secretariat for the Security Council, the Canadian delegation recognized that some special provisions were necessary for such an important body as it would be meeting in permanent session, but they did not want any privileged positions for the Security Council. So they successfully proposed that a Department of Security Council Affairs be set up in the Secretariat. Reid and company were especially keen on providing austere rules for the Secretariat and forbidding interference by governments. They were less shy about trusteeship than at San Francisco and actually served on a subcommittee to draft the text of the resolution on trusteeship later adopted by the Assembly – but that may have been just an acknowledgment of Reid's position as Number One draftsman. Among the other triumphs of Canadian pens was the draft on privileges and immunities for the Secretariat.

Next to economy of language in the Canadian priority came, of course, just plain economy. Wilgress chaired the subcommittee for a Working Capital Fund, and the Canadian delegation proposed an amendment, which was adopted, to ensure centralized cash control from the start. Canada continued to keep a wary eye on the scale of contributions, showing a particular concern over suggestions that no one country should pay more than a certain percentage of the budget – a position that was logical enough in preventing too much influence by the United States but which meant that Americans would be paying less per capita than Canadians. It was the campaign for simple and direct language, a break with jargon and traditional formalities, the effort 'to make United Nations documents more easily understandable by the ordinary man,' in which the report of the Department of External Affairs took special pride.[65] This effort, along with that to provide sound rules and regulations, was not completed when the General Assembly began its first session in January 1946. So a good deal of continuing effort by Reid and his colleagues throughout the early Assembly sessions went into a committee set up at the Assembly to study procedures and economize time.

An interesting position taken by Canada in the preparatory stages was its opposition to an American site for the United Nations. An American site was supported by the Russians, the Chinese, the Australians, and the Latin Americans. Canada joined the British and the French in preferring a European site. This somewhat quixotic policy ran counter to traditional Canadian positions. In favour of a European site the Canadian delegation argued that the most urgent problems with which the United Nations would have to deal related to Europe, yet the Canadian objection to the League of Nations had been that it was too much concerned with the problems and interests of Europeans. Canadian postwar policy, furthermore, was dominated by a fear of American reversion to isolationism and haunted by the ghost of Henry Cabot Lodge, but the principal argument for having the UN based in the United States was that it would keep the Americans involved – a calculation which proved to be well-founded. A factor that might have had some influence was the view held by many officials in London and Washington that if the site were to be in the US, there could not be a North American as secretary-general. The preference for Europe was attributable partly to the professional diplomats who were at that time and continued to be somewhat Eurocentric. The government was embarrassed because Graydon (PC) and Knowles (CCF), who were on the delegation to the Preparatory Commission and the General Assembly, had committed themselves publicly to supporting a Canadian site.[66] There had been some pressure from interested groups in favour of such sites as Navy Island in the Niagara River. The delegation saw an outside possiblity that if there were deadlocks over Europe or the United States, Canada might be proposed as a compromise. However, cabinet opposed a Canadian site, and the delegation was told to say that Canada lacked accommodation, residences, hotels, and possible sites were far from centres of population. Such a humiliating posture could have had only one source and, when the delegation resisted, Robertson sent a personal note to Wilgress saying that the instructions represented 'views held strongly by the Prime Minister who is firmly opposed to the selection of a Canadian site.'[67] When the decision for the United States was made, Canada supported an Atlantic base in New York as against San Francisco which the Asians and Australians favoured.

Of particular concern to the Canadians was a respectful winding up of the League of Nations and an orderly transfer of its assets and responsibilities to the United Nations. This reflected a belief in the practical values for a political institution of continuity and tradition and an anxiety that the valuable experience already gained by the League in such functional activities as narcotic control be the sound basis of institutions in the United Nations system. The argument was stressed particularly by Hume Wrong, who had left Geneva in the fateful days of 1940 and who was to be the Canadian representative at the final session of the League in April 1945. He favoured the winding up of the League in an orderly and dignified manner. 'Much of the practical experience on which the United Nations must build is derived from the League and the United Nations should be regarded in the light of an heir and successor of the League rather that a new experiment in international collaboration.'[68] He had an interest not only in the spirit of the transfer but a practical concern with, for example, the continuation of serial publications, services relating to epidemics, treaties and conventions on drugs, and the retention of able members of the League secretariat.

In these good intentions, Canada, along with Commonwealth and other League members, were not in serious conflict with the wishes of United States officials but they had to contend with the political prejudice in the United States and the Soviet Union against an institution with which their relations had been, to say the least, embarrassing. In fact, most of what Canada wanted on this subject, except generous respect for the late institution, was obtained at the winding up in Geneva.

ELECTIONS

When the General Assembly got under way in London, Canada received an embarrassing setback. It lost out to Australia for a seat on the first Security Council. Although all the instructions and memoranda were careful to state that Canada had no assurance of election, there was an attitude of confidence. Some of the restraint shown at San Francisco in curbing the Security Council may have been, perhaps unconsciously, inspired by an assumption that in the proper kind of Security Council Canada would be a more or less regular member. There was, of course, to be no vulgar campaigning for office. When in late 1945 various Latin American ambassadors approached Canadians, from the prime minister down, for support in elections to various offices, they were given little homilies about Canada's neither giving nor expecting pledges. The prime minister was more of a politician. He could not, of course, miss the chance to savour such a nice moral principle, but when he told Robertson that 'an eye may be kept on the situation,' the latter recognized a hint and suggested to Wilgress in London that when this matter arose he should explain that Canada was not giving or taking pledges but 'we consider that the standing of Canada among the United Nations is such as to make this country an obvious choice for the first Security Council'[69] – in the language of diplomacy a campaign speech if ever there was one. The idea that Australia or Mexico might get the nod over Canada upset King's idea of Canada's status in the world.[70] Officials recognized that Australia had a right to membership in accordance with the qualifications for which Canada had argued and they discussed the problem with the Australians. Evatt had been good enough to say that while Canada and Australia should both be elected, Australia would be content with a one-year term while Canada was entitled to the two-year term, in accordance with the special provisions for the first elections.[71] A reason for wanting both countries elected was Ottawa's anxiety that the League practice of considering only one Commonwealth country at a time eligible for a Council seat should not be revived or established.

There was some lack of proportion in the Canadian estimate of the country's importance in an already expanding United Nations. Even officials were a little bemused by the good will Canadians were inspiring. Canada and Canadians were candidates for too many offices in 1946. Although Lester Pearson was not pressing for the role of secretary-general and the government was officially neutral on the subject, everyone knew that his name was being considered, as was that of Norman Robertson. John Read was a candidate, and a successful one, for the International Court of Justice.[72] Canada was obviously thinking of itself for the Security Council, for ECOSOC, and for the Atomic Energy Commission. All these presumptions, combined with the sermons on good behaviour, might well have got Canada off to a bad start, and it was a triumph of the personality of the principal characters involved that they held their ground.

Whatever might be said about capacity to contribute taking precedence in Article 23 over geography, there was in practice no escaping the fact that the first qualification had to apply, if it did, within a framework provided by the second. Various parts of the world had to be represented – Latin America, Eastern and Western Europe, the Middle East, Asia. The only question was whether the candidates from the various regions would be selected on the basis of capacity or by a system of rotation. It would be very hard, furthermore, to break the practice by which regions would choose their own nominees, and such a practice would almost inevitably lead to rotation. Voting without nominations could not only be anarchic, it could lead to distorted patterns. In the instructions to the Canadian delegation to the Assembly this fact of regional representation was taken for granted. It was recognized that the Security Council was going to consist of the Executive Committee from San Francisco minus three. As they had been selected on a regional basis, they would have to be dropped on that basis. Canada and Australia were left without easily identifiable regions, both clearly qualified by capacity but liable to lose out if they proved unreasonable – or too proud to accept the obvious category of 'other Commonwealth states.' The Canadian delegation's judgment was so clouded by righteousness that they were unable to see that the British would have to ration their favours to Commonwealth countries by supporting some for one council and some for another.[73]

In fact, Canada proved remarkably popular. For the Economic and Social Council it got forty-six out of fifty-one votes on the first ballot and a three-year term. For the Security Council, however, the regional candidates won out first. Short of the thirty-four votes necessary for election were Canada, with 33, and Australia with 28. In the run-off Canada led Australia the first time but fell behind in the next vote, primarily because Mexico had been chosen as one of the Latin Americans and there was a feeling in other countries that three North American members would be too much. St Laurent graciously stood down.

The members were no more likely to accept three Commonwealth than three North American members of the Council. At that time Canada, Australia, New Zealand, South Africa, and even India formed a recognizable category in the eyes of other states. Certainly in the preparations for the United Nations they had appeared as a vigorous group which, if it did not act as a voting bloc, was a consulting team with more coherence in perspective than most of the regional groups. When the great powers (by loose gentleman's agreement the nature of which was disputed) and others fell into the habit of recognizing 'regional' categories for candidates in both the Security and Economic and Social Councils, the Commonwealth was a category with a very short list which provided Canada with its best possible chance to get a seat once a decade. As it emerged from adolescence and developed a new and more proprietary interest in the changing Commonwealth, Canada became more comfortable in the Commonwealth seat – until it disappeared in the Charter revision of 1965.

As for regional representation there was a good deal to be said for it in a council called upon to deal with disputes in all parts of the world. A very small power is quite as likely as a more powerful middle power to offer constructive UN diplomacy. A Security Council in which Canada and a few other accepted middle powers occupied semi-permanent positions might well have been a more rigid body – and for Canada the adjustment to the rise or recovery later on of other 'middle powers' would have been more painful. An anxiety to maintain its status as a middle military power might even have introduced an ambiguous factor into the framing of a national Canadian defence policy. Altogether this cause, on which so much effort had been spent, was perhaps better lost.

9

Economic and Social Functions

The economic and social functions, which have become the major preoccupation of the United Nations, merit special attention. They received much less at the creation than the security issues, even in Canada, although they were in theory the Canadian priority. The essence of Canadian functionalism was the belief that it was as an economic power that Canada deserved particular consideration. In 1945, however, the economic and social role of the United Nations seemed related to long-term problems rather than to the transitional questions of relief and reconstruction which preoccupied the European countries and required also the urgent attention of Canadian officials. In discussing, therefore, the establishment of the UN's economic and social functions it is necessary to treat in this chapter a more extended period of postwar history than is covered in most of this volume.

Public interest is no indication of the amount of effort which went into the laying of an economic and social infrastructure. The part played by Canadians in the conferences at Hot Springs, Bretton Woods, Chicago, where the great agencies to deal with food and money and aviation were set up,[1] was closer to the international centres of power than was their activity at San Francisco. The deference to Canadian views and interests in the establishment of the specialized agencies was due to their intellectual quality and to the fact they were not merely special pleading but a responsible effort to design effective international institutions. It was also attributable to the bargaining power Canada had as one of the two or three countries capable of providing relief and assistance and of thinking beyond the present emergencies.

Canada's own plight was in a way typical of the postwar situation. It was luckier than most countries but nevertheless faced with urgent economic problems, particularly financial adjustments, a plight which made the Canadians useful critics of the blander assumptions into which Americans fell. Self-interest and internationalist convictions led both Americans and Canadians to support measures to open the clogged channels of trade and finance. They were dedicated to the development of international economic institutions primarily for this purpose. Officials in Washington and Ottawa knew they had problems with their own politicians in accepting the domestic implications of their liberal internationalism, but they had few doubts that they were on the right path. The British and other victims of the war believed in international economic institutions as well, but they were inclined to see them as a means, at least in the first instance, of sharing internationally the intolerable burdens they had to face right away, after the common effort against aggression. They saw the issue less in terms of the spreading benefits of free enterprise and somewhat more in terms of orderly protection. They had to envisage a transitional stage before they could play their part in the economic and social Utopia promised in the Charter. Canadians required both protection and opportunity and were in the strategic position to play that middle role which international economics and politics required of them.

Canadian official attitudes on these functions of the international organization were very different in 1945 from what they had been after the First World War.[2] In the last days of the League, however, Canada was giving some support to the recommendations of the Bruce Committee in favour of a substantial and autonomous League programme on economic and social questions. Mackenzie King told the Commons on 30 March 1939 when speaking of the League that 'in the anarchy and passion of to-day, such a centre of co-ordination, such a focus of good-will, is more needed than ever. It will have to operate on a more limited and less spectacular stage, building up its technical and social and economic activities, accustoming peoples and governments to work together, until eventually they may find it possible to use the tried and tested instrument for greater ends.' Confidence in economic and social institutions as the alternative to international provisions for security was characteristic only of the truest believers, but the conviction that they were essential, along with 'collective security,' for a lasting peace was widely held. In August 1944 Mackenzie King said, '... real security requires international action and organization in many other fields – in social welfare, in trade, in technical progress, in transportation, and in economic development. The general aim must be to lower the temperature of nationalism, while preserving its good features, and thus to diminish national rivalries and reduce the importance of frontiers.'[3] He could not, however, get away at that time with the argument that such action would dispense with the necessity of security provisions in the United Nations. In one of the first External Affairs memoranda on postwar organization Hume Wrong approached the question from the opposite direction: 'It is generally agreed that an effective security system is a necessary foundation for all post-war planning, and that international plans for civil aviation, monetary stabilization, commercial policy and so on can only be effective in an atmosphere of international security.'[4]

In a diffuse way the idea that the key to peace was a full belly was widely held in Canada. One of the least internationally minded members of the cabinet, James G. Gardiner, the minister of agriculture, said in his blunt way in 1946 in support of the Food and Agriculture Organization: 'You can have all the U-N-O's you like, but people who could not get food would fight for it.'[5] Before talks began on establishing an International Trade Organization the minister of trade and commerce, James MacKinnon, stated: 'There could be no stronger assurance of peace than to have the conference achieve its objectives of lower tariffs, elimination of restrictive trade practices and the establishment of economic cooperation as the key to world prosperity.'[6] Almost everyone seemed to have been influenced, whether they knew it or not, by J.M. Keynes's classic book, *The Economic Consequences of the Peace*, published in 1920, wherein he denounced the Treaty of Versailles which, he wrote, 'includes no provisions for the economic rehabilitation of Europe.' 'The Council of Four,' he charged, 'paid no attention to these issues ... It is an extraordinary fact that the fundamental economic problems of a Europe starving and disintegrating before their eyes, was the one question in which it was impossible to arouse the interest of the Four.'[7]

Keynes's lesson was widely accepted in London and Ottawa but perhaps not as single-mindedly as by the New Dealers in Washington. Cordell Hull believed that trade conflict and discrimination were the root cause of wars. Arthur Krock of the *New York Times*, summarizing the mood of Washington, said, 'economic freedom for all is the basic American foreign policy for the prevention of war.'[8] The Canadian planners may not have gone so far, but the influential officials in Finance and External Affairs were on the side of the New Deal enthusiasts in the State Department and the White House because these Americans were fighting the battle of internationalism against the conservatives in the Treasury, in Congress, and in the financial community. The Americans who fought for the International Bank and fund were Rooseveltian radicals, deeply suspicious of bankers and international finance – more radical than the consensus of the Canadian cabinet. To understand the intense Canadian activity and the sense of triumph in the Bretton Woods conference it is essential to realize that the Canadians felt involved in a decisive internal struggle in Washington on which the future of an international order depended. John Deutsch, who was involved in these negotiations, has said that 'Canadians often served as ambassadors between the State Department and Treasury.'[9] That kind of international order served the apparent interests of both the United States and Canada, but those in the three capitals who fought the battle of Bretton Woods saw it as a crusade not for the extension of an American 'empire' but for a very much reformed new world, invigorated by the prosperity of America.[10] The enemies were the 'reactionaries' on both sides of the Atlantic.

To assess the Canadian approach – in practice as well as in theory – to the United Nations as a system through which to promote economic and social progress, it is necessary to look not only at the principles professed in preparatory papers but also at the performances in and the adjustment to the councils and agencies while, in the first few years of existence, they were being fashioned in action. The forging of certain basic attitudes at the major wartime conferences and in the experience of UNRRA[11] have already been described. Attention must now be directed to the establishment of the Economic and Social Council and the family of specialized agencies.

ECOSOC

In the Canadian view the Economic and Social Council, shielded from international politics, would be the nerve centre of the social and economic system of the UN, if only feasible schemes to that end could be worked out. The importance Canadians attached to ECOSOC is obscured by the fact that they did not find it necessary to fight very hard for their point of view. Before Dumbarton Oaks Canada indicated that it favoured 'general supervision by the Assembly of international economic and social activities, and possibly also the creation of an economic and social council on the lines of the United States proposal,' preferring 'to see these matters separated from the scope of the World Council except insofar as they relate directly to security.'[12] Once the Russians had been persuaded at Dumbarton Oaks to the inclusion of economic and social questions (rather than their relegation to a totally separate organization), and it looked as if these would be the responsibility of a 'functional committee' attached to the Assembly, Canadians were sufficiently reassured to concentrate their attention on the set-up of the Security Council and a place for 'middle powers.' On the eve of the Commonwealth Conference before San Francisco it was Wrong's view that the general scheme for economic and social issues set out in the Dumbarton Oaks proposals seemed acceptable, apart from some minor drafting changes in the interest of clarity.[13] By the time the delegation reached San Francisco, however, the exercise in clarification had become a complete revision of that section of the draft Charter.

On paper the delegation at San Francisco was quite successful. Canadian amendments to the Charter empowered the Economic and Social Council to take the initiative in concluding agreements with existing agencies (Article 93:1) and in setting up new agencies (Article 59), to participate in deliberations with the specialized agencies (Article 70), to obtain reports from them on the steps they had taken to implement its recommendations and those of the Assembly (Article 64:2), and to co-ordinate their work through recommendations to the General Assembly and the UN members (Article 63:2). These amendments, however, did not place a radically new interpretation on the great-power draft; they bent it somewhat and made more explicit the provisions Canada liked. In the view of Douglas Anglin the Canadian delegation did much to undo its good work in strengthening the powers of ECOSOC by inflating its functions and authority in other respects as well. It was saddled with enormous responsibilities for promoting higher standards of living, full employment, conditions of economic and social progress and development. It was to make or initiate studies or reports and not just recommendations on matters within its competence and to perform services for members in specialized agencies. 'ECOSOC has been called upon to serve as a forum for discussion and negotiation of economic, social and even political matters, and as the body directly responsible for a vast range of activities carried on through its many commissions, committees and boards. It is not surprising, therefore, that it has been unable to carry out effectively what perhaps ought to have been its primary purpose, the coordination of the work of the specialized agencies.'[14]

It is a fair judgment on ECOSOC as a co-ordinator, but the basic illusion was that it could be shielded from politics, for economics have increasingly become the politics of the United Nations. Ironically, the way in which co-ordination was made as non-political as possible was to turn it over to the international bureaucrats. The Preparatory Commission in London in 1946 foresaw the troubles ECOSOC would have and asked the secretary-general to establish a co-ordinating committee of himself and the officers of the agencies. The Administrative Committee on Co-ordination got under way in 1947. It was certainly not what Canadians had considered desirable in theory, but it has worked effectively and quietly to secure at least a minimum of financial and programme control and Canadians have accepted it as something that worked.

Canadians initially took ECOSOC very seriously. The Council consisted at first of eighteen members elected by the General Assembly. It had no permanent members although in practice the principal industrial countries were always elected. At the first session of the Assembly Canada was elected with widespread support for a three-year term. For some officials this appointment was more important than election to the Security Council – a point of view in which there might have been some element of sour grapes. The Council, however, soon began to drown in oratory, in the contemplation of its own organization, and the proliferation of commissions. Canadians were very active in the first three years, usually represented at sessions by a strong delegation headed by a cabinet minister. The deputy minister of welfare, G.F. Davidson, was chairman of an ad hoc committee concerned with agreements with the specialized agencies and Canadians became members of a number of the commissions set up.

After the three-year term, however, disillusion set in. The Department of External Affairs in its report, *Canada and the United Nations 1951-1952*, was complaining about 'over-ambitious and over-elaborate schemes of co-ordination' which might result in a structure 'so cumbrous that it would defeat its own simple objective.'[15] Canada went back later for a further term on ECOSOC but by that time it was clear that the Council, which spent most of its time debating economic and social issues in platitudinous or propagandist tones, was not the body to do anything so hardheaded as co-ordinate. In any case, everything discussed in ECOSOC, much of which had already been chewed over in the functional commissions, was argued out again in the second and third committees of the General Assembly to which it was responsible. Such co-ordination of the work of the specialized agencies as was achieved was being done through the international bureaucracy under the watchful eye of the General Assembly. Canada, like other western countries, also became less enthusiastic about ECOSOC as a supervisor of the specialized agencies because the communist countries largely boycotted the agencies but nevertheless had their opportunity in ECOSOC to discuss the work of bodies to which they did not belong.

The Canadian performance in ECOSOC was more reticent than might have been expected, given the priority accorded it in Ottawa's view of the new United Nations. When the Council got under way it became spendthrift and irresponsible; at least in the eyes of Canadians with their prejudice in favour of thrift and accountability. Canadians liked thrift in speeches and procedures as well, but ECOSOC turned purple. It was not long before it was inevitably concentrating its attention on the needs of the underdeveloped members. Canadians were sympathetic and recognized that, by Article 55, this was a legitimate concern of the United Nations, but it had not been a priority in their thinking. They had assumed that the prosperity coming to the advanced countries when the barriers were down would, with the greater degree of self-government engendered by the United Nations, inevitably raise the standards of the poorer countries as well. At any rate they were not prepared for the budgetary nightmares the less developed countries were proposing. There was so much that needed to be done in the world, they realized, but the resources of the United Nations were limited and they came largely from a small group of which Canada was one of the most vulnerable. It was the 'bottomless pit' in an even more threatening guise than had appeared in the context of European relief. So the Canadian representatives gave lectures on accountability and shied away from initiatives.

Two close observers of Canadian policy, F.H. Soward and Edgar McInnis, noted in 1956 that Canadians had more than once taken positive initiatives in helping create institutions like ECOSOC that the situation seemed to demand, but they had been less enthusiastic about subsidiary bodies and, in the actual operation of such institutions, had been 'helpful supporters' or 'realistic critics' rather than leading advocates. 'In the field of world economics, as in that of security, there is an ever-present consciousness that the ability to implement a given project of major proportions rests ultimately with a few leading states, and the tendency is to wait for their initiative as an indication of how far they are prepared to go, and to judge the practical possibilities in the light of their attitudes. This is typically the role of a middle power, and one to which Canada may possibly be more habitually resigned than is warranted by Canadian resources and capacities.'[16]

THE SPECIALIZED AGENCIES

In the meantime the specialized agencies were being established under their own steam and by national representatives who were not always in collusion with their colleagues specializing in the architecture of the United Nations. The launching of the Food and Agriculture Organization, the International Monetary Fund, and the International Bank for Reconstruction and Development have been described in chapter 2. It would be excessive to describe here the Canadian activity in setting up all these bodies, although the space devoted to them in no way reflects the relative importance or the proportion of man hours dedicated to this aspect of the United Nations. Notice will be taken only of policies that illustrate particular Canadian attitudes to the UN structure. Terminology is a problem. The specialized agencies are definitely part of the United Nations system to which they are constitutionally attached. Misunderstandings arise from the tendency, faute de mieux, to speak of the United Nations 'proper' as the Security Council, the Assembly, and the New York establishment in general.

The International Labour Organization was already in existence. It had been created in 1919 in association with the League of Nations, but instead of suffering liquidation had continued its work throughout the war from Montreal. For these reasons its relationship to the proposed new structures had unique features. The ILO, the bureaucracy supported by its tripartite (labour, employers, and government) constituencies in the member states, had been jealous of its autonomy vis-à-vis the League, and it was suspicious and defensive in the face of proposals to co-ordinate and subordinate it within the all-encompassing world body people were talking about during the latter war years. It had shown its vitality in wartime by, among other things, holding a conference in 1944 at which the so-called Philadelphia Charter, a world code for labour, was drawn up. It had good reason to fear for its survival, however, as there was a widespread disposition to wipe the slate clean. Early American proposals for a postwar order implied there should be some new body to do what the ILO had been doing.[17] As Anglin aptly put it: 'The know-it-alls in Washington and elsewhere had little patience for the Geneva old hands whose experience they dismissed as inapplicable to the changed circumstances of the world. This contempt for the past accounts for the apparently deliberate attempt to snub the ILO, most notably for failing to invite it to the Hot Springs Food and Agricultural Conference.'[18] It was an attitude shared by only a few in Ottawa, where there was a greater disposition than in Washington to recognize the advantages where possible of building from a living organism.

Both the United States and the Soviet Union had been members of the ILO, but the USSR ceased to be a member when it was expelled from the League in 1939. The Soviet Union was not only antagonistic to the ambitions of the ILO but had in mind promoting the claims of a rival body, the World Federation of Trade Unions, as a specialized agency. In the eyes of the western countries the WFTU was not an intergovernmental agency and it was, furthermore, at that time powerfully influenced by communist-dominated trade unions. The Canadian delegation came into conflict with the Russians at San Francisco over a Canadian amendment which, having in mind the ILO, specifically defined specialized agencies as 'intergovernmental' organizations. The Canadian position was strongly supported and it prevailed.

The officials of the International Labour Office then spoiled their good case for autonomy by making unacceptable claims. They produced a report for discussion at Philadelphia[19] that suggested the organization should not be simply one among other agencies but a forum for the general exchange of views, responsible for *scrutinizing* all international economic and financial policies and measures adopted by governments as well as by other international organizations. These proposals were not well received by the major powers, whose officials were at that time concerning themselves with ways and means of linking or co-ordinating the new system of international institutions. The Canadian delegation argued that the scope and functions of the ILO should be specifically restricted to its rightful fields and its relations with the other agencies on the basis of equality. The ILO's scope should not be reduced, but neither should it be accorded primacy. Two amendments to the Philadelphia Charter made this clear. The second was a Canadian proposal which said that the ILO should 'examine and consider' rather than 'scrutinize,' as it had proposed, 'all international economic and financial policies and measures.'

The ILO fought also for special status on the basis of its long standing and its unique structure. As its authority derived not merely from governments, it ought not to be supervised by purely intergovernmental bodies. At least the ILO wanted right of access to the Assembly rather than to a subordinate Economic and Social Council. At Philadelphia, Paul Martin, representing Canada, proposed a committee to study the question, and he became chairman of it. When the committee met in London in January 1945 the Economic and Social Council had already been designed at Dumbarton Oaks, and the forces arraigned behind the ILO did not like it. Although the same governments were represented in the specialized agencies as would be represented in all the United Nations organizations, each had its own constituency within the national governments and it could not be assumed that there would be no conflict. A difference now began to appear between Paul Martin, who as parliamentary assistant to the minister of labour was deeply involved in the ILO, and those concerned with the agenda for San Francisco. In his report to the House of Commons Martin said the ILO was more than just another functional agency and was entitled to a special place. He asked the Canadian delegation to San Francisco to 'consider carefully the wisdom of having the international labour office's future predicated upon a relationship to a body on which the workers and employers of the world are not represented'[20] – that is, ECOSOC. Martin, however, was not on the delegation at San Francisco because in April he had moved from the Labour post to become secretary of state. The Canadian delegation did not support his position, which was put forward by the British; and it was eventually withdrawn.

The first postwar conference of the ILO took place in Montreal in the autumn of 1946 at which a matter of particular importance to Canada was raised. The uncertainty of the jurisdiction of the federal and provincial governments in Canada over labour matters had led in 1937 to a ruling of the Judicial Committee of the Imperial Privy Council that denied the right of the federal government to take action in the provincial domain on the grounds that it was fulfilling an international obligation arising out of its membership in the ILO. The Canadian government secured a clarification at the Montreal conference. An amendment required federal governments to take action similar to that of unitary governments on questions that fell within federal jurisdiction. It also required periodical conferences with provincial authorities and reports to the ILO on questions which fell within provincial competence. These amendments were duly approved by the Canadian parliament in 1947 – but such declarations certainly did not solve the persisting legal and political problems of provincial jurisdiction in United Nations decisions.[21]

The constitutional embarrassment was partly responsible for the Canadian attitude towards the United Nations Educational, Scientific, and Cultural Organization, characterized by Professors Soward and McInnis as 'dutiful interest punctuated by chronic exasperation.'[22] The project seemed to lack the practicality of international co-operation in trade or aviation, nutrition or monetary matters. And it raised the difficult subject of education over which the federal government had no authority. There was no branch of the federal bureaucracy to develop an interest and make plans, as the Departments of Agriculture, Finance, or Transport had involved themselves in other agencies. In all the rhetoric about the postwar world collaboration in matters cultural and educational occupied a prominent place, but in terms not very appealing to the pragmatists in Ottawa or the provinces. However, the creation of such an international organization was authorized in the United Nations Charter, and the Canadian government would have been criticized internally as well as externally if it had not taken part.

No Canadian cabinet minister attended the meeting in London in November 1945 that drafted a constitution for UNESCO. The organization was, like most of the others, to have an assembly and an executive board, and Canada was, in spite of its lack of official zeal, appointed to the Executive Committee. There were to be national commissions representative of the educational, scientific, and cultural organizations of the country to serve as liaison bodies with UNESCO. Although such a commission was a useful device for a country that lacked a ministry of education, the government was in no hurry. It was not until August 1946 that parliament got round to approving participation in UNESCO. The prime minister talked of the Canadian national commission in modest terms and expressed the misgivings held in Ottawa about the budget. This concern over a disposition to high spending and feeble accounting by the artistic community persisted. The assessed contribution paid by Canada was larger, however, than that paid to agencies that it preferred.

After listing a number of the 147 specific proposals before the first general conference, Edmond Turcotte, who had been on the Canadian delegation, commented enthusiastically: 'A short survey such as the present barely scratches the surface of a programme covering fields as vast as human genius itself.'[23] That was the problem. The geniuses assembled in Paris were convinced that 'wars begin in the minds of men' and they wanted to knock down the barriers to understanding and create world unity by pious resolutions and the holding of an infinite number of conferences in the City of Light. They wanted not only to revamp history books and sponsor a 'UNESCO hour' devoted to international understanding on world-wide radio networks, they also had some concrete ideas about tackling illiteracy and facilitating scientific exchanges and translations. One aspect of their work that the government took seriously was the restoration of works of art as an act of postwar reconstruction. For this purpose it set up the Canadian Council for Reconstruction through UNESCO, partly as a token for the more controversial National Commission, but it was allowed to wind up in 1951 without replacement.

The aloofness of officials, attributable to extreme caution about federal interference in education and a deep suspicion of grandiosity, was somewhat out of touch with strong opinions about Canada's neglected role in UNESCO that were held by many articulate citizens.[24] Delegations to UNESCO assemblies consisted largely of non-officials selected on geographical, professional, and, alas, even political grounds, with eventually some representation from provincial Departments of Education. Liaison with the headquarters in Paris was maintained by an officer in the Canadian embassy, and a Temporary Advisory Committee for UNESCO was set up within the Department of External Affairs which kept in touch with various non-governmental organizations. There developed a special commitment to UNESCO among those who had served on delegations and there was pressure on the government from them to take action. Nevertheless, in 1948 the prime minister indicated that he was not proceeding at that time with setting up the National Commission, and in 1949 it was one of the questions referred to the Royal Commission on National Development in the Arts, Letters, and Sciences. The National Commission with a professional base was not in fact set up until 1957.

The World Health Organization, on the other hand, was one of the agencies to which the Canadian government gave unhesitating support. It was largely the steps taken in the health field that had converted Canadians before the war to a positive attitude to social and economic programmes within the League structure. There had, of course, been a long history of international co-operation in coping with epidemics and establishing rules of quarantine. The federal government had a strong Department of National Health and Welfare with a staff accustomed to international conferences and conventions. There was no dissent in parliament when membership in the WHO was approved on 6 August 1946. Canada was the first state to deposit its ratification – even though this agency was authorized to assume powers and responsibilities closer to international administration than those exercised by other agencies. No more than other international institutions, however, could WHO bind its members. The Canadian view was that WHO should provide experts and consultants but not establish or maintain by itself public health programmes in individual states. Operational activity should be undertaken only in emergencies such as epidemics. The Canadian insistence on financial austerity was notable, and Canada was active in securing adoption at the first Assembly of the principle that states which got help from WHO should pay for it if they had the means. As in other cases, the Canadian contribution was also personal. Dr Brock Chisholm, the deputy minister of health, laboured hard as rapporteur of the Technical Preparatory Committee to create WHO and then became its dynamic first director-general.

The Canadian government also played its part in the creation or adaptation of other international institutions. At a conference in Geneva in 1948 an Inter-Governmental Maritime Consultative Organization was envisaged. The Canadian representative was chairman of the preparatory committee, but this committee ran into difficulties after the preliminary meetings in 1948 and the organization was not set up for some years. Canada was a participant in the World Meteorological Organization, the convention for which was signed on 11 October 1947 although it did not come into existence until March 1950. The International Telecommunications Union and the Universal Postal Union had been in existence for many years and were brought into the new United Nations system at various conferences following the war. At an international telecommunications conference at Atlantic City in 1947 an administrative council of eighteen members was established and Canada was elected to it. Canada had interests to protect, including getting a place in the crowded radio spectrum. During the war the CBC had set up an international service to project the Canadian image and join in allied propaganda. In the self-consciousness of 1945 there was a determination to maintain this Canadian presence on the air waves, and this necessitated a fight for frequencies in the ITU. As for the Universal Postal Union, Canada had been a member since 1878 and Canadians were their usual diligent selves at the first postwar congress in Paris in 1947 which prepared for the sanction of the UPU as a specialized agency of the United Nations in 1948.

The proposed specialized agency to which Canada attached most importance never came into existence. This was the International Trade Organization. The crusaders in Washington had insisted on Article VII of the Lend-Lease agreements, which pledged the parties to eliminate 'all forms of discriminatory treatment in international commerce, to the reduction of tariffs and other trade barriers.' The question, however, was what the International Trade Organization would actually do, as it obviously was not going to be in a position to determine the trade and tariff policies of member governments. The ITO was regarded at first as part of a package with the International Bank and the Monetary Fund. However, diplomats did not get down to concrete discussions until long after Bretton Woods – well after the end of the war and the San Francisco Conference. The expansion of trade was not the easiest subject on which to get allied agreement beyond generalities. It was not a matter on which there could be much progress with the Russians. The gap between the plight of the Europeans and that of the North Americans was such that there had to be concentration on the emergency before the Utopia of free trade could be reached. Delay was attributable also to differences of opinion among the planners in Washington, including congressional resistance to what Senator Vandenberg called an attempt 'to spell out a do-gooder program for the whole world.'[25] ECOSOC in February 1946 set up a Preparatory Commission of eighteen countries, including Canada, to prepare an agenda for an International Conference on Trade and Employment and also a draft charter for an International Trade Organization. A preliminary draft charter was not completed until August 1947. Canada accorded provisional agreement to this draft.

In the meantime, however, the countries concerned were getting down to business on the actual matter of reducing tariffs. These bilateral negotiations contributed to something in the nature of a multilateral structure. According to the principle of non-discrimination, each country was entitled to tariff reductions made by other participating countries. An incredible number of agreements were in fact reached in Geneva in exceedingly complex negotiations. It was estimated that half the world's trade was involved. On 30 October 1947 twenty-three countries signed the General Agreement on Tariffs and Trade. Although Canadians did not flag in their anxiety to set up an ITO, they plunged into the GATT negotiations with zeal and had reason for satisfaction with the results. There was no doubt of Canada's position as one of the three or four major trading nations at that moment, and under the direction of its widely experienced trade commissioner turned ambassador, Dana Wilgress, the Canadian delegation played a central role. Canada did agree to make substantial concessions in its own tariffs. Nearly two-thirds of its imports would be affected in some way. The negotiations came at a time of crisis in Canada's financial relations with the United States, and the need to open up the American market to replace lost markets in Britain and Europe was uppermost in Canadian minds.[26] The concessions made by the Americans were encouraging. Spokesmen in Ottawa enthusiastically greeted the Geneva Conference, not only the specific gains in tariff negotiations but the general commitment of the contracting parties to establish most-favoured-nation treatment among themselves and follow the rules covering trade relations set down in the general provisions of the agreement. It was a wide commitment to good behaviour of a kind Canada strongly favoured. The agreements, however, were subjected to considerable criticism in parliament, partly because they were not easy to understand, and ratification by parliament was delayed.

Enthusiastic Canadian officials next set off for Havana where the United Nations Conference on Trade and Employment began in November 1947 to prepare a revised charter for the ITO. After extensive debate that included, needless to say, problems of the voting power to be accorded great and small, a final act was signed on 24 March 1948 by fifty-four countries, including Canada. It was inevitably a compromise that satisfied few. Provisions were made for the charter to come into effect after ratification by a sufficient number of countries. An Executive Committee of the Interim Commission was given the task of preparing the way for the first session of the new organization and Wilgress was chairman. The organization envisaged would have had certain similarities with ICAO in that there would be an initial agreement on trade principles with an organization to supervise their application or revision. ICAO, however, had been accepted before the war was over. By this time it was too late.

The enthusiasm for the 'creation' was waning. Instead of concocting long-range structures, politicians and diplomats were desperately engaged in the actual tariff negotiations and in the setting up of the structure provided for under the Marshall Plan. The Canadian government remained faithful and indicated that it would seek parliamentary approval of the charter of the ITO in its 1949 session, but in Washington the politicians had lost their enthusiasm. At the end of 1950 the State Department announced that the charter would not be resubmitted to Congress. With strong Canadian support, the GATT became in itself a continuing institution, eventually producing its own secretariat and furthering some at least of the causes intended for the ITO. Judged by functionalist Canadian principles it may be that a body which actually grew out of a strongly felt need to negotiate was off to a more practical start than an agency the functions of which remained nebulous.

INTEGRATION AND AUTONOMY

The relationship of the specialized agencies to the United Nations evolved from contention between those interested in creating an integrated international system and those whose needs and purposes were more specific. The differences were not so much between countries as between people of different inclinations within the various governments. Canadian policy inevitably swung between the will to create order out of chaos and the fear of erecting an unworkably centralized structure. It was not a simple struggle between political philosophers in the Department of External Affairs and officials of the functional ministries, but the prejudice in favour of autonomy was naturally stronger among the latter. The ground was, in fact, cut from under the feet of centripetal designers by the fact that powerful agencies, established or on their way before Dumbarton Oaks and San Francisco, were like feudal baronies which could not be brought under control. Nor could there be, as Canadian planners had at first contemplated, a rational allocation of responsibilities in advance between the functional agencies and the proposed functional commissions of ECOSOC.

The supple approach to this question is well expounded in the draft instructions prepared under Hume Wrong's worldly-wise direction for the first session of the General Assembly:

It is in general desirable from many points of view that the relationship between the United Nations and these bodies [specialized agencies] should be clearly defined in order to avoid overlapping of activities, competition for personnel, unequal scales of remuneration, and rivalry in particular fields of activity. The pattern of association, however, cannot be uniform, although certain standard clauses may be included in all agreements with specialized agencies.

With regard to the financing of the specialized agencies, the arguments in favour of a single budget for the major international organizations are strong. Such a budget would have separate chapters for each specialized agency as well as for the Secretariat, the Court of International Justice and so on. The adoption of a central budget, however, raises the question of the degree of authority of the Assembly over the finances of the specialized agencies. The general line to be taken is that the 'financial autonomy' of specialized agencies is not a real issue, since all of them are, like the United Nations itself, established by intergovernmental agreements, and it is primarily the responsibility of national governments to see that their delegations are instructed to approve fair financial provisions for all the international organizations to which they belong. This does not mean, however, that the delegation should press for complete centralization in the United Nations budget of the finances of all the specialized agencies. Some of them, indeed, will be self-financing through charges levied on their own operations; this group would include the International Monetary Fund and the International Development Bank. For others it may be appropriate, because of the nature of their operations, that contributions should be assessed on a special scale, thus necessitating a separate budget.[27]

On the whole the Canadian government favoured a substantial measure of constitutional and financial integration along with functional autonomy, although the way in which the attitude was interpreted varied considerably among officials and ministers. Canada opposed a wartime effort of the ILO to detach itself from the League of Nations budget because this would have prejudiced the chances for a co-ordinated structure in the new United Nations system. It was active in bringing the ILO in line when it made its claims at Philadelphia to act as co-ordinator and to have special status. On the other hand Canada did support special concessions to the IMF and the IBRD because their particular kind of international responsibility required them to have complete financial autonomy. There was nothing in the Charter, said Paul Martin, 'which precluded the Council from recognizing the inherent differences in the functions and nature of the various agencies.'[28] However much a tidy and hierarchical structure might have appealed to some officials, those in Ottawa who had done so much to create the bank and fund would insist on their operating without interference from a highly political central body.

Canada tried in vain to get more United Nations control over constitutional amendments by the agencies, a common United Nations budget, and a high degree of administrative consolidation. Canada put less emphasis, however, on constitutional integration and uniformity of membership when this emphasis began to conflict with its wish that the agencies should, insofar as possible, be isolated from the politics of the Cold War which gripped the Assembly and ECOSOC. By 1949 Canada was admitting that a unified budget was impossible because the United Nations system as it was emerging was not constitutionally capable of coping with such an arrangement. There was a change also in the concept of an integrated UN system on questions of security. In the formative stage the relationship of agencies like ICAO to international security was stressed. For several years, and particularly on the occasion of international crises, Canada insisted didactically on the obligation of the agencies to serve the general cause of the United Nations when security was at stake. The idea that the United Nations might be a meshed structure in which, for example, the agencies would look after the transport or health functions of a grand collective security operation lapsed as the United Nations security system emerged as something very far from that dream.

Canadian policy was flexible enough to be contradictory. It was contradictory because of internal differences over the treatment of various agencies and also because the government in practice sought equilibrium. It wanted as much co-ordination and autonomy as were attainable and consistent with each other. Whatever the talk of control by ECOSOC or the Assembly, it is clear from the Canadian drafts at San Francisco that what was envisaged was that ECOSOC would make recommendations and not issue directives to the agencies. Although Canada wanted to strengthen the regulatory and perhaps even disciplinary authority of UN bodies, it should not be assumed that they wanted them to be legislative.[29] The ultimate authority, including that over budgets, must be held in the last resort by governments. Canadian statements can be misleading if taken out of context. At times they stressed the dangers of chaos and at others the advantages of autonomy, and rightly so, for the effort to find equipoise between growth and discipline remains the constant problem of international organization.

Canada stressed the need for member states to co-ordinate policy at the national level and harmonize instructions given their delegates. Because the bureaucracy was close-knit there was reasonably good, if informal, co-ordination in Ottawa. In December 1949 an attempt was made to copy the British Steering Committee on International Organization by setting up an interdepartmental committee on international organization, but it proved top-heavy and not very effective. More effective were interdepartmental bodies such as the Inter-Departmental Committee on the Food and Agriculture Organization and the close liaison maintained by the United Nations Division of External Affairs with those responsible for the specialized agencies in the functional departments. Douglas Anglin suggested that co-ordination was too effective. 'The immense care taken in the formulation of Canadian policy almost inevitably ensures that it will rarely be bold and imaginative.'[30] There may be notable here the strong hand of the Department of Finance through the medium of Sidney Pollack, for many years the one man in the civil service who regularly attended, and maintained a close interest in the work of, the General Assembly and the various specialized agencies as well. His job was to scrutinize and advocate economy and the Department of Finance view prevailed often because of his extraordinary competence and the respect and even awe with which he was held in United Nations circles, especially the Secretariat.

A useful description of the domestic practice in the early years is contained in the Canadian reply to the secretary-general's questionnaire of 1951 to member states concerning their own administrative procedures for dealing with United Nations questions. It emphasized the paramount importance of cabinet. 'It is the chief instrument of co-ordination because it bears the ultimate responsibility for co-ordination.' The task of cabinet, however, was facilitated to the extent that there was preliminary consultation among the other government departments. The description of the system in Ottawa was used to offer a homily: 'Ever since the United Nations was established Canada has emphasized that, because of the autonomous character of each of the Specialized Agencies and because of the differences in the membership of the United Nations and the Agencies, effective co-ordination between the programmes, budgets and administrative practices of these organizations could be achieved only if each country took steps to ensure that its delegations to the meetings of the organizations pursued co-ordinated and mutually consistent policies.'[31] This was perhaps the prescription rather than the consistent practice. Canadian policies as expressed in Geneva, Paris, or New York were at times contradictory, and this homily was a little rash. Nevertheless, it was a reasonably practical and flexible system for a time when the number and the magnitude of United Nations operations was limited – as was also the band of concerned ministers and bureaucrats clustered around Parliament Hill.

REGIONALISM AND FUNCTIONALISM

On economic and social institutions Canada was as chary of regionalism as it was when security was involved.[32] There was wide agreement with the views of Mitrany who had written in 1943: 'There is little promise of peace in the mere change from the rivalry of powers and alliances to the rivalry of whole continents, tightly organized and capable of achieving a high degree of, if not actual, self-sufficiency. Continental unions would have a more real chance than individual states to practice the autarchy that makes for division.'[33] At the ECOSOC meeting of 1 August 1947 Paul Martin said Canada was 'concerned lest in the future regionalism and regional autarchy play the dangerous role which nationalism and national autarchy have played in recent years.' The Canadian governor of the International Monetary Fund said to the seventh annual meeting of the Board of Governors on 9 September 1952: 'The real payments problems ... are not regional in character. They are world-wide. Each country has to get into equilibrium with the rest of the world and it cannot achieve that end by purely regional arrangements.'[34] This emphasis on global internationalism was reinforced by specific fears of a breach between North America and Europe, moves to promote an exclusive

Commonwealth, the emergence of continentalism in Europe, and by inherited uneasiness about continentalism in North America. For Canada regionalism was the problem, not the answer.

Canada saw in functionalism an alternative to regionalism and to an unwieldy centralized authority. Canada got itself elected to most of the functional commissions set up by ECOSOC and argued that these should be worldwide rather than regional. W.A. Mackintosh was the first chairman of the Economic and Employment Commission and C.H.L. Sharman later became chairman of the Commission on Narcotic Drugs. Canadian experts were appointed to the Commission on Population, Statistics, and Social questions. J.T. Marshall of the Dominion Bureau of Statistics became chairman of the Statistical Commission, and G.F. Davidson, deputy minister of health and welfare, was a strong member of the Social Commission. They were all experts. However, many countries sent diplomats, political friends, and other convenient appointees, and the concept of the UN as a place where experts could collaborate apolitically – a concept emphasized in Canadian planning – was undermined. Commissions and subcommissions flourished out of hand. By 1951 Canada was joining with others to weed out some of the commissions and control proliferation. Against regional economic commissions, however, Canada fought a losing battle. Canada did accept the early establishment of economic commissions for Europe and Asia but they resisted pressure from the Latin Americans to set up the Economic Commission for Latin America. The argument against ECLA was that there was not the same functional justification as for Europe and the Far East – Latin America was not in need of postwar reconstruction.

To a later generation the Canadian position betrays a reprehensible unawareness of the needs of regions like Latin America. The concept of 'aid and development' as a major function of a United Nations is not notably evident in Canadian planning. No one seemed to think about Africa at all. Canadians merely reflected current attitudes before the idea of direct technical and capital assistance seized the imagination of Western governments – after the Marshall Plan and the Chinese Revolution and after it became clear that the vast British Commonwealth was going to be transformed into units responsible for their own welfare and desperately in need of help if they were to continue in their inherited democratic way. Latin America and Africa and a good deal of Asia were in 1945 concealed behind imperial structures. Latin America was regarded as an American responsibility, and its real condition was obscured by its affluent representatives at the United Nations. London, Paris, Brussels, and Lisbon were responsible for Africa and there was little that other countries could do there even if they wanted to. Canadians, fearful of having a depressed Europe on their hands indefinitely, were canny about further commitments of incalculable dimensions. The United Nations was accepted as an instrumentality for raising the standards of living of depressed countries, but largely by unclogging the channels of trade, development, and finance. The communist states were certainly not in favour of extensive economic powers of any kind for the UN. Few people grasped the revolutionary implications for the United Nations of the requirements of the dark continents when the imperial structures had dissolved and its constituent parts would turn to the international community not just for development but for sustenance.

One area where Canadian leaders showed some interest in a regional body was the Arctic. Officials were anxious that the defence arrangements they were discussing with the Americans in the north not be regarded as hostile or exclusive, and government leaders went out of their way to welcome cooperation in non-military matters with other northern countries. In a speech to the New York Rotary Club on 7 February 1946 Pearson said: 'We want to work ... not only with the U.S.A., but with the other Arctic countries, Denmark, Norway, and the Soviet Union, in exploiting to the full the peaceful possibilities of the northern hemisphere. Particularly is this true of the U.S.S.R. ...' In a speech in Princeton on 14 May of the same year St Laurent called on the five Arctic powers to work out co-operative measures within the UN for the development of the economic and communications resources of the northern territories. During 1947 there were further suggestions from the same source but, as there was no interest shown by the Russians in that icy period, the suggestion lapsed.

When the regional economic commissions became a fact, Canada, of course, sought to subordinate them to ECOSOC with close financial control by that body and to keep them advisory, not operational. It did not want at this time to become a member of any of the commissions, but it wanted to reserve the right to participate. This was met by a clause which specified in the case of each commission that any member of the United Nations could participate in a consultative capacity in the consideration of any matter of particular concern. Canada was careful to steer clear of ECLA but was less reticent about sending observers to meetings of the ECE and ECAFE.

Needless to say, Canada also opposed regionalization of the specialized agencies. It had accepted the principle in UNRRA because relief and reconstruction problems could be seen regionally, although donors like Canada from outside the regions were of necessity involved – for *functional* reasons. There was also some reason for regional councils in ICAO because of the significance of geography in aviation. Canada opposed the deliberate regionalization of the FAO. It accepted the validity of bodies that had come into existence to serve a specific regional – and functional – purpose such as the International Commission for Northwest Atlantic Fisheries and the International North Pacific Fisheries Commission and opposed their integration into FAO. Those officials who had developed their own ways of protecting Canada's fish were no more going to agree, on doctrinal grounds, to intervention in these arrangements than the finance men would agree to the subordination of IMF or IBRD – or than the whole government would agree to interference in practical, established, continental bodies like the International Joint Commission.

Canada's particular reasons for caution over regionalism are illustrated in the long dispute over the principle in the World Health Organization. The issue was the incorporation of the already existing Pan American Sanitary Organization as the western hemisphere regional body of WHO. Canada opposed regional proliferation of the agencies on the grounds that these institutions should create a solid base before their limited funds and talents went into regional offices with all their trappings and their inevitable demands for autonomy. It also opposed the pretensions of the Pan-Americans to set themselves apart from the general rules of the United Nations, in security as well as economic and social questions. Although there were people in Ottawa who would have liked to see Canada join the Pan American family, there was also prejudice against it, a dislike of the hegemonial role of the United States, and resentment of the politicking of the Latins.

PASO posed the ticklish question of which hemisphere Canada belonged to, the western or the northern. The mystical symbolism attached to the Isthmus of Panama and the fortuitous naming of the two continents after the same Italian had created an assumption in Washington and further south, but not necessarily in Canada, that the western hemisphere was a natural region. But in functional bodies dealing with health, agriculture, or labour, Canada had little in common with South America. It did have much in common with the United States, but this bilateral region was too lop-sided to be politically attractive. Such a fear may seem incompatible with the insistence on keeping existing bilateral North American institutions such as the International Joint Commission autonomous. The latter, however, were practical means of reducing frictions by enabling Canada to bargain as an equal. Their purpose was not to create a regional entity with a common front or a single voice in world councils. It is true that regional offices or conferences of United Nations agencies were not primarily designed for consensus-making either, but there was a worrying ambiguity about the Pan-American fraternity (later institutionalized as the Organization of American States). The

Bogota Charter of 30 April 1948 specified in Article 100: 'In concluding agreements with international agencies of a world-wide character, the Inter-American Specialized Organizations shall preserve their identity and their status as integral parts of the Organization of American States, even when they perform regional functions of international agencies.'[35] There was about Pan America a suspicious emphasis on unity of which Canada had learned to be wary in the Commonwealth.

The dilemma over WHO was explained in the official report, *Canada and the United Nations, 1950*: '... PASO has focussed its attention on the principal health problems of the area which are largely those of a tropical or sub-tropical nature, whereas Canada's contacts in health matters have been traditionally with those countries having similar problems, namely, the United States, the United Kingdom, and the countries of Western Europe.'[36] Nevertheless, both PASO and WHO declared Canada a member of PASO and of the Regional Committee of the Western Hemisphere for WHO, a curious dyad, concocted as a compromise solution to the furious debate over the 'integration' of PASO with WHO. Still Canada refused to join. Canadians did, however, participate in the debate, waging the battle for the ultimate authority of the universal body.

In retrospect the Canadian resistance may seem excessive and the whole debate scholastic.[37] It was one of those perpetual arguments which, as is characteristic of the United Nations, develops a momentum of its own after positions become entrenched. On Canada's part there seemed to be a sound principle at stake, spiced with a particular animus, and it was hard to let go. What was emerging was what might be described as an acceptance of regionalism when it could be justified as functionalism. That approach was consistent with the general view of international organization as a response to needs rather than an imposed framework. To base international government on the arbitrary division of the world into regional constituencies was to fly in the face of historic reality. Latin America was perhaps an entity of sorts, and Europe had aspirations, but Asia was a region only in geographical terms. Where there were, however, agencies to perform valid functions in a region or where countries of a region wanted to combine for consultation, protection, or to pursue unity, they could be encouraged to do so ad hoc, as long as other countries and continents were not constrained to do likewise and such organization was not seen as the basis of universal federal structures.

HUMAN RIGHTS

One of the commissions of which Canada was not a member was that on human rights. For various reasons the Canadian government kept a low profile. It was the Americans, with their declaratory tradition, the Bill of Rights and all that, who pressed hard for strong or at least strong-sounding provisions about human rights. The Russians and British were sceptical and went along because it was hard to come out in opposition to goodness and truth. At San Francisco, however, there was considerable support from lesser powers for the promotion of respect for human rights and fundamental freedoms as a purpose of the United Nations. There had been little enthusiasm in Ottawa for adding to the Charter anything like a statement of the rights of man or a declaration of the duties of states, and not much attention was given to such a project. 'Such additions are likely to be discussed at San Francisco,' Hume Wrong warned the legal adviser, 'but I imagine that there is not much prospect of their adoption in spite of the ardent support given by Mr. Escott Reid.'[38] What Wrong, and Robertson also, were especially concerned about – because the prime minister was excessively concerned over it – was that defenders of provincial rights could regard the Charter as an invasion. Wrong's view was that the only aspect of the proposals which might be regarded as touching the provincial field of jurisdiction was the injunction to 'promote respect for human rights and fundamental freedoms,' but 'unless this is made a great deal more specific, I think that its acceptance could hardly be regarded as a violation of the B.N.A. Act.'[39]

The attempt to spell out the rights bothered Canadian officials. There seemed something rather Yankee about the whole idea, contrary to the Canadian/British tradition where, it was well known, human rights were more faithfully respected in practice than in the unbridled republic, in spite of its written constitution. There was the more serious objection that customs and practices differed so widely throughout the United Nations, the attempt to reach a consensus on rights would only promote conflict and incite the kind of vapid moralizing which the Ottawa men disliked. There could be no international enforcement measures; they must be the responsibility of the sovereign government – or the subsovereign province. It was not that Canada was uninterested in or had a bad record in human rights. That was made almost offensively clear in official statements on the subject. The chairman of the Canadian delegation insisted to the General Assembly in 1948 when the Universal Declaration of Human Rights was being voted upon: 'So far as the position of Canada in regard to the maintenance and extension of human rights is concerned, we shall, in the future, as we have in the past, protect the freedom of the individual in our country where freedom is not only a matter of resolutions but also of day-to-day practice from one end of the country to the other.'[40]

Despite these objections, the Commission on Human Rights produced in a very few years the Universal Declaration of Human Rights and the Canadian government was faced with the kind of dilemma to which it would grow much more accustomed – what to do in the face of a majority which has not accepted the Canadian way. The draft declaration was considered at length by a joint committee of the Commons and Senate.[41] The committee had many general and specific criticisms, mostly in accord with those of the government. It was not a question of not taking the declaration seriously. Perhaps they took it too seriously. The vagueness of some of the proclaimed rights was criticized because they could not be turned into legislation or interpreted in a court of law. It could be argued, of course, that the declaration was intended simply to set goals to be aimed at, but the Canadian prejudice was against subscribing to a declaration of intentions that was not already or could not be promptly put on the statute books. This attitude sprang from an admirable dislike of hypocrisy but also a failure of imagination. The United Nations was set for a long history of ringing declarations by no means always reflecting the practices of members who subscribed to them. The setting of standards to aim at and the encouragement of aspirations has been one of its accomplishments. The Parliamentary Joint Committee favoured a concise statement of general principles rather than the sprawling pronouncement intended to include everyone's favourite right. Lawyers saw real trouble in Canada's being bound to all sorts of fanciful 'rights,' including some which legitimized Marxist economics. At one time one bemused delegation was said to have proposed a declaration of 'the right to old age.'

What especially worried the Canadians and others was the determined effort to include social and economic rights. It was increasingly recognized in Canada that legal rights could be worth little for the jobless, but there was a distinction as set out in a Canadian submission in 1951: 'Generally speaking ... economic and social rights cannot be protected and encouraged in the same way as civil and political rights. The latter involve limitations on the powers of governments and legislatures to interfere with the rights of the individual. Economic, social and cultural rights, on the other hand, are not so much individual rights as responsibilities of the state in the field of economic policy and social welfare which usually require for their effective implementation detailed social legislation and the creation of appropriate administrative machinery. There is thus a fundamental difference in the nature of the two categories of rights.'[42] These economic rights were pressed by the developing countries, and also by the Australians who had put up a great battle to get into the Charter recognition of the right to 'full employment.' This was a grand slogan of the times and the Ottawa Keynesians certainly favoured it as a goal of postwar governments. American legislators were wary as it smacked of socialism. But what did 'full employment' mean exactly, and was it necessarily an inflexible rule for all countries and all times? Canada proposed a compromise at San Francisco, 'the highest possible level of employment,' but this was a little too sensible to be accepted.

The Declaration of Human Rights came to a vote in the Assembly late in 1948. It was a notable feat of reconciliation, for which a Canadian, J.P. Humphrey, formerly of McGill University, was largely responsible – a distinguished member of the Secretariat and the lone Canadian hero in the human rights struggle. In committee it was adopted without a single negative vote, but Canada and the Soviet bloc abstained. A stubborn conviction of righteousness in Ottawa led to this blunder. Preoccupation of the senior members of the delegation with political issues regarded as more important allowed a situation to develop without adequate calculation. Lester Pearson had just arrived in Paris, where the Assembly was being held, in his new role as secretary of state for external affairs. He moved quickly to pick up the pieces and persuaded the government to alter its stand in the plenary session. He did so with an explanation of the vote that explicitly stated: '... in regard to any rights which are defined in this document, the federal government of Canada does not intend to invade other rights which are also important to the people of Canada, and by this I mean the rights of the provinces under our federal constitution.' The value of the declaration as aspiration was recognized: Canada had decided to vote in favour 'in the hope that it will mark a milestone in humanity's upward march.' However, 'We do not believe in Canada that legislation should be placed on our statute books unless that legislation can indicate in precise terms the obligations which are demanded of our citizens, and unless those obligations can be interpreted clearly and definitely in the courts.' Freedoms in Canada had developed 'within the framework of a system of law derived both from statutes, and from the judgments of the courts' and although Canada had now subscribed to the general statement of principles it had no intention of departing from its own procedures. The speech contained a vigorous attack on the Soviet approach to human rights, just in case there were doubts about the company Canada had been keeping in the committee vote, and the Canadian political philosophy of the day was made clear: 'Without those free institutions, which can only flourish in a liberal democratic society, there can be no human rights.'[43]

This was the best way out of an embarrassing situation. Cabinet ministers had not yet been exposed enough abroad. As a civil servant newly transformed into a politician and suspected of internationalism, Pearson had to toe the line. It was a considerable achievement to get his colleagues to switch the vote. The statement, however, was legalistic and a little smug, a style he shunned when he grew more confident of his position. The Canadian attitude continued squeamish when commissions and committees settled down to the long task of drafting covenants that would be binding legal agreements. One favourable turn was that the economic and social rights were to be placed in a separate covenant, but the same problems persisted.

Much energy was put into securing a 'federal clause' recognizing the special problem of federal governments which lacked domestic power over all human rights. In this struggle Canada, of course, had allies in other federal states. From Ottawa's perspective their position was unassailable: 'I deem it expedient, however, to repeat here what has been said in previous years that the aim of the Canadian Government in insisting on the insertion of a suitable federal clause is not to escape obligations under the Covenants. Time and again we have let it be known that in our opinion such a clause would not relieve federal governments of any obligation which it might constitutionally be capable of implementing ... The present situation in Canada ... is that international agreements dealing with matters coming exclusively within the jurisdiction of the Canadian provinces do not become the law of the land even though these agreements may be approved or ratified by the federal government ...'[44] Some countries seemed malevolently obtuse in not recognizing the sacredness of Canadian constitutional principles. Yet to others it was a very unsatisfactory situation when a member state of the United Nations was incapable of making commitments, that it was placing certain areas outside the law.

An important maturing experience for Canada and other 'liberal democratic' societies was the experiment in promoting 'freedom of information.' Not surprisingly those who had fought the Nazis had strong views on government control of the media as a cause of war. Canada, with strong support from Canadian journalists, was enthusiastic about the conference which the General Assembly in late 1946 authorized the Economic and Social Council to call. Freedom of the press was so sacred and so obvious a right that little opposition was expected, except, of course, from the Soviet bloc whose perverse minority views would simply have to be isolated. An impressive Canadian delegation consisting of diplomats, journalists, and a representative of the CBC attended a month-long conference in Geneva in the spring of 1948 and Canada endorsed the draft convention on the international transmission of news, the right of correction, and draft articles for inclusion in the declaration and the covenants on human rights. However, certain reservations were made. It was becoming clear that for many people, especially those in the developing countries, freedom of information was not synonymous with the unlimited right of powerful foreign news media to report and say unchallenged whatever they liked. There must be a right of correction. However, this proposed search for truth began to look too much like censorship to the highly sensitive press representatives. Eventually the Canadians decided a convention on the subject would do more harm than good and in 1952, after consulting the Canadian media, agreed with other like-minded members to oppose opening the convention for signature.

The experience, however, was perhaps worth more than would have been the subscription to an imprecise and contradictory declaration. It is a principal purpose of the United Nations to increase awareness by revealing complexity. Certainly some of the proposals for checking the right of the western press to slander and distort would have also checked their freedom to make known. However, the self-assurance of the western countries needed pricking, with reference to freedom of the press and of some other human rights they held sacred. An argument for the educational benefits of even the most controversial United Nations projects and debates is that it is doubtful if a Canadian representative in the seventies would speak with such unguarded immodesty about the state of human rights in Canada as the representatives did without hesitation in the postwar decade.

Conclusion

Recollections in tranquillity of untranquil times tend to excessive clarification. I have tried to catch facets of a vision which flashed briefly. We were dealing not in plans but hypotheses that were instantly put to the test. To see this era in terms of dreams betrayed, of unforeseen disasters, or even of predictions fulfilled is to impose on history the values of drama. What happened was neither precisely expected nor unexpected. We took for granted that events would move rapidly and in various directions. The endeavour was to maintain some control over them, to have in advance, therefore, some plans and even more fall-back positions and to keep a quick eye for opportunities to seize.

The system was adapting rapidly from the moment – or moments – of its conception. It was largely the advent of atomic power and the unravelling of empires which rendered the world of San Francisco out of date. The Cold War had been anticipated; it was in fact already a factor in the shaping of peace by the 'allies' in wartime. In basing the provisions for security on great-power consensus, the drafters were displaying not blindness but rather a shrewd endeavour to perpetuate the *sine qua non* of world peace at as high or low a common denominator as could be maintained. It seems to me after three or more decades that they were essentially right. The girdle put 'round about the earth,' rent or distorted though it may be, has held. The United Nations system has grown broader and deeper. Its embrace has become global and the challenges, therefore, infinitely greater than those foreseen in Ottawa or anywhere else in 1945. The frustrations it suffers are attributable to the intractability of the agenda more than to weakness of the structure.

The importance of the Cold War in altering the practice and the framework of the United Nations cannot be dismissed, but it can be exaggerated. For Canada the experience of ending the war and getting the United Nations into operation involved an extensive adjustment of idea to reality, most of which would have been required even if the rift among the great powers had not widened. During a period of transition the language of disappointment predominated, the blame being placed on the powers and especially the Russians for upsetting the consensus on which peace and progress were to rest. By 1947 the lessons were being digested. A new look was taken at international politics and a new phase of creative energy reached.

The times and the conceptions of this period were extraordinary. We err by thinking of it as the dawn of a new heaven and a new earth. Everything was impermanent. Canada's economic, military, and diplomatic capacities were swollen; its position was not one that the country could expect to maintain or would seriously want to. Unfortunately, however, the adjustment to a more normal rating has too often been regarded as decline and fall so that Canada's steady rise in real consequence has been obscured. A country sick of war and depression seized, understandably enough, on a dream of peace and plenty and of status which has appeared in recollection more concrete than it was in fact. The dream was encouraged by the language of political leaders – not for cynical reasons but because they thought the utopian clichés were required for inspiration and encouragement. The world would never be the same again, it was true, but in many respects it was the same old world.

Beneath the rhetoric the Canadian vision of 'world government' was not as different as it seemed from the prewar calculations. The favourite theme was the necessity to surrender sovereignty to a higher authority, but the Canadian government was not prepared itself to do any such thing – and rightly so. The United Nations was an association of sovereign states for collaborative action. As a new generation of diplomats coped with the actuality of international institutions, their principles began to sound more like the discredited views of the thirties, not because they were tired or had become reactionary but because those more astringent calculations of what a world 'government' could do looked sounder as old problems recurred. What was new was the more active and positive will in Canadian foreign policy. The political contradictions remained stubborn. Mackenzie King had been forced to adjust to a changed world and a changed country, but his scepticism about the surrender of decisions to other powers reflected deeply-rooted Canadian concerns.

External Affairs was, on the whole, well out in front of the government, but it would be a mistake to see this as a simple struggle between utopian officials and unimaginative politicians. For officials like Robertson and Wrong, the inhibitions of their own and other governments were not just errors to be corrected, they were the facts of life to be reckoned with in planning any kind of international community and any soundly based Canadian foreign policy. In this study I may seem to have portrayed the bureaucrats as wiser than the politicians. I recognize, however, that it is a moot question whether civil servants are ever advocating wise policies if these are out of touch with politics. It is their duty, of course, to warn their masters of politically unpalatable factors. In this case they also provided an appropriate kind of leadership by formulating goals and schemes to attract the support of cabinet. It was a notable contradiction of a favoured bromide of political scientists, that the bureaucracy always exert a conservative influence on policy.[1]

Where the bureaucrats were out of step with the prime minister and his more elderly colleagues was in their estimate of the positive force which their country was now ready to exert in the world. Impatience had been building during the war. When Hume Wrong arrived in Ottawa from London he was distressed by the attitudes on the highest level and he wrote privately: 'A clear call to arms depicting Canada as a North American democracy fighting for North American issues and values would have united the country and greatly influenced the United States. Canada would have been among the leading countries, instead of figuring as a sutler of the Allies and often as a querulous camp follower.'[2] Querulousness had become such a habitual stance that there were those in Ottawa who seemed actually to welcome reverses to Canadian claims, for these nourished and justified a sense of grievance. It was easier, furthermore, to complain than to contribute.

A somewhat simplistic inclination of 1945 was to do whatever had not been done in the thirties. That attitude was certainly detectable in Ottawa, but, on the whole, and particularly in the realm of policy rather than planning, I think the effort was made to absorb the lessons while building on what was sound, recognizing the League and dominion status as notable steps on the way. Many of our assumptions about what had gone wrong before have carried weight because they were conclusions reached after a bitter experience. They were based, however, on hypotheses that can never be proved. The assumption that all would have been well if Canada and other countries had supported Article 10 and collective security is one such unprovable hypothesis. Another is, of course, that if we had done so or made the pledge to Britain, the country would have been rent in twain. It is at least as valid to contend that the League would have succeeded if it had been universal or nearly so. Here the Canadian record was good, for we had argued insistently that everything should be done to attract the Americans and the other recalcitrant major powers. Universal collective security is a dubious doctrine in any case, but in a rump League, as all Canadian governments insisted, it was a provocation to disaster – and it kept the Americans out.

Members of the United Nations had to learn within a few years that the beautiful doctrine of collective security was not feasible even with the Americans in. It was based on a simplistic view of the causes of war and an ingenuous assumption that there would always be a wide consensus about acts of 'aggression.' It was a system calculated, furthermore, to turn small wars into large ones. That is very much what King, Skelton, and company had been saying. Their conviction that the function of the League was conciliation and economic appeasement may have been irrelevant in the context of the late thirties, but it is arguable that a League stiffened by so vital a force as the United States could at an earlier stage have used its more powerful capacity for persuasion and intimidation to discourage the aggressors, provide for peaceful change on a principle of rough justice, and get at the causes of economic and political tension. It is ironic, but illustrative of the real change in Canada's stance, that Canada's major contribution to security in the United Nations has been dedicated to preventing by 'peacekeeping' the escalation of small wars into large ones.

Such things have been possible in the United Nations, even though the record of accomplishment has been mixed. What saved the United Nations for these, its valid functions, was the eventual recognition of the impracticality of universal collective security and the provision for basic security thereafter in functional associations for collective defence, the most notable being NATO and the Warsaw Pact. The United Nations was thereby relieved of a military responsibility it could never fulfil. In the security provided to the major antagonists by their alliances, the members of the United Nations, large and small, could start groping with the problems of conciliation, peaceful change, and economic 'appeasement.' Collective defence and the balance of terror are not, of course, an ultimate guarantee of peace. Disarmament is a much greater need than the drafters of the Charter envisaged, but the problem is not solved by positing an illusory international force or some other comfortable formula. For the foreseeable future peace has to be managed and conflict controlled arduously and persistently by and through the United Nations and other instrumentalities.

It would be hard to argue that all this was precisely foreseen in the East Block before the war, although Hume Wrong in Geneva was on the track. He recognized that it was folly to ask the League in the late thirties to enforce collective security against the Nazis. Nevertheless, something had to be done to resist such naked aggression, and this, he said, had to be done by the European powers and their associates willing and able to do so.[3] In 1938 Canada was not ready for such a commitment; in 1948 it was. A universal guarantee remained, however, a dubious proposition although in 1945 we were still clutching that noble illusion. As forecasts of the United Nations that was to emerge in the fifties, Canadian views of the thirties, including those of King himself, stand up reasonably well. Canadian thinking on the shape of peace from the thirties to the fifties was an evolution rather than a revolution – in the best Canadian tradition. Wars and rumours of wars were part of our education. Perhaps also Canada had to go through a phase of saying no, within the Commonwealth and the world organization, to well-meant but unsound propositions, such as the single empire voice, universal collective security, or a one-sided pledge to help in Europe's civil wars. It had to do so not just in the national interest but in order to help clear the ground for sounder premises on which to build a new Commonwealth and a United Nations.

On the eve of war political leaders and officials, for all their doubts about the League, had still proclaimed the essentiality of international organization of some kind, and that faith remained axiomatic throughout the war. Afterwards, Louis St Laurent could state with little fear of contradiction: 'If there is one conclusion that our common experience has led us to accept, it is that security for this country lies in the development of a firm structure of international organization.'[4] That conviction seemed to be shared by all but a few in the country, although the obligations involved were not clearly perceived and scepticism revived when the complexities of international organization unfolded. For a brief period, however, there was a near consensus, the previous doubts of the nationalists, imperialists, or pacifists having been submerged by events.

It was the world that changed, not just Canadian policy. '... let us not forget,' said St Laurent, 'that much which forms the basis of our agreement in that respect is the result of circumstances over which we have had little if any control.'[5] It was not a complaint of victimization; it was a recognition that the foreign policy of a power – especially a secondary power – is to a large extent adjustment to the way of the world.

One circumstance was the greatly increased power of North America, of Canada itself, and of the United States whose role in international organization had shifted from peripheral to central. Canada's altered conviction about international organization was a less spectacular conversion than that of the Americans, but it was in its own way just as radical. The United States, in spite of its formal dissociation from the League, had always had to act like a world power. Canada had led a more sheltered life. For three-quarters of a century at least it had consciously found security and a considerable degree of prosperity in the shadow of the Anglo-American entente. It was in the happy position of being able to avoid entangling involvements and pursue a passive foreign policy. The United States, however, had had to take positions of some kind on issues from Manchuria to Spain because its power was a factor even when withdrawn. If it was isolationist vis-à-vis European security and the League, it was a power to be reckoned with in Asia and Latin America and in economic questions everywhere. Canada could and largely did keep as uninvolved as possible, content to be a lesser power, albeit one whose sovereign independence and overseas trade were consistently asserted.

It is too simple, however, to say that Canada, as a result of the war, moved from isolationism to internationalism, because Canadian policy was never fundamentally isolationist. Certainly there was a strong hankering for isolation, but that was not the path chosen when the tests came. Where Canada differed from the United States was in its decisive action in crisis, in 1914 and in 1939, actions which seem uncharacteristically bold in comparison with the cautious peacetime policies of its governments. Canadians, or at least those responsible for the decisions, were convinced that the country's fundamental interest was involved in the issues of the great wars at the time they commenced. They believed that American interests were as much involved as theirs. 'We have gone into this war voluntarily,' Mackenzie King noted in November 1939. 'We are in it at great cost while our powerful neighbour is out of it at great material advantage, though I regret to say at equally great loss of moral power and influence.'[6] Canada would not have gone to war if it had not had the British tie, but it would not have gone if a majority of Canadians had not believed in a cause greater than the call of the blood.

Twice the United States went the same way later. In both wars Canadians sensed that an international security system on which they depended and for which they had some responsibility was threatened, just as the Americans had. Again they ended as partners in the same crusade for world order. This time the United States remained involved and took over leadership. That made a crucial difference to Canada, not because of a preference for American leadership but because the United States commitment altered the basis of international organization and made many things possible. It undermined, furthermore, the argument of those Canadians who had said Europe's quarrels were not of vital interest to North Americans.

The shift of power among the giants had not, however, solved the old Canadian dilemma over the relationship between policy-making and responsibility. The challenge to Canadian rights would come more often now from the United States and the USSR than from Britain. The abstract right of a country to participate in policy-making that might involve it in military operations would hardly be denied by anyone. But how to provide for it? The allied war effort, which had been largely in the hands of a great-power directorate, was not a welcome precedent. The effort to find ways and means had been a central theme of the debate between the wars, whether the subject was the empire or the League, and it remained a central theme when the new international institutions were set up. Before 1939 Canadians seemed to prefer the ambiguity which clouded the degree of commitment. Now they seemed ready to pledge support to a truly international body if their rights were precisely accorded. Some of the wiser heads, however, saw advantages in not trying to define the undefinable. In a sparkling memorandum General Maurice Pope asked 'if this disability is one we can overcome, even in a measure,' and added: 'Is it not one to which all but the Great Powers are subject?' He cited the Low Countries but also the fact that even a great power like the United States was unable to influence British and French policies but was 'literally dragged into two world wars.' He could not for a moment imagine that Canada could have influenced British policy over Munich or Poland but nevertheless we decided it was in our interest to go to war. And so it would be. 'In these circumstances,' he concluded 'that our cautious wait-and-see policy over the years has not been unsound.'[7] The problem was inescapable, but it becomes scholastic at times, and tiresome. There is no answer, no rule-of-thumb prescription. One grows impatient with the amount of time spent on the devising of formulas for participation rather than on the substance of policy. Yet the devising of structure was at the end of the war a large part of the substance. And as far as any power less than super is concerned, the concoction of solutions is futile without the means to put them across.

Meanwhile a new generation of policy-makers was perceiving that demanding rights did not get Canada very far. Making themselves useful did. Within the Empire/Commonwealth and within the League Canada had grappled with these contradictions. The easiest answer to the unanswerable had seemed to be to opt out, but in 1939 Canadians learned that they could opt out only of the policy-making. If they had stayed out of the war in 1939, they could hardly have done so when all their best friends were involved by 1942 and the wartime alliance formally became the 'United Nations.' By 1945 the country seemed determined on participation at both levels, in making the policies and sharing the burdens. Mackenzie King, who had been through all this in the Commonwealth, was less sanguine and perhaps more prescient, but he kept his doubts to his diary. His officers extended the area of Canadian responsibility. The quality of their contribution to policy-making was much more effective than querulous complaint in strengthening the country's hand. He worried, nevertheless, about all the troubles they would get him into.[8]

Unaware as they may have been of the problems of more distant continents, the Canadians of 1945 were in one respect more internationalist than a succeeding generation. They thought of themselves as members of an alliance and were less obsessively preoccupied with the United States. Britain loomed large in their calculations, and Western Europe, and, although imperial attitudes were in transition, the sense of being part of a world-girdling network persisted, whether it was cherished or deplored. It is hard for a later generation to recognize the importance of the British factor in Canadian policy-making of the forties and even the fifties because they know that the shift of power had already taken place. The events of these times have been distorted by the fact that most of the historians are American and they, especially the 'revisionists' who blame their own government for the Cold War, have established what Raymond Aron calls 'the myth of American omnipotence.' Aside from the fact that the recovery of Britain and France was expected, images persisted. The war may have undermined British power; it glorified its reputation. The aura of a great power persisted for at least a decade. Canadian policy-makers usually – although by no means always – thought the British were wiser and more experienced in the game of international politics than were the raw Americans. Mackenzie King, in spite of his resistance to being committed to British policy, consistently and sincerely expressed agreement with the main lines of British thinking on the shaping of peace, as he had before the war. There was more divergence on economic policies because of the very different circumstances of the two countries, but at least for the first few years after the war this was subordinated to a common interest in British recovery. For the officials, however, an aspect of the new internationalism was a determination to create closer relations with non-Anglo-Saxons and become more widely eclectic in taking advice. That was the point of a greatly expanded foreign service.

What the United States did or wanted was recognized as more consequential than what the British or Australians or Indians thought, but the Commonwealth association found its meaning often in a common need to cope with the Americans – not necessarily to oppose them. The apparent intention of the Americans to take a leading role in this firm structure of world organization was welcomed by all, but for Canada and the other countries it posed all kinds of problems in dealing with the United States. For Canada it was a whole new dimension of relations to be worked out. After nearly two centuries the bilateral issues, boundary waters or tariffs or rum-running, were close to the formula stage, although critical economic and cultural issues were about to emerge. Now, however, both the United States and Canada had decided to be world powers – one super and one middle – and they would each have their own policies on a host of global problems where their interests or their perspectives might clash. The acceptance by both countries of the greater vulnerability of North America and their rejection of isolation posed dilemmas of association in defence never before faced. So, in addition to the complexities of finding a place in new and old international organizations, there were raised for Canada in a new form the endemic questions about life with a great neighbour. At the same time there were new opportunities to buffer that relationship in wider institutions, even though Canadians were not very clear in practice how or whether to use them for that purpose.

The wars left Canada an industrial power of consequence, but as ever dependent on world trade and increasingly aware of international order as the national interest of a great trading nation. One of the new features, Robert Spencer notes, was 'a frank recognition that practically everything in international politics was of interest to Canada.'[9] The wars inspired a new kind of nationalism, with deeper roots among ordinary people, and provided Canada with a share of the glory and tragedy it had missed by achieving nationhood in a gentlemanly way. The Second World War was an anguishing experience for Canadians as people, but for the country as an entity it was exhilarating and profitable. By 1945 there were fewer reservations in the recognition by other countries of Canada as an independent actor in world politics and considerably more than a small power in its own right. It took the second war to drive Canadians into the establishment of an adequate foreign service with truly international commitments, but the ground work had been laid.

The growing sense of national purpose was marred, however, by another rift among Canadians over participation in foreign wars. The shift of the war effort by 1945 from an imperial to a broader international base went a considerable way to heal the rift, but it is hard to estimate the long-range consequences of the confrontation between francophones and anglophones over conscription in two world wars. Public opinion polls taken at the end of the war reveal agreement on the basic commitment to participation in international institutions but dramatic differences in the willingness to make commitments to the United Nations and in attitudes to the Soviet Union or Britain or on immigration for example.[10] On the surface, however, there was in 1945 a broader consensus on foreign policy than before or since.

In the long run perhaps the most significant change from 1919 to 1945 in Canadian attitudes to a world organization was the gradual acceptance and then strong advocacy of economic and social functions. The altered will to accept responsibility in security questions was important and symbolic, but that is not a realm in which Canada is ever likely to be of major consequence unless it becomes a casus belli or a battleground. In economics Canada has become a major power, and economic and social questions are by far the greatest preoccupation of the United Nations and the Commonwealth. In retrospect it can be seen that this is where we mattered most in the time of creation, in the setting up of the great functional agencies and drafting the economic and social functions of the United Nations. The change of attitude had come during the war. James Gibson, who was on the prime minister's staff at the time, has distinguished the Mutual Aid legislation of 1943 as a height-of-land because 'responsibility appropriate to function appeared to overtake any immediate preoccupation with status.'[11] This recognition of inescapable responsibility remained, of course, inconstant. We had begun to see the United Nations quite properly as an instrument to serve our economic interests. This it has done, but we perhaps did not realize the extent to which it would enmesh us in commitments to action on a national and international scale.

The old Canadian illusion that 'internationalism' is a policy we can choose or reject is less prevalent, of course, but it still pops up by inference. In fact we probably could renounce 'peacekeeping' or membership in NATO, but much as we might chafe over the policies of the General Agreement on Tariffs and Trade or the International Monetary Fund or even the north-south dialogue in the United Nations Conference on Trade and Development, we could not spring ourselves loose from the consequences of these policies.

On the economic and social functions we began with a major miscalculation, however. A central theme of Canadian planning for the United Nations was the hope that the functional approach would take economic and social questions out of 'politics.' For this reason the Canadian delegation worked hard at San Francisco for the establishment of a separate council to deal with economic and social problems and regarded this, when achieved, as a great advance over the League in that it 'avoided their subordination to political issues.' As chairman of the first FAO conference Lester Pearson, on 1 November 1945, said: 'This approach to international progress and understanding ... is, of course, essentially a non-political and non-diplomatic approach to the solution of international problems. But it is the best approach because it is concerned with the welfare of the individual, not the pride and prejudice of the nation.' By 1948, however, the Department of External Affairs was disillusioned: 'If it was ever the hope of those who framed the United Nations Charter that, by establishing a separate and independent Council to deal with international economic and social questions, they would be able to insulate the discussion of such matters from the political tensions and schisms of the times, those hopes have now been proven to be illusory.'[12]

Disillusionment is, as Hume Wrong pointed out, the clearing away of illusion.[13] The recognition that economics was politics, at home as well as abroad, was a basic step in the learning experience the United Nations provided. It did not, however, alter the priority accorded in Canadian policy to improving the livelihood of mankind. 'No Hollywood producer of historical romances will ever be able to make much out of the meetings of the committees on statistics or agricultural production,' Pearson had said in the same FAO speech. 'But millions of workers may some day live better lives because of these meetings. That is an objective more desirable to achieve, I suggest, than the altering of a boundary or the policing of an election.' Pearson was to win fame and the Nobel Prize for his part in establishing the 'policing' of a boundary in 1956, but that spectacular performance was no more important than his constructive work, largely behind the scenes, to get UNRRA and FAO and other functional bodies launched.

What were the other major failures of vision? First in importance, without doubt, was not grasping fully the implications of real universality, the extent to which the United Nations would be regarded by an expanded membership as an agency not just to keep the peace but to change the world. Secondly, the atomic bomb was certainly not foreseen or at least comprehended by those who did most of the planning. In a sense it merely confirmed the special status conferred by the Charter on the great powers in security, but in fact it altered the whole basis on which security could be calculated. The concept of forces delegated to the United Nations which is enshrined in the Charter and which had preoccupied Canadian thinking up to San Francisco became meaningless. Security henceforth had to be pursued by mutual deterrence and détente. Atomic power led also to a bipolarization of two superpowers which has strained the United Nations almost to breaking-point. This state of affairs was not entirely unforeseen, and, insofar as it was, we hoped it would be a temporary phase – as in the long run it may well prove to be. The challenge of Soviet power or rather Soviet intractability was not unexpected. Canada was prepared to go further than many other countries in accommodating Soviet biases in order to keep them in the structure.

What we less adequately grasped, however, was the nature of the challenges to a multilateral institution of the overweening power of the United States.

So anxious were the Canadians and their allies – and the Russians as well – to get the United States involved and, above all, to get them to accept responsibilities, that they encouraged an American disposition to unilateralism. In the absence of the consensus on which a strong United Nations authority could rest, the United States has become at times a kind of surrogate United Nations. It is only fair to recognize that it has done so partly out of moral arrogance but to a large extent because we have wanted it to throw its weight around, both its resources and its diplomacy. This asymmetry may not make for a healthy international system, but it is certainly better than one in which the United States again refused to accept the responsibility of power. I doubt if anything we could have done at the creation would have corrected the distortion, given the real balance of power in the world and the default of other putative powers. In encouraging American good habits the world community might have done more to restrain its bad habits. What the Americans needed at this time was candid friends to challenge their unilateral inclinations. On the whole I think that the record of the Commonwealth countries, including Canada, was particularly commendable. We argued all the way, losing most of the arguments perhaps but giving a proud loner some education in the constraints of the international life on which he was now embarking.

Whatever the lessons to be learned on the way and the faultiness of much of the original design, the basic Canadian approach to international structure was proving valid. One can note this approach as early as the Canadian submission to the Imperial Conference of 1937, stating that the 'powers and duties of the League develop by usage and experience.'[14] It was set out in a prescient article by Pearson in 1944.[15] He referred to the idea of convening a great United Nations assembly starting from the top and working down, with a general political council that would throw off various constituent bodies. He admitted that that might have been more 'spectacular' but 'This time the approach has been different and has been along functional lines. This means the calling of special conferences to deal with special subjects and to set up permanent postwar bodies covering these subjects, leaving the vital political organization to be constructed later. This procedure means working from the ground up, going from the specific to the general, from the easier, if you like, to the more difficult.' Canadian policy has continued in this lapidary tradition established by the early Canadian designers and practitioners, the laying of a universal structure stone by stone rather than by the imposition on a refractory humanity of an over-arching plan. In doing so it has been in accord with the way the United Nations and other international institutions have grown organically and functionally. It should be noted, however, that advances have been made not by the 'surrender of sovereignty' but by the agreement of sovereign states to discipline themselves. That catch phrase succeeded only in frightening off both politicians and electors who were quite prepared to limit their own freedom of action when multilateral agreement proved essential.

Wrong, Pearson, Glazebrook, R.G. Riddell, and many of the other planners were historians by training and instinct. So was I, and that is probably why I found their approach so congenial at the time and in retrospect. A danger of the historical perspective is that it encourages complacent optimism, the fallacy of inevitable progress. On the other hand a degree of optimism is essential for policy-makers, especially those involved in the creation of a world. They do have to believe that something can be done even if the odds are against it. They, like historians, have to identify, undistracted by utopian fantasies, just how much has been accomplished and the directions in which we are moving. After the first session of the United Nations General Assembly, Louis St Laurent observed, 'We have advanced from barbarism to a sort of international feudalism.' He was a lawyer, but one of the historians, Gerry Riddell, wrote it for him. It was a shrewd estimate of the state that had been reached, with an awareness that in the light of history the feudal system, with all its bloody faults, did mark a considerable step forward in the control of anarchy.

Notes

NOTE ON SOURCES

Unless otherwise specified, documents referred to may be found in the Department of External Affairs records. The *Documents on Canadian External Relations* covering the war years, publication of which is expected shortly after the appearance of *The Shaping of Peace*, will facilitate the researcher's task. United Nations documents may be found in the CIIA and other United Nations depository libraries while League of Nations documents are housed in the League of Nations Archives, UN Library, Geneva. All polls mentioned were conducted by the Canadian Institute of Public Opinion and are available in the CIPO's Toronto office.

PREFACE

1 Ernst B. Haas, 'Turbulent Fields and the Theory of Regional Integration,' *International Organization*, XXX, spring 1976, 180
2 Edward Hallett Carr, *The Twenty Years' Crisis, 1919-1939*, 2nd ed. (London 1946), 62
3 Louis St Laurent, 'The Foundation of Canadian Policy in World Affairs,' Department of External Affairs, *Statements and Speeches*, 47/2, 13 Jan. 1947

CHAPTER 1: TRIAL AND ERROR, 1914-45

1 Raymond Aron, *The Imperial Republic: The United States and the World 1945-1973* (Cambridge, Mass. 1974), xxiv
2 In particular, James Eayrs, *In Defence of Canada*. II: *Appeasement and Rearmament* (Toronto 1965); Richard Veatch, *Canada and the League of Nations* (Toronto 1975); Norman Hillmer and Robert Bothwell, eds., *The In-Between Time: Canadian External Policy in the 1930s* (Toronto 1975); and G.P. de T.

Glazebrook, *A History of Canadian External Relations*. II: *In the Empire and the World, 1914-1939* (Toronto 1966)

3 See Robert Craig Brown, *Robert Laird Borden*. I: *1854-1914* (Toronto 1975), 149.

4 See, for example, Keith Feiling, *The Life of Neville Chamberlain* (London 1946), 349. For King's Papers see, for example, Eayrs, *Appeasement and Rearmament*, 60ff, 226-31.

5 J.L. Granatstein and R. Bothwell, 'King Foreign Policy, 1935-1939,' in Hillmer and Bothwell, eds., *The In-Between Time*, 222

6 For a revealing description of the springs of Bennett's foreign policy on this and other subjects see Donald C. Story, 'The Foreign Policy of the Government of R.B. Bennett: Canada and the League of Nations, 1930-35' (PHD thesis, University of Toronto, 1976). See also R. Bothwell and J. English, 'The Riddell Incident,' in Hillmer and Bothwell, eds., *The In-Between Time*, 122-34.

7 See, for example, Newton Rowell to the League Assembly, 20 Nov. 1920, as cited in Margaret Prang, *N.W. Rowell: Ontario Nationalist* (Toronto 1975), 358.

8 See Veatch, *Canada and the League of Nations*, chapter 7.

9 Ibid., 51

10 *Mike: The Memoirs of the Right Honourable Lester B. Pearson*. I: *1897-1948* (Toronto 1972), 130

11 Quoted by F.H. Soward in Alexander Brady and F.R. Scott, eds., *Canada after the War: Studies in Political, Social and Economic Policy for Post-war Canada* (Toronto 1943), 127; and noted in a valuable critical survey, 'Watchman What of the Night? The Canadian Academic Community and the Threat of War, 1931-1939,' by Charles Spencer in a University of Toronto undergraduate paper, 1976

12 Quoted in Hillmer and Bothwell, eds., *The In-Between Time*, 191

13 Memorandum, 16 Feb. 1937, 'Re Monroe Doctrine,' in John A. Munro, ed., *Documents on Canadian External Relations*. VI: *1936-1939* (Ottawa 1972), 178. For views of Christie and Skelton see John A. Munro, 'Loring Christie and Canadian External Relations, 1935-1939,' paper presented to Canadian Historical Association annual meeting, Winnipeg, 3 June 1970; and Norman Hillmer, 'The Anglo-Canadian Neurosis: The Case of O.D. Skelton,' in Peter Lyon, ed., *Britain and Canada: Survey of a Changing Relationship* (London 1976).

14 The revealing exchanges on refugee policy are to be found in *Documents*, VI, chapter 5.

15 See memorandum by L.C. Christie, 29 March 1939, 'Note on the proposals for a Canadian embargo on war materials to Germany, Italy and Japan,' in ibid., 1147-50.

16 'Re Monroe Doctrine,' ibid., 177-8
17 Memorandum, 'Canada and the Polish War,' ibid., 1247
18 *Mike*, I, chapter 7
19 In a memorandum dated 18 February 1933 Robertson took issue with the Skelton position by saying that it 'does not seem desirable to raise the question of "status" in a situation of this seriousness.' He added that 'the desire evident in Drummond's conversation with Riddell that she should in her own right and on account of her interest in Pacific problems be invited to sit on the Committee, is ample recognition of her international position.' Bennett's telegram of instruction of the same date addressed to the high commissioner in London used Robertson's argument that 'refusal to serve on it might be interpreted as evasion of responsibility.'
20 Despatch 36, 11 June 1938, Secretary of State for External Affairs to Permanent Delegate, Geneva, *Documents*, VI, 802; and N.A. Robertson, memorandum, 29 Nov. 1938, 'Canada and the Refugee Problem,' ibid., 837-43
21 H. Blair Neatby, 'Mackenzie King and National Unity,' in H.L. Dyck and H.S. Krosby, eds., *Empire and Nations* (Toronto 1969), 58
22 *Documents*, VI, 1104-10
23 J.W. Pickersgill, ed., *The Mackenzie King Record.* I: *1939-1944* (Toronto 1960), 434
24 Memorandum, 30 Nov. 1938, 'Some proposals Concerning Canada and the International Labour Organisation,' *Documents*, VI, 636-48
25 Ibid., 1129-31
26 Memorandum, 4 Nov. 1936, 'League of Nations,' ibid., 907
27 Memorandum, 20 May 1936, 'Italian Conquest of Ethiopia and the Situation Confronting the League – Question of Amendment of the Covenant and Canada's Relations Thereto,' ibid., 895
28 Dominions Secretary to SSEA, 30 July 1938, ibid., 933
29 SSEA to Dominions Secretary, 18 Aug. 1938, ibid., 937
30 Canada, House of Commons, *Debates*, 18 June 1936, 3862-73
31 J.S. Macdonald, memorandum, 20 May 1936, *Documents*, VI, 887
32 Memorandum, 12 April 1937, 'Imperial Conference 1937: South African Proposals Respecting a Public Declaration as to International Status and Form of Participation in Treaties,' ibid., 141

CHAPTER 2: THE WARTIME EXPERIENCE

1 See, for example, the references to the Ivy Lea and Kingston speeches in James Eayrs, *In Defence of Canada.* II: *Appeasement and Rearmament* (Toronto 1965), 183-4.
2 *Foreign Relations of the United States, Conferences at Washington and Quebec 1943* (Washington 1970), 397

3 For a thorough account of this exercise and a perceptive analysis of the personalities involved see Don Munton and Don Page, 'Planning in the East Block: The Post-Hostilities Problems Committee in Canada 1943-5,' *International Journal*, XXXII, autumn 1977, 687-726.

4 Charles Ritchie, *The Siren Years: A Canadian Diplomat Abroad, 1937-1945* (Toronto 1974), 195

5 DEA, 'Report of the Canadian Delegates to the Twenty-First Assembly of the Leagues of Nations,' Conference series, 1946, no 2, 25

6 A private note written in January 1940

7 Lincoln Bloomfield, 'Nuclear Spread and World Order,' *Foreign Affairs*, LIII, July 1975, 749

8 Dean Acheson, *Present at the Creation: My Years in the State Department* (New York 1969), epigraph

9 Canada, House of Commons, *Debates*, 17 Feb. 1943, 501

10 J.W. Pickersgill and D.F. Forster, eds., *The Mackenzie King Record*. III: *1945-1946* (Toronto 1970), 31

11 J.W. Pickersgill, ed., *The Mackenzie King Record*. I: *1939-1944* (Toronto 1960), 683

12 Munton and Page, 'Planning in the East Block,' 696

13 *Debates*, 9 Feb. 1943, 286

14 These fears were shared in DEA. On 19 October 1943 Wrong drafted a telegram expressing concern about allied support of the king and Badoglio in Italy and the royalist régimes in Yugoslavia and Greece, but King did not send it.

15 FRUS, *Conferences at Washington and Quebec 1943*, 397

16 See chapter 5, 144.

17 Brooke Claxton, 'The Place of Canada in Post-War Organization,' *Canadian Journal of Economics and Political Science*, X, Nov. 1944, 412

18 See chapter 7, 212ff.

19 As, for instance, the argument against leaving occupation forces in Germany. See chapter 4, 109-12.

20 See R. Warren James, *Wartime Economic Co-operation: A Study of Relations between Canada and the United States* (Toronto 1949), 20.

21 See chapter 6, 176.

22 See chapter 3.

23 Report of Delegation Meeting, San Francisco, 11 May 1945

24 In A.L.K. Acheson, J.F. Chant, and M.F.J. Prachowny, eds., *Bretton Woods Revisited* (Toronto 1972), 44

25 This doctrine was of such importance in Canadian official thinking that it crops up in many sections of this book. For the most extensive treatment see 72-3 of this chapter.

26 USSEA to High Commissioner, London, 4 Aug. 1942
27 In London the Dominions Office championed the Canadian cause while the Foreign Office, wedded to its preference for great power action, raised difficulties. The Treasury and others wanted to keep the Canadians sweet in hope of more aid. An interesting account of the British view as contained in their archives is to be found in J.L. Granatstein, *Canada's War: the Politics of the Mackenzie King Government, 1939-1945* (Toronto 1975), 300ff.
28 Robert Sherwood, *Roosevelt and Hopkins: An Intimate History* (New York 1948), 707
29 *Mike: The Memoirs of the Right Honourable Lester B. Pearson*. I: *1897-1948* (Toronto 1972), 130
30 Memorandum for Prime Minister by Under-Secretary reporting on a conversation with the British High Commissioner, 18 Jan. 1943
31 Prime Minister to Canadian Minister, Washington, 8 Feb. 1943; and USSEA to Pearson, 7 Feb. 1943
32 Pearson to Robertson, 27 Feb. 1943
33 Reported in Robertson to Pearson, 4 March 1943
34 SSEA to Canadian Minister, Washington, 26 Feb. 1943
35 SSEA to Canadian Minister, Washington, 9 March 1943
36 Robertson, memorandum for the Prime Minister, 2 April 1943
37 DEA memorandum to Cabinet War Committee, 6 April 1943
38 SSEA to Canadian Minister, Washington, 7 April 1943
39 Allard (Washington) to Robertson, 14 June 1943
40 The 'take cognizance of' formula was successfully used years later by the Canadian government for a similar purpose of avoiding commitment when, in concluding the agreement on relations with the People's Republic of China, they simply 'took note' of the Chinese declaration that Taiwan was a part of China. (Joint Communiqué, '2 The Chinese Government reaffirms that Taiwan is an inalienable part of the territory of the People's Republic of China. The Canadian Government takes note of this position of the Chinese Government,' Mitchell Sharp, *Statements and Speeches*, no 70/19, 13 Oct. 1970)
41 *Debates*, 18 April 1944, 2158
42 For Canada's policy on refugees see chapter 3.
43 *Mackenzie King Record*, I, 211
44 *Mike*, I, 247
45 John Perry, 'Why U.N.R.R.A. has failed,' *Harper's*, Jan. 1946
46 Canada, not having been a recipient of Lend-Lease assistance, was, of course, the only major ally not bound to the United States by an Article VII commitment, although the Americans, at least, regarded Hyde Park as a pledge of the same kind.

47 Wrong to Pearson, personal, 20 March 1945, enclosing memorandum for USSEA signed H.W., 19 March 1945
48 *Mike*, I, 247
49 Ibid., 248
50 Grant Dexter, *Canada and the Building of Peace* (Toronto 1944), 91
51 *Mike*, I, 249
52 Address to Institute of Post-War Reconstruction, New York University, 15 Dec. 1943
53 In Acheson, Chant, Prachowny, eds., *Bretton Woods Revisited*, 37
54 R.F. Harrod, *The Life of John Maynard Keynes* (London 1951), 579
55 Ibid., 541-2
56 Ibid., 553-4
57 Louis Rasminsky, 'International Credit and Currency Plans,' *Foreign Affairs*, XXII, July 1944, 599
58 Rasminsky in Acheson, Chant, Prachowny, eds., *Bretton Woods Revisited*, 34
59 Harrod, *Life of John Maynard Keynes*, 570-1
60 Tentative Draft Proposals of Canadian Experts for an International Exchange Union, 9 July 1943 (tabled in Commons, 12 July 1943)
61 H.D. White, assistant to the secretary of the Treasury, Washington, to W.C. Clark, deputy minister of finance, Ottawa, 24 July 1943
62 Acheson, Chant, Prachowny, eds., *Bretton Woods Revisited*, 36
63 Ibid., 40-1
64 'International Credit and Currency Plans,' 587-603
65 *Debates*, 14 Dec. 1945, 3506
66 Ibid., 6 Dec. 1945, 3057
67 Good accounts of these interrelated discussions are to be found in R.S. Sayers, *History of the Second World War: Financial Policy 1939-1945* (London 1956); and in Robert Bothwell and John English, 'Canadian Trade Policy in the Age of American Dominance and British Decline, 1943-1947,' *Canadian Review of American Studies*, VIII, spring 1977, 52-65.
68 Acheson, Chant, Prachowny, eds., *Bretton Woods Revisited*, 47
69 Dexter, *Canada and the Building of Peace*, 128
70 *Debates*, 17 March 1944, 1578
71 When asked on 4 August 1943 by CIPO whether a 'joint board' should be set up to regulate international airlines or countries should be free to start international airlines as they pleased, 61 per cent of Canadians favoured the 'joint board' and 23 per cent were for 'free competition.'
72 *Debates*, 2 April 1943, 1778
73 Memorandum, Paul T. David, bureau of the budget, 1 Sept. 1943, '... access to the rich market of the United States is our greatest trading point; we ought

not to give that access for anything less than access to all parts of the British Commonwealth,' FRUS, *Conferences at Washington and Quebec 1943*, 1323.

74 C.D. Howe Press Conference, London, 18 Oct. 1943, *The Times* (London), 19 Oct. 1943

75 *Proceedings of the International Civil Aviation Conference, Chicago, Illinois, November 1-December 7, 1944*, vol 1 (Washington 1948), 82

76 Ibid., 111

77 Beatrice Bishop Berle and Travis Beal Jacobs, eds., *Navigating the Rapids 1918-1971: from the Papers of Adolf A. Berle* (New York 1973), 342

78 Ibid., 484

79 Ibid., 485

80 Stokely W. Morgan, 'The International Civil Aviation Conference at Chicago and what it means to the Americas,' Department of State *Bulletin*, XII, 7 Jan. 1945, 38

81 *Navigating the Rapids*, 252

82 Ibid., 365-6. For a more accurate account of Keenleyside's thinking and some further views of Berle, see R.D. Cuff and J.L. Granatstein, *Canadian-American Relations in Wartime: from the Great War to the Cold War* (Toronto 1975), 98-101.

83 The arguments are very effectively stated by Edward Warner, at that time vice chairman of the Civil Aeronautics Board, in 'The Chicago Air Conference,' *Foreign Affairs*, XXIII, April 1945, 406-21.

84 Anson C. McKim (1st Canadian representative on ICAO Council), 'World Order in Air Transport,' *International Journal*, II, summer 1947, 229

85 *Debates*, 17 March 1944, 1577

86 Wrong to Massey, 4 Aug. 1942

87 *Debates*, 17 March 1944, 1579

88 On covering note dated 4 November 1943, with memorandum by Wrong of 3 November

89 David Mitrany, *A Working Peace System* (Chicago 1966) (first published 1943)

90 A.J. Miller, 'Canada at San Francisco: A Reappraisal of the Influence of the "Functional Concept"' (unpublished paper)

91 Douglas Anglin, 'Canadian Policy Towards International Institutions, 1939-1950' (PHD thesis, Oxford, 1956), 298

CHAPTER 3: RELIEF, REHABILITATION, AND RECONSTRUCTION

1 David Corbett, *Canada's Immigration Policy* (Toronto 1957), xi

2 'Today and Tomorrow' column, New York *Herald Tribune*, 25 Feb. 1948

3 Quoted in J.L. Granatstein, *Canada's War: the Politics of the Mackenzie King Government, 1939-1945* (Toronto 1975), 49

4 For details of Mutual Aid Agreements see F.H. Soward, *Canada in World Affairs, 1944-1946* (Toronto 1950), 74-5.

5 In a CIPO poll of March 1944 70 per cent outside Quebec approved of mutual aid whereas in Quebec it was approved by only 33 per cent.

6 Canada, House of Commons, *Debates*, 21 April 1944, 2242

7 UN Doc A/C.2/86/Rev. 1, 'Revised Draft Resolution'

8 Canada, Department of External Affairs, *The United Nations 1946*, Report of the second part of the first session of the General Assembly of the United Nations held in New York, October 23-December 15, 1946, 85

9 Ibid., 234

10 Ibid., 235

11 Ibid.

12 Ibid., 85

13 Max Freedman, 'The General Assembly,' *International Journal*, II, spring 1947, 112

14 The extent to which the Canadian reputation in United Nations circles depended on the personal contribution of able Canadians zealous in the general cause was particularly illustrated in the case of Adelaide Sinclair, who, as executive assistant to the deputy minister of welfare and later as deputy executive director of UNICEF, was justly credited with a major part in establishing the United Nations' best-run agency – a cause she often had to support by doing battle within the Canadian government apparatus.

15 From its establishment in 1949 until 1975 Canada contributed $33 million in cash to UNRWA and ranks third in total contributions. UNKRA lasted from 1950 to 1958, during which time Canada contributed $7,500,000, ranking sixth in total contributions.

16 For detailed accounts of the Anglo-Canadian economic negotiations see Robert Bothwell and John English, 'Canadian Trade Policy in the Age of American Dominance and British Decline, 1943-1947,' *Canadian Review of American Studies*, VIII, spring 1977, 52-65; and R.D. Cuff and J.L. Granatstein, *American Dollars – Canadian Prosperity: Canadian-American Economic Relations 1945-1950* (Toronto 1978).

17 Letter, A.F.W. Plumptre to the author, 19 March 1974

18 *Debates*, 7 Sept. 1945, 11

19 J.W. Pickersgill and D.F. Forster, eds., *The Mackenzie King Record*. III: *1945-1946* (Toronto 1970), 167

20 When asked on 25 May 1946 whether the loan to Britain would benefit Canada, 64 per cent in Ontario and 26 per cent in Quebec said yes.

21 Letter from Louis Rasminsky to the author, 17 Oct. 1975
22 *Debates*, 3 Dec. 1945, 2845, 2846
23 See 'The Cold War' in the forthcoming second volume of this study.
24 Graham Towers, annual report to the minister of finance, Feb. 1947
25 'Aide-mémoire from the U.S. Government,' released to press 17 Nov., Department of State *Bulletin*, XVII, no 439, 30 Nov. 1947, 1055
26 This is not to say, as some American historians have argued, that Soviet misbehaviour was either fabricated or exaggerated to gain support for an economic programme designed to gain control for the United States or for North America over the European economy. The fear of the Soviet Union, whether or not it was based on sound perceptions, was strategic rather than economic – and it was real.
27 High Commissioner, London, to DEA, 16 March 1948
28 Inter-Departmental Committee on External Trade, Minutes of Meeting, Sept. 1948
29 For a thorough and balanced treatment of Canada's refugee policy during the period considered in this chapter see Gerald E. Dirks, *Canada's Refugee Policy: Indifference or Opportunism?* (Montreal 1977), esp. chaps. 3-6, and Irving Abella and Harold Troper, 'The line must be drawn somewhere: Canada and Jewish Refugees, 1933-9,' *Canadian Historical Review*, LX, 2, June 1979, 178-209.
30 Records of 1st Assembly of the League of Nations, 169-70
31 DEA, Report on the first part of the first session of the General Assembly of the United Nations (London, January 10-February 14), Conference series, 1946, no 1, 60, 61
32 Dirks, *Canada's Refugee Policy*, 125ff
33 USSEA, San Francisco, to SSEA, Ottawa, 27 May 1945
34 About 80 per cent gave a flat no to a CIPO question of 14 December 1946 as to whether immigration should be planned by the United Nations.
35 For a good discussion of the Keynesian attitudes in Ottawa, see Corbett, *Canada's Immigration Policy*, 112.
36 Letter, 23 June 1939, Dr. O.D. Skelton, USSEA, to F.C. Blair, director of immigration, Department of Mines and Resources
37 Dirks, *Canada's Refugee Policy*, 74-86
38 Prime Minister to Wrong, 11 June 1938, John A. Munro, ed., *Documents on Canadian External Relations*. VI: *1936-1939* (Ottawa 1972), 801-5
39 *Debates*, 9 July 1943, 4560
40 CIPO samples of 2 and 30 Oct. 1946
41 Freda Hawkins, *Canada and Immigration: Public Policy and Public Concern* (Montreal 1972), 17
42 *Debates*, 4 March 1947, 1005

43 Ibid., 1 May 1947, 2645
44 Ibid., 2646

CHAPTER 4: PEACEMAKING

1 Christie's memorandum, from which this is quoted, is reproduced in 'Canada's International Status: Developments at the Paris Peace Conference, 1919,' *External Affairs*, XVI, April 1964, 162-72.
2 Statement of 2 August 1946, 'Report of the Canadian Delegation at the Paris Peace Conference,' *Votes and Proceedings* of the House of Commons, 10 Feb. 1947
3 Canada, House of Commons, *Debates*, 30 Jan. 1947, 13
4 Montreal *Star*, 18 Jan. 1947
5 For an extensive, documented account of post-hostilities planning see Don Munton and Don Page, 'Planning in the East Block: the Post-Hostilities Problems Committee in Canada 1943-5,' *International Journal*, XXXII, autumn 1977, 687-726.
6 *Debates*, 27 Sept. 1945, 492
7 Wrong, memorandum for the USSEA, 5 July 1943
8 For a more detailed account of this whole question of occupation forces together with appropriate references and quotations, see James Eayrs, *In Defence of Canada*. III: *Peacemaking and Deterrence* (Toronto 1972), 183ff.
9 Ibid., 184
10 SSEA to Dominions Secretary, London, 30 July 1943
11 C.P. Stacey, *Arms, Men and Governments: the War Policies of Canada, 1939-1945* (Ottawa 1970), 65
12 See Dale Thomson, *Louis St. Laurent: Canadian* (Toronto 1969).
13 *Debates*, 3 March 1947, 975
14 Ibid., 954
15 See, for example, the detailed account of planning in the memoirs of Lord Gladwyn who was closely involved throughout and well aware of Canadian and Australian representations. *The Memoirs of Lord Gladwyn* (London 1972)
16 The most meticulous and reliable account of the Paris Peace Conference is to be found in F.H. Soward, *Canada in World Affairs, 1944-1946* (Toronto 1950), 198-215, which, although it was written shortly after the event, requires no amendment from the unpublished record.
17 Commentary for Canadian delegation to the Paris Peace Conference, chapter 1, 19-20
18 For administrative reasons of no political significance, Canada had failed to declare war on Bulgaria and took no part in consideration of the treaty with that country.

19 J.W. Pickersgill and D.F. Forster, eds., *The Mackenzie King Record*. III: *1945-1946* (Toronto 1970), 281

20 Ibid., 279

21 BBC broadcast from Paris, 1 Sept. 1946

22 Despatch of 26 Aug. 1946 from The Hague

23 *Mackenzie King Record*, III, 292-3

24 Canadian Delegation, Paris, to DEA, Sept. 1946

25 Claxton's detailed report to the SSEA was tabled in the House of Commons on 10 February 1947 along with copies of the treaty texts. The report was printed as an appendix to *Votes and Proceedings* of the same date and the treaties are found in Canada, *Treaty Series*, 1947, nos 4-7.

26 Brooke Claxton, 'Canada at the Paris Conference,' *International Journal*, II, spring 1947, 130

27 F.H. Soward, 'A Survey of Canadian External Policy,' prepared for DEA 1952, chapter 5, 2

28 For a description of this issue see G.K.N. Trevaskis, *Eritrea – a Colony in Transition: 1941-1952* (London 1960), 81-102.

29 SSEA to London, 7 Aug. 1948

30 DEA United Nations Division memorandum to Acting USSEA, 21 Sept. 1950

31 Memorandum for Cabinet War Committee, 'cessation of hostilities and immediate organization in Europe,' 26 July 1943

32 Wrong to Ritchie, 27 Nov. 1943

33 Reported in Robertson to the Canadian Minister, Washington, 3 Dec. 1943

34 Dominions Secretary to SSEA, 21 Aug. 1944

35 *Debates*, 30 Jan. 1947, 5ff

36 The text of the submission is printed in R.A. MacKay, *Canadian Foreign Policy 1945-1954: Selected Speeches and Documents* (Toronto 1971), 44-6.

37 From a memorandum prepared in March 1948 for presentation in London, Washington, and Paris. Quoted in Soward, 'Survey,' chapter 5, 31

38 The various exchanges between Robertson and DEA in March and April are reported in Soward, 'Survey,' chapter 5, 31-2.

39 *Debates*, 5 May 1948, 3632-3

40 The text of the Canadian submission on Germany is to be found in *Debates*, 30 Jan. 1947, and, with a commentary by G.P. de T. Glazebrook, in *International Journal*, II, spring 1947, 132-43.

41 Soward, 'Survey,' chapter 5, 34

42 Terms used by King at the Commonwealth Prime Ministers meeting, May 1946

43 Soward, 'Survey,' chapter 5, 29

44 From concluding section of the Canadian submission to the Council of Foreign Ministers

45 *Debates*, 25 Feb. 1947, 762
46 J.W. Pickersgill, *The Mackenzie King Record*. I: *1939-1944* (Toronto 1960), 630
47 Prime Minister, London, to Prime Minister, Ottawa, 13 Aug. 1945
48 Prime Minister, Ottawa, to Prime Minister, London, 15 Aug. 1945
49 Wrong memorandum to Prime Minister, 25 Aug. 1945, and memorandum, Wrong to Robertson, 1 Sept. 1945
50 Instructions prepared for first meeting of Far Eastern Advisory Commission in Washington on 30 Oct. 1945
51 Vincent Massey to Lord Addison, 27 Dec. 1945
52 A sensitive and revealing account of Norman's work in Japan is contained in Charles Taylor, *Six Journeys: A Canadian Pattern* (Toronto 1977).
53 A Departmental memorandum for the prime minister of 21 Nov. 1945 said of Norman: 'For the last two months he has, in effect, been the head of the United States Army Counter-Intelligence Division in Japan.' Following the comment is a recommendation that Norman be appointed representative of the FEAC, and, in the margin: 'I approve, W.L.M.K. 30-11-45.'
54 *Keesing's Contemporary Archives*: VI, *1946-1948*, 7629
55 *Debates*, 16 Nov. 1949, 1837
56 The DEA views are set out at length in a memorandum of 15 Feb. 1950, for the Interdepartmental Committee on Reparations and Peace Treaty Implementation, entitled 'Prospects of a Peace Treaty for Japan.'
57 *Debates*, 22 Jan. 1950, 133, 134
58 Ibid., 255-6
59 DEA, Louis St Laurent, 'Canada's Relations with Asia,' *Statements and Speeches*, no 52/33, 5 Sept. 1952
60 *Debates*, 11 Feb. 1953, 1854
61 Ibid., 30 Jan. 1947, 10
62 Robert A. Spencer, *Canada in World Affairs, 1946-1949* (Toronto 1959), 53-4
63 *Debates*, 8 April 1952, 1300
64 Ibid., 13 Sept. 1945, 134-5; 12 Dec. 1945, 3344
65 Statement by prime minister, ibid., 12 April 1946, 809-10
66 Canadian positions in the developing Cold War will be discussed in detail in the forthcoming volume 2 of this work.
67 'Canada at the Paris Conference,' 130

CHAPTER 5: THE COMMONWEALTH, 1944-7

1 J.W. Pickersgill, ed., *The Mackenzie King Record*. I: *1939-1944* (Toronto 1960), 598-9

2 A DEA memorandum, 'Recent Trends in United States-Canada Relations,' prepared by H.L. Keenleyside, 27 Dec. 1941, foresaw the problem. 'We may find that the Americans are not as conscious of our position and our problems in this regard as the British have become through a long period of education.' 'Our position,' he defined as 'that of a separate nation fighting in this war as such.'

3 Prime Minister, Canberra, to Prime Minister, Ottawa, 3 July 1941

4 Prime Minister, Ottawa, to Prime Minister, Canberra, 2 Aug. 1941

5 Prime Minister, Pretoria, to Prime Minister, London, 23 Aug. 1941

6 Canada, House of Commons, *Debates*, 28 Jan. 1942, 106

7 *Robert Laird Borden: His Memoirs*, II (Toronto 1938), 622

8 Washington Embassy to DEA, 9 Aug. 1944

9 These are described in more detail in chapter 2.

10 See chapter 2, Bretton Woods section.

11 See chapter 2, Chicago section.

12 Robert Sherwood, *Roosevelt and Hopkins: An Intimate History* (New York 1948), 707

13 *Proceedings of the International Civil Aviation Conference*, Chicago, Illinois, November 1-December 7, 1944 (Washington, DC 1948), I, 562; II, 1317-18

14 For example, Howard Green, *Debates*, 9 July 1943, 4564-5

15 Lord Cranborne tended to take the Canadian position that existing means of consultation were very satisfactory. He knew only too well that Canadian opposition could not be overcome. See his answer in the House of Lords, 2 Nov. 1943, with reference to the Australian prime minister's proposal and his remarks during the prime ministers' meeting in London in May 1944.

16 For further words on this proposal see chapter 8, 'Drafting the Charter,' section on 'The Commonwealth and the United Nations.'

17 These are the subjective reflections of the author based on his experience of liaison with the Foreign Office from Canada House during the years 1944-7.

18 Curtin's various statements on this subject may be found in Nicholas Mansergh, *Documents and Speeches on British Commonwealth Affairs, 1931-1952*, I (London 1953), 562-4.

19 Speech to the Toronto Board of Trade, 24 Jan. 1944, reproduced in ibid., 575-9

20 Pearson to Robertson, 1 Feb. 1944

21 Charles Ritchie to Hume Wrong, 9 March 1944

22 It was trotted out years later by Conservative leaders such as Edward Heath seeking to justify Britain's turning to Europe instead of the Commonwealth.

23 This quotation is from a Report on Prime Ministers Meetings, London, May 1944, undated and initialled JWH which the author, who was general factotum

to the delegation, was asked to make. Material on the conference is based on this report and on the author's notes and occasionally his recollections, checked against the official records of the conference produced by the Dominions Office.

24 Appendix I to report of the conference. Statement made by the prime minister of Canada on 11 May 1944

25 Non-verbatim report of 12th meeting, Prime Ministers Conference, 11 May 1944

26 Statement of 11 May, ibid.

27 As late as 1954 he revived the idea with St Laurent but got no response. High Commissioner, London, to SSEA, 11 March 1954

28 Holmes, London, to Wrong, 1 May 1946

29 'We should not under-estimate our improved chances of influencing the British since the San Francisco Conference. There is no doubt of the profound impression made on the United Kingdom authorities – as well as those of other countries – by the Canadian delegation at U.N.C.I.O. The important thing about this Canadian contribution was that it was not in a limited sphere in which we were considered to be specially interested but in the broadest sphere of world affairs. We are now looked upon as a country which has sound and responsible ideas on important problems.' Memorandum for Pearson, 10 Sept. 1945, initialled JWH, the Canada House officer responsible for liaison with the Dominions and Foreign Offices on political and security questions

30 Testimony of the author as eye-witness

31 See chapter 4, 119ff.

32 Draft memorandum for Pearson from Holmes, London, 10 Sept. 1945

33 Ibid.

34 Canada House to SSEA, 3 June 1946

35 A survey of the exchanges between Ottawa and London on this issue is to be found in F.H. Soward, 'A Survey of Canadian External Policy,' compiled for DEA, 1952, chapter 3, 61-6. See also Memorandum for the Advisory Committee on Post-Hostilities Problems of 17 July 1944, exchanges between Robertson and Massey of 21 and 28 March 1945, the report on the prime ministers' meetings of 1946 from Canada House, 3 June 1946, and a memorandum for the prime minister of 13 Nov. 1946 concerning the UK White Paper entitled 'Central Organization for Defence,' published in October; and a penetrating and amusing memorandum for Robertson by Maurice Pope, 2 Aug. 1945.

36 See chapter 6, 174ff.

37 Minutes of Meetings of British Commonwealth Prime Ministers, London, May 1946

38 Canada House to SSEA, 3 June 1946
39 Holmes to Wrong, 1 Sept. 1945. When Wrong cited this comment in a memorandum to the prime minister of 4 Sept. 1945 he discreetly substituted 'Evatt' and 'Bevin.' King would not have approved of such familiarity on the part of a first secretary.
40 The Canadian public was dimly aware of the new Commonwealth emerging, contradictory in its attitudes and inclined to think in old patterns. Polls taken in 1944 showed a considerable majority, outside Quebec, which seemed to favour a common foreign policy but many of the same people wanted Canada free to act by itself. CIPO polls of 25 March and 17 May 1944

CHAPTER 6: NORTH AMERICA

1 R.D. Cuff and J.L. Granatstein, *Canadian-American Relations in Wartime: From the Great War to the Cold War* (Toronto 1975); James Eayrs, *In Defence of Canada*. III: *Peacemaking and Deterrence* (Toronto 1972); A.F.W. Plumptre, *Three Decades of Decision: Canada and the World Monetary System, 1944-75* (Toronto 1977)
2 Cited in Eayrs, *Peacemaking and Deterrence*, 325
3 See chapter 8, 252-4, and chapter 9, 286-90.
4 Secretary of State for External Affairs to Dominions Secretary, 16 June 1946, in Donald Page, ed., *Documents on Canadian External Relations*, XII: *1946* (Ottawa 1977), 1600
5 For detailed accounts of continental defence in this period see James Eayrs, *In Defence of Canada*. II: *Appeasment and Rearmament* (Toronto 1965) and III: *Peacemaking and Deterrence*; C.P. Stacey, *Arms, Men and Governments: The War Policies of Canada, 1939-1945* (Ottawa 1970); Stanley Dziuban, *Military Relations between the United States and Canada, 1939-1945* (Washington, DC 1959); and J.L. Granatstein, *Canada's War: the Politics of the Mackenzie King Government, 1939-1945* (Toronto 1975).
6 James Eayrs, *Appeasement and Rearmament*, 177ff; John Michael Little, 'Canada Discovered: Continentalist Perceptions of the Roosevelt Administration, 1939-1945' (PHD thesis, University of Toronto, 1975)
7 Little, 'Canada Discovered,' 127, and N.H. Hooker, ed., *The Moffat Papers: Selections from the Diplomatic Journals of Jay Pierrepont Moffat, 1919-1943* (Cambridge, Mass. 1956), 328-9
8 Stacey, *Arms, Men and Governments*, 350ff
9 A more extensive analysis of the PJBD will be included in volume 2.
10 In the preparation of this section I have profited greatly from the researches and insights of Danford Middlemiss of the University of Alberta who has

completed a University of Toronto doctoral thesis, 'A Pattern of Co-operation: the Case of the Canadian-American Defence Production Sharing Arrangements, 1958-1963,' and of John Kirton of the University of Toronto whose extensive work on defence production has appeared in summary version in Andrew Axline, et al., eds., *Continental Community? Independence and Integration in North America* (Toronto 1974).

11 Plumptre, *Three Decades of Decision*, 25

12 Little, 'Canada Discovered,' 333

13 Ibid., 429ff, contains an interesting account of Morgenthau's efforts.

14 Plumptre, *Three Decades of Decision*, 62-4

15 R. Warren James, *Wartime Economic Co-operation: A Study of Relations between Canada and the United States* (Toronto 1949), 22

16 Beatrice Bishop Berle and Travis Beal Jacobs, eds., *Navigating the Rapids 1918-1971: from the Papers of Adolf A. Berle* (New York 1973), 365. See also chapter 2, 67-9, for more of Berle's views of North America.

17 Canada, *Treaty Series, 1941* (Ottawa 1943)

18 Canada, House of Commons, *Debates*, 28 April 1941, 2289

19 See Kal J. Holsti and Thomas Allen Levy, 'Bilateral Institutions and Trans-governmental Relations between Canada and the United States,' *International Organization*, XXVIII, autumn 1974, 875-901.

20 United States, Department of State *Bulletin*, V, 27 Dec. 1941, 579

21 'Canada's Relations with War-time Agencies in Washington,' *Canadian Journal of Economics and Political Science*, XI, Aug. 1945, 411

22 Granatstein, *Canada's War*, 90

23 James, *Wartime Economic Co-operation*, 13

24 See chapter 2, 30-3.

25 See chapter 7, 198-9.

26 Quoted in James, *Wartime Economic Co-operation*, 133

27 Middlemiss, 'A Pattern of Co-operation,' 43-4

28 John J. Kirton, 'Canadian-American Integration in Defence Production 1941-1971: Causes, Courses, Consequences' (MA thesis, Carleton University, School of International Affairs, 1973)

29 The text of the Report of the Advisory Committee on Post-Hostilities Problems, 'Post-war Canadian Defence Relationship with the United States: General Considerations,' 23 Jan. 1945, is reproduced as Document 1 in Eayrs, *Peacemaking and Deterrence*, 375-80.

30 A summary of the exchange is in F.H. Soward, 'A Survey of Canadian External Policy,' compiled for DEA, chapter 3, 67ff.

31 Associate Under-Secretary of State for External Affairs to Secretary of the Cabinet, 24 June 1946, *Documents*, XII, 1569

32 Correspondence concerning weather stations may be found in ibid., 1543ff, and concerning the revision of ABC-22, 1598ff.

33 Ibid., USSEA to Deputy Minister of Transport, 24 June 1946, 1533-4

34 *Debates*, 1 Feb. 1943, 20-1

35 Dzuiban, *Military Relations*, 322

36 *Treaty Series, 1948*, no 1, 'Exchange of Notes,' 7 and 15 May 1945

37 Eayrs, *Peacemaking and Deterrence*, 345

38 J.W. Pickersgill and D.F. Forster, eds., *The Mackenzie King Record*, III: *1945-1946* (Toronto 1970), 92

39 Cited in Robert Bothwell and John English, 'Canadian Trade Policy in the Age of American Dominance and British Decline, 1943-1947,' *Canadian Review of American Studies*, VIII, spring 1977, 58-9

40 FRUS, *The Conferences at Washington and Quebec 1943* (Washington 1970), 653ff

41 Cited in Bothwell and English, 'Canadian Trade Policy,' 59

42 *Public Papers of the Presidents: Harry S. Truman, 1949* (Washington 1964), 218

43 Ibid., 107

44 Assistant Secretary of State for Economic Affairs (Thorp) memorandum to Under-Secretary of State (Lovett) in FRUS, *1948*, IX (Washington 1972), 406. See also the less inhibited views of Adolf Berle in *Navigating the Rapids*, 365-6.

45 Robertson to Prime Minister, 12 Dec. 1943

46 See J.L. Granatstein and R.D. Cuff, 'Canada and the Marshall Plan, June-December 1947,' paper presented to the Canadian Historical Association Annual Meeting, Fredericton, 5 June 1977

47 Wrong to DEA, 22 May 1948

48 Wrong to DEA, 23 Dec. 1947

49 Abbott to St Laurent, 26 July 1948

50 Cited in Soward, 'Survey,' chapter 7, 50

51 Quoted in ibid., 41

52 Cited in Robert A. Spencer, *Canada in World Affairs, 1946-1949* (Toronto 1959), 263

53 Wrong to DEA, 21 July 1948

54 Report from Pierce in Paris of a conversation of 26 July 1948, quoted in Soward, 'Survey,' chapter 7, 45

55 Quoted in ibid., 17

56 DEA to London, 9 Sept. 1947

57 DEA to Robertson, 2 Sept. 1947

58 Robertson to DEA, 19 June 1947; Soward, 'Survey,' chapter 7, 5

59 Soward, 'Survey,' chapter 7, 20

60 Letter to the author from Louis Rasminsky, 17 Oct. 1975
61 Soward, 'Survey,' chapter 7, 26
62 Ibid., 11
63 Ibid., 28
64 FRUS, *1945*, II (Washington 1967), 1069-70, 1087-8
65 Robertson for prime minister, 22 Dec. 1941
66 *Mike: The Memoirs of the Right Honourable Lester B. Pearson*. I: *1897-1948* (Toronto 1972), 254
67 See Cuff and Granatstein, *Canadian-American Relations*, 92
68 James, *Wartime Economic Co-operation*, 3
69 Harold A. Innis, *Essays in Canadian Economic History*, edited by Mary Q. Innis (Toronto 1956), 406
70 *Debates*, 6 June 1947, 3863-87; 9 June, 3913-26
71 *Mackenzie King Record*, III, 211
72 *Debates*, 12 Feb. 1948, 1168
73 See chapter 7.
74 See Cuff and Granatstein, 'The Perils of Exemptionalism,' in *Canadian-American Relations*, 156-63, and the response in Plumptre, *Three Decades of Decision*, 82-5.
75 Holsti and Levy, 'Bilateral Institutions,' 878

CHAPTER 7: THE ATOMIC TRIAD

1 'An Outsider Looking In,' Canada's Tomorrow Conference, Quebec, 13-14 Nov. 1953. I am indebted to Professor Paul Ambrose of Shippensburg State College for drawing my attention to this apt quotation. His 1966 dissertation for the University of Pennsylvania, 'Canada Becomes a Potential Nth Country: 1943-1951,' and his unpublished paper, 'Canada and the North Atlantic Atomic Triangle,' are the most complete accounts of Canada's atomic relations and have been of great value in the preparation of this chapter.
2 C.S.A. Ritchie, 'Control of the Atomic Bomb by the United Nations Organization,' Department of External Affairs, 8 Sept. 1945
3 The best published accounts of the wartime and postwar atomic policies are the official British and American accounts, both of which are admirably objective and contain, especially the British, a good deal of information about the Canadian involvement. Margaret Gowing, *Britain and Atomic Energy, 1939-1945* (London 1964), and *Independence and Deterrence: Britain and Atomic Energy 1945-1952*. I: *Policy Making*; II: *Policy Execution* (London 1974); and Richard G. Hewlett and Oscar Anderson, Jr, *History of the United States Atomic Energy Commission*, I: *The New World, 1939-1946*; Hewlett and Francis

Duncan, II: *Atomic Shield, 1947-1952* (University Park, PA 1962, 1969). For a more detailed account of Canadian policies see Wilfrid Eggleston, *Canada's Nuclear Story* (Toronto 1965); and James Eayrs, *In Defence of Canada*. III: *Peacemaking and Deterrence* (Toronto 1972), 258-318.

4 'Its existence had given Britain the foundations of a peacetime nuclear reactor programme, and Canada a flying start into the nuclear age, with all the implications this held for her science and industry.' Gowing, *Policy Making*, 8

5 Gowing, *Britain and Atomic Energy*, 103

6 Ibid., 193, and Eggleston, *Canada's Nuclear Story*, 64-6

7 Martin J. Sherwin, *A World Destroyed: The Atomic Bomb and the Grand Alliance* (New York 1975), 71-6

8 J.W. Pickersgill and D.F. Forster, eds., *The Mackenzie King Record*, II: *1944-1945*, 327-451

9 Gowing's conclusion, however, after reading the documents, is that it would probably not have made a difference if the bomb had been destined for Europe. Mackenzie King, however, confided to his diary that it was fortunate the bomb was used on the Japanese 'rather than upon the white races of Europe.' See Eayrs, *Peacemaking and Deterrence*, 276. It is an appalling comment. However, those interested in the curious workings of King's mind should see this in the context of all the impetuous extravagances of expression in the diary.

10 Wrong to Mackenzie, 22 Oct. 1945

11 'Memorandum on Attlee's letter of 25 September to President Truman regarding the forthcoming exchange of views on the atomic bomb,' 6 Nov. 1945, drafted by C.S.A. Ritchie and signed by Wrong

12 J.W. Pickersgill and D.F. Forster, eds., *The Mackenzie King Record*, III: *1945-1946*, 42

13 DEA memorandum of 6 Nov. 1945

14 Quotations drawn from memoranda annexed to Washington despatch to Ottawa, 21 Nov. 1945

15 The Canadian report on the meeting is contained in Pearson's despatch of 21 Nov. 1945 to SSEA.

16 For example, André Fontaine, *History of the Cold War*, I (New York 1968), 268ff

17 Memorandum on Atomic Warfare, initialled LBP, 8 Nov. 1945, attached to letter of 21 Nov. 1945 to DEA, reproduced in J.A. Munro and A.I. Inglis, 'The Atomic Conference of 1945 and the Pearson Memoirs,' *International Journal*, XXIX, winter 1973-4, 94-9

18 Volume II of this study, forthcoming

19 Gowing, *Britain and Atomic Energy*, 95

20 American messianism was a problem for Canadians because the best internationalists in Washington took it for granted that the United States was not like other powers. See a discussion of this phenomenon in connection with the formation of ICAO in chapter 2.

21 Andrew Pierre, *Nuclear Politics: the British Experience with an Independent Strategic Force, 1939-1970* (London 1972)

22 Gowing, *Policy Making*, 117, 277-8

23 Ibid., 98

24 Ibid., 134

25 Pearson to Robertson, 14 Dec. 1945; Wrong to Ignatieff, 15 May 1946. Howe wrote to Heeney, 17 May 1946, saying that 'under date of May 13 I sent you a reply which I now find is wholly in error.' This concerned the amounts of uranium Eldorado was producing and under contract to supply to the United States. Fortunately the inaccuracies balanced out and did not radically affect a reply sent to the United Kingdom.

26 Howe to Bateman, 11 Dec. 1945

27 Howe to Pearson, 30 Nov. 1945

28 Pearson to Robertson, 4 Dec. 1945

29 King to Attlee, 1 May 1946

30 Pearson to Heeney, 3 May 1946

31 DEA to London, 1 May 1946

32 Heeney to Howe, 20 March 1946

33 House of Commons Standing Committee on External Affairs, *Minutes of Proceedings and Evidence*, no 2, 7 April 1954, 44

34 Hewlett and Anderson, *The New World, 1939-1946*, 501

35 Heeney to Wrong, 10 Dec. 1947

36 Wrong to Heeney, 24 Sept. 1947

37 Heeney to Wrong, 11 Sept. 1947

38 Pearson to Howe, 2 Dec. 1947

39 Wrong to DEA, 19 Dec. 1949

40 Heeney to Wrong, 11 Sept. 1949

41 Eggleston, *Canada's Nuclear Story*, 145

42 Howe to Heeney, 8 Sept. 1947

43 Gowing, *Policy Making*, 138

44 Canada, House of Commons, *Debates*, 5 Dec. 1945, 2959

45 Howe to Malcolm MacDonald, 23 March 1946

46 Gowing, *Policy Making*, 134. She notes, however, that it was Howe and Mackenzie, not King, who wanted the British piles.

47 Memorandum, Wrong to Pearson, 16 Dec. 1946

48 Gowing, *Policy Making*, 328

49 Wrong to Heeney, 24 Sept. 1947
50 *The Journals of David E. Lilienthal*. II: *The Atomic Energy Years, 1945-1950* (New York 1964), 381, 385; and Hewlett and Duncan, *The Atomic Shield, 1947-1952*, 480ff
51 *The Private Papers of Senator Vandenberg*, ed. Arthur H. Vandenberg, Jr (Boston 1952), 267
52 J.E. Hodgetts, *Administering the Atom for Peace* (New York 1964), 57
53 *Debates*, 4 Feb. 1947, 81
54 Hodgetts, *Administering the Atom*, 177-8
55 Three specialized bodies were set up to control nuclear energy in Canada: Eldorado Mining and Refining Ltd, responsible for procurement of uranium and for all processes from exploration to manufacture; Atomic Energy of Canada Ltd, to handle research and development; Atomic Energy Control Board, primarily concerned with regulation. A succinct account of their work is to be found in ibid., 50-7.
56 CIPO polls of 3 Oct. 1945, 26 Jan., and 8 June 1946

CHAPTER 8: DRAFTING THE CHARTER

1 Skelton to Massey, 14 March 1939, in John A Munro, ed., *Documents on Canadian External Relations*. VI: *1936-1939* (Ottawa 1972), 1411
2 Dated 23 Feb. 1944. For a survey of the work of the Post-Hostilities Problems Committees see Don Munton and Don Page, 'Planning in the East Block: the Post-Hostilities Problems Committee in Canada 1943-5,' *International Journal*, XXXII, autumn 1977. This article contains also an excellent analysis of the officials involved.
3 Pearson to Robertson, 1 Feb. 1944
4 Pearson to DEA, 8 Sept. 1944
5 Reproduced in R.A. MacKay, *Canadian Foreign Policy 1945-1955: Selected Speeches and Documents* (Toronto 1971), 6-10
6 Canada, House of Commons, *Debates*, 1st sess, 28 March 1945, 300
7 See his comments on the unwisdom for a secondary power of planning from the foundation upwards, chapter 4, 107.
8 Wrong memorandum, 'Canadian planning for the international settlement,' 23 Feb. 1944
9 Wrong, 'Note for Mr. Robertson,' 24 Feb. 1944, with comments by Robertson
10 Wrong to Reid, 11 Oct. 1944
11 It was all the more creative because of the respect all these men had for each other and their close personal ties. This was evident to a junior officer who was fortunate enough to work for each of them.

12 A very interesting account of American and British views on the qualifications of these two Canadians is contained in James Barros, 'Pearson or Lie: The Politics of the Secretary-General's Selection, 1946,' *Canadian Journal of Political Science*, x, March 1977, 65-92.

13 Wrong to Pearson, 1 Feb. 1944

14 USSEA, San Francisco, to SSEA, Ottawa, 10 June 1945

15 Canadian views put forward to Dumbarton Oaks participants are summarized in a memorandum of 18 September 1944, initialled JWH and entitled 'The Dumbarton Oaks Conference on World Organization: Canadian Interests.'

16 SSEA to Secretary of State for Dominions Affairs, London, for Churchill from King, 28 Sept. 1944

17 Undated scribbled note probably written in the early summer of 1944

18 Wrong to Canadian High Commissioner, Canberra, 20 Feb. 1945

19 See chapter 4

20 See note 16 above.

21 Memorandum, 'Questions arising from Dumbarton Oaks,' intended for London Conference, 2 March 1945

22 For example, in memoranda by Wrong of 25 April and MacKay of 11 July 1944. Sir Charles Webster in the Foreign Office argued that 'if Canada and Brazil do not agree the whole existence of a World Organization is threatened.' P.A. Reynolds and E.J. Hughes, *The Historian as Diplomat: Charles Kingsley Webster and the United Nations, 1939-1946* (London 1976), 51

23 CIPO polls of 20 Jan., 20 Nov. 1943; 10 Jan. 1945; and 13 July 1946

24 Memorandum signed H.H. Wrong and entitled 'Military Aspects of the Dumbarton Oaks Proposals, February 19th 1945'

25 See chapter 9, 290-5.

26 *Mike: The Memoirs of the Right Honourable Lester B. Pearson*. I: *1897-1948* (Toronto 1972), 271-2

27 See note 24 above.

28 See chapter 5.

29 See Reynolds and Hughes, *The Historian as Diplomat*, 31.

30 Massey to Robertson, London, 23 April 1945

31 Ibid.

32 SSEA to Secretary of State for Dominions Affairs, London, 4 Sept. 1944

33 Reid and Pearson were more enthusiastic about public discussion of Canadian policy than were Wrong and Robertson, who were closer to the throne. Reid wanted to publish his draft charter to get discussion going and Pearson wanted to put the record straight when the *New York Times* had misrepresented Canadian positions. Neither request was granted. There was legitimate concern that Canada would jeopardise its sources if it made public its views on British and

American papers shown them in confidence. Wrong went rather far, however, when he doubted the wisdom of presenting other governments before San Francisco with a summary of Canadian views because 'a document of this sort would certainly become public property and might prove embarrassing if we were unable to secure the amendment of the proposals on the lines we desire and nevertheless wished to lay the Charter before Parliament for ratification.' Memorandum for the prime minister from Wrong, 15 March 1945

34 Fraser called a British statement 'contemptible' and 'most dishonest.' Senator Connally (US) asked him to withdraw this unparliamentary language. Robertson reported to DEA: 'All told it was an extraordinary and deplorable exhibition of Commonwealth public manners. Pearson intervened effectively just before the close of debate and managed, I think, to put Commonwealth differences in a little better light and perspective from that in which they had been exhibited by the principal protagonists.' USSEA, San Francisco, to SSEA, 10 June 1945

35 *Debates*, 28 March 1945, 311

36 20 April diary entry, quoted in *Mike*, I, 273-4

37 Memorandum on Delegation Meeting, 9 May 1945

38 The practice of mixed delegations was continued by Canada in composing delegations to the General Assembly until 1947. Eventually it was realized, however, that it was a principle which did not accord well with the Canadian system of responsible government. Unanimity was essential on the Charter itself, but it was inevitable and proper that issues considered in the Assemblies should be ones on which there might be political divisions at home. As each country was allowed only five representatives and five alternates on an Assembly delegation, it was difficult to know what status to accord opposition leaders. King did not want all three opposition parties represented on the delegation and in particular he did not want either John Diefenbaker or Donald Fleming at all. It was Pearson who suggested the formula for advisers. (Memorandum for SSEA, 13 Aug. 1947). The compromise was a provision for 'parliamentary observers' from all parties which has done a great deal ever since to expose members of parliament to the realities of the United Nations.

39 Canada, DEA, Conference Series, 1945, no 2, 'Report on the United Nations Conference on International Organization held at San Francisco, 25th April-26th June, 1945' (Ottawa 1945), 10, 11

40 Ibid., 23

41 Report of Delegation Meeting, 21 May 1945

42 Ibid., 11 June 1945

43 Ruth B. Russell with Jeannette Muther, *A History of the United Nations Charter* (Washington, DC 1958), 735-41

44 *Debates*, 1198
45 'Report on the United Nations Conference,' 32
46 Ibid., 36
47 Report of Delegation Meeting, 19 May 1945
48 Russell, *A History of the United Nations Charter*, 662
49 *Debates*, 16 Oct. 1945, 1199
50 See also the discussion of regionalism in economic and social functions, chapter 9, 286ff.
51 Robertson, London, to Wrong, 13 May 1944
52 Sir Charles Webster, the historian-adviser to the Foreign Office on international organization, was contemptuous of Churchill's concept and gives a gleeful account in his diary notes of the role of the dominions in forcing him to abandon them. Reynolds and Hughes, *The Historian as Diplomat*, chapter 3
53 *Article 51*: 'Nothing in the present Charter shall impair the inherent right of individual or collective self-defense if an armed attack occurs against a Member of the United Nations, until the Security Council has taken the measures necessary to maintain international peace and security. Measures taken by Members in the exercise of this right of self-defense shall be immediately reported to the Security Council and shall not in any way affect the authority and responsiblitiy of the Security Council under the present Charter to take at any time such action as it deems necessary in order to maintain or restore international peace and security.'
   Article 53
   '1. The Security Council shall, where appropriate, utilize such regional arrangements or agencies for enforcement action under its authority. But no enforcement action shall be taken under regional arrangements or by regional agencies without the authorization of the Security Council, with the exception of measures against any enemy state, as defined in paragraph 2 of this Article, provided for pursuant to Article 107 or in regional arrangements directed against renewal of aggressive policy on the part of any such state, until such time as the Organization may, on request of the Governments concerned, be charged with the responsibility for preventing further aggression by such a state.
   '2. The term enemy state as used in paragraph 1 of this Article applies to any state which during the Second World War has been an enemy of any signatory of the present Charter.'
54 Report of Delegation Meeting, 15 June 1945
55 Leland M. Goodrich, Edvard Hambro, and Patricia Simons, *Charter of the United Nations: Commentary and Documents*, 3rd rev. ed. (New York 1969), 645

56 'In the philosophy of power politics China is an obligation and a danger and not an asset. Inclusion as a party to the Declaration [ie, a proposed Four-Power Declaration on security after the war] is a question of "face" and a departure from the basic principle as I see it. It is, however, vain to propose the exclusion of China in view of the attitude adopted by the United States Government.' Wrong memorandum for the prime minister, 22 Sept. 1943

57 Report of delegation meeting, 14 May 1945

58 H.W., Memorandum for the Prime Minister, San Francisco, 11 May 1945

59 'Report on the United Nations Conference,' 19

60 Report of delegation meeting, 24 May 1945

61 Read to Robertson, from Washington, 17 April 1945

62 'Report on the United Nations Conference,' 49, 53

63 The delegation's intention, as reported in a telegram from San Francisco of 23 May 1945, was: 'In view of the terms of our own amendment, which is designed to establish independent status of a real international secretariat, I think we shall have to oppose Great Powers' amendment, but shall do so in very moderate language.'

64 He was also indefatigable. He not only proposed after Dumbarton Oaks that Canada produce its own redraft of the Charter in the interest of greater clarity and more popular appeal, he did the job himself. As he reported to Norman Robertson: 'In Chicago [where he had been very active at the Civil Aviation Conference] I got into the habit of drafting dozens of Convention Articles overnight. I have not yet been able wholly to break myself of that bad habit, to which I have lately been succumbing between the hours of eight and midnight. Consequently I am sending you by bag on Saturday, as a Christmas present, a redraft of the Charter and in my redraft have incorporated 75 per cent to 90 per cent of the Constitutional Articles of the Permanent Aviation Convention.' Washington to SSEA, 21 Dec. 1944. In Ottawa Robertson and Wrong doubted that this would, as Reid thought, 'run a good chance of being taken as the basis of discussion.'

65 DEA, *Conference Series, 1946*, no 1, 'Report of the first part of the first session of the General Assembly of the United Nations' (Ottawa 1946), 43

66 Wilgress, London, to Robertson, 8 Dec. 1945

67 Robertson for Wilgress, 6 and 10 Dec. 1945

68 Draft initialled H.W. enclosed with Memorandum for the Prime Minister, 28 Dec. 1945

69 Robertson to Wilgress, 11 Dec. 1945

70 Memorandum for the prime minister by N.A. Robertson, 26 Nov. 1945, with marginal comments by WLMK

71 Robertson to the prime minister, ibid. Beside Robertson's comment that Australia was disposed to concede 'Canada's prior claim,' King noted ungenerously 'we certainly have.' He commented also: 'If Mexico were on the Security Council and Canada *not* this would surely raise a question here.'

72 Read was a senior and essential member of the Canadian delegation to the first session of the General Assembly but he illustrated his personal and national dedication to austere principles by walking out on the delegation the instant he was elected to such a high judicial position and had nothing more to do with it.

73 Wilgress to Robertson, London, 24 Dec. 1945

CHAPTER 9: ECONOMIC AND SOCIAL FUNCTIONS

1 See chapter 2, 47ff.

2 See chapter 1, 8ff, 20ff.

3 Canada, House of Commons, *Debates*, 4 Aug. 1944, 5909-10

4 7 August 1943

5 *Canadian Information Service Weekly*, 1 March 1946, 5

6 Ibid., 12 April 1946

7 J.M. Keynes, *The Economic Consequences of the Peace* (New York 1920), 226

8 Quoted by Richard Gardner in A.L.K. Acheson, J.F. Chant, and M.F.J. Prachowny, eds., *Bretton Woods Revisited*, (Toronto 1972), 22

9 In ibid., 46

10 Polls taken during the latter years of the war confirm the view that the public regarded 'free trade' with the United States and with the world at large as a desirable situation.

11 See chapter 2, 33ff.

12 DEA telegram to Dominions Office, para 12, 2 Aug. 1944

13 'Questions arising from Dumbarton Oaks,' intended for London Conference, 2 March 1945

14 D.G. Anglin, 'Canadian Policy Towards International Institutions 1939-1950' (PHD dissertation, Oxford, 1956), 165

15 DEA, *Canada and the United Nations 1951-1952* (Ottawa 1952), 92

16 F.H. Soward and Edgar McInnis, *Canada and the United Nations* (New York 1956), 187

17 See, for example, *The Memoirs of Cordell Hull*, II (New York 1948), 1302.

18 Anglin, 'Canadian Policy,' 160

19 International Labour Conference, 26th session, Report 1: *Future Policy, Programme and Status of the International Labour Organization* (Philadelphia 1944), 39-43, 185-8

20 *Debates*, 20 March 1945, 44

21 See, for example, the section on human rights, 290ff.
22 Soward and McInnis, *Canada and the United Nations*, 202
23 'The World of UNESCO,' *International Journal*, I, autumn 1946, 368-9
24 That the attitude of the officials, viewed in retrospect, was somewhat priggish and unimaginative is hereby acknowledged by one of them.
25 Quoted in Ruth B. Russell with Jeannette Muther, *A History of the United Nations Charter* (Washington, DC 1958), 616
26 See chapter 3, 91-3.
27 (Draft) Instructions for the Canadian Delegation to the General Assembly of the United Nations, 27 Dec. 1945, initialled HW, under cover of Memorandum for the prime minister, 28 Dec. 1945
28 Official Records of the Economic and Social Council, Fifth Session, 271 Summary record
29 See doubts about assumptions of legislative power expressed by Wrong and Rasminsky at San Francisco, chapter 8, 257.
30 Anglin, 'Canadian Policy,' 169
31 *Canada and the United Nations, 1951-52*, appendix 3, 152-4. The report contains a thorough description of the responsibilities of Canadian departments and the means of co-ordination characteristic, with some alterations, of the first decade or so of UN policy.
32 See chapter 8, 252ff.
33 David Mitrany, *A Working Peace System* (Chicago 1966), 12
34 International Monetary Fund, *Summary Proceedings of the Seventh Annual Meeting of the Board of Governors* (Washington 1952), 121
35 Reproduced in *International Conciliation*, no 442, June 1948, 432
36 DEA, *Canada and the United Nations, 1950* (Ottawa 1951), 123
37 The details of the controversy over a number of years cannot be recounted here, but a good account can be found in Anglin, 'Canadian Policy,' 243-58.
38 Memorandum for the Legal Adviser, signed HW, 23 March 1945
39 For consideration of human rights in the context of domestic jurisdiction see chapter 8, 256-7.
40 DEA, *Canada and the United Nations, 1948* (Ottawa 1949), 248
41 Special Joint Committee of the Senate and the House of Commons on Human Rights and Fundamental Freedoms, *Minutes of Proceedings*, including the second and final report, 21 and 23 June 1948
42 UN Doc E/CN.4/515/Add 13, 16 March 1951
43 *Canada and the United Nations, 1948*, 248, 249
44 Statement by Canadian representative in 3rd Committee of the General Assembly, 2 Nov. 1954, cited in R.A. MacKay, *Canadian Foreign Policy 1945-1954: Selected Speeches and Documents* (Toronto 1971), 168

CONCLUSION

1 See, for example, W.D. Coplin, *Introduction to International Politics: A Theoretical Overview* (Chicago 1974), 74ff.
2 from a private letter.
3 Chapter 1, 17-18
4 'The Foundation of Canadian Policy in World Affairs,' *Statements and Speeches*, no 47/2, 13 Jan. 1947
5 Ibid.
6 David R. Murray, ed., *Documents on Canadian External Relations*. VII: *1939-1941, Part I* (Ottawa 1974), 192
7 Memorandum addressed to Robertson, Wrong, and Heeney, 2 Aug. 1945
8 See, for example, J.W. Pickersgill and D.F. Forster, eds., *The Mackenzie King Record*. IV: *1947-1948* (Toronto 1970), 135-6.
9 Robert A. Spencer, *Canada in World Affairs, 1946-1949* (Toronto 1959), 2
10 See polls mentioned on 28, 97, 224, 242.
11 'Root and Branch in Canadian Foreign Policy,' from notes for a seminar at Darwin College, University of Kent at Canterbury, 10 May 1972
12 DEA, *Canada and the United Nations, 1948* (Ottawa 1949), 85
13 See chapter 2, 26.
14 John A. Munro, ed., *Documents on Canadian External Relations*. VI: *1936-1939* (Ottawa 1972), 935-7
15 'Canada and the Postwar World,' *Canadian Affairs*, 1 April 1944

Index